THOMAS'
CONCISE
TELECOM and
NETWORKING
DICTIONARY

THOMAS'
CONCISE
TELECOM and NETWORKING DICTIONARY

Thomas M. Thomas, II

McGraw-Hill

New York   St. Louis   San Francisco   Auckland   Bogotá   Caracas
Lisbon   London   Madrid   Mexico City   Milan   Montreal
New Delhi   San Juan   Singapore   Sydney   Tokyo   Toronto

McGraw-Hill

A Division of The McGraw-Hill Companies

Copyright © 2000 by The McGraw-Hill Companies, Inc. All rights reserved. Printed in the
United States of America. Except as permitted under the United States Copyright Act
of 1976, no part of this publication may be reproduced or distributed in any form or by
any means, or stored in a data base or retrieval system, without the prior written permission
of the publisher.

1 2 3 4 5 6 7 8 9 0   AGM/AGM   0 5 4 3 2 1 0

ISBN 0-07-212253-6

The sponsoring editor for this book was Steven Elliot and the production supervisor
was Clare Stanley. It was set in Garamond by Patricia Wallenburg.

Printed and bound by Quebecor/Martinsburg.

PREFACE

Did you ever sit in a classroom reading a brief with all your peers or reading an article written by some Networking Guru and wonder what the heck does that acronym or obscure term mean? Let me raise my hand and be the first to say, "Yes, I have!" At times like these, I wished I had an easy-to-read, concise, and complete dictionary—not one full of overwhelming and confusing definitions. This is your solution and my primary reason for putting this dictionary together.

My other goal was to include and expand various definitions by including *quality* web sites from across the Internet, which you can use to expand your knowledge. I believe this is very important because the information found on the Internet is like a huge library full of books—but all the books are thrown on the floor. So how do you find useful information in a reasonable amount of time? I have added URLs with a number of the definitions, to allow you to get more information on that topic.

Who Should Use This Dictionary?

Everyone! I have tried to make this dictionary useful to all the people involved in this increasingly technical and connected world. To this end, I have tried to make the definitions clear, concise, useful, and educational. It is my hope that anyone can pick up this dictionary, read a definition, and understand what it means.

If you have suggestions, corrections, or additions that you'd like to see appear in the next edition of this dictionary, e-mail me at *telecom@netcerts.com*. If your correction, new definition, or suggestion is accepted then we will thank you in the next edition of this book.

DEDICATION

There can be no doubt in my mind that the person with the most impact on making this dictionary a reality is my very lovely wife Rose. She was my inspiration, guide, confidant, and drill sergeant on those nights I wanted nothing to do with writing. To my wife I say *"Thank you for all your help, humor, and understanding while I wrote this book. Without your love and support, my life would be a much poorer place. Are you ready for the next twelve years?"*

The other person was my father. It was almost a year ago when my father was visiting my family and me, when we wandered into my local Border's Bookstore (where else would an author hangout?). While browsing the shelves, we noticed another dictionary, and we were both very impressed with it. He decided to purchase it as a birthday present for me. Not long after that, I decided to write a dictionary that everyone could use. *"Dad, thank you for planting the seed of an idea that grew into this dictionary."*

In closing, without the blessing and support of the Lord Jesus Christ, none of this would have been possible. To him I owe an eternal debt of gratitude.

ACKNOWLEDGMENTS

I have come to realize that there are so many people involved in this incredible process that I will probably miss acknowledging someone's effort, although I hope not! I would like to thank Steve Elliot, who shared my vision, a vision that went through many changes... many more than we ever thought! Jennifer Perillo, for her impeccable timing. John Streck, for his keen insight and observations. John Bass, for being able to provide excellent suggestions and humor that was greatly appreciated. John Vacca, for his thoroughness in finding places on the Internet that I never knew existed and for sharing his resume. Marcus Goncalves, for his insight and dedication to excellence and Francis "Franny" Kelly for being a true professional and a good friend.

ABOUT THE AUTHOR

Thomas M. Thomas, II is the founder of NetCerts.com (www.netcerts.com), a leading training and education site for those seeking Cisco® certifications. He was previously a Course Developer for Cisco Systems and was a Group Leader of the Advanced Systems Solutions Engineering Team for MCI's Managed Network Services. In his spare time, he has authored *OSPF Network Design Solution* and *Thomas' Telecom & Networking Dictionary*. He also likes to work with the Research Triangle Park, North Carolina Chapter of the Cisco Professional Association Worldwide (www.ciscopaw.org). Tom is currently working as an Instructor/Consultant for Chesapeake Network Solutions (www.ccci.com).

TECHNICAL REVIEWERS

As the leading publisher of technical books for more than 100 years, McGraw-Hill prides itself on bringing you the most authoritative and up-to-date information available. To ensure that our books meet the highest standards of accuracy, we have asked a number of top professionals and technical experts to review the accuracy of the material you are about to read.

We take great pleasure in thanking the following technical reviewers for their insights:

John Bass has worked in the networking industry for over ten years as an engineer, consultant, and author of numerous trade magazine articles. He is currently the Technical Director of Centennial Networking Labs at North Carolina State University. John develops test tools and system tests for networking and server equipment for publications, manufacturers, and network administrators.

Marcus Goncalves is a Senior IT/Enterprise Applications Analyst for Automation Research Corporation, and has several years of experience as an internetworking consultant. He has published more than 15 books, and is a regular contributor to magazines such as *BackOffice, Compaq Enterprise, CIO, Start, Developer's*, and *WEBster*.

John Streck has degrees from Renssesslaer Polytechnic Institute at Troy, New York: a BS in Electrical Engineering in 1972 and an MS in EE in 1974. He was granted his P.E. license in 1977. Currently, he is Associate Director for Advanced Technology Development at North Carolina State's Information Technology group, as well as a member of the Senior Technical Staff for North Carolina State's Centennial Networking Labs.

Ed Taylor is the Chief Information Architect for Information World, a consulting and network engineering firm in Dallas, Texas. He has served as network consultant for Fortune 500 companies and is a former network architect for IBM.

John Vacca is an information technology consultant and internationally known author based in Pomeroy, Ohio. Since 1982, John has authored of 29 books and more than 360 articles in the areas of Internet and Intranet security, programming, systems development, rapid application development, multimedia and the Internet. John was also a configuration management specialist, computer specialist, and the computer security official for NASA's space station program (Freedom) and the International Space Station Program, from 1988 until his early retirement from NASA in 1995. John can be reached on the Internet at jvacca@hti.net.

THOMAS'
CONCISE
TELECOM and NETWORKING
DICTIONARY

1+ dialing The ability to dial "1" plus the long distance number for calls within the North American Dial Numbering Plan.

10Base2 10 Mbps, baseband Ethernet, deployed in185-meter segments. The IEEE 802.3 sub-standard for ThinWire, coaxial.

10Base-2A 10-Mbit/s baseband network using thin Ethernet coaxial cable.

10Base5 The original IEEE 802.3 cabling standard for Ethernet which uses coaxial cables (type RG-8). The name derives from the fact that the maximum data transfer speed is 10 Mbps, it uses baseband transmission, and the maximum length of cables is 500 meters (1640 feet) length and a maximum of 100 MAUs. The maximum end-to-end propagation delay for a coaxial segment is 2165ns (nanoseconds). Maximum attenuation for the segment shall not exceed 8.5dB (17dB/km) for each 500m segment. 10Base5 is also known as *thick Ethernet, ThickWire,* or *ThickNet.*

10Base-5A 10-Mbit/s baseband network using thick Ethernet coaxial cable.

10BaseF 10 Mbps, baseband, over fiber optic cabling. The IEEE 802.3 substandard for fiber optic Ethernet that refers to the 10BaseFB, 10BaseFL, and 10BaseFP standards for Ethernet over fiber optic cabling.

10Base-FB Part of the IEEE 10Base-F specification providing a synchronous signaling backbone that allows additional segments and repeaters to be connected to the network.

10Base-FL IEEE 10Base-Fiber specification designed to replace the Fiber-Optic Inter-Repeater Link (FOIRL) standard providing Ethernet over fiber optic cabling; interoperability is provided between the old and new standards. 10BaseFL is a part of the IEEE 10BaseF specification and, although able to interoperate with FOIRL, it is designed to replace the FOIRL specification. 10BaseFL segments can be up to

3,280 feet (1,000 meters) long if used with FOIRL, and up to 1.24 miles (2,000 meters) if 10BaseFL is used exclusively in the deployment.

10Base-FP Part of the IEEE 10Base-F specification that allows the organization of a number of end nodes into a star topology without the use of repeaters. *See* 10Base-FB, 10Base-FL, *and* 10Base-FP.

10Base-FT The IEEE specification for baseband Ethernet over fiber optic cabling. *See* 10Base-FB, 10Base-FL, *and* 10Base-FP.

10Base-T IEEE 802.3 physical layer specification enabling telephone UTP cable to be used for 10 Mbps Ethernet over two pairs of unshielded twisted pair wiring (UTP). One of several adaptations of the Ethernet (IEEE 802.3) standard for Local Area Networks (LANs). The purpose of the 10Base-T standard was to provide a simple, inexpensive, and flexible means of attaching devices to the ubiquitous twisted-pair cable. 10Base-T is a multisegment 10-Mbps baseband network operating as a single collision domain.

10Broad36 10-Mbps Ethernet specification using broadband coaxial cable, which is part of the IEEE802.3 standard 10Broad36, has a distance limitation of 3,600 meters. *See* Ethernet *and* IEEE 802.3.

100Base-F Standard for fiber optic cabling used with Fast Ethernet, often used to mean Fast Ethernet with fiberoptic cabling.

100Base-FX The 100Base-FX system is designed to allow fiber optic segments of up to 412 meters in length. The 100Base-FX specification requires one pair of multimode fiber (MMF) cable per link. The typical fiber optic cable used for a fiber link segment is a graded index MMF cable with 62.5 micron core and 125 micron cladding. The wavelength specified is 1,350 nanometers, with an 11dB loss budget per link.

100Base-T Fast Ethernet. An IEEE 802.3 physical layer specification for 100-Mbps Ethernet over different grades of unshielded twisted-pair wiring (UTP). Fast Ethernet offers a natural migration from traditional 10-Mbps Ethernet, because it uses the same CSMA/CD access mechanism. Officially, the 100BASE-T standard is IEEE 802.3u. There are several different cabling schemes that can be used with 100BASE-T, including:

100BASE-TX: Two pairs of high-quality twisted-pair wires.

100BASE-T4: Four pairs of normal-quality twisted-pair wires.

100BASE-FX: Fiber optic cables.

The physical medium for 10Base-T is twisted-pair wiring. 10Base-T networks are typically installed utilizing existing unshielded telephone wiring and typical telephony installation practices. Thus, the end-to-end path may include different types of wiring, cable connectors, and cross-connects. Typically, a DTE connects to a wall outlet using a twisted-pair patch cord. Wall outlets are connected through building wiring and to a cross connect to the repeater hub in a wiring closet. Also known as *UTP, twisted pair,* and *twisted sister.*

100Base-T4 An IEEE 802.3 specification for baseband Fast Ethernet over four pairs of Category 3, 4, or 5 unshielded twisted-pair (UTP) wire. Physical segments are limited to 100 meters in length to ensure that the round trip timing specifications are met. The 100Base-T4 standard operates over four pairs of wires, with a signaling system that makes it possible to provide 100-Mbps Ethernet signals over standard voice-grade cabling systems. This signaling method uses three wire pairs for transmit and receive, while the fourth pair is used to listen for collisions. 100Base-T4 specifies a segment of up to 100 meters in length, but two 100-meter 100Base-T4 segments can be connected together through a single Class I or Class II repeater. A system with a total maximum diameter of 200 meters between any two DTEs is therefore provided. 100Base-T4 requires a *transmit/receive signal crossover.* The standard recommends that buildings are cabled straight through and ports on the hub/repeater perform the crossover internally. If two stations are linked together with a single 100Base-T4 segment, or if the repeater hub does not implement the signal crossover internally, then a crossover cable must be provided for proper operation.

100Base-TX An IEEE 802.3 specification for Fast Ethernet over two pairs of Category 5 unshielded twisted-pair (UTP), or Type 1 shielded twisted-pair (STP) wire. The first pair of wires is used to receive data; the second pair is used to transmit data. The maximum distance for a segment is 100 meters. Two 100-meter transmission segments can be connected together through a single Class I or Class II repeater, thereby providing up to 200 meters between DTE devices.

100Base-VG A joint AT&T and Hewlett-Packard proposal for a 100 Mbps, four-pair, category 3 Ethernet. It is being standardized by the IEEE 802.12 working group.

100Base-X A Grand Junction Networks' proposal for 100 Mbps Ethernet using two pairs of category 5 wire and CSMA/CD. It is being standardized by the IEEE 802.13 working group.

100VG-AnyLAN A new 100-Mbps LAN technology originally developed by Hewlett-Packard and currently refined and described in the IEEE 802.12 standard. 100VG-AnyLAN departs from traditional Ethernet in that it uses a centrally controlled Demand Priority access protocol instead of CSMA/CD. It builds on the positive aspects of both token ring and Ethernet to run at 100 Mbits/s with resilience and high realization of potential. Generally considered better technically than Fast Ethernet, the alternative, but it has been less than successful in the marketplace.

110 type block A wire block that terminates 100 to 300 pairs of wire. It has excellent electrical characteristics and a relatively small physical foot print. It organizes pairs horizontally in order to connect them.

1003.4 POSIX real-time extensions.

1003.6 POSIX security extensions.

1003.7 POSIX system management extensions.

1003.8 POSIX networking extensions.

24th channel signaling *See* A&B bit signaling.

2780 An SNA batch processing standard used to communicate with IBM mainframes or compatible systems.

2780/3780 A model of remote batch terminals used in IBM bisynchronous environments. Bisync gateways are also known as 2780/3780 emulators.

3COM One of the top four networking companies in the world; a manufacturer of hubs, routers, switches, modems, NICs. 3Com was founded in 1979 by Dr. Robert Metcalfe, who was a co-inventor of Ethernet. The company's name was derived from the words *computer, communication*, and *compatibility*.

3-D audio A specialized technique for giving more depth to traditional stereo sound.

3-D graphics A specialized technique that makes a two-dimensional space, such as a computer monitor, appear as a three-dimensional space.

3-D software Software that represents 3-dimensional objects such as CAD/CAM, action computer games, or animation software on a computer.

32 bit word A measurement in four-octet (byte) increments.

32-bit The number of bits that can be processed or transmitted in parallel, or the number of bits used for single element in a data format.

3002 An AT&T definition for a standard telephone circuit.

3090 IBM mainframe, sometimes called Sierra.

3174 *See* controller.

3270 Display Stations Terminals for IBM mainframe computers.

3270 IBM's interactive communications terminal standard used to communicate with an IBM mainframe or compatible system. Often

used to generically define Systems Network Architecture (SNA).

3270 Refers to a 3270 data stream (arrangement of data).

3274 A cluster controller for IBM equipment, often called a terminal concentrator. *See* controller.

3480, 3490 The IBM designation for families of half-inch magnetic tape drives typically used on mainframes and AS/400s. The 3480 drives use 18-track cartridges at 38,000 bpi to yield 200MB. The 3490 uses built-in compression to obtain 400MB. The 3490e records 36 tracks and uses longer tape to hold 800MB. Tape libraries are available that hold from a handful to thousands of cartridges. The 3490 drives provide transfer rates of at least 3MB per second. Drives are available that use the ESCON and Fast SCSI-2 interfaces to obtain up to 20MB/sec.

370 Architecture/370 Extended Architecture IBM architecture for mainframe computers, including the 3090 processors.

370 block mux channel *See* block multiplexer channel.

3705 An IBM communications controller. A Physical Unit (PU) type 4 in SNA, used to connect token ring networks, cluster controllers, non-IBM SNA gateways, and other devices to a PU Type 5 host.

3725 *See* 3705.

3770 Refers to remote job entry.

3780 A batch protocol used to communicate with an IBM mainframe or compatible system.

4B/5B local fiber 4-byte/5-byte local fiber. A fiber channel physical media with FDDI or ATM.

4.4 Berkeley Software Distribution (4.4BSD) A version of the Berkeley University family of UNIX products.

4.4BSD 4.4 Berkeley Software Distribution.

401xA series of Tektronix graphics terminals. A de facto standard for identifying graphics terminals.

43401 A Bell specification for a circuit that consists of two dry, twisted, unswitched, pairs of conductors used in direct, point-to-point communications.

5250 (*a*) Reference to a 5250 data stream (arrangement of data). (*b*) IBM terminal used on the System/3X and AS/400 lines.

66-type block (*Illustration*) A type of wire connecting block that is used for twisted-pair cabling cross connections. It holds 25 pairs in one to four vertical columns.

680x0 The family of microprocessors made by Motorola and used in systems like Apple's Macintosh and Sun's computers and workstations.

8+ dialing The ability to dial an "8" to get access through a PBX or home telephone system to the public telephone network. *See* 1+ and 9+ dialing.

8B/10B local fiber 8-byte/10-byte local fiber. Fiber channel physical media that supports speeds up to 149.76Mbps over multimode fiber.

802.x The set of IEEE standards for the definition of LAN protocols.

802.1d IEEE standard for spanning tree.

802.1p The IEEE standard that adds important filtering controls to the 802.1d standard; designed with VLANs in mind.

802.1Q The IEEE encapsulation standard, which calls for adding 4 bytes to a packet to tag it for virtual LAN purposes. *See* VLANs and tagging.

802.2 IEEE standard for the control of the lower part of layer 2 Logical Link Control of the seven-layer OSI reference model.

802.3 IEEE broadband bus networking system that uses the CSMA/CD protocol. Ethernet has become the commonly used name, although it is one trademarked version of 802.3.

802.4 IEEE standard for the token bus medium access method.

802.4I EEE standard that governs broadband bus and broadband token bus. Usually used in industrial applications.

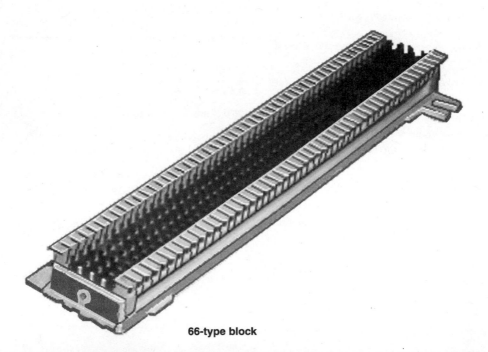

66-type block

802.5 IEEE standard that governs the characteristics and operation of token-ring networks.

802.6 IEEE standard that governs metropolitan area networks (MANs).

802.9 Integrated voice and data LAN IEEE standard.

802.10 IEEE standard for packet tagging for security within LANs; also used by some companies (such as Cisco Systems) to tag packets for virtual LANs.

802.11 IEEE standard for wireless LANs which use Ethernet bridges with roaming to join them to the network.

802.12 IEEE standard that specifies the physical layer and the MAC sublayer of the data-link layer of the seven-layer OSI reference model.

80x86 Family of microprocessors made by Intel; used in PC and clone computers.

9+ dialing The ability to dial a "9" to get access through a PBX or home telephone system to the public telephone network *See* 1+ and 8+ dialing.

9370 Mid-range IBM processor.

A&B bit signaling Procedure used in T1 transmission facilities, in which each of the 24-T1 channels devotes one bit of every sixth frame to the carrying of control-oriented signaling information. Also called *24th channel signaling*.

A/UX Apple's version of UNIX, which runs on some versions of the Macintosh. The *A/UX toolbox* is a library that enables a program running under the A/UX operating system to call Macintosh user interface toolbox and operating system routines.

AA *See* accidental administrator.

AAA *See* authentication, authorization, and accounting.

AAF *See* Advanced Authoring Format.

AAL *See* ATM adaptation layer.

AARP *See* AppleTalk Address Resolution Protocol.

Abend Abnormal end of task.

ABM *See* asynchronous balanced mode.

abort Abnormal termination of a program or process.

ABR *See* available bit rate.

absolute address A fixed logical address in memory.

abstract service primitive (ASP) In the AppleTalk session protocol, an attached support processor.

abstract syntax Machine-independent types and values, defined using an abstract syntax notation 1.

abstract syntax notation (ASN)/Abstract Syntax Notation 1 (ASN.1) A standard heavily used by OSI and OSI-inspired protocols, including X.500, H.323, SNMP and LDAP, that defines a grammar used to write textual descriptions of messages. One of several encoding rules is then used to construct the actual binary messages. ISO Standard X.680 defines the ASN.1 grammar. *Basic Encoding Rules (BER), Canonical Encoding Rules (CER),* and *Distinguished Encoding Rules (DER),* are specified in ISO Standard X.690. *Packed Encoding Rules (PER)* are specified in ISO Standard X.691. This language, used to describe abstract entities or concepts in a machine such as a router or switch, is commonly used by SNMP.

With its well-defined syntax, automated tools such as *MIB Browsers* can be constructed to compile ASN.1 definitions into subroutines that can encode and decode ASN.1 messages, thus simplifying the design of programs implementing ASN.1-based protocols.

 For more information on MIB browsers, see *http://www.mg-soft. com.*

Abstract Windows Toolkit (AWT) The Java API that enables programmers to develop Java applications with GUI components, such as windows, buttons, and scroll bars.

AC *See* access control.

AC-3 Coding system used by Dolby Digital. The two terms, AC-3 and *Dolby Digital,* are used interchangeably.

ACAP *See* Application Configuration Access Protocol.

ACB name In SNA, the name of a microinstruction. A name typically specified on the VTAM application (APPL) definition statement.

accelerated graphics port (AGP) An interface specification developed by Intel Corporation. AGP is based on PCI, but is designed especially for the throughput demands of 3-D graphics.

accelerator board An expansion board which can serve multiple purposes; one of which is graphics acceleration.

accept In a VTAM application program, to establish a session with a logical unit in response to a CINIT request.

acceptable use policy (AUP) Also known as *terms of service (TOS)*. A contract specifying what a subscriber can and cannot do while using an ISP's service. Issues covered under the AUP might include liability disclaimers, unacceptable behaviors, billing policies, and more.

access control (AC) Mechanisms and policies that restrict access to computer resources. For example, an *access control list (ACL)* defines the kinds of access granted or denied to users of an object.

access control byte The byte following the start delimiter of a token or frame that is used to control access to the token-ring network, hence its name.

access control entry (ACE) A single entry within an access control list (ACL). Default protection for directories, or security alarms that specify the method of identification and associated access rights to be granted or denied to the holders of the identification.

access control list (ACL) A list defining the kinds of access granted or denied to users of an object.

access method A technique for moving data between main storage and input/output devices and for telecommunications.

access method control block A control block that links an application program to VSAM or VTAM.

access priority The maximum priority that a token can have for the adapter to use it for transmission.

access rate The bit-per-second (bps) rate at which a user can transmit over the network's lines.

access time The time a program or device takes to locate a piece of information and

make it available to the computer for processing and use.

access unit A unit that allows multiple attaching devices access to a token-ring network at a central point. Sometimes these devices may also be referred to as *concentrators*.

accidental administrator (AA) A person "accidentally" responsible for their network or IT department whose primary duties and training are in other fields.

ACE *See* access control entry.

ACF *See* advanced communications function.

acknowledgment (ACK) A positive response message sent by a protocol, such as TCP, which acknowledges the reception of a transmitted packet from the receiving end station. ACKs can be separate packets or piggybacked on reverse-traffic packets.

ACL *See* access control list.

ACM *See* Association for Computing Machinery.

ACP *See* ancillary control process.

ACPI *See* advanced configuration and power interface.

acquire In VTAM, to take over resources that were formerly controlled by an access method in another domain.

ACR *See* allowed (or available) cell rate.

Acrobat A suite of programs developed by Adobe Systems, Inc. for creating and distributing electronic documents in PDF (Portable Document Format).

 For more information, see http://www.adobe.com.

acronym Technically, a word that is formed by combining some parts (usually the first letters) of other terms. For example, modem is the acronym derived from proper title: modulator/demodulator. Various cultural groups, newsgroups, chat rooms, and e-mail users have spawned a rich set of acronyms and abbreviations for common phrases. A few common ones are listed below.

Acronym	Meaning
ASAP	As Soon As Possible
BTW	By The Way
FWIW	For What It's Worth
FYI	For Your Information
IMHO	In My Humble Opinion
IMO	In My Opinion
LOL	Laughing Out Loud
ROTFL	Rolling On The Floor Laughing
TIA	Thanks In Advance
RTFM	Read the Friggin Manual

ACSE *See* association control service element.

activate To initialize a resource.

active Operational. The state of a resource when it has been activated and is running.

active application An application currently capable of being used by a user.

active hub Multiported device that amplifies LAN transmission signals.

active monitor A function in a single adapter on a token-ring network that initiates the transmission of tokens and provides token error recovery facilities. Any active adapter on the ring has the ability to provide the active monitor function if the current active monitor fails.

active program Any program that is loaded into memory and ready to be executed and/or an operational program in progress.

active server pages (ASP) A means for Web developers to activate their Web pages with dynamic live database-driven content. The code that produces this content is all server side; it runs on the server. The benefit of server-side scripting is that the end result is raw HTML. An example is the NetCerts website (*http://www.netcerts.com*), which is constructed primarily of ASP pages.

active session The session in which a user is currently interacting with the computer; that is, the user can be a human or a program.

active window The terminal window where current operations are in the foreground.

ActiveX A set of technologies developed by Microsoft, largely based on OLE (Object Linking and Embedding) and COM (Component Object Model).

ActiveX Data Objects (ADO) Microsoft's newest high-level interface for data objects.

ACTLU In SNA, a command used to start a session with a logical unit.

ACTPU In SNA, a command used to start a session with a physical unit.

AD Proper name for an addendum document to an OSI standard

adapter (*a*) Short for expansion board. (*b*) The circuitry required to support a particular device. For example, video adapters enable the computer to support graphics monitors, and network adapters enable a computer to attach to a network. Adapters can be built into the main circuitry of a computer or they can be separate add-ons that come in the form of expansion boards. *See* MAC address.

adapter address Twelve hexadecimal digits that identify a LAN adapter.

adapter card A hardware card that provides the interface between the computer (DTE) and the physical network circuit. *See* NIC

adaptive differential pulse code modulation (ADPCM) A form of pulse code modulation (PCM) that produces a digital signal with a lower bit rate than standard PCM.

adaptive routing A method of routing packets of data or data messages in which the system's intelligence selects the best path. This path might change with traffic patterns or link failures.

adaptive session-level pacing A form of session-level pacing in which session components exchange pacing windows that may vary in size during the course of a session. This allows transmission within a network to adapt dynamically to variations in availability and demand of buffers on a session-by-session basis. Session-level pacing occurs within independent stages along the session path according to local congestion at the intermediate nodes.

add-in (*a*) A component that can be added to a computer or other device to increase its capabilities. They can come in the form of expansion boards, cartridges, or chips. (*b*) A software program that extends the capabilities of larger programs.

additive increase rate (AIR) The cell rate at which a source station can transmit after increasing its rate by the routing information field.

add-on A product designed to complement another product.

address A designation referencing a particular location. This could refer to memory, adapter card identification, data structure location in storage, and other such points referenced.

address class The original Internet IP routing scheme was developed in the 1970s, and sites and hosts were assigned IP addresses from one of the following three classes: *Class A, Class B*, and *Class C*. The address classes differ in both their size and number of networks/hosts allowed within each. Class A addresses are the largest, but there are just a few of them. Class B's are medium in size. Class C's are the smallest, but they are numerous. Classes D and E are also defined, but not used in normal operation. Specific information regarding the ranges, networks, and hosts allowed for each class are shown in the following table.

The official description of IP addresses is found in RFC 1166, *Internet Numbers*. To

Summary of IP Address Classes

Class A: 0nnnnnnn hhhhhhhh hhhhhhhh hhhhhhhh
  First bit is always 0, with 7 network bits, and 24 host bits
  Range of addresses as defined in the initial byte: 0–127
  126 Class A addresses exist (0 and 127 are reserved)
  16,777,214 hosts can be assigned on each Class A

Class B: 10nnnnnn nnnnnnnn hhhhhhhh hhhhhhhh
  First two bits are always 10, with 14 network bits, and 16 host bits
  Range of addresses as defined in the initial byte: 128–191
  16,384 Class B addresses exist
  65,532 hosts can be assigned on each Class B

Class C: 110nnnnn nnnnnnnn nnnnnnnn hhhhhhhh
  First three bits are always 110, with 21 network bits, and 8 host bits
  Range of addresses as defined in the initial byte: 192–223
  2,097,152 Class C addresses exist
  254 hosts can be assigned on each Class C

Class D: 1110mmmm mmmmmmmm mmmmmmmm mmmmmmmm
  First four bits are always 1110, with 28 multicast address bits
  Range of addresses as defined in the initial byte: 224–247
  Class Ds are reserved for multicast addresses - see RFC 1112

Class E: 1111rrrr rrrrrrrr rrrrrrrr rrrrrrrr
  First four bits are always 1111, with 28 reserved address bits
  Range of addresses as defined in the initial byte: 248–255
  Class E addresses are reserved for experimental use

receive an assigned network number, contact your Internet Service Provider. *See* IP addressing *and* RFC 1166.

address mapping Technique that allows different protocols to interoperate by translating addresses from one format to another. For example, when routing IP over X.25, the IP addresses must be mapped to the X.25 addresses so that the IP packets can be transmitted by the X.25 network. *See* address resolution.

address mask Bit combination used to describe which portion of an address refers to the network or subnet and which part refers to the host. Sometimes referred to simply as the mask. Each class of IP address has a default mask. *See* subnet mask, address class, and IP addressing.

Address Resolution Protocol (ARP) The TCP/IP protocol used to dynamically bind a high level IP address to low level physical (MAC) hardware addresses. ARP works across single physical networks and is limited to networks that support hardware broadcast. *See* RARP and Inverse ARP.

address space Addresses used to uniquely identify network-accessible units, sessions, adjacent link stations, and links in a node for each network in which the node participates. The set of all legal addresses in memory for a given application. The address space represents the amount of memory available to a program. Interestingly, the address space can be larger than physical memory through a technique called *virtual memory*.

address space manager (ASM) A program used to control and manage the use of address space.

addressing In data communication, the way in which a station identifies the station to which it is supposed to send data. *See* address class *and* IP addressing.

adjacency A relationship formed between neighboring OSPF routers for the purpose of exchanging link state information. *See* OSPF, ABR, *and* DR.

adjacent In an internetwork, devices, nodes, or domains that are directly connected by a physical connection. *See* adjacencies.

adjacent control point A control point directly connected to an APPN, LEN, or composite node.

adjacent link station A link station directly connected to a given node by a link connection over which network traffic can be carried.

adjacent NCPs Network control programs connected by subarea links with no intervening NCPs.

adjacent nodes Two nodes connected by at least one path that connects no other node.

adjacent SSCP table A table identifying SSCPs into which VTAM can enter a session.

adjacent subareas Subareas connected by one or more links with no intervening subareas.

administrative distance A rating of the trustworthiness of the route to a destination, typically the best route is the route with the "lowest" administrative distance. The higher the value, the lower the trustworthiness rating.

admission control *See* traffic policing.

ADN *See* Advanced Digital Network.

ADO *See* ActiveX Data Objects.

ADPCM Adaptive differential pulse code modulation.

ADSL *See* asymmetric digital subscriber line.

ADSP *See* AppleTalk data stream protocol.

ADSU *See* ATM DSU.

Advanced Authoring Format (AAF) A multimedia file format introduced by Microsoft in 1998. AAF provides a common file format so that users can develop a multimedia presentation in one application and then edit it in a second application.

Advanced Communications Function (ACF) A group of IBM licensed programs.

advanced communications function (ACF)/ network control program (NCP) A program that resides in the communications controller and interfaces with the SNA access method in the host processor to control network communications, it is also the primary SNA NCP. *See* SNA, ACF, *and* NCP.

advanced configuration and power interface (ACPI) A power management specification developed by Intel, Microsoft, and Toshiba.

Advanced Digital Network (ADN) Usually refers to a 56Kbps leased line.

advanced integration module (AIM) New series of add-on boards available for certain routers like the 2600 series.

Advanced Interactive eXecutive (AIX) A specialized version of UNIX produced by IBM. AIX runs on a variety of computers, such as PCs and workstations.

Advanced Micro Devices (AMD) A manufacturer of chips for personal computers. AMD is challenging Intel with a set of Intel-compatible microprocessors through the manufacturing of its "K" line.

Advanced Peer-to-Peer Network (APPN) An upper-layer networking protocol based on peer technology. The fundamental difference between APPN and SNA is that the former is "peer" oriented whereas the latter is hierarchical by design. An APPN *end node* can register its local LUs with a network node server. The server can also have links to multiple nodes, but can have only one CP-CP session with a network node at any one time. This type of node can attach to subarea SNA as a peripheral node.

An APPN *interchange node* can be characterized by its functions, which include controlling network resources, performing CDRM functions in subarea networks, and owning NCPs. This type of node is extremely flexible and it appears to be an APPN node to an APPN network, as well as a subarea node to a subarea network. This node can reside between an APPN network and a subarea network, thus providing integration between the two. An APPN *LEN node* provides end-user services

without explicit, direct use of CP-CP sessions. An APPN *network node* performs the following functions or services:

- Distributed directory services
- Intermediate routing services within an APPN network
- Network services for specific end nodes
- Intermediate session routing

This type of node is also the management service focal point. The APPN network node cooperates with other network nodes to maintain a network topology database, which is used to select optimal routes for LU-LU sessions based on requested classes of service.

advanced power management (APM) An API developed by Intel and Microsoft, which allows developers to include power management features via the Built In Operating System (BIOS). APM defines a layer between the hardware and the operating system that effectively shields the programmer from hardware details while allowing proper power management. APM is widely used in laptop computers.

advanced program-to-program communication (APPC) (*a*) A protocol based on T2.1 architecture utilizing LU6.2 to accomplish peer communications. The basic meaning of APPC is communication protocol used between programs, such as transaction programs. This type of protocol permits communication between programs written in different languages. (*b*) IBM SNA software running on LU 6.2 devices, which allows high-speed communication between applications on different computer systems within a distributed computing environment. APPC is responsible for the establishment and tear down of connections between the communicating applications. It consists of two interfaces, a programming interface and a data-exchange interface. The programming interface replies to requests from applications requiring communication and the data-exchange interface, which establishes the communication sessions between applications. *See* LU6.2.

Advanced Research Projects Agency (ARPA) United States government entity focused upon what would become known as "The Internet."

Advanced Research Projects Agency Network (ARPANET) A large wide-area network created by the United States Defense Advanced Research Project Agency and the precursor to the Internet, established in 1969.

advanced SCSI programming interface (ASPI) An interface specification used to send commands to a SCSI host adapter.

Advanced Streaming Format (ASF) A streaming multimedia file format developed by Microsoft.

advertising The process within a router during which routing or service updates are sent at specified intervals so that other routers on the internetwork can maintain a complete list of usable routes. *See* link state protocols *and* distance vector protocols *for different methods of advertising*.

AEP *See* AppleTalk Echo Protocol.

AFC *See* application foundation classes.

AFP *See* AppleTalk Filing Protocol.

agent A program that performs some information gathering or processing task (typically a small one) in the background.

aggregate control The control of the multiple streams using a single timeline by the server. For audio/video feeds, this means that the client may issue a single play or pause message to control both the audio and video feeds.

AGP *See* accelerated graphics port.

AI *See* artificial intelligence.

AIFF *See* Audio Interchange File Format.

AIM *See* advanced integration module.

AIR *See* additive increase rate.

AIS *See* alarm indication signal.

AIX *See* Advanced Interactive eXecutive.

alarm Message notifying an operator or administrator of a network problem. *See* event and trap.

alarm indication signal (AIS) One of the OAM function types used for fault management. Typically an all-ones signal is transmitted to test the functions of a circuit, such as a T1. *See* T1, CC, *and* RDI.

alert An alarm message sent to a network management server such as HP OpenView, to identify a problem or an impending problem. In SNA, a message sent to a management subsystem typically using the network management vector transport (NMVT) protocol.

alert box A small box that appears on a computer's display screen to provide the user with information or a warning about a potentially damaging operation. Alert boxes are also called *message boxes*.

alertable In a DECnet network architecture, a synchronous alert that delivers data to specific points.

algorithm A clearly-defined mathematical formula used to solve a problem or run an operation.

alias An alternative name for an object, such as a variable, file, or device.

alias file A file that contains a pointer to another file, directory, or volume.

alias name A naming convention sometimes used to refer to a name, which means the same as the alias or that refers to another name which may be used as a pointer.

aliasing (*a*) In computer graphics, aliasing is the process by which smooth curves and other lines become jagged because the resolution of the graphics device or file is not high enough to represent a smooth curve. (*b*) In digital sound, aliasing is static distortion resulting from a low sampling rate-below 40 kilohertz (Khz).

alignment The arrangement of text or graphics relative to a the margin or to other objects.

alignment error In IEEE 802.3 networks, an error usually caused by frame damage due to collisions, which occurs when the total number of bits of a received frame is not divisible by eight.

allocation class According to DEC documentation, this is a unique number between 0 and 255 that the system manager assigns to a pair of hosts and to the dual-path devices that the hosts make available to other nodes in a VMS cluster.

allowed (or available) cell rate (ACR) The available bandwidth, measured in cells per second, for a given QoS class, which is dynamically controlled by the network devices.

all-routes broadcast frame A frame that has bits in the routine information field set to indicate the frame is to be sent to all LAN segments in the network. The destination address is not examined and plays no role in bridging.

all-stations broadcast frame A frame whose destination-address bits are set to all ones. All stations on any LAN segment on which the frame appears will copy it.

alphanumeric Describes the combined set of all letters in the alphabet and the numbers 0 through 9.

Alta Vista A well-known Internet firm, which provides search services, commerce, and media content on the Internet.

For more information, see
http://www.altavista.com.

alternate mark inversion (AMI) Also known as *binary coded alternate mark inversion*. AMI is a line-code type used on T1 and E1 circuits, which requires the sending device maintain a ones density. In AMI, zeros are represented by 01 during each bit cell, and ones are represented within each bit cell by alternating between 11 or 00. *See* ones density.

alternate route A route which is not the primary method of moving data from point to point.

ALU *See* arithmetic logic unit.

AM *See* amplitude modulation.

AMD *See* Advanced Micro Devices.

American National Standards Institute (ANSI) A voluntary organization that creates standards in programming languages, electrical specifications, communications protocols, and many other issues affecting the computer industry.

American Standard Code for Information Interchange *See* ASCII.

American Wire Gauge (AWG) A wire diameter specification, in which the lower the AWG number, the larger the physical wire.

AMI *See* alternate mark inversion.

Amiga A family of personal computers originally produced by Commodore Business Machines. Current popular Amiga models include the Amiga A1200 and the Amiga A4000T.

For more on Amiga, see
www.amiga.com.

ampersand (&) When used in the command line of most UNIX operating systems, it places the task or tasks in background operation.

amplitude The maximum value of varying wave forms.

amplitude modulation (AM) (*Illustration*) A modulation technique, which allows information to be conveyed via the amplitude of the carrier signal as shown in the figure below. *See* FM, PAM, and modulation.

analog (*Illustration*) Almost everything in the electronic world can be described or represented in one of two forms: analog or digital. The principal feature of analog representations is that they are continuous in form and

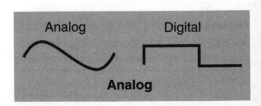

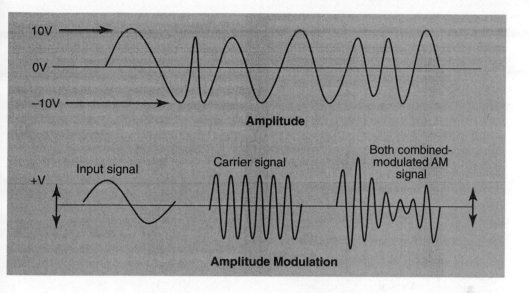

Amplitude

Amplitude Modulation

Input signal   Carrier signal   Both combined-modulated AM signal

appearance. In contrast, digital representations consist of values measured at discrete intervals such as "on" and "off" or 1 and 0. When an analog signal is transmitted over wires or through the air, the transmission conveys information through a variation of some combination of signal amplitude, frequency, and phase. *See* cycle.

ancillary control process (ACP) A computing process that is acting as an interface between application software and a specific I/O driver.

ANI *See* automatic number identification.

animated GIF A type of GIF image that can be animated by combining several different images into a single GIF file. When viewed the image appears animated.

animation A simulation of movement created by displaying a series of pictures, or frames. Cartoons on television is one example of animation. Animation on computers is one of the chief ingredients of multimedia presentations. There are many software applications that enable a user to create animations that can be displayed on a computer monitor.

annotation A comment attached to a particular section of a document.

anonymous FTP One of the earliest methods of Internet file transfer, anonymous FTP uses the *File Transfer Protocol (FTP)* along with some simple conventions. FTP was designed to let a user connect a remote system on which he had an account, authenticate using a user ID/password combination, then navigate a directory hierarchy and retrieve files. Anonymous FTP extends this idea by allowing users without accounts to use FTP for retrieving "public" data. To do this, a user connects to an anonymous FTP server with a normal FTP client, offering *anonymous* as a user ID and sending an identifying string, typically an e-mail address, as password. Servers configured for anonymous FTP will accept almost anything as password, so this information is really based on an "honor code." Once connected in this manner, the user can examine the server's file repository and download anything of interest, using FTP's standard capabilities. Anonymous FTP servers typically implement various security measures to prevent anonymous users from access to anything but an area designated for public information.

ANSI *See* American National Standards Institute.

ANSI Character Set A collection of special characters and codes adopted by the American National Standards Institute.

anycast address A method developed for IPv6, of sending a datagram or packet to a single address with more than one interface. The packet is usually sent to the "nearest" node in a group of nodes, as determined by the routing protocol's measure of distance. *See* multicast *and* unicast.

APaRT *See* automated packet recognition/ translation.

API *See* application program interface.

APM *See* advanced power management.

APPC *See* advanced program-to-program communication.

append To add something at the end.

APPL *See* application program.

Apple event According to Apple documentation, a high-level function that adheres to the specialized Apple event interprocess messaging protocol.

Apple event handler According to Apple documentation, a defined function that extracts pertinent data from an Apple event.

Apple event interprocess messaging protocol A standard defined by Apple Computer, Inc., for communication among applications. According to Apple documentation, high-level events that adhere to this protocol are called *Apple events*.

Apple event parameter According to Apple documentation, a keyword specifying a descriptor record containing data which the target application of an Apple event must use.

Apple file exchange A program that permits file transfer between Apple computers and DOS-based computers.

Apple key A special key on Macintosh computers, labeled with the Apple logo, which serves as the Command key for Apple systems.

AppleShare file server Software that permits users to perform tasks in AppleTalk networks.

AppleShare print server A Macintosh computer-software combination that manages network printing.

applet A small, specialized program, designed to be executed from within another application, hence the name. Unlike a normal application, applets cannot be executed directly from the operating system. With the growing popularity of *object linking and embedding (OLE)*, applets are becoming more widely used. A well-designed applet can be invoked from many different applications, this makes them very useful on the Internet.

AppleTalk (*Illustration*) Inexpensive local-area network (LAN) architecture developed by and built into all Apple computers and laser printers.

AppleTalk Address Resolution Protocol (AARP) An AppleTalk-based protocol that assists nodes in determining their AppleTalk addresses. *AARP probe packets* are transmitted by the AppleTalk Address Resolution Protocol to determine whether a randomly selected node ID is being used by another node in a nonextended AppleTalk network. If the node ID is not being used, the sending node uses that node ID. If the node ID is being used, the sending node chooses a different ID and sends more AARP probe packets to determine if the new ID is in use. *See* ARP and AppleTalk.

AppleTalk data stream protocol (ADSP) An AppleTalk protocol that provides the capability for maintaining a connection-oriented session between entities on an Internet.

AppleTalk Echo Protocol (AEP) A protocol used to test connectivity between AppleTalk nodes. One node sends a packet to another node and, in return, the sender receives a duplicate, or echo, of that packet.

AppleTalk Filing Protocol (AFP) The protocol used between an application and a file server. AFP is a client of ASP.

AppleTalk Internet router Software operating on an Apple computer that simulates a router and allows it to support up to eight AppleTalk networks.

AppleTalk Phase 2 Introduced in June 1989 by Apple Computers, AppleTalk Phase 2 extended the capability of AppleTalk Phase I

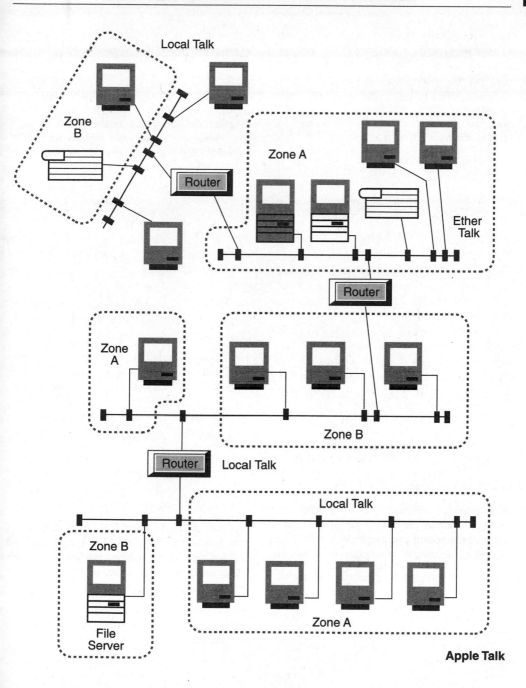

Apple Talk

networks; for example, it allows for the support of token ring networks and provides more efficient routing techniques. It is included in System/7 software.

AppleTalk session protocol (ASP) An AppleTalk session protocol used to establish and maintain logical connections between a workstation and a server.

AppleTalk transaction protocol (ATP) An AppleTalk protocol that functions in many ways like a connection-oriented protocol. For example, ATP aligns the packets into the order in which they need to be received, based on sequence numbers, and if any packets have been lost, automatic retransmission of a packet(s) is automatically performed.

AppleTalk transition queue An operating system queue.

AppleTalk transition Informational message indicating specific occurrences of transitions that relate to the AppleTalk transition queue.

AppleTalk Update-Based Routing Protocol (AURP) AppleTalk traffic encapsulation type placed in the header of a non-AppleTalk protocol, such as TCP/IP. AURP encapsulation allows the connection of two or more discontiguous AppleTalk internetworks across a non-AppleTalk network through a connection known as an *AURP tunnel*. AURP maintains routing tables for the entire AppleTalk WAN by exchanging routing information between exterior routers. *See* AURP tunnel *and* exterior router.

application A program or group of programs designed for end users. Software can be divided into two general classes: *systems software* and *applications software*.

Application Configuration Access Protocol (ACAP) An e-mail protocol being developed by the IETF to complement IMAP4.

application foundation classes (AFC) A set of Microsoft foundation classes written entirely in Java.

Application layer The seventh and highest layer of Systems Network Architecture (SNA) and Open Systems Interconnection (OSI). It supplies functions to applications or nodes allowing them to communicate with other applications or nodes.

application program (APPL) Software that provides functions needed by a user whenever requested. *See* applet *and* application program interface.

application program interface (API) A set of routines, protocols, and tools for building software applications.

application program major node In a VTAM, a group of application program minor nodes.

application result handler A program designed to perform predefined functions of results generated from applications.

application server A computer connected to a network, which is used solely to provide processing power for application programs in support of users.

application service element (ASE) A definition that explains the capabilities of an entity used within an application.

application specific integrated circuit (ASIC) A chip designed for a particular application.

application transaction program The program built around LU6.2 protocols. A program written around the LU6.2 protocols for or by a user to process the user's application; in an SNA network, an end user of a type 6.2 logical unit.

APPN *See* advanced peer-to-peer networking.

APPN end node An end node that provides full SNA end-user services and supports sessions through dynamic registration between its local control point and the CP in an adjacent network node.

APPN intermediate routing The capability of an APPN network node to accept traffic from one adjacent node and pass it on to another.

APPN intermediate routing network Portion of an APPN network consisting of network nodes and their connections.

APPN network A type 2.1 IBM network that has at least one APPN node within it.

APPN network node A type 2.1 (T2.1) node that, besides offering full SNA end-user services, provides intermediate routing services within a T2.1 network, and network services to its local LUs and attached T2.1 end nodes in its domain; it can also attach to a subarea network as a peripheral node.

APPN+ Next-generation high performance routing APPN that replaces the label-swapping routing algorithm with source routing.

Archie A software based tool for finding files stored on anonymous FTP sites, provided you know the exact name or substring of the file being requested.

architecture A design. Can refer to either hardware or software.

archival backup A type of backup in which all files are copied to a backup storage device. Archival backups are also called *full backup*.

archive To copy files to a long-term storage device for backup and archival purposes.

area Logical set of network segments and their attached network devices. Areas are usually connected to other areas via *routers*, making up a single *autonomous system*. Areas can be found within CLNS, DECnet, or OSPF networks. *See* autonomous system, OSPF, CLNS, *and* DECnet.

area border router (ABR) The name given to a router, running OSPF and located on the border of one or more OSPF areas that connect to the OSPF backbone, commonly known as Area 0. As a result ABRs are considered members of both the OSPF backbone and the attached areas. ABRs maintain routing tables describing both the backbone topology and the topology of the other OSPF areas. *See* OSPF.

argument list A vector of entries representing a procedure parameter list and possibly a function value.

arithmetic logic unit (ALU) That part of a computer which performs all arithmetic computations, such as addition and multiplication, and all comparison operations. The ALU is one component of the *central processing unit (CPU)*.

ARM *See* asynchronous response mode.

ARP *See* Address Resolution Protocol.

ARPA *See* Advanced Research Projects Agency.

ARPANET *See* Advanced Research Projects Agency Network.

artificial intelligence (AI) The branch of computer science concerned with making computers behave like humans. The term was coined in 1956 by John McCarthy at the Massachusetts Institute of Technology.

AS/400 Application System/400, a popular line of IBM minicomputers.

For more information, see *www.ibm.com*.

AS *See* autonomous system.

ASBR *See* autonomous system boundary router.

ASCII (*Illustration*) This is the de facto worldwide standard for the code numbers used by computers to represent all upper- and lowercase Latin letters, numbers, punctuation, etc. This character set lists and defines letters, symbols, numbers, and specialized control functions. There are 128 standard ASCII codes, each of which can be represented by a 7-digit binary number: 0000000 through 1111111, with each letter assigned a number from 0 to 127. For example, the ASCII code for uppercase M is 77. Most computers use ASCII codes to represent text, which makes it possible to transfer data from one computer to another. This is in contrast to a *binary file*, in which there is no one-to-one mapping between bytes and characters.

ASE *See* application service element.

ASF *See* Advanced Streaming Format.

ASIC *See* application specific integrated circuit.

ASM *See* address space manager.

ASN/ASN.1 *See* abstract syntax notation.

ASP *See* abstract service primitive.

ASPI *See* advanced SCSI programming interface.

assembler A program that translates programs from assembly language to machine language.

Least significant bits (hexadecimal)

Most significant bits

(hexadecimal)

(hexadecimal)	000 (0)	001 (1)	010 (2)	011 (3)	100 (4)	101 (5)	110 (6)	111 (7)
0000 (0)	NUL	DLE	SP	0	@	P	`	p
0001 (1)	SOH	DC1	!	1	A	Q	a	q
0010 (2)	STX	DC2	"	2	B	R	b	r
0011 (3)	ETX	DC3	#	3	C	S	c	s
0100 (4)	EOT	DC4	$	4	D	T	d	t
0101 (5)	ENQ	NAK	%	5	E	U	e	u
0110 (6)	ACK	SYN	&	6	F	V	f	v
0111 (7)	BEL	ETB	'	7	G	W	g	w
1000 (8)	BS	CAN	(	8	H	X	h	x
1001 (9)	HT	EM	)	9	I	Y	I	y
1010 (A)	LF	SUB	*	:	J	Z	j	z
1011 (B)	VT	ESC	+	;	K	[	k	{
1100 (C)	FF	FS	,	<	L	\	l	
1101 (D)	CR	GS	-	=	M	]	m	}
1110 (E)	SOH	RS	.	>	N		n	~
1111 (F)	SI	US	/	?	O		o	DEL

DEFINITIONS OF ASCII CONTROL CODE ABBREVIATIONS

ACK - ACKNOWLEDGE
BEL -BELL
BS - BACKSPACE
CAN - CANCEL
CR - CARRIAGE RETURN
DC - DIRECT CONTROL
DEL - DELETE IDLE
DLE - DATA LINK ESCAPE
EM - END OF MEDIUM
ENQ - ENQUIRY
EOT - END OF TRANSMISSION
ESC - ESCAPE
ETB - END OF TRANSMISSION BLOCK
ETX - END OF TEXT
FF - FORM FEED

FS - FORM SEPARATOR
GS - GROUP SEPARATOR
HT - HORIZONTAL TAB
LF - LINE FEED
NAK - NEGATIVE ACKNOWLEDGE
NUL - NULL
RS - RECORD SEPARATOR
SI - SHIFT IN
SO - SHIFT OUT
SOH - START OF HEADING
STX - START OF TEXT
SUB - SUBSTITUTE
SYN - SYNCHRONOUS IDLE
US - UNIT SEPARATOR
VT - VERTICAL TAB

ASCII

assembly language A programming language derived from *machine language*. Whereas machine languages consist entirely of numbers, assembly languages use names instead of numbers. Thus it is easier for programmers to read assembly languages rather than machine languages.

association control service element (ACSE) A convention used by the OSI model to establish, maintain, or terminate a connection between two different applications. Used to establish and terminate associations between applications.

Association for Computing Machinery (ACM) An organization composed of United States computer professionals. Founded in 1947, the ACM publishes information relating to computer science, holds seminars, and creates and promotes computer standards.

AST *See* asynchronous system trap.

asymmetric digital subscriber line (ADSL) (*Illustration*) A method for moving data over regular phone lines. Currently ADSL is not widely deployed but telcos are promising quick expansions within many metropolitan areas. Even though ADSL is deployed over regular phone lines it is much faster than a regular phone connection, and the wires coming into the subscriber's premises are the same (copper) wires used for regular phone service. This allows for easy installation at the customer's premise. An ADSL circuit must be configured to connect two specific locations, and as a result it is similar to a leased line in its operation. ADSL supports data rates of from 1.5 to 9 Mbps when receiving data (known as the *downstream rate*) and from 16 to 640 Kbps when sending data (known as the *upstream rate*). ADSL is often discussed as an alternative to ISDN, allowing higher speeds in cases where the connection is always to the same place. *See* XDSL.

asymmetric digital technology An xDSL technology in which modems are attached to twisted-pair copper lines.

asynchronous Not synchronized; that is, not occurring at predetermined or regular inter-

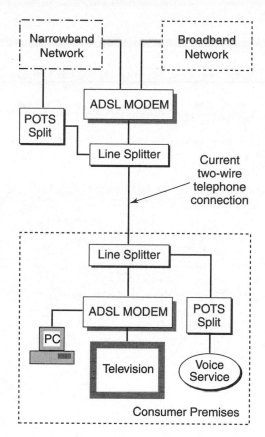

vals. All lower-level data communications protocols can be classified as either *synchronous* or *asynchronous*. Asynchronous transmissions are clocked, or synchronized, one byte at a time. Synchronous transmissions are clocked in groups of bytes.

asynchronous balanced mode (ABM) An HDLC communication mode supporting peer-oriented and point-to-point communications between two stations that allows either station to initiate a transmission.

asynchronous response mode (ARM) An HDLC communication mode involving one primary station (router) and at least one secondary station, where either the primary or the secondary stations can initiate a data transmission session. *See* HDLC, primary *and* secondary station.

asynchronous system trap (AST) A method of identifying a specific event via a software-simulated interrupt.

asynchronous time-division multiplexing (ATDM) An asynchronous and intelligent TDM where time slots are allocated to the users on demand (dynamically).

asynchronous transfer An efficient approach for transmitting information using time slots on a demand basis (ATDM, ATM) rather than on a periodical one (TDM, STM).

asynchronous transfer mode (ATM) (*Illustration*) A telecommunications concept defined by ANSI and CCITT standards committees for the transport of a broad range of user information including voice, data, and video communication on any user-to-network interface (UNI). ATM might well be positioned to be the high-speed networking tool of the next century. ATM can be used to aggregate user traffic from multiple existing applications onto a single UNI. The ATM concept aggregates a myriad of services onto a single access arrangement. Some of these applications include:

- PBX-to-PBX lines/trunks
- Host-to-host computer data links
- Video conferencing circuits
- LAN-to-LAN bridged or routed traffic
- Multimedia networking services between high-speed devices
- Workstations
- Supercomputers
- Routers

asynchronous transmission A method of data transmission which allows characters to be sent at irregular intervals by preceding each character with a *start bit*, and following it with a *stop bit*. No clocking signal is provided. *See* synchronous transmission.

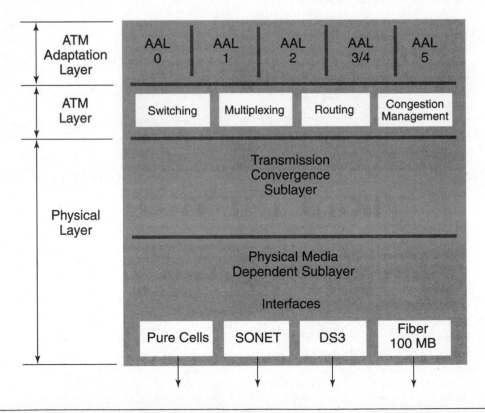

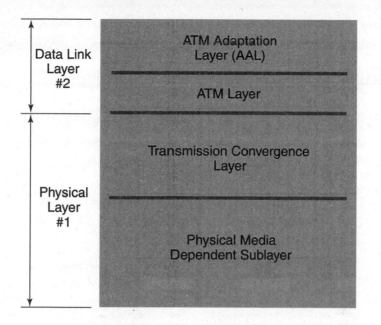

AT attachment packet interface (ATAPI)
An extension to EIDE (also called *ATA-2*) that
enables the interface to support CD-ROM
players and tape drives.

AT bus The expansion bus on the IBM PC/AT
and compatible computers. The bus is the collection of wires and electronic components that
connect all device controllers and add-in cards.

AT command set The standard language
used to control modems.

ATAPI *See* AT attachment packet interface.

ATDM *See* asynchronous time-division
multiplexing.

ATM *See* asynchronous transfer mode.

ATM adaptation layer (AAL) (*Illustration*) A
collection of standardized ATM-based protocols
that provides services to higher layers by adapting user traffic to a cell format. The AAL is divided into the *convergence sublayer (CS)* and the
*segmentation and reassembly (SAR) sublay-
ers*. At present, the four types of AAL recommended by the ITU-T are AAL1, AAL2, AAL3/4,
and AAL5. AAL type 1. A ATM protocol standard
used for the transport of constant bit rate (CBR)
traffic (i.e., audio and video) and for emulating

TDM-based circuits (i.e., DS1, E1). AAL type 2. A
ATM protocol standard for supporting time-
dependent variable bit rate (VBR-RT) of connection-oriented traffic (i.e., packetized video
and audio). AAL type 3 and 4. A ATM protocol
standard for supporting both connectionless
and connection-oriented variable bit rate (VBR)
traffic. Used also to support SMDS.

AAL type 5 ATM protocol standard for supporting the transport of lightweight variable bit
rate (VBR) traffic and signaling messages. Also
used to support frame relay services.

**ATM channel/data service unit (ATM
CSU/DSU)** A device that converts information
bits (i.e., transmitted over the telephony network) or frame-based information into (or
from) a stream of ATM cells. *See* CSU, DSU, *and*
DXI.

ATM DSU (ADSU) A type of terminal adapter
that is used to access an ATM network via a
HSSI-compatible device. *See* DSU, ATM, *and*
HSSI.

ATM Forum Originally founded by a group of
vendors and telecommunication companies,
this formal standards body is comprised of various committees responsible for making rec-

ommendations and producing implementation specifications for ATM.

For more information see, *www.atmforum.com*.

ATM layer The second layer of the ATM protocol stack model that constructs and processes ATM cells. Its functions also include *usage parameter control (UPC)* and support of *quality of service (QoS)* classes.

ATMF *See* ATM Forum.

ATM-service access point (ATM-SAP) The physical interface at the boundary between the AAL and the ATM layer. *See* SAP *and* PHY-SAP.

AToMMIB or ATM MIB IETF-defined management information base (MIB) for managing VP/VC links and ATM PVC-supported services and interfaces.

ATP *See* AppleTalk Transaction Protocol.

attachment unit interface (AUI) The portion of the Ethernet standard that specifies how a cable is to be connected to an Ethernet card. AUI specifies a coaxial cable connected to a transceiver that plugs into a 15-pin socket on the network interface card (NIC).

attenuation A decrease in magnitude of current, voltage, or electrical or optical power of a signal in transmission between points. It may expressed in *decibels* or *nepers*.

Audio Interchange File Format (AIFF) A common format for storing and transmitting audio.

Audio Video Interleave (AVI) The file format for Microsoft's Video for Windows standard.

AUI *See* attachment unit interface.

AUP *See* acceptable use policy.

AURP tunnel Logical connection created in an AURP-based WAN, which contains two discontiguous AppleTalk internetworks. An AURP tunnel functions as a single, virtual data link between the two AppleTalk internetworks physically separated by a foreign networks (such as a

TCP/IP network, for example). *See* AppleTalk Update-Based Routing Protocol (AURP).

authentication A process of establishing identity. *See* authorization.

authentication, authorization, and accounting (AAA) A security method that allows you to implement three unique aspects of security into a cohesive whole. These unique aspects are *authentication, authorization*, and *accounting*. AAA uses protocols such as RADIUS, TACACS+, and Kerberos to administer and control its security functions.

authority zone A section of the DNS domain-name tree for which one name server is the authority. *See* DNS.

authorization The process of granting or denying a user access to a network resource. To gain authorization, authentication must first be verified. *See* authentication.

auto-answer A feature supported by many modems, which enables a computer to accept incoming calls even if the user is not present.

automated packet recognition/translation (APaRT) A method that recognizes specific data link-layer encapsulation packet types and, when these packet types are transferred from one physical medium to another, translates them into the native packet format of the destination device. This allows a server or other device to be connected to either FDDI or CDDI with no network or application reconfiguration being necessary.

automatic call reconnect An automatic rerouting feature that routes a call away from a failed trunk line.

automatic log-on In SNA, a process by which VTAM automatically creates a session-initiation request to establish a session between two logical units (LUs). The result of this request is the SNA BIND command from the primary logical unit (PLU) to the secondary logical unit (SLU). Hence, a LU-LU session is established if the BIND image is correct and other parameters are accurate.

automatic number identification (ANI) A service that provides the telephone number of an incoming call. ISDN, the standards for transmissions on telephone lines, supports ANI.

autonomous confederation Autonomous system groups that rely on their own internal network connectivity and routing table information more than they rely on the same information received from other autonomous systems or confederations.

autonomous system (AS) An internetwork that is part of the Internet and has a single routing policy. Each autonomous system is assigned an *autonomous system number*.

autonomous system boundary router (ASBR) A router located between an OSPF autonomous system, in a nonstub area, and a non-OSPF network, such as a network running RIP or BGP. ASBRs will run both OSPF and another routing protocol, such as RIP. *See* ABR, non-stub area, *and* OSPF.

AutoSuggest A feature that automatically determines when an attempted connection needs some kind of intermediate device, and then scans the device library for the appropriate device models to use. Some examples of automatically suggested intermediate devices include adding an RJ-45 AUI transceiver, adding a modem to the DCE end of the connection, and adding an ISDN terminal adapter to the DTE end of the connection.

AUX *See* auxiliary port.

auxiliary port (AUX) The logical name in DOS systems for the standard communications port. This is usually the same as *COM1*.

available bit rate (ABR) A best-effort service type where the network makes no absolute guarantee of cell delivery. The available bit rate provides only best effort delivery. *See* CBR *and* UBR.

avatar (*a*) A graphic which represents a real person in a cyberspace system. (*b*) A common name for the superuser account on UNIX systems.

average cell rate The mean number of cells that the source can inject into a network over a given virtual connection (VC).

average cell transfer delay The arithmetic average of a number of cell transfer delays (CTD). *See* mean cell transfer delay.

AVI *See* Audio Video Interleave.

AWK An interpreted programming language included in most versions of UNIX.

AWT *See* Abstract Windows Toolkit.

AXP A DEC hardware and operating system architecture.

B8ZS *See* bipolar 8 zero substitution.

back end A specialized node or software program used by frame relay, which provides services to a front-end device. *See* client, front end, *and* server.

back pressure The propagation of network congestion information upstream through an internetwork. A good example of this is an Ethernet switch that signals the endstation on a port by raising the carrier signal to prevent further transmissions until the congestion within the switch drops to an acceptable level. This back pressure to the end stations minimize retransmissions due to pack loss within the switch.

backbone A group of network devices that provides connectivity between subnetworks in an enterprise-wide network. This group can either be connected through LAN or WAN technologies. The backbone serves as a central communications highway for LAN-to-LAN traffic. *See* network.

backbone LAN segment In a multisegment LAN configuration, a centrally located LAN segment to which other LAN segments are connected by means of bridges or routers.

background (*a*) In a multitasking computer that is executing several tasks or programs at the same time, the currently processed task is the *foreground process*, and those on hold are the *background processes*. (*b*) The area of a display screen not covered by characters and graphics.

background process An applications process that does not require the total attention of the operating system to function.

backoff Retransmission delay randomly determined and enforced by contentious MAC protocols after a network node with data to transmit determines that the physical medium is already in use, typically through the detection of a collision.

backplane (*a*) A circuit board containing sockets into which other circuit boards can be plugged in. In PCs, the backplane is the circuit board that contains sockets for expansion cards. Backplanes can be classified as active or passive. *Active backplanes* contain logical circuitry that performs computing functions in addition to the sockets. *Passive backplanes* contain almost no computing circuitry. (*b*) The physical connection between an interface processor or card and the data buses and power distribution buses inside a chassis.

backside bus A microprocessor bus that connects the CPU to a Level 2 cache. A backside bus usually runs at a faster clock speed than the *frontside bus* that connects the CPU to main memory.

backup To copy files to a second "backup" medium in case the first medium fails.

backup path In an IBM token-ring network, an alternative path for signal flow through access units and their main ring-path cabling.

backup server A program or device that copies files so that at least two up-to-date copies always exist.

backward compatible A program or product that is compatible with earlier models or versions of the same product.

backward error correction (BEC) An error-correction scheme where the sender retransmits any data to be found in error, based on the feedback from the receiver.

backward explicit congestion notification (BECN) Bit set by a frame relay network in frames traveling in the opposite direction of frames encountering a congested path. The DTE receiving frames with the BECN bit set can request that higher-level protocols take flow control action as appropriate. *See* FECN.

backward learning Algorithmic process used for routing traffic that surmises routing information by assuming symmetrical network conditions are in existence throughout the entire internetwork. For example, if <RouterA> receives a packet from <RouterB> through <RouterC>, the backward-learning routing algorithm will assume that <RouterA> can easily reach <RouterB> through <RouterC>.

bad sector A portion of a disk that cannot be used because it is flawed.

BAF RACE II project R2024.

BAK file In many systems, a file with a .BAK extension, indicates that the file is a backup.

balanced configuration A point-to-point network configuration in an HDLC network, using two combined stations. *See* HDLC.

balun (balanced/unbalanced) An impedance-matching transformer. Baluns are small passive devices that convert the impedance of coaxial cable so that its signal can run on twisted-pair wiring. They are used often so that IBM 3270-type terminals, which traditionally require coaxial cable connection to their host computer, can run on twisted pair.

bandwidth (BW) Transmission capacity of a communications medium. The amount of data that can be transmitted in a fixed amount of time. Bandwidth is usually expressed in *bits per second* or *bytes per second* for digital devices. For analog devices, bandwidth is expressed in *cycles per second* or *Hertz (Hz)*. A subtle difference should be noted with the definition of bandwidth: the number of bits a communications line may transmit may not be the total bandwidth for data because some bits may be used for control signals. This leaves a lesser amount as *real bandwidth* for the user. For example, an OC3 SONET line, in ATM, which is rated at a 155 Mbits really only has 149.76 of real data bits available to the user.

Bandwidth-on-Demand (BOD) A protocol used with Multilink PPP to add additional dial-up connections, as necessary, to increase bandwidth. *See* PPP.

bar chart In presentation graphics, a type of graph in which different values are represented by rectangular bars.

BARRNet *See* Bay Area Regional Research Network.

base address An address that is a reference point for other addresses.

BASE disk In SNA, and specifically the VM operating system, this is the disk containing text decks and macroinstructions for VTAM, NetView, and VM/SNA console support (VSCS).

base priority The priority a VM system assigns to a process when it is created. Normally, it comes from the authorization file.

baseband transmission A type of digital data transmission in which each medium (wire) carries only one signal, or channel, at a time. In contrast, *broadband transmission* enables a single wire to carry multiple signals simultaneously.

BASIC Beginner's All-purpose Symbolic Instruction Code. BASIC is one of the earliest and simplest high-level programming languages. It was developed by John Kemeney and Thomas Kurtz in the mid-1960s.

basic encoding rules (BER) Rules for encoding data units described in the ISO ASN.1 standard. *See* ASN.1.

basic information unit segment (BIU segment) In SNA, data contained within a path information unit (PIU). It consists of either a request (or response) header (RH) followed by all or part of a request (or response) unit (RU), or only part of an RU.

basic logical object An object in a specific logical structure which has no subordinate.

basic rate interface (BRI) Low-speed ISDN connection providing up to 128 Kbps of data, two phone lines, or both. It consists of two B (Bearer) channels and one D (Data) channel. The specification that provides two 64-kbps data B-channels that can carry voice or data and one 16-kbps control D-channel which carries call-control information, all sharing the same physical medium. Another type of ISDN configuration is called *primary-rate interface (PRI)*, and consists of 23 B-channels (30 in Europe) and one D-channel.

Basic Research and Human Resources (BRHR) HPCC program component designed to support research, training, and education in computer science, computer engineering, and computational science. *See* HPCC.

BASize *See* buffer allocation size.

batch file A file that contains a sequence, or batch, of commands. Batch files are useful for storing sets of commands that are always executed together because you can simply enter the name of the batch file instead of entering each command individually. In DOS systems, batch files are often called BAT files because their filenames end with a .BAT extension.

batch processing Executing a series of non-interactive jobs all at one time. The term originated in the days when users entered programs on punch cards. They would give a batch of these programmed cards to the system operator, who would feed them into the computer.

baud The number (frequency) of signaling changes that can occur within a second. The term is named after J.M.E. Baudot, the inventor of the Baudot telegraph code. Technically, baud is the number of times per second that the carrier signal shifts value—for example a 1,200 bit-per-second modem actually runs at 300 baud, but it moves 4 bits per baud (4 x 300 = 1,200 bits per second). *See* bit *and* modem.

bay A site in a personal computer where a hard or floppy disk drive, CD-ROM drive, or tape drive can be installed.

Bay Area Regional Research Network (BARRNet) Regional network serving the San Francisco Bay Area. BARRNet is composed of the University of California, Stanford University, Lawrence Livermore National Laboratory, and NASA Ames Research Center. BARRNET is now part of the BBN Planet network. *See* BBN Planet.

BB *See* begin bracket.

BBN Planet Internet network composed of the former regional networks BARRNET, NEARNET, and SURAnet. BBN Planet is also a subsidiary company of BBN that operates a nationwide. *See* BARRNet, BBN, NEARNET, and SURAnet.

BBS *See* bulletin board system.

Bc *See* burst, committed.

B-channel Bearer channel. 64kb dta transmission channel used in ISDN. A B-channel can be specified as *clear* in that all 64 Kbytes are available to the user or *restricted* where some of the 64k bits are used for switch-to-switch signaling. *See* ISDN *and* D-channel.

Be *See* burst, excess.

beacon A token-ring frame sent by an adapter indicating that it has detected a serious ring problem, such as a broken cable or a multistation access unit. An adapter sending these frames is said to be *beaconing*.

BEC *See* backward error correction.

Because It's Time NETwork (or Because It's There NETwork) (BITNET) A network of educational sites separate from the Internet.

BECN *See* backward explicit congestion notification.

begin bracket In SNA, the value of the begin-bracket indicator in the request header (RH). It is the first request in the first chain of a bracket. Its value denotes the start of a bracket.

beginning of message (BOM) A PDU type that represents the beginning of a message.

Bell 103 A standard defining asynchronous, full-duplex communication for transmitting data over telephone lines at transmission rates of 300 baud within the United States. Europe and Japan use the CCITT V.21 protocol.

Bell 212A A standard that defines asynchronous, full-duplex communication for transmitting data over telephone lines at transmission rates of 1,200 bps within the United States. Europe and Japan use the CCITT V.22 protocol.

Bellcore Bell Communications Research, Inc.

Bellman-Ford routing algorithm *See* distance vector routing algorithm.

bells and whistles Fancy features provided by an application.

BER *See* bit error rate.

Berkeley broadcast A nonstandard IP broadcast address using all zeros instead of all ones in the host portion.

Berkeley Software Design, Inc. (BSDI) A commercial supplier of Internet and networking software based on the BSD (Berkeley) version of UNIX.

BERT *See* bit error rate tester.

best effort A QoS class in which no specific traffic parameters and no guarantees are provided. Other best effort transmission types include UBR and ABR. *See* service types.

best-effort delivery A description of network technologies that do not provide reliability at link levels.

BF *See* boundary function.

BGP *See* Border Gateway Protocol.

bias A dc voltage used in electronic circuitry which holds a desired time spacing of transient states from a mark to a space.

B-ICI *See* broadband-intercarrier interface.

BIGA *See* bus interface gate array.

big-endian The historical name of a technique that identifies the most-significant bytes in multi-byte data types. In systems that support big-endian architectures such as mainframes, the leftmost bytes are the most significant. In *little-endian* supported architectures such as PCs, the rightmost bytes are most significant. For example, consider the number 1,025 (2 to the tenth power plus one) represented in a 4-byte integer.

00000000 00000000 00000100 00000001

Big-Endian representation of 1,025	Little-Endian representation of 1,025
00	0000000000000001
01	0000000000000100
02	0000010000000000
03	0000000100000000

Note that the example above shows only big- and little-endian byte orders. The bit ordering within each byte can also be big- or little-endian, and some architectures actually use big-endian ordering for bits and little-endian ordering for bytes, or vice versa.

Converting data between the two numbering systems is sometimes referred to as the *NUXI problem*. Imagine the word UNIX stored in two 2-byte words. In a big-endian system, it would be stored as UNIX. In a little-endian system, it would be stored as NUXI.

The terms big-endian and little-endian are derived from the Lilliputians of *Gulliver's Travels*, whose major political issue was whether soft-boiled eggs should be opened on the big side or the little side. Likewise, the big-/little-endian computer debate has much more to do with political issues than technological merits.

binary arithmetic (*Illustration*) For some important aspects of Internet engineering, most notably IP addressing, an understanding of binary arithmetic is critical. Many strange-looking decimal numbers can only be understood by converting them (at least mentally) to binary. To convert a number from decimal to binary, begin at leftmost bit position. If the number is larger than or equal to the bit's weight, write a 1 in the bit position, subtract the bit's weight from the number, and continue with the difference. If the number is less than the bit's weight, write a 0 in the bit position and continue without any subtraction. Here's an illustration of converting 141 to binary (top of next page).

There is a simpler way to convert bytes back and forth between binary and decimal; akin to memorizing multiplication tables. The byte can split into two four-bit halves, each half called a *nibble*. Memorize the decimal values for the high nibble (all multiples of 16). The low nibble is trivial. Every number between 0 and 255 is the sum of one of the high nibble values and one of the low nibble values. Write the high nibble next to the low nibble, and this is the byte value in binary. Conversely, an eight-bit binary byte can be split in half, each nibble

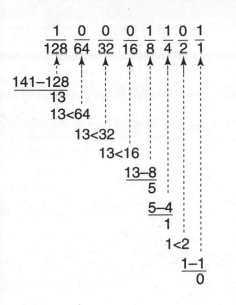

converted to decimal and two decimal numbers added together.

binary coded alternate mark inversion
See AMI.

binary compatible Two files having the exact same data format, down to the binary level; that means they have the same pattern of zeroes and ones in the data portion of the file. The file header, however, may be different.

binary file A computer-readable, but not human-readable, file. An example of a binary file is *executable programs*, which are stored in binary files, as are most numeric data files. *See* ASCII.

binary format A format for representing data used by some applications.

binary large object (BLOB) A collection of binary data stored as a single entity in a database management systems (DBMS).

binary numbers A number system that has just two unique digits, 1 and 0. Computers are based on the binary numbering system. All mathematical operations that are possible in the decimal numbering system (addition, subtraction, multiplication, division) are equally possible in the binary system. The decimal system is used in everyday life because it seems more natural (we have ten fingers and ten toes). For the computer, the binary system is more natural because of its electrical nature (charged versus uncharged).

Let's compare and contrast how numbers are represented as shown in the following figures.

High Nibble		Low Nibble	High Nibble		Low Nibble
0	0000	0	128	1000	8
16	0001	1	144	1001	9
32	0010	2	160	1010	10
48	0011	3	176	1011	11
64	0100	4	192	1100	12
80	0101	5	208	1101	13
96	0110	6	224	1110	14
112	0111	7	240	1111	15

$$137 = 128 + 9 = \boxed{1000}\ \boxed{1001}$$

Decimal and Binary Equivalents

Decimal	Binary
1	1
2	10
3	11
4	100
5	101
6	110
7	111
8	1000
9	1001
1	1010
16	10000
32	100000
64	1000000
100	1100100
256	100000000
512	1000000000
1000	1111110100

binary synchronous communication (BSC) A telecommunication protocol using a standard set of transmission control characters and control character sequences. A set of IBM operating procedures for synchronous transmission used in teleprocessing networks.

binary synchronous/bisynchronous transmission (bisync) A type of synchronous communications used primarily in mainframe networks.

binary tree A tree structure in which each node has at most two leafs that are often used for sorting data.

binary-coded decimal (BCD) (*Illustration*) A numbering format for representing decimal numbers in which each digit is represented by four bits (a nibble). For example, the number 374 would be represented as: 0011 0111 0100 in binary-coded decimal. More examples are shown in the figure.

bind To assign a value to a symbolic placeholder. In SNA, this is a request for session activation between network accessible units (NAUS) BIND image

BIND pacing In SNA, a technique used to prevent a BIND standoff. It is a technique used by the address space manager (ASM).

Binhex BINary HEXadecimal. A method for converting non-text files (non-ASCII) into ASCII. This is needed because Internet e-mail

Powers of 2	Value
2 × 0	1
2 × 1	2
2 × 2	4
2 × 3	8
2 × 4	16
2 × 5	32
2 × 6	64
2 × 7	128
2 × 8	256
2 × 9	512
2 × 10	1024
2 × 11	2048
2 × 12	4096

decimal	BCD
0	0000
1	0001
2	0010
3	0011
4	0100
5	0101
6	0110
7	0111
8	1000
9	1001

Bindary Coded Decimal (BCD)

can only handle ASCII files. *See* ASCII, binary numbers, MIME, *and* UUENCODE.

biometrics The study of measurable biological characteristics such as fingerprints. This science is quickly becoming an integral part of the *smart card* (credit cards having some interactive processing) technology.

BIOS Basic input/output system. Built-in software that determines what a computer can do without accessing programs from a disk. The BIOS contains code which controls the keyboard, monitor, disk drives, and other functions. The BIOS checks all of these components to make sure they are operating properly. The BIOS is usually placed in a ROM chip (called a *ROM BIOS*). This chip is second in importance only to the CPU.

biphase coding Bipolar coding scheme originally developed for use in Ethernet. The biphase signal contains no direct current energy. It does, however, have clocking information embedded within it, thereby removing the need for separate clocking leads.

bipolar 8 zero substitution (B8ZS) A special line type that is used on T1 and E1 circuits for testing purposes. During these tests, a special code is sent after eight consecutive zeros which are interpreted by the remote end. *See* AMI *and* ones density.

bipolar Circuit characteristic that has both negative and positive electrical polarity. Contrast with *unipolar*.

B-ISDN *See* Broadband Integrated Services Digital Network.

bisync *See* binary synchronous.

bisynchronous transmission *See* binary synchronous/bisynchronous transmission.

bit Abbreviation for *binary digit*. A digital representation of the smallest possible unit of information. It can be in one of two states—off or on, 0 or 1. The meaning of the bit, which can represent almost anything, is unimportant at this point. The thing to remember is that all computer data—a text file on disk, a program in memory, a packet on a network—is ultimately a collection of bits.

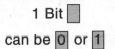

1 Bit
can be 0 or 1

If one bit has two different values, how many values do two bits have? The answer is four (2^2). Likewise, three bits have eight values (2^3). For example, if a computer display had eight colors available, and a user wished to select one of these in which to draw a diagram, three bits would be sufficient to represent this information. Each of the eight colors would be assigned to one of the three-bit combinations, and the user could pick one of the colors by picking the right three-bit combination.

2 Bits = 4 Possible Different Values
3 Bits = 8 Possible Different Values

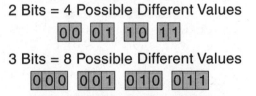

A common and convenient grouping of bits is the *byte* or *octet*, composed of eight bits. If two bits have four combinations, and three bits have eight combinations, how many combinations do eight bits have? Multiply eight 2s together—one two for each bit. 2 x 2 = 4 (2^2), so the number of combinations of two bits is four. 2 x 2 x 2 = 8 (2^3), so the number of combinations of three bits is eight. Do this eight times—compute 2 to the 8th power—to see that a byte has 256 possible values.

1 Byte = 8 Bits

If a byte has 256 possible states, its exact state can be represented by a number from 1 to 256. However, since zero is a very important number, a byte is more typically represented by a number from 0 to 255. This is very common, with bit pattern 00000000 representing zero, and bit pattern 11111111 representing 255. The numbers matching these two patterns, and everything in between, can be computed by assigning a weight to each bit, multiplying each bit's value (0 or 1) by its weight, and then adding the totals. For example, here's how 217 is represented as 11011001 in binary:

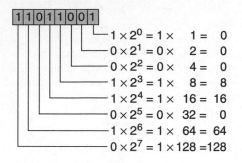

$$1 \times 2^0 = 1 \times \quad 1 = \quad 0$$
$$0 \times 2^1 = 0 \times \quad 2 = \quad 0$$
$$0 \times 2^2 = 0 \times \quad 4 = \quad 0$$
$$1 \times 2^3 = 1 \times \quad 8 = \quad 8$$
$$1 \times 2^4 = 1 \times \ 16 = \ 16$$
$$0 \times 2^5 = 0 \times \ 32 = \quad 0$$
$$1 \times 2^6 = 1 \times \ 64 = \ 64$$
$$0 \times 2^7 = 1 \times 128 = 128$$

$$1 + 8 + 16 + 64 + 128 = 217$$

The most common bit patterns in Internet engineering are those with a string of one bits, followed by a string of zero bits. Here are all such bytes, along with their decimal representation, computed just like the example using 217.

1 1 1 1 1 1 1 1	255
1 1 1 1 1 1 1 0	254
1 1 1 1 1 1 0 0	252
1 1 1 1 1 0 0 0	248
1 1 1 1 0 0 0 0	240
1 1 1 0 0 0 0 0	224
1 1 0 0 0 0 0 0	192
1 0 0 0 0 0 0 0	128
0 0 0 0 0 0 0 0	0

bit error rate (BER) The ratio of received bits that contain errors.

bit error rate tester (BERT) A test device that determines the bit error rate within a communications channel. *See* bit error rate (BER).

bit rate The number of bits of data transmitted over a communications line each second.

bit stuffing The practice of adding bits to a stream of data in order to prevent data from being interpreted as control information.

bitmap Generally speaking, bitmap is an array of data bits used for graphic images.

bitmap device A device that displays bitmaps.

bitmap font A font that is created from a matrix of dots.

bit-mapped graphics format (BMP) A graphics format used in the Windows environment. By convention, graphics files in the BMP format end with a .BMP extension.

BITNET *See* Because It's Time NETwork (or Because It's There NETwork).

bit-oriented protocol Data-link layer protocols that can transmit frames regardless of frame content. This results in a very efficient and reliable protocol that can operate in a full-duplex mode. Compare with *byte-oriented protocol*.

bits/s *See* bits-per-second.

bits-per-second (Bps) A measurement of how fast data is moved from one place to another. A 28.8 modem can move 28,800 bits per second. *See* bandwidth *and* bit.

BIU segment *See* basic information unit segment.

black hole Routing term for an area of a network that, because of problems within the network, allows packets to enter, but does not allow them to emerge. An example could be a router that does not respond correctly with an ICMP message which states that packets it is receiving are too large and must be fragmented.

blind carbon copy A copy of an e-mail message sent to a recipient without the recipient's address appearing in the message. This feature is very useful if you want to send a copy of a message to many people without each of them seeing who the other recipients are.

bloatware Software that requires considerable disk space and RAM.

BLOB *See* binary large object.

block multiplexer channel A United States channel standard that implements the FIPS-60 standard, also referred to as *OEMI channel* and *370 block mux channel*.

blocking A condition in switches have no paths available to complete a circuit.

BMP *See* bit-mapped graphics format.

BN *See* boundary node.

BNC connector British Naval Connector or Bayonet Nut Connector or Bayonet Neil Consulman. A bayonet-locking connector for slim coaxial cables. A type of connector used with the 10base2 Ethernet coaxial cables, such as the RG-58 A/U cable.

BOD *See* Bandwidth-on-Demand.

Bolt, Beranek, and Newman Inc. (BBN) High-technology company located in Massachusetts which developed and maintained the ARPANET core gateway system. *See* Internet and BBN Planet.

BOM *See* beginning of message.

bomb To fail, as in when a program ends prematurely or aborts.

boot Bootstrap. The starting-up of a computer, which involves loading the operating system and other basic software. A *cold boot* occurs when the computer is turned on from an off position. A *warm boot* occurs when the computer is reset while already on. The term "bootstrap" refers to a strap attached to the top of a boot that assists in pulling the boot on. Hence, the expression "pull oneself up by the bootstraps."

boot flash Flash memory used to store an emergency copy of IOS in Cisco routers. If installed, it will take the place of boot ROM. Boot flash can be rewritten multiple times, versus ROM, which can be written only once.

bootable diskette A diskette from which you can boot your computer.

BOOTP *See* Bootstrap Protocol.

bootstrap block That part of the index file on a system disk which contains a program that loads the operating system into memory.

Bootstrap Protocol (BOOTP) An Internet protocol (IP) documented in RFC951, which enables a diskless workstation to determine its own IP address, the IP address of the BOOTP server, and which file to be loaded into memory in order for the workstation to boot.

Border Gateway Protocol (BGP) The dynamic routing protocol used between ISPs to manage extremely large routing tables. BGP enables groups of routers (called *autonomous systems*) to share routing information so that efficient, loop-free routes can be established. BGP is commonly used within and between Internet Service Providers (ISPs). The protocol is defined in RFC 1771.

bot Program that runs automatically.

boundary function (BF) In SNA, protocol support for attached peripheral nodes.

boundary node (BN) A network node that performs the function of transforming network addresses to local addresses. A boundary node can also be a network device that sits in one domain with a network link to another domain.

BPDU *See* bridge protocol data unit.

Bps *See* bits-per-second.

bracket In SNA, one or more chains of RUs and their responses that are exchanged between session partners.

bracket protocol A data flow control protocol in which session partners exchange data via IBM's SNA bracket protocol.

branch In tree structures, a single section of the tree that ends with a leaf.

Break key A key on computer keyboards which temporarily interrupts the computer's communications line.

BRHR *See* Basic Research and Human Resources.

BRI *See* basic rate interface.

bridge (*Illustration*) (*a*) An interface connecting two similar or dissimilar LAN media types. (*b*) A device that connects two LANs. It performs its functions at the data link control (DLC) layer.

bridge forwarding Process that uses entries in a filtering database to determine whether frames with a given MAC destination address can be for-

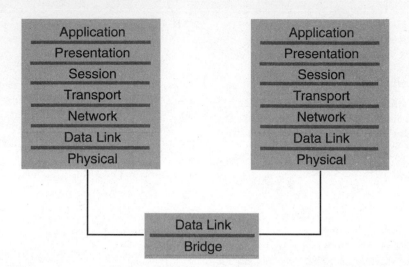

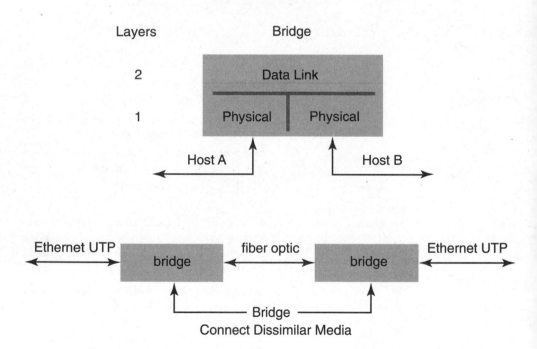

Bridge
Connect Dissimilar Media

warded to a given port or ports. Described in the IEEE 802.1 standard. *See* IEEE 802.1.

bridge ID The bridge label, combined with the address of the adapter connecting the bridge to the LAN segment with the lowest LAN segment number.

bridge label A two-byte hexadecimal number that the user can assign to each bridge.

bridge number The bridge identifier that the user specifies in the bridge program configuration file. The bridge number distinguishes between parallel bridges.

bridge protocol data unit (BPDU) A spanning-tree protocol hello packet that is sent out at regular intervals to exchange information among switches/bridges in the network. *See* spanning tree, PDU, *and* bridging.

bridge static filtering Process in which a bridge maintains a filtering database consisting of static entries. Each static entry equates a MAC destination address with a port that can receive frames with this MAC destination address and a set of ports on which the frames can be transmitted. Defined in the IEEE802.1 standard. *See* IEEE 802.1.

bridging A method of path selection (*contrast routing*). In a bridged network, no correspondence is required between addresses and paths. Put another way, addresses don't imply anything about where hosts are physically attached to the network. Any address can appear at any location. In contrast, routing requires more thoughtful address assignment, corresponding to physical placement. Bridging relies heavily on broadcasting. Because a packet may contain no information other than the destination address, and that implies nothing about the path that should be used, the only option may be to send the packet everywhere. This is one of bridging's most severe limitations, because this is a very inefficient method of data delivery, and can trigger *broadcast storms*. In networks with low-speed links, this can introduce crippling overhead. *See* translational *and* transparent bridging.

Broadband Integrated Services Digital Network (B-ISDN) An ITU-T-introduced protocol platform to support the integrated, high-speed transmission of data, audio, and video in a seamless fashion. Asynchronous transfer mode (ATM) has emerged as a suitable transport standard. B-ISDN data may be transmitted over fiber optic telephone lines at data rates of 1.5 million bits per second (bps).

broadband transmission Data transmission type in which a single physical medium (wire) can carry several channels at once. Used in cable television (and in other forms) to allow multiple high-speed signals to share the bandwidth of a single cable via frequency division multiplexing.

broadband-intercarrier interface (B-ICI) An interface that supports service connections (such as CRS, CES, SMDS, FR) across public ATM networks and/or carriers.

 For more information, go to *http://www.atmforum.com* and search on B-ICI for a summary of the specification.

broadcast The simultaneous transmission of data to more than one destination. A source sends one copy of a message to all the nodes on the network even if any node does not want to receive such messages. *See* anycast, unicast, multicast, *and* IP multicasting.

broadcast address Generally, a MAC destination address of all ones. It is reserved for sending to all stations on a internetwork. Compare with *multicast address* and *unicast address*.

broadcast and unknown server (BUS) A server that forwards multicast, broadcast, and unknown-destination address traffic to the attached LECs. *See* LANE.

broadcast domain The part of a network that receives the same broadcasts.

broadcast message A message from one station sent to all other users. On a token-ring LAN, the destination address is unspecified, thus all devices receive the message.

broadcast network A network that supports more than two attached routers, and has the capability to address a single physical message to all of the attached routers.

broadcast search In APPN, the simultaneous search to all network nodes in the form of a request for some type of data.

broadcast storm A state in which a message that has been broadcast across a network results in even more responses. Each response then results in still more responses, in a snowball effect. A severe broadcast storm can block all other network traffic, resulting in a network meltdown. Broadcast storms can usually be prevented by carefully configuring a network to block illegal broadcast messages.

brouter In local area networking, a device that combines the dynamic routing capabilities of an internetwork router with the capability of a bridge to interconnect LANs.

browse With regard to functions that can be performed on an entity, browse merely permits viewing.

browser Client application software for accessing data on the World Wide Web. *See* client, URL, WWW, Netscape, Mosaic, *and* home page.

BSC *See* binary synchronous communication.

BT *See* burst tolerance.

Btrieve According to Novell documentation, this is a complete indexed record management system designed for high-performance data handling.

BTW By the way. A shorthand appended to a comment written in an online forum, e-mail or other electronic communication types.

bubble sort A simple but popular sorting algorithm. Although bubble sorting is simple, it is rather inefficient compared to other sorting techniques like *merge sorts* or *heap sorts*.

buffer (*a*) A temporary storage area, usually in RAM, used to hold input or output data. (*b*) In data transmission, a temporary storage location for information being sent or received. Usually located between two different devices that have different abilities or speeds for handling the data.

buffer allocation size (BASize) A 1-byte field in the CPCS-PDU header to indicate to the receiving end the buffer space that needs to be reserved for reassembling the CPCS-PDU.

bug An error or defect in software or hardware that causes a program to malfunction. Legend has it that the term originated when a moth was discovered trapped in the components of the first digital computer.

building backbone The link between the building and campus backbone.

bulletin board system (BBS) A computerized meeting and announcement system that allows users to carry on discussions, upload and download files, and make announcements without users being connected to the computer at the same time.

burn-in Initial testing of computer equipment. The theory behind the use of the burn-in techniques is that most of the weak parts will fail during early operation, prior to shipment to the end user. Most computer equipment undergoes a burn-in test at the factory before being released for sale.

burst, committed (Bc) Negotiated tariff metric that represents the maximum amount of data (in bits) that a frame relay internetwork is committed to accept and transmit. *See* Be *and* CIR.

burst, excess (Be) Negotiated tariff metric in a frame relay internetworks. *See* Bc and DE.

burst mode To send data at the maximum transmission rate for a short interval of time.

burst tolerance (BT) Proportional to the MBS, a measure (*leaky bucket parameter*) for conformance checking of the SCR

burstiness A source traffic characteristic that is defined as the ratio of the peak cell rate (PCR) to the average cell rate. It is a measure of the intercell spacing. *See* MBS.

bus (*a*) A network configuration in which nodes are interconnected through a bi-directional transmission medium. (*b*) A collection of wires through which data is transmitted from one part of a computer to another. A sort of highway on which data travels within a computer.

bus interface gate array (BIGA) A Catalyst-5000 Switch technology which allows the switch to receive and transmit frames from its packet-switching memory to its MAC local buffer memory without the intervention of the host processor.

bus network A network in which all nodes are connected to a single wire (the bus) that has two endpoints. Ethernet 10Base-2 and 10Base-5 networks, for example, are bus networks.

bus topology One of the three principal topologies used in LANs. All devices are connected to a central cable, called the *bus* or *backbone*. Bus networks are relatively inexpensive and easy to install. Ethernet systems use a bus topology. *See* ring topology *and* star topology.

BW *See* bandwidth.

bypass mode Operating mode on FDDI and token ring networks when an interface has been removed from the ring.

bypass relays Relays or switches that eliminate failed or powered-down stations from the ring. These devices are attached to nodes on the ring and operate normally until a failed node is detected. In normal operation, a bypass relay lets information through uninterrupted. However, when a node attached to a relay fails or is powered down, the bypass relay reroutes the signal away from the failed station and back onto the ring. As PCs and

workstations connect to the ring, power-downs become even more prevalent and important to protect against.

byte (*Illustration*) A set of eight bits that represent a single character. *See* bit.

Byte Eight bits, also known as an octet.

10101010 – A mathematical representation of one byte.

ⅡⅠⅡⅠⅡ – An electronic representation of one byte.

Byte

---

byte reversal Process of storing numeric data with the least-significant byte first. Used for integers and addresses on devices with Intel microprocessors.

bytecode The compiled format for Java programs.

C A high-level programming language developed by Dennis Ritchie and Brian Kernighan at Bell Labs in the mid-1970s. C is popular both for its size—it requires less memory than other languages—and its flexibility. C is often used in business and engineering programs. Most famously, the UNIX operating system was written in C.

C++ A high-level programming language developed by Bjarne Stroustrup at Bell Labs. C++ adds object-oriented features to its predecessor, C. C++ is often used in graphical applications.

CA *See* certification authority *and* channel adapter.

cable loss The amount of radio frequency signal attenuation caused by a cable.

cable range Range of network numbers valid for use by nodes on an extended AppleTalk network. The cable range value can be a single network number or a contiguous sequence of several network numbers. Node addresses are assigned based on the cable range value.

cable riser Cable running vertically in a multistory building to serve the upper floors.

cable TV (CATV) Communication system where multiple channels of programming material are transmitted to homes using broadband coaxial cable. Formerly called *Community Antenna Television*.

cable A physical transmission medium that consists of copper wire or optical fiber wrapped in a protective cover.

CAC *See* connection admission control.

cache A high-speed storage buffer. It can be either a reserved section of main memory or an independent high-speed storage device. The two types of caching commonly used in personal computers are *memory caching* and *disk caching*.

CAD *See* computer-aided design.

CADD *See* computer-aided design and drafting.

CAE *See* computer-aided engineering.

CAI *See* computer-assisted instruction.

California Education and Research Federation Network (CERFnet) A large TCP/IP network, founded in 1988 by the San Diego Supercomputer Center and based in Southern California, which connects hundreds of higher-education centers internationally while also providing Internet access to subscribers.

call admission control In ATM networks, a method for traffic management that determines whether the network can offer a path with enough bandwidth for a requested VCC.

call control function (CCAF) The function that contains call processing logic and control.

call handler (CH) A programmable, remote digital announcer capable of handling up to three lines at a time.

call priority Defines which calls can or cannot be placed during a bandwidth reservation. It also determines when calls are reconnected in a circuit switched system.

call progress signal Communication from the data circuit-terminating equipment (DCE) to the calling data terminal equipment (DTE) indicating the status of a call.

call request packet In X.25 communications, a call supervision packet transmitted by a data terminal equipment (DTE) source to ask for a call establishment through the network.

call setup time The time required to establish a call between DTE devices in a switched network.

call To invoke a program, routine, or subroutine.

call-connected packet A data terminal equipment (DTE) packet transmission indicating data circuit-terminating equipment (DCE) acceptance of the incoming call.

calling The process of transmitting selection signals to establish a connection between data stations.

CAM content-addressable memory (*See* associative memory). *See* computer-aided manufacturing.

campus A networking environment in which users of voice, video, and data transmissions are spread out over a broad geographic area, as in a university, hospital, medical center, etc. There may be several LANs on a campus. They will be connected with bridges and/or routers communicating over telephone or fiber optic cable.

campus backbone A link between buildings that contains the cabling and resources for a campus-area network (CAN).

Canadian Standards Association (CSA) Agency within Canada that certifies products that conform to Canadian national safety standards.

cancel To terminate.

CAN-M *See* cooperative network architecture for management.

CAPI *See* common ISDN application programming interface.

capture (*a*) To save a programs particular state. (*b*) To download a graphic from a source.

CardBus The 32-bit version of the PCMCIA PC card standard that also supports bus mastering and operation speeds up to 33 MHz.

cards *Adapter cards* or *network interface cards (NICs)* are circuit boards installed in a device's chassis slots to provide network communication capabilities to and from other devices.

caret A symbol (^) generally found above the number 6 key on computer keyboards, and often used to indicate the control key.

carrier In data communication, a continuous frequency capable of being modulated.

carrier sense A device (transceiver, interface board, or other entity) capable of detecting a constant frequency. The channel access method used by the Ethernet and ISO 8802-3 LANs.

carrier-sense multiple access with collision detection (CSMA/CD) A protocol utilizing equipment capable of detecting a carrier, which permits multiple access to a common medium. This protocol also has the ability to detect a collision, because this type of technology is broadcast oriented. *See* Ethernet.

cascading style sheets (CSS) A feature of HTML that gives both Web site developers and users more control over how pages are displayed.

CASE *See* common application service element *and* computer-aided software engineering.

Castanet Software that helps administrators install and update applications and information across a network. If a company chose to upgrade its version of Microsoft Excel, for example, an administrator could use Castanet to update the software across the network without having to physically install the program on each computer. Castanet was developed by Marimba, Inc.

casual connection In SNA, a connection made in subarea networks with PU T5 nodes attached via a boundary function using low-entry networking capabilities.

catalog In SNA, a list of pointers to libraries, files, or data sets.

Category1 cabling The cabling is most commonly used for telephone communication systems; it is typically not suitable for transmitting data. It is one of five grades of *Unshielded Twisted Pair (UTP)* cabling as described in the EIA/TIA-586 standard. Compare with *Category2 cabling, Category3 cabling, Category4 cabling*, and *Category5 cabling*. *See* UTP.

Category2 cabling One of five grades of UTP cabling described in the EIA/TIA-586 standard. Category2 cabling is capable of transmitting data at speeds up to 4Mbps. Compare with *Category1 cabling, Category3 cabling, Category4 cabling*, and *Category5* cabling. *See* EIA/TIA-586 and UTP.

Category3 cabling One of five grades of UTP cabling described in the EIA/TIA-586 standard. Category3 cabling is used in *10BaseT* or low speed ATM networks capable of transmitting data at speeds up to 10Mbps. Compare with *Category1 cabling, Category2 cabling, Category4 cabling,* and *Category5* cabling. *See* UTP.

Category4 cabling One of five grades of UTP cabling described in the EIA/TIA-586 standard. Category4 cabling is used in *token ring* networks and is capable of transmitting data at speeds up to 16Mbps. Compare with *Category1 cabling, Category2 cabling, Category3 cabling,* and *Category5* cabling. *See* UTP.

Category5 cabling (*Illustration*) One of five grades of UTP cabling described in the EIA/TIA-586 standard. Category5 cabling is used for running *copper distributed-data interface (CDDI)* and can transmit data at speeds up to 100Mbps. Compare with *Category1 cabling, Category2 cabling, Category3 cabling,* and *Category4* cabling. A type of UTP commonly used with ATM interfaces for higher-speed cell transmission (more than 50 Mbps). *See* UTP.

catenet A type of network, such as the Internet, in which hosts are connected to diverse networks, which themselves are connected with routers.

cathode-ray tube (CRT) A device, found in computer display terminals and televisions, that works by moving an electron beam back and forth across the back of the screen. Each

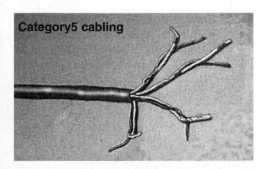
Category5 cabling

time the beam makes a pass across the screen, it lights up phosphor dots on the inside of the glass tube, thereby illuminating the active portions of the screen. By drawing many such lines from the top to the bottom of the screen, it creates an entire screenful of images.

CATV *See* cable TV.

CAV *See* constant angular velocity.

CBEMA *See* Computer & Business Equipment Manufacturers Association.

CBR *See* constant (or continuous) bit rate.

CBT *See* computer-based training.

CC *See* continuity cell.

CCAF *See* call control function

CCB *See* channel control block *and* connection control block.

CCD *See* charge-coupled device.

CCIS *See* common channel interoffice signaling.

CCITT High-Level Language (CHILL) A strongly typed, block-structured language, which essentially consists of data objects, actions performed upon the data objects, and description of program structure.

CCITT *See* Consultative Committee on International Telegraphy and Telephony.

CCO *See* Cisco Connection Online.

CCP *See* console command processor.

CCR *See* commitment, concurrency, and recovery, *and* current cell rate.

CCS *See* common channel signaling, common communications support, *and* console communication service.

CCU *See* central control unit *and* communications control unit.

CCW *See* channel command word.

CDDI *See* Copper Distributed Data Interface (CDDI).

CDF *See* channel definition format.

CDI *See* change direction indicator.

CDMA *See* code-division multiple access.

CDP *See* Cisco Discovery Protocol.

CDPD *See* cellular digital packet data.

CDRM *See* cross-domain resource manager.

CD-ROM Compact disc-read-only memory. A type of optical disk capable of storing large amounts of data. A single CD-ROM has the storage capacity of 700 floppy disks, enough memory to store about 300,000 bytes of text.

CD-ROM player A device that can read information from a CD-ROM. Also called a *CD-ROM drive*.

CDRSC *See* cross-domain resource.

CDS *See* central directory server.

CDV *See* cell delay variation.

CDVT *See* cell delay variation tolerance.

CEI *See* connection end-point identifier.

Celeron A line of Intel microprocessors designed for low-cost PCs, first introduced in 1998.

cell Basic ATM transmission unit. It is a 53-byte packet, comprised of a 5-byte header and a 48-byte payload. User traffic is segmented into cells at the source and reassembled at the destination.

cell delay variation (CDV) A QoS parameter that measures the difference between a single cell's transfer delay (CTD) and the expected transfer delay. It gives a measure of how closely cells are spaced in a virtual circuit (VC). CDV can be introduced by ATM multiplexers (MUXs) or switches.

cell delay variation tolerance (CDVT) The maximum acceptable CDV, which is a parameter specifying the variance in delay between ATM cells.

cell error rate (CER) A QoS parameter that measures the fraction of transmitted cells that contain errors when they arrive at the destination.

cell header A 5-byte ATM header that contains control information regarding the destination path and flow control. More specifically, it contains the GFC, VPI, VCI, PT, CLP, and HEC fields.

For a detailed description, go to the ATM Forum web page at *http://www.atmforum.com*.

cell information field (CIF) The payload (48 bytes) of an ATM cell.

cell layer Same as ATM layer.

cell loss priority (CLP) Field in the ATM cell header that determines the probability of a cell's being dropped if the network becomes congested. Cells with CLP=0 are insured traffic, which is unlikely to be dropped. Cells with CLP=1 are best-effort traffic, which might be dropped in congested conditions to free up resources to handle insured traffic. The CLP is an indication of the priority of a specific cell. During times of network congestion, it is used to decide which cells are lost.

cell loss ratio (CLR) A QoS parameter that gives the ratio of the lost cells to the total number of transmitted cells.

cell misinsertion rate (CMR) A performance measure that is defined as the number of misinserted cells (those that arrive from the wrong source) per (virtual) connection second.

cell missequenced ratio (CSR) A performance measure that is defined as the number of missequenced cells (those that arrive in the wrong order) per (virtual) connection second.

cell rate margin (CRM) A measure of the residual useful bandwidth for a given QoS class, after taking into account the SCR.

cell relay service (CRS) A bearer service offered to the end users by an ATM network that delivers (transports and routes) ATM cells.

cell relay Used for high-speed transmission of multiple types of traffic, including voice, data, and video. Network technology based on the use of small, fixed-size packets, or cells that form the basis of high-speed networks such as ATM, IEEE802.6, or SMDS. Because cells are fixed-length, they can be processed and switched in hardware at high speeds. Cell relay is the basis for many high-speed network protocols including ATM, IEEE 802.6, and SMDS. *See* cell.

cell switch fabric (CSF) *See* switch fabric.

cell transfer delay (CTD) A QoS parameter that measures the average time for a cell to be transferred from its source to its destination over a virtual connection (VC). It is the sum of any coding, decoding, segmentation, reassembly, processing, and queuing delays.

cellular digital packet data (CDPD) A data transmission technology (800- to 900-MHz range) developed for use on cellular phone frequencies to transmit data in packets via data transfer rates of up to 19.2 Kbps. It provides for quicker call set up and better error correction than the use of modems on an analog cellular channel.

cellular radio Technology that uses radio transmissions to access telephone-company networks via a low-power transmitter.

cellular (*Illustration*).

CEN/ELEC *See* Committee European de Normalization Electrotechnique.

Center NIC The authority to create DNS root servers.

central control unit (CCU) A platform upon which numerous functions, such as alarms, the computer interface, and multiple communication speeds, are incorporated.

central directory server (CDS) An APPN network node that provides a repository for network resource locations.

central office (CO) (*Illustration*) A facility that contains the lowest node in the hierarchy of switches that comprises the public telephone network. Any place where the phone company has located telephone switching equipment (see illustration on next page). Premises of a carrier service provider, where customer lines (i.e., telephone lines) are multiplexed and switched to other COs.

central processing unit (CPU) The circuitry that executes instructions. Sometimes called the "brain" of the computer.

centrex Central office exchange service; a PBX service in which switching occurs at a local telephone station instead of at the company premises.

CEP *See* connection end-point.

CEPT *See* Conference of European Postal and Telecommunications Administrations.

CER *See* cell error rate.

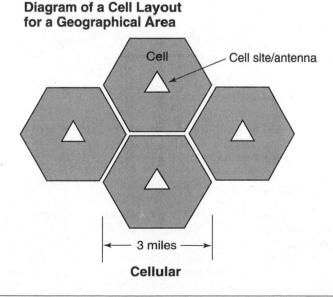

Diagram of a Cell Layout for a Geographical Area

Cell — Cell site/antenna

←— 3 miles —→

Cellular

The Main Parts of a Central Office

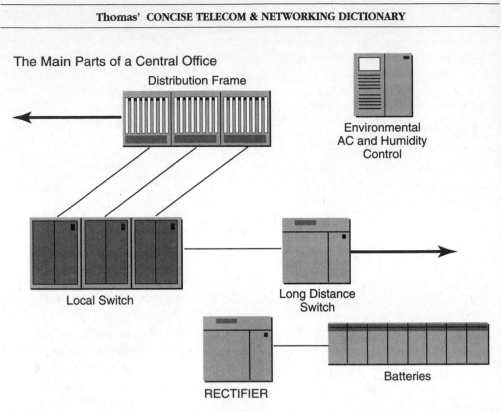

Central Office

CERFnet *See* California Education and Research Federation Network.

CERN European Laboratory for Particle Physics. A research laboratory headquartered in Geneva, Switzerland.

CERT/CC *See* Computer Emergency Response Team/Coordination Center.

certificate authority (CA) An issuer of *security certificates* used in *secure sockets layer (SSL)* connections. *See* security certificate *and* secure sockets layer (SSL).

certification authority (CA) A secure electronic identity conforming to the X.509 standard. It typically contains a user's name and public key. A CA authorizes certificates by signing the contents using its CA signing private key.

Certification for Information System Security Professional (CISSP) A certification reflecting the qualifications of information systems security practitioners. The CISSP examination consists of multiple choice questions, covering topics such as access control systems, cryptography, and security management practices, and is administered by the *International Information Systems Security Certification Consortium (ISC)²*. The (ISC)² promotes the CISSP as an aid to evaluating personnel performing information security functions. The certification was first available in 1989.

CES *See* circuit emulation service.

CFGR *See* configuration.

CGA *See* color/graphics adapter.

CGI *See* common gateway interface.

cgi-bin The most common name of a directory on a Web server in which CGI programs are stored. The "bin" part of "cgi-bin" is a shorthand version of "binary," because most programs were once referred to as "binaries." In real life, most programs found in cgi-bin directories are text files—scripts that are executed by binaries located elsewhere on the same machine. *See* common gateway interface (CGI).

CGM *See* computer graphics metafile.

CH *See* call handler.

chaining Grouping RUs together for the purpose of error recovery in SNA.

Challenge Handshake Authentication Protocol (CHAP) A high-security method of authentication used in PPP.

challenge-response A common authentication technique in which a user is prompted (the challenge) to provide some private information (the response).

change direction indicator (CDI) In SNA, when there is only one end-point with the right to transmit, one of the end-points refrains from transmitting while the other end-point transmits. By setting the change direction indicator, the end-point with the right to transmit is provided with a means to transfer that right to the other end-point.

channel The data path between two nodes.

channel adapter (also **attachment**) **(CA)** These adapters, usually fiber, can be used in either a point-to-point configuration to interconnect two RS/6000 300, 500, 900, R class machines or in conjunction with the 7319 model 110 Fibre Channel Switch 16/1063 to cluster up to 16 machines.

channel command word (CCW) In SNA, an instruction that defines and generates an 8-byte format-1 channel command word for input/output operations.

channel control block (CCB) Stores state information with reference to the connection termination. CCIS *See* common channel interoffice signaling.

channel definition format (CDF) A specification developed by Microsoft that allows Web publishers to push content at users. Once a user subscribes to a CDF channel, any software that supports the CDF format will automatically receive new content posted on the channel's Web server.

channel link A data-link connection between two devices.

channel path identifier (CHPID) A value assigned to each installed channel path of the system. This value uniquely identifies that path to the system.

channel service unit (CSU) A device that manages a digital connection to a digital phone line. CSUs are used to terminate a digital circuit, such as T1, at the customer site. For example, a user could connect two remote routers in two different buildings over a T1 line by using MUXs and CSUs at both building sites. CSUs also perform several protective and diagnostic functions, usually required on a T1 or FT1 or T3 line. *See* DCE.

channel-attached In SNA terminology, this term connotes a serial or parallel data-link protocol. IBM has other data-link protocols, such as SDLC, ESCON, and token ring.

channelized E1 Access link operating at 2.048Mbps. It is subdivided into 30B-channels and an 1D-channel. Supports DDR, frame relay, and X.25. Compare with *channelized T1*. Predominantly used in Europe.

channel-to-channel (CTC) A hardware device connecting two channels on the same computing system or on different systems.

channel-to-channel adapter (CTCA) A hardware device connecting two channels on the same computing system or on different systems.

CHAP *See* Challenge Handshake Authentication Protocol.

character In computer software, a symbol that requires one byte of storage. This includes all the ASCII and extended ASCII characters.

character string A series of characters manipulated as a group.

character-based Programs which are capable of displaying only ASCII (and extended ASCII) characters. Character-based programs treat a display screen as an array of boxes, each of which can hold one character.

character-coded In SNA VTAM, unformatted.

characters per inch (cpi) A typographic measurement specifying the number of characters that can fit on a printed line one-inch long.

characters per second (cps) A unit of measure used to describe the speed of dot-matrix and daisy-wheel printers.

charge-coupled device (CCD) A semiconductor or integrated circuit whose elemental semiconductors devices are connected so that the output of one serves as the input of the next. Digital cameras, video cameras, and optical scanners all use CCD arrays.

chassis A metal frame that serves as the structural support for electronic components. Every computer system requires at least one chassis to house the circuit boards and wiring.

chat room A virtual room where a chat session takes place. Technically, a chat room is really a channel, but the term "room" is used to promote the chat metaphor.

chat Conversational hypertext access technology. Real-time communication between two users via computer. Another term for *IRC*.

Cheapernet Industry term used to refer to the IEEE 802.3 10Base2 standard. Compare with Thinnet. *See* 10Base2, Ethernet, *and* IEEE 802.3.

check box In graphical user interfaces, a box that a user can click to turn an option on or off.

checksum A numeric value used to verify the integrity of a block of data. The value is computed using a checksum procedure. A *crypto checksum* incorporates secret information in the checksum procedure so that it can't be reproduced by third parties that don't know the secret information.

CHILL *See* CCITT High-Level Language.

chip A small piece of semiconducting material (usually silicon) on which an integrated circuit is embedded. A typical chip can contain millions of electronic components (transistors).

chipset A number of integrated circuits designed to perform one or more related functions. The term is often used to refer to the core functionality of a motherboard.

choose To pick a command or option.

Chooser In Apple documentation, an accessory that lets a user select shared devices, such as printers and file servers.

CHPID *See* channel path identifier (ID).

CHRP *See* common hardware reference platform.

CI *See* congestion indication.

CIAC *See* Computer Incident Advisory Center.

CICNet Regional network that was founded in 1988 and connects academic, research, nonprofit, and commercial organizations in the Midwestern United States. CICNet was a part of the NSFNET and was funded by the NSF until the NSFNET dissolved in 1995. *See* NSFNET.

CICS *See* customer information control system.

CID *See* command (*also* connection) identifier *and* communication identifier.

CIDR *See* classless inter-domain routing.

CIF *See* cell information field.

CIM *See* computer-integrated manufacturing.

Cinepak A popular *codec* (compression/decompression technology) for computer video developed by SuperMac Inc.

CINIT A request sent from a SSCP to a primary logical unit requesting that a BIND command be issued.

cipher text Data that have been encrypted with a cipher, as opposed to *plain text*.

CIR *See* committed information rate.

circuit emulation A virtual-circuit (VC) service offered to end users. The characteristics of an actual, digital bit-stream (i.e., video traffic) line are emulated (i.e., a 2- or 45-Mbps signal).

circuit emulation service (CES) An ATM-provided class of service, where TDM-type, constant-bit-rate (CBR) circuits are emulated by the AAL1.

circuit group Grouping of associated serial lines that link two bridges.

circuit PVC *See* frame relay.

circuit switching A method of handling traffic through a switching center, either from local users or from other switching centers, whereby a connection is established between the calling and called parties.

CISC *See* complex instruction set computer.

Cisco Connection Online (CCO)

 For more information see Cisco's Web site *www.cisco.com*.

Cisco Discovery Protocol (CDP) A proprietary Cisco network protocol used by Cisco routers to discover other Cisco networking devices on the network.

CISSP *See* Certification for Information System Security Professional.

cladding (*Illustration*) The surrounding part of a cable that protects the core optical fibers. It is located between the fibers and the cable jacket.

class In object-oriented programming, a category of objects. For example, there might be a class called *shape* that contains objects which are circles, rectangles, and triangles. The class defines all the common properties of the different objects that belong to it.

class 1 repeater A type of Fast Ethernet hub that performs translations when transmitting/repeating incoming signals to allow different media types to be connected to a single collision domain. Only one Class I repeater is allowed per collision domain.

class 2 repeater A type of Fast Ethernet hub that only transmits or repeats an incoming signal to other devices on the same media type (no translations are performed). Only two class 2 repeaters are allowed per collision domain.

class 4 Specifies the parameters for connectionless data transfer. AAL3/4 or AAL5 can be used to support this class.

class A IP address A type of unicast IP address that segments the address space into many network addresses and few host addresses.

class B IP address A type of unicast IP address that segments the address space into a medium number of network and host addresses.

class B station *See* SAS.

class C IP address A type of unicast IP address that segments the address space into many host addresses and few network addresses.

class D IP This specifies multicast host groups in IPv4-based networks.

classical IP IETF-defined protocols for developing IP-over-ATM networks (i.e., IP support for the QoS classes, ARP-over-SVC, and PVC networks) so that common applications (i.e., FTP, Telnet, SMTP, and SNMP) can be supported in an ATM environment. The main issues in the transport of IP over ATM are the packet encapsulation and the address resolution.

classless inter-domain routing (CIDR) An IP addressing scheme that replaces the older system based on classes A, B, and C. With CIDR, a single IP address can be used to designate many unique IP addresses. Faced with the exhaustion of class B address space and the explosion of routing table growth triggered by a flood of new class C addresses, IETF began implementing classless interdomain routing (CIDR), in the early 1990s. CIDR is documented in RFC 1518 and RFC 1519.

The primary requirement for CIDR is the use of routing protocols that support it, such as RIP Version 2, OSPF Version 2, and BGP Version

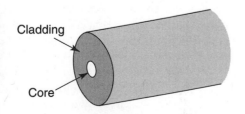

Cladding

Core

4. The *subnetting mask* becomes an integral part of routing tables and protocols. A route is no longer an IP address, broken down into network and host bits according to its class. A route is now a combination of address and mask.

Networks can be broken down into *subnets*, and also combined into *supernets*, as long as they have a common network prefix. CIDR defines address assignment and aggregation strategies designed to minimize the size of top-level Internet routing tables.

A CIDR IP address looks like a normal IP address except that it ends with a slash followed by a number, called the IP prefix. For example:

172.200.0.0/16

The IP prefix specifies how many addresses are covered by the CIDR address, with lower numbers covering more addresses. An IP prefix of /12, for example, can be used to address 4,096 former Class C addresses. CIDR addresses reduce the size of routing tables and make more IP addresses available within organizations.

class-of-service (COS) A designation of the transport network characteristics, such as route security, transmission priority, and bandwidth, needed for a particular session. The class of service is derived from a mode name specified by the initiator of a session. In SNA, this term defines explicit routes, virtual routes, and priority, and is used to provide a variety of services within the network.

class-of-service database In APPN, a database maintained independently by each network node, and optionally by APPN end nodes.

CLAW *See* Common Link Access for Workstations.

cleanup In SNA, the method by which sessions are terminated between LUs. Specifically, it is a network services request that causes a particular LU-LU session to be ended immediately.

clear To erase. A user can clear a screen, clear a variable, or clear memory.

clear-indication packet A call supervision packet that data circuit-terminating equipment (DCE) transmits to inform data terminal equipment (DTE) that a call has been cleared.

clear-request packet A call supervision packet transmitted by a data terminal equipment (DTE) source to ask that a call be cleared.

CLEC *See* competitive local exchange carrier.

CLI *See* command line interface.

click To press and release a mouse button.

client A term used to connote peer technology. Clients are programs used to initiate something. A Web browser is a specific kind of client application which performs the front-end processing of various Internet processes such as FTP and Telnet. *See* browser *and* server.

client-side An event that is occurring on the client side of a client-server system.

clipper chip An encryption chip designed under the auspices of the United States government to enforce security in all devices that might use encryption, including computers, modems, telephones, and televisions. The United States government would control the encryption algorithm, thereby giving it the ability to decrypt any messages it recovered.

CLIST *See* command list.

CLM *See* current load model.

CLNP *See* connectionless network protocol.

CLNS *See* connectionless network service.

clock speed Also called *clock rate*, the speed at which a microprocessor executes instructions and synchronizes all the various computer components. The CPU requires a fixed number of clock ticks (or clock cycles) to execute each instruction. The faster the clock, the more instructions the CPU can execute per second. Clock speeds are expressed in megahertz (MHz), 1 MHz being equal to 1 million cycles per second. The CPUs of personal computers have clock speeds of anywhere from 33 MHz to well over 300 MHz.

clock tick The smallest unit of time recognized by a device. For personal computers, clock ticks generally refer to the main system clock, which runs at 66 MHz. This means that there are 66 million clock ticks (or cycles) per second.

clocking The use of clock pulses to control synchronization.

clone A computer, software product, or device that functions exactly like another, better-known product.

close (*a*) To finish work on a data file and save it. (*b*) In graphical user interfaces, to close a window is to exit an application or file, thereby removing the window from the screen.

closed user group (CUG) A user group whose members can communicate with other users in the group, but not with users outside the group.

CLP *See* cell loss priority.

CLR Cell loss ratio.

CLTP *See* Connectionless Transport Protocol.

CLTS *See* connectionless transport service.

CLU *See* control logical unit.

cluster A network of computers in which only one computer has file system disk drives attached to it.

cluster controller In SNA, the precursor to the establishment controller. It is a device to which terminals and printers attach. IBM's 3274 cluster controllers appear as a PU2.0.

clustering Connecting two or more computers so that they behave like a single computer; typically used for parallel processing, fault tolerance, or load balancing.

CLV *See* constant linear velocity.

CM *See* configuration manager.

CMIP *See* Common Management Information Protocol.

CMIS *See* common management information service.

CMIS/P-over-TCP/IP (CMOT) The use of common management information service over TCP/IP. Succinctly, it is the implementa-

tion of the OSI network management specification over TCP/IP.

CMISE *See* common management information service element.

CMOS *See* complementary metal oxide semiconductor.

CMOT *See* CMIS/P-over-TCP/IP.

CMR *See* cell misinsertion rate.

CMS *See* configuration management service.

CMT *See* connection management.

CMYK Cyan-magenta-yellow-black.

CN *See* composite node.

CNM *See* communication network management.

CNMAP *See* communication network management application program.

CNN *See* composite network node.

CO *See* central office.

coaxial cable (*Illustration*) A cable composed of an insulated central-conducting wire wrapped in another cylindrical conducting wire. The whole thing is usually wrapped in another insulating layer and an outer protective layer. A coaxial cable has great capacity to carry great quantities of information. It is typically used to carry high-speed data and in cable TV. A cable composed of a central-conducting wire wrapped with an insulating sheath (usually a dielectric material of a specific value) with an outer cylindrical conducting sheath, which in turn is wrapped in another insulating and outer protective layer.

COBOL Common Business Oriented Language. A programming language most often used for business applications that run on large computers. COBOL is wordier than other languages, which means COBOL programs can be long; however, this characteristic also makes COBOL programs easy to understand.

COBRA Race II project R2065.

CODASYL *See* Conference on Data Systems Languages.

Coaxial cable crossection

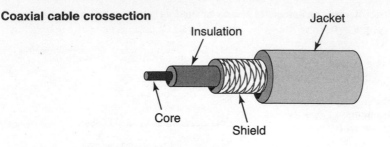

code (*a*) A system of instructions making up software. (*b*) A system of symbols making up cipher text.

codec (*a*) Compressor/decompressor; any technology for compressing and decompressing data. Codecs can be implemented in software, hardware, or a combination of both. (*b*) In telecommunications, short for coder/decoder, a device that encodes or decodes a signal. (*c*) The translation of a binary value into a voltage that can be transmitted over a wire.

code-division multiple access (CDMA) A digital cellular technology, developed by Qualcomm, that uses spread-spectrum techniques, where individual conversations are encoded with a random digital sequence.

COFF *See* Common Object File Format.

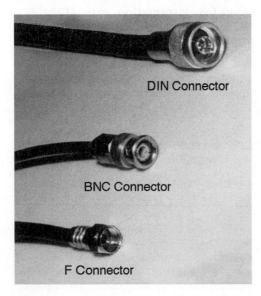

COI *See* connection-oriented internetworking.

cold boot The start-up of a computer from a powered-down state.

COLD *See* computer output to laser disk.

collapse To compress a view of a hierarchy so that only the roots of each branch are visible. The opposite of expand.

collision An event where two or more devices simultaneously perform a broadcast on the same medium. This term is used in Ethernet networks and also in networks where broadcast technology is implemented. *See* collision domain.

collision detection The process of detecting simultaneous transmissions (collisions) on a shared medium. Typically, each transmitting workstation that detects a collision will wait some period of time and try again. Collision detection is an essential part of the *CSMA/CD* access method. Workstations detect collisions if, after sending data, they fail to receive an acknowledgment from the receiving station.

collision domain In Ethernet, the network area within which frames that have collided are propagated. Repeaters and hubs propagate collisions; LAN switches, bridges, and routers do not.

co-location Having a server that belongs to one person or group physically located on an Internet-connected network that belongs to another person or group. Usually this is done because the server owner wants the machine to be on a high-speed Internet connection and/or does not want the security risks of having the server on its own network. *See* Internet, server, *and* network.

color depth The number of distinct colors that can be represented by a piece of hardware or software.

color/graphics adapter (CGA) An old graphics system for PCs. It has been replaced by EGA, VGA, and SVGA.

COM file In DOS environments, a COM file is an executable command file with a .com filename extension.

COM *See* continuation of message, *and* component object model.

comma-delimited A data format in which each piece of data is separated by a comma. This format is preferred because most database systems can easily import and export comma-delimited data. (Also called *CSV*, i.e. comma separate variable.)

command (also **connection**) **identifier (CID)** The authority in charge, identified for a specific training authority document.

command buffer A temporary storage area where commands are kept.

command language The programming language through which a user communicates with the operating system or an application.

command line interface (CLI) The text-based interface common to all IOS-based (Cisco) routers. This text-based interface is being copied as the command interface on network devices besides those sold by Cisco.

command line The line on the display screen where a command is entered.

command list (CLIST) A list of requests from a user at a terminal for the execution of particular tasks.

CLM *See* current load model.

command processor The part of the operating system that receives and executes operating system commands. Every operating system has a command processor. When the command prompt is displayed, the command processor waits for a command.

command (*a*) A request to execute an event. (*b*) According to Digital Equipment, when used in reference to *Digital Command Language (DCL)*, an instruction, generally an English word, entered by the user at a terminal or included in a command procedure.

commitment, concurrency, and recovery (CCR) A method of furnishing an environment for the execution of computer and network operations in a consistent manner, despite failures.

committed information rate (CIR) In frame relay, the information rate the network is committed to provide the user with, under any network conditions.

Committee Européan de Normalisation Electrotechnique (CEN/ELEC) A European technical standard body that together with its members, affiliates, and cooperating partners, is developing and achieving a coherent set of voluntary electrotechnical standards as a basis to a Single European Market/European Economic Area without internal frontiers for goods and services inside Europe.

common application service element (CASE) An Application Service Element (ASE) that is common to many application processes (APs).

common channel interoffice signaling (CCIS) A separate voice circuit using time-division techniques for transmission. It is a digital encoding method of transmitting signaling information between COs for a group of trunks.

common channel signaling (CCS) Independent of the voice or data paths, it uses a separate path for the control signals.

common communications support (CCS) An SAA element consisting of components used for communications between SAA systems, with the purpose of enabling interoperability between SAA systems.

common gateway interface (CGI) A program for transferring information between a World Wide Web server and a *CGI program*. A CGI program is any program designed to accept and return data that conforms to the CGI specification. Usually, a CGI takes data from a Web server and does something with it, like putting the content of a form into an e-mail message, or turning the data into a database query. *See* cgi-bin.

common hardware reference platform (CHRP) A specification for PowerPC based machines, first released in 1996, that can run the Mac OS, Windows NT, or AIX.

common ISDN application programming interface (CAPI) An application programming interface (API) standard used to access ISDN equipment.

Common Link Access for Workstations (CLAW) Data-link layer protocol used by channel-attached RISC System/6000 series systems and by IBM3172 devices running TCP/IP off-load.

Common Management Information Protocol (CMIP) A protocol formally adapted by the International Standards Organization (ISO), and used to exchange network management information over OSI. Typically, this information is exchanged between two management stations. The protocol can be used to exchange information between an application and a management station.

Although designed for OSI networks, it is transport independent. Theoretically, it can run across a variety of transports, including IBM's SNA. It is used with *common management information services (CMIS)*, which defines a system of network management information services. CMIP was proposed as a replacement for the less sophisticated *Simple Network Management Protocol (SNMP)* but has not been widely adopted. CMIP provides improved security and better reporting of unusual network conditions.

common management information service (CMIS) (*a*) A standard that defines a system of network management information services. (*b*) A service to monitor and control heterogeneous networks within the OSI network management service interface.

common management information service element (CMISE) The application service element responsible for relaying systems management information.

Common Object File Format (COFF) A binary file format used in UNIX System V and Windows.

common parent The lowest-level directory that appears in pathnames of multiple files or directories on the same volume.

common part convergence sublayer (CPCS) Part of the AAL convergence sublayer (CS). It must be present in the AAL implementation. Its task is to pass primitives to the other AAL sublayers (SAR, SSCS). It supports the functions of the standardized common part AALs: AAL1, AAL3/4, and AAL5.

common part indicator (CPI) A one-byte field, in the header of the CPCS-PDU in AAL3/4, which indicates the number of bits making up the BASize field.

Common programming interface with C language (CPI-C) An interface that allows applications written in REXX and high-level languages to access APPC/VM functions through a set of program-to-program communication routines.

communication The transmission and reception of data from one computer to another, or from one device to another.

communication adapter A circuit card with associated software that enables a processor, controller, or other device to be connected to a network.

communication control unit (CCU) A communication device that controls transmission of data over lines in a network.

communication controller A control unit whose operations are controlled by one or more programs stored and executed in the unit. In most instances, it manages lines and routing data through a network.

communication identifier (CID) A VTAM key for locating the control blocks that represent a session. This key is created during session establishment and is deleted when the session ends.

communication line Deprecated term for telecommunication line.

communication network management (CNM) The process of designing, installing, operating, and managing distribution of information and control among users of communication systems. The *communication network management interface* is a common point where applications can move data and commands to the access method. These data and commands are associated with communication system management.

communication network management application program (CNMAP) A VTAM application that issues and receives formatted management service request units for PUs. NetView is an example of a CNM application program.

communications control unit (CCU) A programmed transmission control unit designed to assume many of the line control and processing functions for a data communication subsystem.

communications line The physical link (such as wire or a telephone circuit) that connects one or more workstations to a communications control unit or that connects one control unit to another.

communications port (*a*) An access point for data entry to or exit from a communication device such as a terminal. (*b*) On a personal computer or workstation, a synchronous or asynchronous serial port to which a modem can be attached.

communications protocol The set of rules defining a format between devices, which require that the devices agree on the format of the data and how these devices talk to each other. At the very least, a communications protocol must define the following:

■ Rate of transmission (in baud or bps)

■ Whether transmission is to be synchronous or asynchronous

■ Whether data is to be transmitted in half-duplex or full-duplex mode.

In addition, protocols can include sophisticated techniques for detecting and recovering from transmission errors and for encoding and decoding data. The best-known are Xmodem, Kermit, MNP, and CCITT V.42. These protocols can be implemented in either hardware or software.

communications scanner processor (CSP) A communications controller hardware unit providing the connection between lines and the central control unit. It also monitors telecommunication lines as well as data links for service requests.

community antenna television *See* cable TV.

community sharing An SNMP term referring to the administrative relationship between an SNMP agent and its managers to control the access to SNMP MIB (management information base). This relationship is validated every time an SNMP agent wants to transfer data on the Internet. Access to the SNMP community is regulated by the *community name*, which is sent in every packet between a management station and an SNMP agent. The community name is usually an ASCII string that validates that the sending SNMP agents are members of the community.

Compaq One of the world's leading manufacturers of high-quality, low-cost PCs.

For more information, see *www.compaq.com*.

compatible Products which can work together.

competitive local exchange carrier (CLEC) A telephone company that competes with an *incumbent local exchange carrier (ILEC)* such as a *Regional Bell Operating Company (RBOC)*, GTE, ALLNET, etc. With the passage of the Telecommunications Act of 1996, there has been an explosion in the number of CLECs.

compile To transform a program written in a high-level programming language from *source code* into *object code*. Programmers write programs in source code. Source code must go through several steps before it becomes an executable program. The first step is to pass the source code through a compiler, which translates the high-level language instructions into object code.

compiler A program that translates source code into object code.

complementary metal oxide semiconductor (CMOS) A widely used type of semiconductor.

complete sequence number PDU (CSNP) A PDU sent by the designated router in an OSPF network to maintain database synchronization.

complex instruction set computer (CISC) In personal computer technology, an architecture in which the CPU supports as many as 200 instructions. Most PCs. use CISC architecture.

component Generally speaking, a piece of hardware or software that forms part of a larger system.

component object model (COM) A model for binary code developed by Microsoft. The component object model (COM) enables programmers to develop objects that can be accessed by any COM-compliant application. Both OLE and ActiveX are based on COM.

composite end node To a type 2.1 node, a group of nodes that appears to be a single end node.

composite LEN node A group of nodes made up of a single type 5 node and subordinate type 4 nodes. To a type 2.1 node, a composite LEN node appears as one LEN node. Examples of a composite LEN node are NCP and VTAM.

composite network node (CNN) A group of nodes made up of a type 5 node and its subordinate type 4 nodes that appear as a single APPN network node to the APPN network.

composite node In IBM networking, specifically SNA with VTAM, a type 5 node and its owned type 4 nodes that collectively appear as a single node to other APPN nodes in an APPN network.

Compressed Serial Link Internet Protocol (CSLIP) Extension of SLIP that allows just

header information to be sent across a SLIP connection, reducing overhead and increasing packet throughput on SLIP lines when appropriate. *See* SLIP.

computer A programmable machine that responds to a set of instructions, either prerecorded or entered by a user.

Computer & Business Equipment Manufacturers Association (CBEMA) An organization of the top United States providers of information technology.

Computer Emergency Response Team/Coordination Center (CERT/CC) A publicly accessible group dedicated to network security.

computer graphics metafile (CGM) A file format where both vector and raster images are accommodated in a single file.

Computer Incident Advisory Center (CIAC) An organization with the United States Department of Energy that alerts concerned parties with information about security issues, such as viruses, which may affect governmental agencies and the public.

computer interconnect (CI) A fault-tolerant, dual-path bus, with a bandwidth of 70 Mbits/s.

computer literacy The level of expertise and familiarity someone has with computers and their use.

computer output to laser disk (COLD) The storage of data on optical disk.

Computer Science Network (CSNET) Large internetwork consisting primarily of universities, research institutions, and commercial concerns.

computer science The study of computers, including hardware design, software design, artificial intelligence, software engineering, and many other subjects.

computer system A totally complete and working computer, which includes software as well as hardware.

computer-aided design (CAD) A sophisticated combination of hardware and software frequently used by engineers, architects, and designers, to help during the design phase of product development.

computer-aided design and drafting (CADD) Computer-aided design (CAD) systems with additional drafting features.

computer-aided engineering (CAE) Computer systems that analyze engineering designs. CAE systems are able to simulate a design under a variety of conditions to see if it actually works.

computer-aided manufacturing (CAM) Computer systems used to design and manufacture products.

computer-aided software engineering (CASE) A category of software that provides a development environment for programming teams. CASE systems offer tools to automate, manage and simplify the development process.

computer-assisted instruction (CAI) A device that allows the transmission of screens from one monitor to other monitors within a network.

computer-based training (CBT) Training in which students learn by executing special instructional programs on a computer. For example, students can learn new computer applications by practicing with the application using the CBT method.

computer-integrated manufacturing (CIM) A series of computerized tools and techniques aimed to integrate manufacturing processing and design. This may include CAD (part and product design, tool and fixture design), CAPP (process planning), CAM (programming, production planning, machining, assembly), CAQC (quality control, inspection) and ASRS (storage and retrieval of raw material, WIP, finished product) modules.

computer-telephony-integration (CTI) Systems that enable a computer to act as a telephone call center, accepting incoming calls and routing them to the appropriate device or person.

concentrator A type of multiplexer that combines multiple channels, such as dial-up access as provided by an ISP, into a single transmission so that all the individual channels can be simultaneously active.

concurrent Pertaining to the occurrence of two or more activities within a given interval of time.

conductors A piece of wire. For 10BaseT purposes it is solid, copper wire, not stranded.

Conference of European Postal and Telecommunications Administrations (CEPT) An association of the 26 European PTTs, which recommends communication specifications to the ITU-T.

Conference on Data Systems Languages (CODASYL) An organization founded in 1957 by the United States Department of Defense to develop programming languages. CODASYL created COBOL. The organization is no longer extant, but the term CODASYL is still used sometimes to refer to COBOL.

conference A multiparty, multimedia presentation, where "multi" implies greater than or equal to one.

configuration (CFGR) The act of setting up a system's rules. The manner in which the hardware and software of an information processing system are organized and interconnected.

configuration management service (CMS) A service that is responsible for device configurations and device moves, adds, and changes.

configuration manager (CM) A central console used to set up configuration subsets.

configure To set up a program or computer system for a particular application.

congestion (*a*) A network state caused by one or more overloaded network devices. Congestion leads to datagram loss. (*b*) A stable condition where a network becomes flooded with retransmissions. *See* congestion control.

congestion control A resource and traffic management mechanism to avoid and/or prevent excessive situations (buffer overflow, insufficient bandwidth) that can cause the network to collapse. There exist various congestion control methods. *See* flow control.

congestion indication (CI) A bit in the RM cell to indicate congestion. It is set by the destination if the last cell received was marked.

connected Having a physical path from one point to another.

connection In data communications, there are two types of connections, *physical* and *logical*. A physical connection consists of a tangible path between two or more points. A logical connection is the capability to communicate between two or more end-points.

connection admission control (CAC) An ATM function which determines whether a virtual circuit (VC) connection request should be accepted or rejected.

connection control block (CCB) Part of data structure; a record that consists of 242 bytes. AppleTalk Data Stream Protocol (ADSP) uses the CCB to store state information about the connection end.

connection end-point (CEP) Within a SAP, it is a terminator at one end of a layer connection.

connection end-point identifier (CEI) Identifier of a connection end-point, in an SAP.

connection management (CMT) A process used to create and maintain end-to-end frame relay and ATM connections, including dial-up and dial backup connections.

connection network A representation within an APPN network of a *shared-access transport facility (SATF)*, such as a token ring, that allows nodes identifying their connectivity to the SATF by a common virtual routing node to communicate without having individually defined connections to one another.

connection server A program that accepts an open connection request passed to it by a connection listener and selects a socket to respond to the request.

connectionless A type of network protocol that allows a host to send a message without establishing a connection with the recipient. That is, the host simply puts the message onto the network with the destination address and hopes that it arrives. Examples of connectionless protocols include Ethernet, IPX, and UDP.

connectionless network Communications service where packets are transferred from source to destination without the need of a preestablished connection. Examples are IP and SMDS. *See* datagram.

connectionless network protocol (CLNP) An OSI protocol that does not perform retransmissions or error recovery at a transport layer.

connectionless network service (CLNS) An OSI network-layer service that does not require a circuit to be established before data is transmitted. CLNS routes messages to their destinations independently of any other messages. *See* connectionless network protocol (CLNP).

connectionless service A network service that delivers data or packets as separate pieces. An example of this type of service is TCP/IP's Internet protocol (IP).

Connectionless Transport Protocol (CLTP) A protocol that provides end-to-end transport data addressing and error detection, but does not guarantee delivery or provide flow control.

connectionless transport service (CLTS) A service that does not guarantee reliable data transfer.

connection-oriented Communications service where an initial connection between the endpoints (source and destination) has to be set up. Examples are ATM and frame relay. *See* virtual circuit.

connection-oriented internetworking (COI) A set of subnetworks connected physically and thus rendered capable of connection-oriented network service.

Connection-Oriented Network Service (CONS) An OSI protocol that exchanges information over a virtual circuit for packet-switched networks.

connection-oriented service A type of service offered in some networks. This service has three phases: connection establishment, data transfer, and connection release.

connectivity The notion of device communication interchange, even if such devices are diverse.

connector The part of a cable that plugs into a port or interface to connect one device to another. Most connectors are either *male* (containing one or more exposed pins) or *female* (containing holes in which the male connector can be inserted).

CONS *See* Connection-Oriented Network Service.

console command processor (CCP) A module of the CP/M operating system, which is loaded directly below the BDOS module and interprets and executes commands typed by the console user. Part of the PPP protocol negotiation.

console communication service (CCS) A function used in SNA environments that acts as an interface between the control program and the VSCS component of VTAM for VM.

constant In programming, a value that never changes; as opposed to a *variable*, a symbol whose value can vary throughout a program.

constant (or continuous) bit rate (CBR) One of the five ATM classes of service which supports the transmission of a continuous bit stream of information where traffic, such as voice and video, needs to meet certain QoS requirements. *See* quality of service classes.

constant angular velocity (CAV) A technique where a disk rotates at a constant speed for accessing data.

constant linear velocity (CLV) A method used by older CD-ROM players to access data.

Consultative Committee on International Telegraphy and Telephony (CCITT) A standards and specifications body whose published recommendations include definition of terms, basic principles and characteristics, protocol design, description of models, and other specifications.

consumer Defined in the Multicast Transport Protocol as a transport system capable only of receiving user data. It can transmit control packets, such as negative acknowledgments, but can never transmit requests for the transmit token or any form of data or empty messages.

contact manager An application that enables the user to easily store and find contact information, such as names, addresses, and telephone numbers.

contiguous Immediately adjacent.

continuation of message (COM) A PDU that is part of a message.

continuity cell (CC) A cell used to check periodically whether a connection is idle or has failed (i.e., at the cross-connect nodes), to guarantee a continuation in the flow of the information cells. Continuity checking is one of the OAM function types for fault management. *See* AIS *and* RDI.

control block A storage area that holds control information.

control bus The physical connections that carry control and status information between the CPU and other devices within the computer.

control character One of 32 special, non-printing character defined in ASCII.

control LLC Specification for the IEEE 802.x series of standards. It defines the services for the transmission of data between two stations with no intermediate switching stations. There are three versions: LLC1 is connectionless, LLC2 is connection-oriented, and LLC3 is connectionless with acknowledgment.

control logical unit (CLU) A logical unit that resides in a transaction processing facility (TPF) type 2.1 node. It is used to pass private protocol requests between the TPF type 2.1 node and the log-on manager, which is a VTAM application program. Communication flow between the CLU and the log-on manager enables a logical unit controlled by VTAM to establish a session with TPF.

control panel A place that allows a user to set or "control" a feature of some sort.

control point (CP) A component of a node that manages resources of that node and optionally provides services to other nodes in the network. A part of T2.1 architecture. A control program in IBM terminology is that software which runs on a VM host. The CP communicates with the hardware.

control program (CP) A program that performs system-oriented functions such as scheduling and the supervising of program execution for a computer system.

control program facility (CPF) The process within a computer system that schedules and supervises program execution.

Control Program for Microprocessors (CP/M) One of the first operating systems for personal computers, created by Digital Research Corporation. CP/M is now obsolete.

controller A device that coordinates and controls the operation of one or more input/output devices.

convergence The amount of time it takes for a change to a routing topology to propagate throughout the network.

convergence sublayer (CS) The upper half of the AAL. It is divided into two sublayers, the *common part (CPCS)* and the *service-specific (SSCS)*. It is service dependent and its functions include manipulation of cell-delay variation (CDV), source clock frequency recovery, and forward error correction (FEC). Although each AAL has its own functions, in general the CS describes the services and functions needed for conversion between ATM and non-ATM protocols. *See* SAR.

convergence sublayer protocol data unit (CS-PDU) The PDU used at the CS for passing information between the higher layers and the SAR, where they are converted into cells.

conversation Communication between two transaction programs using an LU 6.2 session.

convert To change data from one format to another.

cookie A small file that contains data about the user. A cookie is sent by a Web server (Web site) to a Web browser (your PC), and the browser software is expected to save it and send it back to the server whenever the browser makes additional requests from the server.

Copper Distributed Data Interface (CDDI) A 100-Mbps FDDI LAN standard based on token-ring arbitration protocols and used over unshielded twisted pair (UTP) copper cable on lengths of up to 100 meters. Like all token-ring implementations, redundancy is provided by using a dual-ring architecture. CDDI was a trade name of Crescendo Communications (acquired by Cisco Systems in 1993) and commonly used instead of the general term *twisted pair physical layer medium (TP-PMD)*.

coprocessor A special-purpose processing unit that assists a computer's CPU in performing certain types of operations. For example, a math coprocessor.

copy To duplicate a piece of data to a temporary location. A piece of such duplicated data, such as a file or a directory.

core gateway The primary routers in the Internet.

core network A combination of switching offices and the transmission plant that connects the switching offices. In the United States local exchange, core networks are linked by several competing interexchange networks. In the rest of the world, core networks extend to national boundaries.

core router A router that is part of the backbone, in a packet-switched star topology, and that serves as the single pipe through which all traffic from peripheral networks must pass on its way to other peripheral networks.

Core-Based Trees (CBT) A routing protocol characterized by a single tree shared by all nodes.

corporate network An *internetwork*, a *wide area network*, or an *enterprise network*. A network of networks that connects most or all of a corporation's local area networks. Connections between networks and LANs are made with bridges and routers.

Corporation for Open Systems (COS) A group organized to provide ways of testing OSI implementations, made up of an international consortium of computer users and vendors.

Corporation for Research and Educational Networking (CREN) A group devoted to providing Internet connectivity to its members, which include the alumni, students, faculty, and other affiliates of participating educational and research institutions. *See* BITNET, BITNETIII, *and* CSNET.

corrupted Data that has been damaged in some way.

COS *See* class-of-service *and* Corporation for Open Systems.

cost Arbitrary value, typically based on hop count, media bandwidth, or other measures, that is used to compare various paths through an internetwork. Cost values are used by routing protocols to determine the most favorable path to a particular destination; the lower the cost, the better the path. Sometimes called *path cost*. *See* routing metric.

counter-rotating A method of using two ring networks going in opposite directions.

count-to-infinity A problem that can occur in routing algorithms with slow convergence, in which routers continuously increment the hop count to particular networks, thus counting up to infinity. Typically, some arbitrary hop-count limit is imposed to prevent this problem.

CP/M *See* Control Program for Microprocessors.

CP *See* control point (or program).

CPCS *See* common part convergence sublayer.

CPE *See* customer premises equipment.

CPF *See* control program facility.

cpi *See* characters per inch.

CPI *See* common part indicator.

CPI-C *See* common programming interface with C language.

cps *See* characters per second.

CPU *See* central processing unit.

CPU time The amount of time the CPU is actually executing instructions.

crack (*a*) To break into a computer system. (*b*) To copy commercial software illegally by breaking (cracking) the various copy-protection and registration techniques being used.

crackers Unlike *hackers*, who break into computer systems for the thrill of it, crackers break into computer systems for their own financial gain. *See* hacker.

crash A computer failure, such as a computer that freezes or a program that shuts down unexpectedly. A crash can be the result of a malfunction in either hardware or software.

CRC *See* cyclic redundancy check.

CREN *See* Corporation for Research and Educational Networking.

crimper (*Illustration*) A pliers-like device used to attach connectors to the end of cables.

CRM *See* cell rate margin.

cron A UNIX command for scheduling jobs to be executed sometime in the future.

cross-domain In SNA, a term used to refer to resources in a different domain. *Domains*, in SNA, relate to ownership.

cross-domain keys In SNA, a pair of cryptographic keys used by a system services control point (SSCP) to encipher the session cryptography key that is sent to another SSCP.

cross-domain link A subarea link connecting two subareas in different domains. A physical link connecting two domains.

cross-domain resource (CDRSC) In SNA, a resource (typically software) that resides in another domain, under the control of a different VTAM.

cross-domain resource manager (CDRM) In SNA, the function in the SSCP which controls initiation and termination of cross-domain sessions.

cross-network LU-LU session In SNA, a session between logical units (LUs) in different networks.

cross-network session A session whose path traverses more than one SNA network.

cross-platform The ability of software or hardware to run identically on different platforms. Cross-platform computing is becoming increasingly important as local area networks (LANs) become better at linking machines of different types.

crosstalk Interfering energy transferred from one circuit (or wire) to another.

CRS *See* cell relay service.

CRT *See* cathode-ray tube.

cryptography The art or science concerning the principles, means, and methods for rendering plain information unintelligible and for restoring encrypted information to intelligible form.

CS *See* convergence sublayer.

CSA *See* Canadian Standards Association.

CSF *See* switch fabric.

CSLIP *See* Compressed Serial Link Internet Protocol.

CSMA/CA *See* carrier-sense multiple access with collision avoidance.

CSNET *See* Computer Science Network.

CSNP *See* complete sequence number PDU.

CSP *See* communications scanner processor.

CS-PDU *See* convergence sublayer protocol data unit.

CSR *See* cell missequenced ratio.

CSS *See* cascading style sheets.

CSU *See* channel service unit.

CTC *See* channel-to-channel.

CTCA *See* channel-to-channel adapter.

CTD *See* cell transfer delay.

CTI *See* computer-telephony-integration.

CUG *See* closed user group.

currency The previous, current, and next position of a record in a file. Currency can be either *logical* or *physical*.

current An object that is acting as a reference point.

current cell rate (CCR) A field in the RM cell header that indicates the current complying cell rate a user can transmit over a virtual connection (VC).

current load model (CLM) A service that maintains current usage statistics, such as the effective bandwidth at the VPC and link level

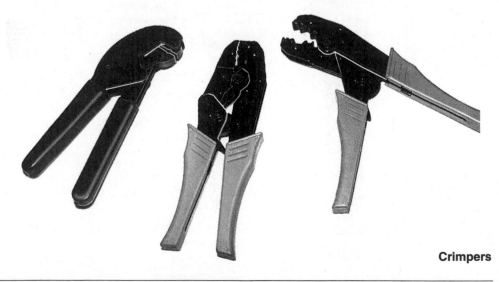

Crimpers

and the number of active and rejected connections per CoS and source/destination pair.

cursor A symbol which shows where the next character will be displayed on a computer monitor.

customer information control system (CICS) An IBM software program that supports real-time transactions between remote users and custom-written transactions. It includes facilities for building, using, and maintaining databases.

customer premises equipment (CPE) Communications equipment that resides at the customer's location. Computer and communications equipment (hardware and software) used by a carrier's customer and located at the customer's site. *See* DTE.

cut buffer A memory area that holds text which has been deleted from a file.

cut To remove an object from a document and place it in a buffer.

CWALL An NCP threshold of buffer availability, below which the NCP will accept only high-priority path information units (PIUs).

cyan-magenta-yellow-black (CMYK) Pronounced as separate letters. CMYK is a color model in which all colors are described as a mixture of these four process colors.

cyberpunk Originally a cultural sub-genre of science fiction, taking place in a not-so-distant over-industrialized society. The term grew out of the work of science-fiction writers William Gibson and Bruce Sterling and has evolved into a cultural label encompassing many different kinds of human, machine, and punk attitudes. It includes clothing and lifestyle choices as well. *See* cyberspace.

cyberspace (*a*) The entire range of information available on the Internet through computer networks. First used by author William Gibson in his sci-fi novel *Neuromancer*. (*b*) A metaphor for describing the non-physical terrain created by computer systems.

cycle (*Illustration*) A complete oscillation of a waveform, either analog or digital.

cycles per second *See* hertz.

cyclic redundancy check (CRC) A common technique for detecting data transmission errors. A number of file transfer protocols, including Zmodem, use CRC in addition to checksum. A bit-errors detection technique that employs a mathematical algorithm, where, based on the transmitted bits, it calculates a value attached to the information bits in the same packet. The receiver, using the same algorithm, recalculates that value and compares it to the one received. If the two values do not agree, the transmitted packet is then considered to be in error.

cylinder A single track location on the platters making up a hard disk.

Cyrix A manufacturer of Intel-compatible microprocessors.

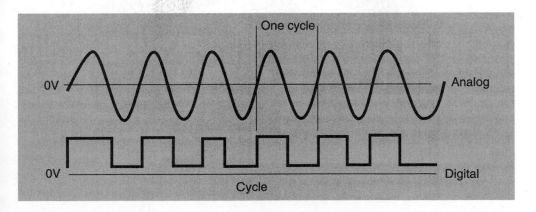

D channel or data channel (*a*) A channel in ISDN lines, used to set up calls and carry out-of-band information about the calls. (*b*) An IBM term used as a synonym for *input/output channel*.

D4 framing *See* SF.

DA *See* destination address.

DAC *See* digital-to-analog converter; dual-attached concentrator.

daemon A process that runs in the background and performs a specified operation at predefined times or in response to certain events. This is a UNIX term, although many other operating systems provide support for daemons; in other systems, daemons may have alternative names. Windows, for example, refers to daemons and *system agents* and *services*. Typical daemon processes include print spoolers, e-mail handlers, and other programs that perform administrative tasks for the operating system. The term comes from Greek mythology, where daemons were evil guardian spirits.

DAF *See* directory access function.

daisy-wheel printer A type of printer that produces letter-quality type. A daisy-wheel printer works on the same principle as a ball-head typewriter. The daisy wheel is a disk made of plastic or metal on which characters stand out in relief along the outer edge. To print a character, the printer rotates the disk until the desired letter is facing the paper. Then a hammer strikes the disk, forcing the character to hit an ink ribbon, leaving an impression of the character on the paper. You can change the daisy wheel to print different fonts.

DAO *See* data access objects *and* disk at once.

DAP *See* Directory Access Protocol.

DARPA *See* Defense Advanced Research Projects Agency.

DARPA Internet Obsolete term referring to the Internet. *See* Internet.

DASD *See* direct-access storage device.

DAT *See* digital audio tape.

data (*a*) Distinct pieces of information, usually formatted in a special way. All software is divided into two general categories: data and programs. Programs are collections of instructions for manipulating data. (*b*) A term often used to distinguish binary machine-readable information from textual human-readable information. (*c*) In database management systems, *data files* store the database information, whereas other files, such as index files and data dictionaries, store administrative information, known as *metadata*.

data access objects (DAO) Objects that work with the Jet database engine. DAO objects are generally created with Visual Basic. Once created, a DAO object can be accessed and manipulated by any application that can use the Jet engine. This includes all of the applications in Microsoft Office, such as MS-Word, MS-Access, and Excel.

data bus connector (DB connector) Type of connector used to connect serial and parallel cables to a data bus. DB connector names are of the format DB-*x*, where *x* represents the number of (wires) within the connector. Each line is connected to a pin on the connector, but in many cases, not all pins are assigned a function. DB connectors are defined by various EIA/TIA standards.

data cable levels A cable grading scheme used by cable manufacturers to identify the designed transmission speed for a given cable.

data channel *See* D channel.

data circuit A pair of associated transmit and receive channels providing a means for two-way data communication.

data circuit-terminating equipment or **data communications equipment (DCE)** A type of serial device connection (for example, a modem). The equipment installed at the user's premises provides all the functions required to establish, maintain, and terminate a connection for data transmission, and the signal conversion and coding between the data terminal equipment device and the line. A DCE device helps the terminal equipment communicate over the network by establishing, maintaining, and terminating the connection in a data conversation. It also provides any encoding or conversion necessary. Examples of DCEs include modems, cluster controllers, multiplexers, and line drivers.

data communication The transmission and reception of data.

data compression Storing data in a format that requires less space than usual. Compressing data is the same as *packing data*. Data compression is particularly useful in communications because it enables devices to transmit the same amount of data in fewer bits. There are a variety of data compression techniques, but only a few have been standardized. The CCITT has defined a standard data compression technique for transmitting faxes (Group 3 standard) and a compression standard for data communications through modems (CCITT V.42bis). In addition, there are file compression formats, such as ARC and ZIP.

data country code (DCC) One of two ATM address formats developed by the ATM Forum for use by private networks. Adapted from the subnetwork model of addressing in which the ATM layer is responsible for mapping network layer addresses to ATM addresses. *See* ICD.

data dictionary In database management systems, a file that defines the basic organization of a database. A data dictionary contains a list of all files in the database, the number of records in each file, and the names and types of each field.

Data Encryption Standard (DES) In computer security, the National Institute of Standards and Technology (NIST) Data Encryption Standard, adopted by the United States government as *Federal Information Processing Standard (FIPS)* publication 46, which allows only hardware implementations of the data encryption algorithm. A popular symmetric-key encryption method, it was developed in 1975 and standardized by ANSI in 1981 as ANSI X.3.92. It was a widely used method of providing secure connections through data encryption until it was broken in July 1998. DES uses a 56-bit key and is illegal to export out of the United States or Canada if the exporter does not meet BXA requirements.

data encryption A means of implementing security whereby data is encrypted and decrypted over WAN lines.

data entry The process of entering data into a computerized database or spreadsheet. Data entry can be performed by an individual typing at a keyboard or by a machine entering data electronically.

data exchange interface (DXI) A frame-based ATM interface between a DTE (such as a router or a local switch) and a DCE. DXI interfaces to the ATM UNI and has been chosen by the ATM Forum as an affordable solution for providing ATM capabilities over WAN.

data-flow control (DFC) Layer 5 of the SNA architectural model. In SNA, a request or response unit (RU) category used for requests and responses exchanged between the data-flow control layer in one half-session and the data-flow control layer in the session partner.

data host node In SNA, a host dedicated to processing applications, that does not control network resources, except for its channel-attached or communication adapter-attached devices.

data independence The separation of data from the programs that use the data.

data integrity The validity of data.

data link A physical link, like a wire, that connects one or more devices or communication controllers.

data-link connection identifier (DLCI) (*Illustration*) Used to indicate a frame relay

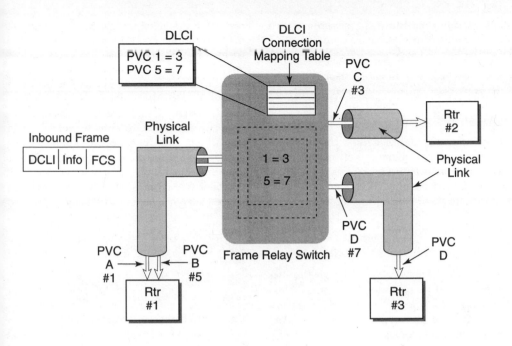

D

port connection to and from a frame relay network. DLCIs are associated with *virtual circuits* as a pair of DLCIs (one at either end) mapped across a frame relay network become a virtual circuit (VC).

data-link control (DLC) (*a*) A set of rules used by nodes at layer 2 within a network. The data link is governed by data-link protocols such as Ethernet, channel, FDDI, and token ring. (*b*) The physical means of connecting one location to another for the purpose of transmitting and receiving data. (*c*) In SNA, the second layer of the seven-layer architecture. In OSI, the second layer of the seven-layer architecture. (*d*) The second lowest layer in the OSI reference model. Every network interface card (NIC) has a DLC address or DLC identifier (DLCI) that uniquely identifies the node on the network. Some network protocols, such as Ethernet and token ring, use the DLC addresses exclusively. Other protocols, such as TCP/IP, use a logical address at the network layer to identify nodes. For networks that conform to the IEEE 802 standards (e.g., Ethernet), the DLC address is usually called the *media access control (MAC)* address.

data-link layer Layer 2 of the OSI reference model. It synchronizes transmission and handles error correction for a data link.

data-link level The conceptual level of control logic between high-level logic and a data-link protocol that maintains control of the data link.

data-link switching plus (DLSW+) A legacy networking protocol. A type of serial device connection (for example, a dumb terminal).

data manipulation language (DML) A set of statements used to store, retrieve, modify, and erase data from a database. There are two types of DML: *procedural*, in which the user specifies the data is needed and how to get it; and *nonprocedural*, in which the user specifies only the data is needed

data migration The process of translating data from one format to another. The process of moving data from one storage device to another.

data mining A class of database applications that looks for hidden patterns in a group of data. For example, data mining software can help retail companies find customers with common interests.

data network An arrangement of data circuits and switching facilities for establishing connections between data terminal equipment. A term commonly found in X.25 network implementations.

data network identification code (DNIC) Part of an X.121 address. DNICs are divided into two parts: the first specifying the country in which the addressed PSN is located and the second specifying the PSN itself. *See* X.121.

data packet A packet used for the transmission of user data on a virtual circuit at the DTE/DCE interface.

data processing A class of programs that organize and manipulate data, usually large amounts of numeric data. Accounting programs are the prototypical examples of data processing applications.

data rate *See* data transfer rate.

data server An application that acts like an interface between a database extension on a computer and a data source.

data service unit or digital service unit (DSU) A device used in digital transmission that connects end-user equipment, such as a router, to a digital transmission circuit or service. DSUs terminate a digital circuit, such as T1, at the customer site. For example, to bring frame relay service into a building, you could connect the incoming digital leased line (fractional T1) to the building's DSU, which in turn could be connected to the building's router via a serial media using the Frame Relay protocol. For frame relay service, DSUs range in speed from 56 Kbps to T3 (51 Mbps).

data set A way in which data, programs, and other representations of information are stored in IBM's MVS operating system environment.

data set ready (DSR) EIA/TIA-232 interface circuit that is activated when a DCE is powered up and ready for use.

data stream (*a*) In SNA, a continuous stream of data elements being transmitted, in charac-

ter or binary digital form, using a defined format. (*b*) A communication channel. Remote logins, file transfers, mail delivery, all use streams. A stream resembles a pipeline. It has two end-points; data is put in one end and comes out the other. None of the data is duplicated, discarded, or reorganized in any way. Two streams can be paired together to form a full duplex connection. All Internet transfers are in the form of *datagrams*. Internet streams are emulated using datagrams by the TCP Protocol. To diagnose Internet operation, a packet decoder such as TCPdump is used to view individual packets. This, along with a knowledge of TCP operation, enables the Internet engineer to assemble a mental picture of network operation.

data structure In programming, a scheme for organizing related pieces of information.

data-switching exchange (DSE) Equipment at a single location that provides switching functions, such as circuit switching, message switching, and packet switching.

data terminal equipment (DTE) (*a*) A source or destination for data. Often used to denote terminals or computers attached to a wide area network. (*b*) That part of a data station which constitutes a data source, data link, or both. (*c*) A device that controls data flowing to or from a computer. The term is most often used in reference to serial communications defined by the RS-232C standard. This standard defines the two ends of the communications channel as being a DTE and *data communications equipment (DCE)* device. In practical terms, the DCE is usually a modem and the DTE is the computer itself, or more precisely, the computer's UART chip. For internal modems, the DCE and DTE are part of the same device. For example, a PC, a printer, and a PBX are all DTE devices, while a modem, multiplexer, and line driver are DCE devices. *See* CPE *and* DCE.

data terminal ready (DTR) EIA/TIA-232 circuit that is activated to let the DCE know when the DTE is ready to send and receive data.

data transfer rate The speed with which data can be transmitted from one device to another. Data rates are often measured in megabits (million bits) or megabytes (million bytes) per second. These are usually abbreviated as Mbps and MBps, respectively. Another term for data transfer rate is *throughput*.

data type (*a*) In programming, classification of a particular type of information. It is easy for humans to distinguish between different types of data. We can usually tell at a glance whether a number is a percentage, a time, or an amount of money. We do this through special symbols—%, :, and $—that indicate the data's type. Similarly, a computer uses special internal codes to keep track of the different types of data it processes. (*b*) In SNA, particularly NetView, these can be alerts, events, or statistics.

data unit (DU) In the OSI environment, the smallest unit of a file content meaningful to an FTAM file action.

data vaulting The process of sending data off-site, where it can be protected from hardware failures, theft, and other threats.

data warehouse A collection of data designed to support management decision making. Data warehouses contain a wide variety of data that present a coherent picture of business conditions at a single point in time. The term generally refers to combining many different databases across an entire enterprise.

database A collection of information organized in such a way that a computer program can quickly select desired pieces of data. Traditional databases are organized by fields, records, and files. A *field* is a single piece of information; a *record* is one complete set of fields; and a *file* is a collection of records. To access information from a database, you need a *database management system (DBMS)*, which is a collection of programs that enables you to enter, organize, and select data in a database.

Database 2 (DB2) A family of relational database products offered by IBM. DB2 provides an open database environment that runs on a wide variety of computing platforms.

datagram In IP networks, a packet. A way of sending data in which a data message is randomly broken into parts and the parts are cor-

rectly reassembled by the receiving machine. Each message part contains information about itself, including its destination and source. Datagrams are small pieces of data, often in the 256- to 2,000-byte range. Datagrams are completely self-contained. They have a source and a destination, but nothing that could be called a connection. A datagram has no relationship to any other datagrams that came before or after. Although most networking communication uses *data streams*, all Internet transfers are in the form of datagrams. Internet streams are actually emulated by the TCP Protocol using datagrams. To diagnose Internet operation, a packet decoder such as TCPdump is used to view individual packets. This, along with a knowledge of TCP operation, enables the Internet engineer to assemble a mental picture of network operation.

datagram delivery protocol (DDP) In AppleTalk networks, a protocol that provides socket-to-socket delivery of data packets.

daughtercard A printed circuit board that plugs into another circuit board (usually the motherboard). A daughtercard is similar to an expansion board, but it accesses the motherboard components (memory and CPU) directly instead of sending data through the slower expansion bus. A daughtercard is also called a *daughterboard*.

DB connector *See* data bus connector.

dB *See* decibel.

DB2 *See* Database 2.

DB-9 (*Illustration*) A physical connector that has nine pins.

DB-15 (*Illustration*) Connector used for data-connectivity applications. It has 15 pins and can be configured for several protocols, including the popular RS-232.

DB-25 (*Illustration*) A connector used for data connectivity applications. It has 25 pins and can be configured for several protocols, including the popular RS-232.

dBASE A popular database management system produced by Ashton Tate Corporation. The original version, called *Vulcan*, was created by

DB-9 Male

DB-9 Female

DB-15 Female

DB-15 Male

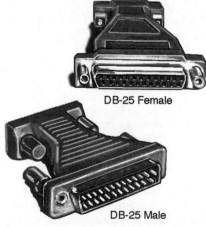

DB-25 Female

DB-25 Male

Wayne Ratliff. In 1981, Ashton-Tate bought Vulcan and marketed it as dBASE II. Subsequent versions with additional features are known as dBASE III, dBASE III+, and dBASE IV, all of which are currently owned and developed by Borland Corporation.

DBCS *See* double-byte character set.

DCA *See* Defense Communication Agency.

DCC *See* data country code *and* direct cable connection.

DCE *See* data circuit-terminating equipment *or* data communications equipment *and* distributed computing environment.

DCL *See* Digital Command Language.

DCLI *See* data-link connection identifier.

DCOM *See* Distributed Component Object Model.

DCS *See* defined context set.

DCT *See* discrete cosine transform.

DDC *See* display data channel.

DDCMP Digital (DEC) data communications message protocol.

DDE *See* dynamic data exchange.

DDM *See* distributed data management.

DDN *See* Defense Data Network.

DDoS Distributed Denial of Service, a type of attack wherein the target site (server or router) is sent packets (ICMP, PING, or TCP SYN) that appears to be normal traffic. In reality, this traffic is not normal and the target site is actually flooded with these false packets preventing legitimate traffic from accessing the site thus denying service to real users. In recent days, these attacks have become distributed in nature as computers throughout the "World Wide Web" join together in order to attack a site.

DDoS Daemon A specialized computer program that was designed for use in controlling and coordinating a DDoS attack. As of this writing, there are four known programs: Tribal Village (TFN), TFN2K, Trinoo, and Stacheldraht, which is German for "barbwire."

You can learn more about these programs at the following URL's:

http://staff.washington.edu/ dittrich/.misc/trinoo.analysis

http://staff.washington.edu/ dittrich/misc/tfn.analysis

http://staff.washington.edu/ dittrich/misc/stacheldraht. analysis

DDP *See* datagram delivery protocol.

DDR *See* Dial-on-Demand Routing.

DDR-SDRAM *See* double data rate-synchronous DRAM.

DDS *See* digital data service.

DE *See* directory entry.

de facto standard A standard that results from technology that has been developed, widely used, and that has achieved some level of popularity. A standard that exists by nature of its widespread use. Compare with *de jure standard*. *See* standard.

de jure standard A standard set by a body or official consensus. A standard that exists because of its approval by an official standards body. Compare with *de facto standard*. *See* standard.

deactivate To take a resource out of service.

deadlock (*a*) Unresolved contention for the use of a resource. (*b*) In APPN, when two elements of a process each wait for action by or a response from the other before they resume the process. (*c*) A condition that occurs when two processes are each waiting for the other to complete before proceeding. The result is that both processes hang. Deadlocks occur most commonly in multitasking and client/server environments.

deallocate In APPC, a LU6.2 application program interface (API) terminates a conversation and makes the session free for a future conversation.

debug To find and remove errors (bugs) from a program or design.

DEC *See* Digital Equipment Corporation.

decibel (dB) Unit of measurement for sound.

decimal Numbers in base 10 (the numbers we use in everyday life). The numbers 9, 100345000, and –256 are all decimal numbers. Note that a decimal number is not necessarily a number with a decimal point in it. Numbers with decimal points (that is, numbers with a fractional part) are called *fixed-point* or *floating-point numbers*. In addition to the decimal format, computer data is often represented in binary, octal, and hexadecimal formats.

Decimal and Binary Equivalents

Decimal	Binary
1	1
2	10
3	11
4	100
5	101
6	110
7	111
8	1000
9	1001
10	1010
16	10000
32	100000
64	1000000
100	1100100
256	100000000
512	1000000000
1000	1111110100
1024	10000000000

decipher To convert enciphered data in order to restore the original data.

declare To define the name and data type of a variable or other programming construct. Many programming languages, including C and

Pascal, require you to declare variables before using them.

DECnet Digital Equipment Corporation's proprietary network protocol. Versions are identified by their phase number, such as Phase IV and Phase V. Phase V is the most recent iteration and supports both OSI protocols and proprietary Digital protocols. Phase IV Prime supports inherent MAC addresses that allow DECnet nodes to coexist with systems running other protocols that have MAC address restrictions. *See* DNA.

DECnet routing Proprietary routing scheme introduced by Digital Equipment Corporation in DECnet Phase III. In DECnet Phase V, DECnet completed its transition to OSI routing protocols (ES-IS and IS-IS).

decoder A device or program that translates encoded data into its original format (e.g., it decodes the data).

decryption In computer security, to decipher or decode. Synonym for deciphering. The reverse application of an encryption algorithm to encrypted data, thereby restoring that data to its original, unencrypted state. Decryption requires a secret key or password. *See* encryption.

dedicated Reserved for a specific use. In communications, a *dedicated channel* is a line reserved exclusively for one type of communication. This is the same as a *leased line* or *private line*. A *dedicated server* is a single computer in a network, which is reserved for serving the needs of the network.

dedicated LAN Network segment allocated to a single device. Used in LAN switched network topologies.

dedicated line A communications line that is indefinitely reserved for transmissions, rather than switched as transmission is required. *See* leased line.

default (*a*) A value or setting that a device or program automatically selects if the user does not specify a substitute. For example, word processors have default margins and default page lengths that you can override or reset. A *default*

drive is the disk drive the computer accesses unless the user specifies a different disk drive. A *default directory* is that directory the operating system searches unless the user specifies a different directory. (*b*) An action that a device or program will take. For example, some word processors generate backup files by default.

default route Routing table entry that is used to direct frames for which a next hop is not explicitly listed in the routing table.

default SSCP list In VTAM, a list of SSCPs to which a session request can be routed when a cross-domain resource manager (CDRM) is not specified.

Defense Advanced Research Projects Agency (DARPA) Formerly ARPA. The government agency that funded research and experimentation with the ARPANET. *See* ARPA.

Defense Communication Agency (DCA) United States government organization responsible for DDN networks such as MILNET. Now called *DISA*.

Defense Data Network (DDN) Used loosely to refer to MILNET and ARPANET, and the TCP/IP protocols they use. More specifically, it is MILNET and associated parts of the connected Internet that connect military installations. The DDN is a military network composed of an unclassified network (MILNET) and various secret and top-secret networks. DDN is operated and maintained by DISA. *See* DISA *and* MILNET.

Defense Information Systems Agency (DISA) United States military organization responsible for implementing and operating military information systems, including the DDN. *See* DDN.

defined context set (DCS) A set of presentation contexts negotiated between peer presentation entities.

definite response (DR) A protocol used in SNA that requests the receiver of the request to return a response unconditionally, whether positive or negative, to that request chain.

definition statement In IBM's VTAM program, a statement describing an element of the network. In IBM's NCP, a type of instruction that defines a resource.

defrag A DOS and Windows utility that defragments the hard disk.

degauss To remove magnetism from a device. The term is usually used in reference to color monitors and other display devices that use a cathode ray tube (CRT). These devices aim electrons onto the display screen by creating magnetic fields inside the CRT. External magnetic forces—such as the Earth's natural magnetism or a magnet placed close to the monitor—can magnetize the shadow mask, causing distorted images and colors. To remove this external magnetic force, most monitors automatically degauss the CRT whenever the monitor is turned on. In addition, many monitors have a manual degauss button that performs a more thorough degaussing of the CRT. There are also external degaussers that degauss the monitor from the outside. Because it may be impossible to remove the external magnetic force, degaussing works by realigning the magnetic fields inside the CRT to compensate for the external magnetism. Magnetic media, such as disks, can also be degaussed, thereby removing all data from the media.

delay The time between the initiation of a transaction by a sender and the first response received by the sender. Also, the time required to move a packet from source to destination over a given path.

delete key Often abbreviated Del; used to remove characters and other objects from a keyboarded data entry.

delete To remove or erase.

Delphi A rapid application development (RAD) system developed by Borland International, Inc. Delphi is similar to Visual Basic from Microsoft, but whereas Visual Basic is based on the BASIC programming language, Delphi is based on Pascal.

DELTA disk In SNA, the virtual disk in a VM operating system that contains program temporary fixes (PTFs) that have been installed but not yet merged.

D

demand priority A centrally-controlled access mechanism that is markedly different from other common LAN technologies. For example, all other Ethernet technologies use carrier sense multiple access/collision detection (CSMA/CD), which allows for multiple nodes to access and uses back-off and retransmit processes when a message exchange causes a collision. In token ring networks, a token passing mechanism is used for message exchange. In 100VG-AnyLAN, demand priority is a deterministic request method that maximizes network efficiency by eliminating collisions and token rotation delays. It uses a hub that can handle multiple transmission requests and can process traffic according to priority, making it useful for servicing time-sensitive traffic such as multimedia and video. Demand priority eliminates the overhead of packet collisions, collision recovery, and broadcast traffic typical in Ethernet networks. *See* 100VG-AnyLAN.

demarc or demarcation point The physical location where the phone company's responsibility for voice and data lines ends within a given building.

demodulation Process of returning a modulated signal to its original form. Modems perform demodulation by taking an analog signal and returning it to its original (digital) form. *See* modulation.

demultiplexing The separation of multiple input streams, which have been multiplexed into a common physical signal, back into multiple output streams. *See* multiplex.

denial-of-service (DoS) attack A type of attack on a network, designed to bring the network to its knees by flooding it with useless traffic. Many DoS attacks, such as the Ping of Death and Teardrop attacks, exploit limitations in the TCP/IP protocols. For all known DoS attacks, there are software fixes that system administrators can install to limit the damage caused by the attacks. But, like viruses, new DoS attacks are constantly being created by hackers.

dense mode PIM *See* PIM dense mode.

dense-mode A category of routing protocol that assumes multicast group members.

density How tightly information is packed together on a storage medium (tape or disk). A higher density means that data are closer together, so the medium can hold more information.

Department of Defense (DoD) United States government organization that is responsible for national defense. The DoD has frequently funded communication protocol development.

Department of Defense Intelligence Information System Network Security for Information Exchange (DNSIX) A collection of security requirements for networking defined by the United States Defense Intelligence Agency.

dependent (also **destination**) **logical unit (DLU)** An LU that depends on the SSCP to provide services for establishing sessions with other LUs. *See* LU *and* SSCP.

dependent logical unit requester (DLUR) The client half of the dependent LU requester/server enhancement to APPN. The DLUR component resides in APPN ENs and NNs that support adjacent DLUs by securing services from the DLUS. *See* APPN, DLU, *and* DLUS.

dependent logical unit server (DLUS) The server half of the dependent LU requester/server enhancement to APPN. The DLUS component provides SSCP services to DLUR nodes over an APPN network. *See* APPN, DLU, *and* DLUR.

DES *See* Data Encryption Standard.

descent line An imaginary line, usually marking the maximum distance below the baseline of the descenders of glyphs in a particular font.

Deschutes One of Intel's Pentium II microprocessors.

description Streams within a presentation, such as the set of encodings, network addresses, and information about the content.

descriptor A data buffer parameter passed for an extended-get or extended-step operation.

descriptor type An identifier for the type of data referred to by the handle in a descriptor record.

designated bridge The bridge that incurs the lowest path cost when forwarding a frame from a segment to the route bridge.

designated router An OSPF router that generates LSAs for a multi-access network and has other special responsibilities in running OSPF. Each multiaccess OSPF network that has at least two attached routers has a designated router elected by the OSPF Hello protocol. The designated router reduces the number of adjacencies required on a multiaccess network, which in turn reduces the amount of routing protocol traffic and the size of the topological database.

desk accessory (DA) On Apple Macintoshes, a utility—a small, standalone program designed to perform one small task.

desktop In graphical user interfaces, the metaphor used to portray file systems. Also short for desktop model computer.

desktop management interface (DMI) An API to enable software to collect information about a computer environment. For example, using DMI, a program can determine what software and expansion boards are installed on a computer.

desktop publishing Using a personal computer or workstation to produce high-quality printed documents. A desktop publishing system allows the user to use different typefaces, specify various margins and justifications, and embed illustrations and graphs directly into the text. The most-powerful desktop publishing systems enable the user to create illustrations, while less-powerful systems let users insert illustrations created by other programs.

destination In a network, any point or location—for example, a node, station, or terminal—to which data is to be sent.

destination address (DA) That part of a message which indicates for whom the message is intended. Synonymous with the address on an envelope. IBM token-ring network addresses are 48 bits in length.

destination logical unit (DLU) The logical unit to which data is to be sent.

destination MAC (DMAC) The MAC address specified in the Destination Address field of a packet. Compare with SMAC. *See* MAC address.

destination service access point (DSAP) The SAP of the network node designated in the Destination field of a packet. Compare to SSAP. *See* service access point (SAP).

Deutsche Industrie Norm (DIN) German national standards organization.

device (*a*) In networking, a generic term describing a modem, host, terminal, or other entity. (*b*) Any machine or component that attaches to a computer. Examples of devices include disk drives, printers, mice, and modems.

device bay A specification developed by Intel, Compaq, and Microsoft that would standardize the size, shape, and connection of computer components, such as disk drives, modems, and audio devices.

device-independent bitmap (DIB) The bit-mapped graphics format used by Windows.

DFC *See* data-flow control.

DHCP *See* Dynamic Host Configuration Protocol.

DIA *See* document interchange architecture.

dialed number identification service (DNIS) A telephony standard that can be set on high-speed data lines.

dial-in In most SNA environments, the motion of inbound traffic toward the host.

dialog box A box that appears on a display screen to present information or request input.

Dial-on-Demand Routing (DDR) Protocol for creating dial-up WAN connections, which are automatically initiated on an as-needed basis. Technique whereby a Cisco router can automatically initiate and close a circuit-switched session as transmitting stations demand. The router spoofs keepalives so that end stations treat the session as active. DDR permits routing over ISDN or telephone lines using an external ISDN terminal adapter or modem.

dial-out In most networking environments, the motion of outbound capabilities to access resources elsewhere.

dial-up (*a*) A type of communications established by a switched-circuit connection using the public telephone network. (*b*) A temporary connection between machines established over a standard phone line, usually by means of modems.

DIB *See* device-independent bitmap, directory information base, *and* dual independent bus.

differential encoding Digital encoding technique whereby a binary value is denoted by a signal change rather than a particular signal level.

differential Manchester encoding Digital coding scheme in which a mid-bit-time transition is used for clocking, and a transition at the beginning of each bit time denotes a zero. The coding scheme used by IEEE 802.5 and token ring networks.

diffusing update algorithm (DUAL) Convergence algorithm used in Enhanced IGRP that provides loop-free operation at every instant throughout a route computation. Allows routers involved in a topology change to synchronize at the same time, while not involving routers that are unaffected by the change. *See* Enhanced IGRP.

digerati The digital version of *literati*; a reference to a group of people seen to be knowledgeable, hip, or otherwise in-the-know in regard to the digital revolution.

digest A message that contains multiple individual postings to a mailing list or newsgroup; for example, the GroupStudy Daily Digest at *http://www.groupstudy.com*.

digital (*Illustration*) Any system based on discontinuous data or events. Computers are digital machines because at their most basic level they can distinguish between just two values, 0 and 1, or off and on. There is no simple way to represent all the values in between, such as

0.25. All data that a computer processes must be encoded digitally, as a series of zeroes and ones.

digital audio tape (DAT) A type of magnetic tape that uses a scheme called *helical scan* to record data. A DAT cartridge can hold from 2 to 24 gigabytes of data. It can support data transfer rates of about 2 MBps.

digital camera A camera that stores images digitally rather than recording them on film. Once a picture has been taken, it can be downloaded to a computer system, manipulated with a graphics program, and printed. Unlike film photographs, which have an almost infinite resolution, digital photos are limited by the amount of memory in the camera, the optical resolution of the digitizing mechanism, and, finally, by the resolution of the final output device.

Digital Command Language According to DEC documentation, a command interpreter in the operating system. It provides a means of communication between the user and the operating system.

digital data communication message protocol (DDCMP) The link-level protocol used by DEC in their network products. DDCMP operates over serial lines, delimits frames by a special character, and includes checksums at the link level. It was relevant to TCP/IP because the original NSFNET used DDCMP over its backbone lines.

digital data service (DDS) The industry standard for digital audio tape (DAT) formats. The latest format, DDS-3, specifies tapes that can hold 24 GB (the equivalent of over 40 CD-ROMs) and support data transfer rates of 2 MBps.

Digital Equipment Corporation (DEC) One of leading producers of workstations, servers, and high-end PCs. DEC also developed one of the leading Internet search engines called *Alta Vista*.

digital light processing (DLP) A technology developed by Texas Instruments used for projecting images from a monitor onto a large screen for presentations.

digital linear tape (DLT) A type of magnetic tape storage device originally developed by DEC and now marketed by several companies.

digital loop The carrier's local loop infrastructure that connects end users.

digital nervous system (DNS) A term coined by Bill Gates to describe a network of personal computers that make it easier to obtain and understand information.

digital network architecture (DNA) Network architecture developed by Digital Equipment Corporation. The products that embody DNA (including communications protocols) are collectively referred to as DECnet. The set of protocols govern the format, control, and sequencing of message exchange for all DEC network implementations. The protocols are layered, and they define rules for data exchange from the physical-link level up through the user-interface level. DNA controls all data that travels throughout a DEC network. DNA also defines standard network management and network generation procedures. *See* DECnet.

digital photography The art and science of producing and manipulating digital photographs.

digital satellite system (DSS) A network of satellites that broadcast digital data.

digital signal 0 (DS-0) Physical interface for digital transmission at the rate of 64 kbps.

digital signal 1 (DS-1) *(Illustration)* Physical interface for digital transmission at the rate of 1.544 Mbps. Also, known as a T-1 standard, it can simultaneously support 24 DS-0 circuits. Also referred to as a T1 or E1 line.

digital signal 2 (DS-2) Physical interface for digital transmission at the rate of 6.312 Mbps.

digital signal 3 (DS-3) Physical interface for digital transmission at the rate of 44.736 Mbps.

DS1 circuit/line types and applications

Line format/coding	framing format	signaling	Application
AMI	SF/D4	in-band	24 voice/modem channels
AMI	ESF	in-band	24 voice/modem channels
AMI	ESF	out-of-band	23 voice/modem or digital/data channels
B8ZS	SF/D4	in-band	24 voice/modem channels
B8ZS	ESF	in-band	24 voice/modem channels
B8ZS	ESF	out-of-band	23 voice/modem or digital/data channels

D

digital signal processing (DSP) Manipulating analog information, such as sound or photographs, that has been converted into a digital form. DSP also implies the use of a data compression technique.

digital signature A digital code that can be attached to an electronically transmitted message that uniquely identifies the sender. Like a written signature, the purpose of a digital signature is to guarantee that the individual sending the message really is who he or she claims to be. Digital signatures are especially important for electronic commerce and are a key component of most authentication schemes. To be effective, digital signatures must be unforgeable. There are a number of different encryption techniques to guarantee this level of security.

digital simultaneous voice and data (DSVD) An all-digital technology for concurrent voice and data (SVD) transmission over a single analog telephone line. DSVD is endorsed by Intel, Hayes, United States Robotics, and others and has been submitted to the ITU for possible standardization.

digital storage architecture (DSA) According to DEC documentation, the specifications from DEC governing the design of and interface to mass storage products. DSA defines the functions to be performed by host computers, controllers, and drives, and specifies how they interact to manage mass storage.

digital storage systems interconnect (DSSI) A data bus that uses the systems communication architecture protocols for direct host-to-storage communications. The DSSI cable can extend to 6 m and has a peak bandwidth of 4 Mbytes.

digital versatile disc or **digital video disc (DVD)** A type of CD-ROM that holds a minimum of 4.7GB (gigabytes), enough for a full-length movie. Many experts believe that DVD disks, called DVD-ROMs, will eventually replace CD-ROMs, as well as VHS video cassettes and laser discs. Unlike DVD-ROMs, the digital-video format includes a content scrambling system (CSS) to prevent users from copying discs. This means that today's DVD-ROM players cannot play DVD-Video discs without a software or hardware upgrade to decode the encrypted discs.

digital-to-analog converter (DAC) A device (usually a single chip) that converts digital data into analog signals.

digitize To translate into a digital form. For example, optical scanners digitize images by translating them into bit maps. It is also possible to digitize sound, video, and any type of movement. In all these cases, digitization is performed by sampling at discrete intervals.

digitizing tablet An input device that enables the user to enter drawings and sketches into a computer. Digitizing tablets are also called *digitizers, graphics tablets, touch tablets*, or simply *tablets*.

Dijkstra's algorithm *See* SPF.

DIMM *See* dual in-line memory module.

DIN *See* Deutsche Industrie Norm.

DIN connector Deutsche Industrie Norm connector. Multipin connector used in some Macintosh and IBM PC-compatible computers, and on some network processor panels.

DIP *See* dual in-line package.

DIP switch A series of tiny switches built into circuit boards. The housing for the switches, which has the same shape as a chip, is the DIP. These switches enable the user to configure a circuit board for a particular type of computer or application. The installation instructions indicate how to set the switches. DIP switches are always *toggle switches*, which means they have two possible positions—on or off, or 1 and 0.

DirecPC A service offered by Hughes Network Systems that provides Internet access through private satellite dishes. Requests for Web pages go through a normal modem connection but pages are delivered through the satellite link at up to 400 Kbps (about 15 times faster than a 28.8 Kbps modem, and 4 times faster than an ISDN connection). To install the DirecPC system, you need to purchase a small satellite dish from Hughes, plus an ISA card to install in your computer. You'll also need a normal Internet connection via an ISP for upstream traffic (e.g., requests for Web pages).

direct cable connection (DCC) A Windows 95 feature that enables two computers to be connected via a serial or parallel cable. Once connected, the two computers function as if they were on a local-area network (LAN). Either computer can access files on the other computer. Because DCC does not require network interface cards (NICs), it is less expensive and simpler. The limitations are that it can connect only two PCs, and the data transfer rate is slower than with a true LAN.

direct memory access (DMA) A technique for transferring data from main memory to a device without passing it through the CPU.

direct search list (DSRLST) In SNA, a message unit that contains a search request sent throughout subarea networks to obtain information about a network resource such as its name, routing information, and status information.

Direct3D An application programming interface (API) for manipulating and displaying three-dimensional objects. Developed by Microsoft, Direct3D provides programmers with a way to develop 3-D programs that can utilize whatever graphics acceleration device is installed in the machine.

direct-access storage device (DASD) (*a*) A device in which access time is effectively independent of the location of the data. (*b*) IBM terminology for a disk drive in mainframe environments.

DirectDraw A software interface standard for transferring video processing from a PC's CPU to the video adapter. When the CPU is not busy, the Windows Graphics Display Interface (GDI) updates the video display. If the CPU is busy, the DCI driver allows an application to send update information directly to the video adapter. DirectDraw can also provide applications such as games direct access to features of particular display devices.

directed broadcast address In TCP/IP-based environments, an IP address that specifies all hosts on a specific network. A single copy of a directed broadcast is routed to the specified network where it is broadcast to all machines on that network.

directed search Search request sent to a specific node known to contain a resource. A directed search is used to determine the continued existence of the resource and to obtain routing information specific to the node. *See* broadcast search.

directory A term whose meaning depends on the environment in which it is used. (*a*) A special kind of file used to organize other files into a hierarchical structure. For example, in UNIX environments a directory is a listing of files and the files themselves. This definition is generally the case in most environments; however, some vendors contend that a significant difference exists. (*b*) In IBM's VM/SP environment, a control program (CP) disk file that defines each virtual machine's normal configuration: the user ID, password, normal and maximum allowable virtual storage, CP command privilege classes allowed, dispatching priority, logical editing symbols to be used, account number, and CP options desired. (*c*) In APPN, a database that lists names of resources and records the CP name of the node where each resource is located. (*d*) The subdivision of a volume, available in the hierarchical file system (HFS). A directory can contain files as well as other directories.

directory access function (DAF) The framework for distributed applications

Directory Access Protocol (DAP) The protocol used between a directory user agent and a directory system agent.

directory entry (DE) An object in the directory information base to model information. It can be an object entry or an alias entry.

directory information base (DIB) A set of directory entries, which contains objects to which the directory provides access. It includes all pieces of information which can be read or manipulated using the directory operations.

directory information shadowing protocol A protocol used for shadowing between two directory service agents in the directory services standard.

directory information tree (DIT) A tree structure of the directory information base.

directory name Name for directory entries in the directory information base.

Directory Operational Binding Management Protocol (DOP) A protocol used by directory service agents to activate showing agreement. This allows directory service agents to establish, modify, and terminate operational bindings.

directory service agent (DSA) An application entity that offers the directory services.

directory service protocol (DSP) The protocol used between two directory system agents.

directory services (DS) According to its use in OSI environments, an application service element that translates the symbolic names used by application processes into the complete network addresses used. A control point component of an APPN node that maintains knowledge of the location of network resources. Services that help network devices locate service providers.

directory user agent (DUA) An application entity that provides the directory services.

DirectX A set of APIs developed by Microsoft that enables programmers to write programs that access hardware features of a computer without knowing exactly what hardware will be installed on the machine where the program eventually runs.

DISA *See* Defense Information Systems Agency.

disable To deactivate.

discarded packet A piece of data, called a *packet*, that is intentionally destroyed.

disconnection Termination of a physical connection.

discovery The act of exploring a network to determine the types and settings of network devices. Discoveries can ferret out network topologies, router, host, and database information, operating system and memory information, and so on.

discovery architecture APPN software that enables a machine configured as an APPN EN to automatically find primary and backup NNs when the machine is brought onto an APPN network.

discovery mode Method by which an AppleTalk interface acquires information about an attached network from an operational node and then uses this information to configure itself. Also called *dynamic configuration*.

discrete cosine transform (DCT) A technique for representing waveform data as a weighted sum of cosines. DCT is commonly used for data compression, as in JPEG

discrete multi-tone (DMT) A wave-modulation scheme that discretely divides the available frequencies.

discretionary controls Security controls that are applied at the user's option.

disk A round plate on which data can be encoded. There are two basic types of disks: magnetic disks and optical disks. On *magnetic disks*, data is encoded as microscopic magnetized needles on the disk's surface. *Optical disks* record data by burning microscopic holes in the surface of the disk with a laser.

disk at once (DAO) A method of recording to CD-R disks, in which all data is written in a single session.

D

disk cache A part of RAM that acts as an intermediate buffer when data is read from and written to file systems on secondary storage devices.

disk compression A type of data compression that works by storing compressed versions of files on the hard disk. A disk compression utility sits between the operating system and the disk drive. Whenever the operating system attempts to save a file to disk, the utility intercepts it and compresses it. Likewise, when the operating system attempts to open a file, the disk compression utility intercepts the file, decompresses it, and then passes it to the operating system.

disk drive A machine that reads data from and writes data onto a disk. A disk drive rotates the disk at high speed and has one or more heads that read and write data.

disk pack A stack of removable hard disks encased in a metal or plastic container.

diskless workstation A workstation or PC on a local-area network (LAN) that does not have its own disk. Instead, it stores files on a network file server. Diskless workstations reduce the overall cost of a LAN because one large-capacity disk drive is usually less expensive than several low-capacity drives. In addition, diskless workstations simplify backups and security because all files are on the file server. Also, accessing data from a large remote file server is often faster than accessing data from a small local storage device. One disadvantage of diskless workstations, however, is that they are useless if the network fails. When the workstation is a PC, it is often called a *diskless PC* or a *Net PC*.

DISP *See* Draft International Standardized Profile.

display data channel (DDC) A VESA standard for communication between a monitor and a video adapter.

display screen The display part of a monitor. Most display screens work under the same principle as a television, using a *cathode ray tube (CRT)*. Consequently, the term CRT is often used in place of display screen.

distance learning A type of education where students work on their own at home or at the office, and communicate with faculty and other students via e-mail, electronic forums, videoconferencing, and other forms of computer-based communication. Distance learning is becoming especially popular with companies that need to regularly retrain their employees, because it is less expensive than bringing all the students together in a traditional classroom setting.

Distance Vector Multicast Routing Protocol (DVMRP) An internetwork gateway protocol, largely based on RIP, that implements a typical dense-mode IP multicast scheme. DVMRP uses IGMP to exchange routing datagrams with its neighbors. *See* IGMP.

distance-vector routing algorithm Class of routing algorithms that iterate on the number of hops in a route to find a shortest-path spanning tree. Distance-vector routing algorithms call for each router to send its entire routing table in each update, but only to its neighbors. Distance-vector routing algorithms can be prone to routing loops, but are computationally simpler than link-state routing algorithms. Also called *Bellman-Ford routing algorithm*. *See* link-state routing algorithm *and* SPF.

Distance-Vector Routing Protocol A routing protocol that requires that each router simply inform its neighbors of its routing table. For each network path, the receiving routers pick the neighbor advertising the lowest cost, then add this entry into its routing table for readvertisement. *Hello* and *RIP* are common D-V routing protocols. Common enhancements to D-V algorithms include *split horizon, poison reverse, triggered updates*, and *holddown*. See the discussion of D-V, or *Bellman-Ford algorithms* in RIP's protocol specification, RFC 1058.

distinguished name (DN) Name of a directory entry.

distortion delay Problem with a communication signal resulting from nonuniform transmission speeds of the components of a signal through a transmission medium. Also called *group delay*.

Distributed Component Object Model (DCOM) An extension of the *Component Object Model (COM)* to support objects distributed across a network. DCOM was developed by Microsoft and has been submitted to the IETF as a draft standard.

distributed computing environment (DCE) An Open Software Foundation (OSF) set of standards for distributed computing. Also, distributed computing in the general sense of the term. DCE services include: Remote Procedure Calls (RPC), Security Service Directory, Service Time, Service Threads, and Service Distributed File Service.

distributed data management (DDM) Software in an IBM SNA environment that provides peer-to-peer communication and file sharing. One of three SNA transaction services. *See* DIA *and* SNADS.

distributed directory database (DDDB) In an APPN architecture, the complete listing of all resources in the network as maintained in individual directories scattered throughout an APPN network.

distributed network directory Synonym for distributed directory database.

distributed processing A network of computers, connected so that the processing of information is initiated in local computers, and the resultant data is sent to a central computer for further processing with the data from other local systems. A LAN is an example of distributed processing.

distributed queue dual bus (DQPD) The IEEE 802.6 standard is a MAN protocol based on 53-byte packets that can support connectionless and connection-oriented, isochronous integrated services. It is implemented as two unidirectional buses configured in a physical ring topology.

distributed system object model (DSOM) A version of SOM that supports sharing binary objects across networks.

DIT *See* directory information tree.

dithering Creating the illusion of new colors and shades by varying the pattern of dots (pixels) that make up the picture. Newspaper photographs, for example, are dithered. When they are viewed closely, it is apparent that different shades of gray are produced by varying the patterns of black and white dots.

Divx Digital video express. A new DVD-ROM format being promoted by several large Hollywood companies, including Disney, Dreamworks SKG, Paramount, and Universal. With Divx, a movie (or other data) loaded onto a DVD-ROM is playable only during a specific time frame, typically two days. As soon as you begin playing a Divx disc, the counter starts. Each Divx player is connected to a telephone outlet and communicates with a central server to exchange billing information.

DIX Ethernet A version of Ethernet developed by Digital, Intel, and Xerox.

DIX DEC, Intel, and Xerox.

DLC *See* data-link control.

DLCI *See* data-link connection identifier.

DLL *See* dynamic link library.

DLP *See* digital light processing.

DLSW+ *See* data-link switching plus.

DLSw *See* data-link switching.

DLT *See* digital linear tape.

DLU *See* destination logical unit.

DLUR *See* dependent logical unit requester.

DLUR node In APPN networks, an EN or NN that implements the DLUR component. *See* DLUR.

DLUS *See* dependent logical unit server.

DLUS node In APPN networks, an NN that implements the DLUS component. *See* DLUS.

DMA *See* direct memory access.

DMAC *See* destination MAC.

DMI *See* desktop management interface.

DML *See* data manipulation language.

DN *See* distinguished name.

DNA *See* digital network architecture.

DNIC *See* data network identification code.

DNIS *See* dialed number identification service.

DNS *See* digital nervous system *and* domain name system (or service).

DNSIX *See* Department of Defense Intelligence Information System Network Security for Information Exchange.

document (*n*) A file created with a word processor. In addition to text, documents can contain graphics, charts, and other objects. (*v*) To enter written explanations. For example, programmers are always exhorted to document their code by inserting comments.

document interchange architecture (DIA) Defines the protocols and data formats needed for the transparent interchange of documents in an SNA network. One of three SNA transaction services. *See* DDM *and* SNADS.

document object model (DOM) The specification for how objects in a Web page (text, images, headers, links, etc.) are represented.

document type definition (DTD) A type of file associated with SGML and XML documents that defines how the markup tags should be interpreted by the application presenting the document.

DoD Four-Layer Model The Department of Defense Four-Layer Model was developed in the 1970s for the DARPA Internetwork Project that eventually grew into the Internet. The core Internet protocols adhere to this model, although the OSI Seven-Layer Model is justly preferred for new designs. The four layers in the DoD model, from bottom to top, are:

1. The *Network-Access Layer*, responsible for delivering data over the particular hardware media in use. Different protocols are selected from this layer, depending on the type of physical network.

2. The *Internet Layer*, responsible for delivering data across a series of different physical networks that interconnect a source and destination machine. Routing protocols are most closely associated with this layer, as is the IP Protocol, the Internet's fundamental protocol.

3. The *Host-to-Host Layer*, handles connection rendezvous, flow control, retransmission of lost data, and other generic data flow management. The mutually exclusive TCP and UDP protocols are this layer's most important members.

4. The *Process Layer*, contains protocols that implement user-level functions, such as mail delivery, file transfer and remote login.

DoD *See* Department of Defense.

DOM *See* document object model.

domain (*a*) A group of computers and devices on a network that are administered as a unit with common rules and procedures. Within the Internet, domains are defined by the IP address. All devices sharing a common part of the IP address are said to be in the same domain. (*b*) A part of the DNS naming hierarchy.

domain name The unique name that identifies an Internet site. English language standard for a computer system's TCP/IP numeric address (example: 10.10.12.1). Domain names always have two or more parts, separated by dots (example: netcerts.com). The part on the left is the most specific, and the part on the right is the most general. A given machine may have more than one domain name but a given domain name points to only one machine. For example, the domain names netcerts.com, mail.netcerts.com, and ftp.netcerts.com, can all refer to the same machine, but each domain name can refer to no more than one machine. Usually, all the machines on a given network have the same right-hand portion of their domain names. It is also possible for a domain name to exist but not be connected to an actual machine. This is often done so that a group or business can have an Internet e-mail address without having to establish a real Internet site. In these cases, some real Internet machine must handle the mail on behalf of the listed domain name. As documented in RFC 1591, top-level domain names take one of two forms. First, they can be *generic domains*, all of which are populated by predominantly American domains. Alternately, a top-level domain can be a United Nations two-digit *country code*, listed in ISO-3166, the most common form for non-American domains.

Generic Domains Country Domains (partial list)

com	commercial
uk	United Kingdom
edu	Educational
fr	France
org	Non-profit Organizations
de	Germany
net	Networking Providers
nl	Netherlands
mil	US Military
us	United States
gov	US Government
au	Australia
int	International Organizations
ax	Antarctica

To be used, domain names must be converted into 32-bit *IP addresses*, using the *DNS Protocol*. Domain name registrations are handled by *InterNIC* in North America, *RIPE* in Europe, and *APNIC* in Asia. Domain-name assignment is completely distinct from IP address assignment.

domain name server In TCP/IP environments, a protocol for matching object names and network addresses. It was designed to replace the need to update /etc/hosts files of participating entities throughout a network.

domain name system (or service) (DNS) (*Illustration*) An Internet service that translates domain names into IP addresses. Because domain names are alphabetic, they are easier to remember. The Internet however, is really based on IP addresses. Every time you use a domain name, therefore, a DNS service must translate the name into the corresponding IP address. For example, the domain name www.example.com might translate to 19.15.32.4. The DNS system is, in fact, its own

network. If one DNS server doesn't know how to translate a particular domain name, it asks another one, and so on, until the correct IP address is returned.

D

DNS uses a distributed database protocol to delegate control of domain name hierarchies among *zones*, each managed by a group of *name servers*. For example, *.NetCerts.com, where * is anything, is completely the responsibility of NETCERTS. NETCERTS is responsible for constructing name servers to handle any domain name ending in NetCerts.com, referred to as their *Zone of Authority (ZOA)*. A zone takes its name from its highest point, so this zone is simply called NetCerts.com. NETCERTS registers its zone with InterNIC, who loads the name server IP addresses into the *root name servers*, which makes this information available to the global Internet. NETCERTS can also make subdelegations, like delegating news. NetCerts.com to their news division. This can be as simple as creating new name server entries with the longer names, but mechanisms exist if the delegate wants to operate an independent name server (RFC 1034).

domain-specific part (DSP) That part of a CLNS address that contains an area identifier, a station identifier, and a selector byte.

dongle A device that attaches to a computer to control access to a particular application.

DOP *See* Directory Operational Binding Management Protocol.

DOS Disk operating system. The term DOS can refer to any operating system, but it is most often used as a shorthand for MS-DOS (Microsoft disk operating system). Originally developed by Microsoft for IBM, MS-DOS was the standard operating system for IBM-compatible personal computers.

DoS attack *See* denial-of-service attack.

dot address The common notation for IP addresses in the form <n.n.n.n> where each number *n* represents, in decimal, one byte of the 4-byte IP address. Also called *dotted notation* or *four-part dotted notation*.

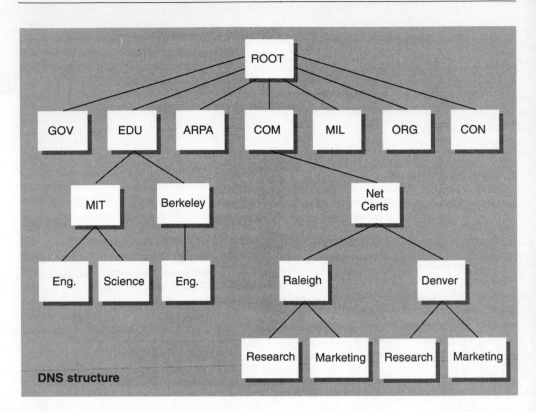

DNS structure

ROOT   The root server contains information about itself and the top-level domains immediately beneath it.

GOV   Refers to government entities.

EDU   Refers to any educational institutions.

ARPA   Refers to any ARPANET (Internet) host ID.

COM   Refers to any commercial organizations.

MIL   Refers to military organizations.

ORG   Serves as miscellaneous category for those not formally covered.

CON   Refers to countries conforming to ISO standards.

dot pitch A measurement that indicates the diagonal distance between like-colored phosphor dots on a display screen. Measured in millimeters, the dot pitch is one of the principal characteristics that determines the quality of display monitors. The lower the number, the crisper the image. The dot pitch of color monitors for personal computers ranges from about 0.15 mm to 0.30 mm. Another term for dot pitch is *phosphor pitch*.

dot-matrix printer A type of printer that produces characters and illustrations by striking pins against an ink ribbon to print closely spaced dots in the appropriate shape.

dots per inch (DPI) A number indicating the resolution of images. The more dots per inch, the higher the resolution.

dotted notation *See* dot address.

dotted-decimal notation The addressing scheme of the Internet protocol (IP). It is the representation of a 32-bit address consisting of four 8-bit numbers written in base 10 with periods separating them.

double click To tap a mouse button twice in rapid succession.

double data rate-synchronous DRAM (DDR-SDRAM) A type of SDRAM that supports data transfers on both edges of each clock cycle, effectively doubling the memory chip's data throughput. DDR-SDRAM is also called *SDRAM II*.

double-byte character set (DBCS) A set of characters in which each character is represented by two bytes. Languages like Japanese, Chinese, and Korean use this method to represent characters.

down Not working. A computer system is said to be down when it is not available to users.

downlink station *See* ground station.

download To copy data (usually an entire file) from a main source to a peripheral device. The term is often used to describe the process of copying a file from an online service to one's own computer. Downloading can also refer to copying a file from a network file server to a computer on the network.

downstream physical unit (DSPU) (*a*) A controller or a workstation downstream from a gateway that is attached to a host. (*b*) In SNA, a PU that is located downstream from the host.

dpi, DPI *See* dots per inch.

DQDB *See* distributed queue dual bus.

DR *See* definite response.

Draft International Standardized Profile (DISP) A directory information shadowing protocol.

drag In graphical user interfaces, to movie an icon or other image on a display screen. To drag an object across a display screen, the user usually selects the object with a mouse button (*grab*s it) and then moves the mouse while keeping the mouse button pressed down.

drain In APPC, to honor pending allocation requests before deactivating a session with a partner logical unit.

DRAM *See* dynamic RAM.

dribbleware Software characterized by frequent updates, fixes, and patches. The term is somewhat derogatory, indicating software that was released without sufficient testing or before all features could be added.

drive bay An area of reserved space in a personal computer where hard or floppy disk drives (or tape drives) can be installed.

driver A program that controls a device. Every device, whether it be a printer, disk drive, or keyboard, must have a driver program. Many drivers, such as the keyboard driver, come with the operating system. For other devices, it may be necessary to load a new driver when connecting the device to a computer.

drop cable A cable connecting individual network devices, such as PCs, to the main trunk cables of a network.

drop Point on a multipoint channel where a connection to a networked device is made.

DRSLST *See* direct search list.

DS *See* directory service(s).

DS-0 *See* digital signal 0.

DS0 (*Illustration*) A data circuit carrying 56Kbps or 64Kbps of information. It may be its own line, or one channel in a DS1 (T1/E1). Can also be referred to as a 56- or 64-Kbps leased line.

DS-1 *See* digital signal 1.

Bandwidth	Equivalent DS0	Equivalent DS1	Equivalent DS3	comments
64Kb/s	1	*	*	one phone line
1.544Mb/s	24	1	*	popular service
3.152Mb/s	48	2	*	equipment
2.048Mb/s	32	1	*	European
6.312Mb/s	96	4	*	equipment
8.448Mb/s	96	4	*	European
44.736Mb/s	672	28	1	popular service
34.368Mb/s	512	16	1	European
139.264Mb/s	2016	80	6	long haul radio
51.84Mb/s	672	28	1	electrical STS-1
51.84Mb/s	672	28	1	SONET OC-1
255.520Mb/s	2,016	84	3	SONET OC-3
622.080Mb/s	8,064	336	12	SONET OC-12
2.488Gb/s	32,256	1,344	48	SONET OC-48
9.953Gb/s	129,024	5,376	192	SONET OC-192

DS-2 See digital signal 2.

DS-3 See digital signal 3.

DSA See directory service agent.

DSAP See destination service access point.

DSE See data switching exchange.

DSOM See distributed system object model.

DSP See digital signal processing, directory service protocol, *and* domain specific part.

DSPU See downstream physical unit.

DSR Data set ready.

DSRLST See direct search list.

DSS See digital satellite system.

DSU See data service unit.

DSVD See digital simultaneous voice and data.

DSX-1 Cross-connection point for DS-1 signals.

DTD See document type definition.

DTE See data terminal equipment.

DTE/DCE The interface between data terminal equipment (DTE) and data circuit-terminating equipment (DCE); one of the most common in networking.

DTMF See dual-tone multifrequency.

DTR See data terminal ready.

DU See data unit.

DUA See directory user agent.

dual counter-rotating rings Network topology in which two signal paths, whose directions are opposite one another, exist in a token-passing network. FDDI and CDDI are based on this concept.

dual homing Network topology in which a device is connected to the network by way of two independent access points (points of attachment). One access point is the primary connection, and the other is a standby connection activated in the event of a failure of the primary connection.

dual independent bus (DIB) A new bus architecture utilized in Intel's Pentium Pro and Pentium II microprocessors.

dual in-line memory module (DIMM) A small circuit board that holds memory chips. A *single in-line memory module (SIMM)* has a 32-bit path to the memory chips whereas a DIMM has 64-bit path. Because the Pentium processor requires a 64-bit path to memory, it is necessary to install SIMMs two at a time. Using DIMMs, memory can be installed one DIMM at a time.

dual in-line package (DIP) A type of chip housed in a rectangular casing with two rows of connecting pins on either side.

dual IS-IS *See* integrated IS-IS.

DUAL *See* diffusing update algorithm.

dual-attached concentrator (DAC) FDDI or CDDI concentrator capable of attaching to both rings of an FDDI or CDDI network.

dual-homed station Device attached to multiple FDDI rings to provide redundancy.

dual-tone multifrequency (DTMF) The system used by touch-tone telephones. DTMF assigns a specific frequency, or tone, to each key so that it can easily be identified by a microprocessor. Each key press generates two tones, one for the row and one for the column on the keyboard.

duplex Pertaining to communication in which data can be sent and received at the same time.

DVD *See* digital versatile disc or digital video disc.

DVMRP *See* Distance Vector Multicast Routing Protocol.

DXI *See* data exchange interface.

dynamic In a generic sense, something done on the fly. A more specific explanation is performing an operation that does not require a predetermined or fixed time.

dynamic address resolution Use of an address resolution protocol to determine and store address information on demand.

dynamic configuration *See* discovery mode.

dynamic data exchange (DDE) An interprocess communication (IPC) system built into the Macintosh, Windows, and OS/2 operating systems. DDE enables two running applications to share the same data. For example, DDE makes it possible to insert a spreadsheet chart into a document created with a word processor. Whenever the spreadsheet data changes, the chart in the document changes accordingly.

Dynamic Host Configuration Protocol (DHCP) A protocol for assigning dynamic IP addresses to devices on a network. With dynamic addressing, a device can have a different IP address every time it connects to the network. In some systems, the device's IP address may change while it is still connected. DHCP also supports a mix of static and dynamic IP addresses. *Dynamic addressing* simplifies network administration because the software keeps track of IP addresses rather than requiring an administrator to manage the task. This means that a new computer can be added to a network without the trouble of manually assigning it a unique IP address. Many ISPs use dynamic IP addressing for dial-up users. DHCP client support is built into Windows 95 and NT workstations. The NT 4 server includes both client and server support.

dynamic HTML Web content that changes each time it is viewed.

dynamic link library (DLL) A library of executable functions or data that can be used by a Windows application. Typically, a DLL provides one or more particular functions and a program accesses the functions by creating either a static or dynamic link to the DLL.

dynamic path update A generic reference to the process of changing network path parameters for sending information without regenerating complete configuration tables.

dynamic RAM (DRAM) A type of physical memory used in most personal computers. The term dynamic indicates that the memory must be constantly refreshed (reenergized) or it will lose its contents. *Random-access memory (RAM)* is sometimes referred to as DRAM (pronounced dee-ram) to distinguish it from *static RAM (SRAM)*. *See* main memory.

dynamic window A window that may change its title or reposition any of the objects within its content area.

E.164 An ITU-T–defined 8-byte address format. In ATM, it is typically used in public networks and is provided by the telecommunication carriers, while 20-byte NSAP format addresses are used within private networks.

E-1 (*Illustration*) European Digital Signal 1. The European standard for digital physical interface at 2.048 Mbps. It consists of 32 64-Kbps channels. Channels can be ordered as needed from the phone company.

E-2 (*Illustration*) European Digital Signal 2. The European standard for digital physical interface at 8.448 Mbps. It can simultaneously support 4 E-1 circuits.

E-3 (*Illustration*) European Digital Signal 3. The European standard for a digital physical interface at 34.368 Mbps. It can simultaneously support 16 E-1 circuits. Compare with T3. *See* DS-3.

E-4 European Digital Signal 4. European standard for digital physical interface at 139.264 Mbps.

early deployment (ED) IOS releases, which deliver support for new features and platforms in their regular maintenance updates.

early token release A method of token passing, which allows the token to be released prior to completion of transmission by the station. It is used on 16-Mbps token-ring networks.

EARN *See* European Academic Research Network.

EB *See* end bracket.

EBCDIC *See* Extended Binary-Coded Decimal Interchange Code.

ECC memory *See* error-correcting code memory.

	Total Bandwidth	total number of 64Kb/s Channels	Number of Channels used for Out of Band Signaling
T1	1.544 Mb/s	24	1
E1	2.048Mb/s	32	2

	Total Bandwidth	total number of 64Kb/s Channels	Equivalent E1/T1 Carried
T2	6.312 Mb/s	96	4
E2	8.448 Mb/s	128	4

	Total Bandwidth	total number of 64Kb/s Channels	Equivelent E1/T1 Carried
T3	44.736 Mb/s	672	28
E3	34.368 Mb/s	512	16

echo In data communication, a reflected signal on a communications channel.

echo cancellation A technique used by ADSL, V.32, and V.34 modems that isolates and filters unwanted signal energy from echoes caused by the main transmitted signal.

echoplex A processing mode, in which keyboard characters are echoed on a terminal screen upon return of a signal from the other end of the line, thus indicating that the characters were received correctly.

ECMA *See* European Computer Manufacturers Association.

ED *See* early deployment.

edge connector That part of a printed circuit board which plugs into a computer or device. The edge connector generally has a row of broad metallic tracks that provide the electrical connection.

EDI *See* electronic data interchange.

EDIFACT *See* electronic data interchange for administration, commerce, and transport.

editor A program that enables the user to create and edit text files.

EDO DRAM *See* extended data output dynamic random access memory.

EEMS *See* enhanced expanded memory specification.

EEPROM *See* electrically erasable programmable read-only memory.

EFCI *See* explicit forward congestion indication.

EGA *See* enhanced graphics adapter.

EGP *See* Exterior Gateway Protocol.

EIA *See* Electronic Industries Association.

EIA/TIA 32E Interface Between Data Terminal Equipment and Data Circuit-Terminating Equipment Employing Serial Binary Data Interchange (July, 1991). A common physical layer interface standard, developed by EIA and TIA. It supports unbalanced circuits at signal speeds of up to 64 kbps. EIA/TIA 232 E closely resembles the V.24 specification and was formerly called RS-232. This standard is applicable to the interconnection of data terminal equipment (DTE) and data circuit-terminating equipment (DCE) employing serial binary data interchange.

EIA/TIA-232 Common physical layer interface standard, developed by EIA and TIA, which supports unbalanced circuits at signal speeds of up to 64-Kbps. Closely resembles the V.24 specification. Formerly known as RS-232.

EIA-232D Electronics Industries Association-232D. The official designation for RS-232 (Recommended Standard-232), an Electronics Industries Association standard asynchronous serial line, which is used commonly for modems, computer terminals, and serial printers.

EIA-530 Two electrical implementations of EIA/TIA-449: RS-422 (for balanced transmission) and RS-423 (for unbalanced transmission). *See* RS-422 *and* RS-423.

EIDE *See* enhanced IDE.

Eiffel An advanced programming language created by Bertrand Meyer and developed by his company, Interactive Software Engineering (ISE). The language was introduced in 1986; a basic Windows compiler is available at no charge.

EIGRP *See* Enhanced Interior Gateway Routing Protocol.

EISA *See* extended industry standard architecture.

ELAN *See* LAN emulation.

electrically erasable programmable read-only memory (EEPROM) Similar to *flash memory* (sometimes called *flash EEPROM*). The principal difference is that EEPROM requires data to be written or erased one byte at a time whereas flash memory allows data to be written or erased in blocks, thus making flash memory faster.

electromagnetic interference (EMI) A type of noise resulting from currents induced in electric conductors.

electromagnetic interference/radio frequency interference (EMI/RFI) Random, airborne electrical signals that may interfere with or cause noise in network cabling. To test for EMI or RFI, turn on a radio near the cabling.

electromagnetic pulse (EMP) A sudden outpouring of radiation from the detonation of a nuclear device. These pulses may bombard network systems with interference and noise, thus rendering most networks inoperable.

electronic commerce Conducting business on line. This includes, for example, buying and selling products with digital cash and via electronic data interchange (EDI).

electronic data interchange (EDI) A set of standard data formats for electronic information exchange. The electronic communication of operational data, such as orders and invoices, between organizations.

electronic data interchange for administration, commerce, and transport (EDIFACT) Data exchange standard administered by the United Nations; regarded as a multi-industry EDI standard.

Electronic Frontier Foundation A foundation that addresses social and legal issues arising from the impact of computers on society.

Electronic Industries Association (EIA) A trade association representing the United States high-technology community. It began in 1924 as the Radio Manufacturers Association. The EIA sponsors a number of activities on behalf of its members, including conferences and trade shows. In addition, it has been responsible for developing some important standards, such as the RS-232, RS-422, and RS-423 standards for connecting serial devices.

electronic software distribution (ESD) A system for selling software over a network. ESD systems provide secure communications that customers use to download and pay for software. These systems can operate over the Internet or on a direct modem-to-modem connection. ESD systems can also allow users to use software for a trial period before purchasing.

electronically programmable ROM (EPROM) A *read-only memory (ROM)* used to hold programs that cannot be changed once they have been loaded into the ROM chip. On Cisco routers, EPROM memory is used to store a scaled-down copy of IOS for emergency boot-up and to allow access to Flash to change IOS code.

electrostatic discharge (ESD) The rapid discharge of static electricity from one conductor to another of a different potential. An electrostatic discharge can damage the integrated circuits found in computer and communications equipment.

element A term with differing meanings, depending on networking environment. In SNA, the particular resource within a subarea that is identified by an element address.

element address In IBM documentation, a value in the element address field of the network address identifying a specific resource within a subarea.

e-mail client An application that runs on a personal computer or workstation and enables you to send, receive, and organize e-mail.

e-mail or **email** Electronic mail. The transmission of messages over communications networks. The messages can be notes entered from the keyboard or electronic files stored on disk.

EMI *See* electromagnetic interference.

EMI/RFI *See* electromagnetic interference/radio frequency interference.

emoticon A small icon, usually viewed lying on its side, composed of punctuation characters that indicates how an e-mail message should be interpreted (that is, the writer's mood). For example, a :-) emoticon indicates a smile, or that the message is meant as a joke and shouldn't be taken seriously.

Emoticons	Emoticon Meaning
(*_)	An orange or tomato
(\O/)(\O/)	Angels

Emoticons	Emoticon Meaning
( )	A snowball
:-(	Sad
:-)	Joking
:-<	Frowning
:-0	Bored
;-)	Winking
@>-}—	A rose
[_][_][_]	Squares of chocolate
0=(~~~	A dagger

EMP *See* electromagnetic pulse.

emulation The ability of a program or device to imitate another program or device. Many printers, for example, are designed to emulate Hewlett-Packard LaserJet printers because so much software is written for HP printers. By emulating an HP printer, a printer can work with any software written for a real HP printer.

emulation program (EP) A program that simulates the functions of another program. A generic example could be a 3270 terminal emulation program. Other possibilities also exist.

EN *See* end node.

ENA *See* extended network addressing.

enable To make functional. In a loose sense, it means to activate.

enabled The state of being capable of performing work.

encapsulate In the internetworking community, to surround one protocol with another protocol for the purpose of passing the foreign protocol through the native environment.

Encapsulated PostScript (EPS) Pronounced as separate letters. The graphics file format used by the PostScript language. EPS files can be either binary or ASCII. The term EPS usually implies that the file contains a bit-mapped representation of the graphic for display purposes. In contrast, PostScript files include only the PostScript commands for printing the graphic.

encipher *See* encrypt.

encrypt To scramble data or to convert it to a secret code that masks the meaning of the data to any unauthorized recipient. In VTAM, to convert clear data into enciphered data.

encryption The translation of data into a secret code. Encryption is the most effective way to achieve data security. To read an encrypted file, you must have access to a secret key or password that enables you to decrypt it. Unencrypted data is called *plain text*; encrypted data is referred to as *cipher text*.

end bracket (EB) A term specifically used in SNA. It is the value of the end bracket indicator in the request header (RH) of the first request of the last chain of the bracket. The value denotes the end of the bracket.

end key A special cursor control key on PC keyboards and Macintosh extended keyboards. It moves the cursor to the end of a line, or in combination with the Ctrl or Alt key, to the end of a file.

end node In APPN, a node that can receive packets addressed to it and send packets to other nodes. It cannot route packets from other nodes.

end system-to-intermediate system (ES-IS) An OSI protocol that defines how end systems (hosts) announce themselves to intermediate systems (routers). *See* IS-IS.

end user The individual who uses a product after it has been fully developed and implemented or marketed.

end-node domain That area defined by an end-node control point, attached links, and its local LUs.

end-user license agreement (EULA) That type of license used for most software. It specifies what rights the user of the software has, and what restrictions on use, distribution, and modification also apply.

end-user verification LU6.2 identification check of end users by means of identifiers and passwords on the attach function management headers (FMHs).

Energy Sciences Network (ESnet) A data communications network managed and funded by the United States Department of Energy Office of Energy Research (DOE/OER). It interconnects the DOE to educational institutions and other research facilities.

Engineering Task Researchers, closely aligned to the Internet Architecture Board.

enhanced expanded memory specification (EEMS) An enhanced version of the original EMS, which enables DOS applications to use more than 1MB (megabyte) of memory.

enhanced graphics adapter (EGA) A graphics display system for PCs, introduced by IBM in 1984. EGA supports 16 colors from a palette of 64 and provides a resolution of 640 x 350.

enhanced IDE A newer version of the IDE mass storage device interface standard developed by Western Digital Corporation. It supports data rates of between 4 and 16.6 MBps, about three to four times faster than the old IDE standard. In addition, it can support mass storage devices of up to 8.4 gigabytes, whereas the old standard was limited to 528 MB. Because of its lower cost, enhanced EIDE has replaced SCSI in many areas.

Enhanced Interior Gateway Routing Protocol (EIGRP) A Cisco proprietary dynamic routing protocol.

enhanced keyboard A 101- or 102-key keyboard from IBM that supersedes the keyboard for the PC/AT computer.

enhanced small device interface (ESDI) An interface standard developed by a consortium of the leading personal computer manufacturers. It is used to connect disk drives to PCs. ESDI is two to three times faster than the older ST-506 standard. To use an ESDI drive, a computer must have an ESDI controller.

ENR *See* Enterprise Network Roundtable.

Enter key A key that moves the cursor (or insertion point) to the beginning of the next line, or returns control to whatever program is currently running.

enterprise network The computer network of (usually) a large commercial organization. It may include mail servers, Web servers, Web sites, and e-commerce facilities, as well as a client/server database system.

Enterprise Network Roundtable (ENT) An ATM Forum-associated group of ATM users who provide feedback on ATM-related issues and also present users with completed interoperable capabilities and functionality.

enterprise resource planning (ERP) A business management system that integrates all facets of the business, including planning, manufacturing, sales, and marketing. As the ERP methodology has become more popular, software applications have emerged to help business managers implement ERP.

enterprise system connection (ESCON) IBM channel architecture that specifies a pair of fiber optic cables, with either LEDs or lasers as transmitters and a signaling rate of 200 Mbps.

entity The information transferred as the payload of a request or response.

entry point A type 2.0, 2.1, 4, or 5 node that provides distributed network management support. It sends network management data about itself and the resources it controls to a focal point for centralized processing. It receives and executes focal-point-initiated commands to manage and control its resources.

EP *See* emulation program.

EPOC An operating system from Psion Software, designed specifically for mobile, ROM-based computing devices. EPOC16 is a 16-bit version of the operating system that has been available for several years and is embedded in many handheld devices.

EPOC32 is a newer, 32-bit operating system that supports preemptive multitasking. EPOC is competing head-to-head with Windows CE in the grow PDA market.

EPROM *See* electronically programmable ROM.

EPS *See* Encapsulated PostScript.

equalization Technique used to compensate for communications channel distortions.

ER *See* explicit rate.

erasable optical disk A type of optical disk that can be erased and loaded with new data. In contrast, most optical disks, called *CD-ROMs*, are read-only.

ergonomics The science concerned with designing safe and comfortable machines for humans. For example, one branch of ergonomics deals with designing furniture that avoids causing backaches and muscle cramps. In the computer field, ergonomics plays an important role in the design of monitors and keyboards.

ERP *See* enterprise resource planning.

error control Technique for detecting and correcting errors in data transmissions.

error detection In communications, a class of techniques for detecting garbled messages. Two of the simplest and most common techniques are called *checksum* and *cyclic redundancy checking (CRC)*. More sophisticated strategies include MNP and CCITT V.42 .

error rate In data transmission, the ratio of the number of incorrect elements transmitted to the total number of elements transmitted.

error-correcting code Code having sufficient intelligence and incorporating sufficient signaling information to enable the detection and correction of many errors at the receiver.

error-correcting code memory (ECC memory) A type of memory that includes special circuitry for testing the accuracy of data passing in and out of memory.

escape sequence A sequence of special characters that sends a command to a device or program.

ESCD *See* extended system configuration data.

ESCON *See* enterprise system connection.

ESCON channel IBM channel for attaching mainframes to peripherals such as storage devices, backup units, and network interfaces. This channel incorporates fiber channel technol-ogy. The ESCON channel replaces the bus and tag channel. *See* bus, enterprise system connection (ESCON), parallel channel, *and* tag channel.

ESD *See* electronic software distribution *and* electrostatic discharge.

ESDI *See* enhanced small device interface.

ESF *See* extended superframe format.

ES-IS routing In Open Systems, a routing exchange protocol that provides an automated means for ISs and ESs on a subnetwork to dynamically determine the existence of each other. It also means to permit an IS to inform an ES of a potentially better route toward a destination. *See* end system-to-intermediate system (ES-IS).

ES-IS *See* end system-to-intermediate system.

ESnet *See* Energy Sciences Network.

Ethernet (*Illustration*) A very common method of networking computers in a LAN. A data-link-level protocol. It (Version 2.0) was defined by Digital Equipment Corporation, Intel Corporation, and the Xerox Corporation in 1982. The Ethernet specification serves as the basis for the IEEE 802.3 standard, which specifies the physical and lower software layers.

Ethernet handles about 10,000,000 bits per second and can be used with almost any kind of computer. It specifies a data rate of 10 Mbits/s, a maximum station distance of 2.8 km, a maximum number of stations (1,024), a shielded coaxial cable using baseband signaling, functionality of CSMA/CD, and a best-effort delivery system. *See* bandwidth *and* LAN.

Ethernet hub *See* hub.

Ethernet meltdown When Ethernet protocol is used as the data-link-layer protocol in a network. It is an event that causes saturation or near-saturation on an Ethernet data link. This scenario usually results from illegal or misrouted packets and lasts a short time.

EtherTalk In Apple and Ethernet environments, the software that enables AppleTalk protocols to run over industry-standard Ethernet technology.

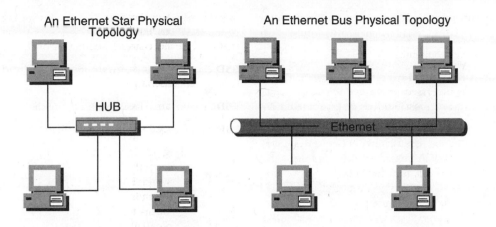

An Ethernet Star Physical Topology

An Ethernet Bus Physical Topology

HUB

Ethernet

ETHERNET TYPES

PROTOCOL	PHYSICAL TOPOLOGY	WIRING USED
10 BASE 2	BUS	RG 58 COAX (50 ohm)
10 BASE 5	BUS	RG 8 COAX (50 ohm)
10 BASE T	STAR	CAT 4 or 5 UTP/STP*
100 BASE T	STAR	CAT 5 UTP/STP*

* unshielded twisted pair / shielded twisted pair

ETR *See* early token release.

ETSI *See* European Telecommunications Standards Institute.

EULA *See* end-user license agreement.

EUnet European Internet. European commercial Internet service provider. EUnet is designed to provide electronic mail, news, and other Internet services to European markets.

European Academic Research Network (EARN) A European network connecting universities and research institutes. EARN merged with RARE to form TERENA. *See* TERENA.

European Computer Manufacturers Association (ECMA) A group of European computer vendors who have performed substantial OSI standardization work.

European Telecom A consortium of manufacturers, service carriers, and others responsible for establishing and maintaining standards for electronic communications in Europe.

European Telecommunications Standards Institute (ETSI) The corresponding body of ANSI in Europe, involved in providing and adapting standards for the European telecommunications.

event (*a*) A predefined occurrence in a given network. In NetView, a record indicating irregularities of operation in physical elements of a network. (*b*) An action or occurrence detected by a program. Events can be user actions, such as clicking a mouse button or pressing a key, or system occurrences, such as running out of memory.

exabyte Two to the 60th power (1,152,921,504,606,846,976) bytes. An exabyte is equal to 1,024 petabytes.

Exabyte Corporation A manufacturer of mass storage devices.

exception A condition, often an error, that causes the program or microprocessor to branch to a different routine. The terms *interrupt* and exception are very close in meaning. Both can be used to refer to either hardware or software. The only real difference is that an exception usually indicates an error condition.

exchange identification (XID) In SNA, a specific type of basic link unit used to convey node and link characteristics between adjacent nodes. In the SNA network, XIDs are exchanged between link stations before and during link activation to establish and negotiate link and node characteristics, and after link activation to communicate changes in these characteristics.

Exchange SPX A transport-layer protocol similar to TCP. Together with IPX, it provides connection services similar to TCP/IP.

Excite A World Wide Web search engine developed by Excite, Inc. In addition to providing a full-text index of approximately 50 million Web pages, Excite also enables users to search from its list of over 60,000 reviewed sites. Sites are rated with a five-star rating system.

EXE file An executable file with an .EXE extension.

executable file A file in a format that the computer can directly execute. Unlike source files, executable files cannot be read by humans. To transform a source file into an executable file, you need to pass it through a compiler or assembler.

executable image An image that can be run in a process. When run, an executable image is read from a file for execution in a process.

execute To perform an action, as in executing a program or a command.

executive A generic term for the collection of procedures included in the operating system software that provides the operating system's basic control and monitoring functions.

exit An instruction that terminates the execution of a program or a portion of that program.

exit program *See* exit routine.

exit routine One of two types of routines: installation exit routes or user exit routes.

expansion board A printed circuit board that can be inserted into a computer to give it added capabilities.

expansion bus A collection of wires and protocols that allows the expansion of a computer by inserting printed circuit boards.

expansion slot An opening in a computer where a circuit board can be inserted to add new capabilities to the computer. Nearly all personal computers, except portables, contain expansion slots for adding more memory, graphics capabilities, and support for special devices. The boards inserted into the expansion slots are called *expansion boards, expansion cards, cards, add-ins,* and *add-ons.*

explicit forward congestion indication (EFCI) A 1-bit field in the PTI that contains information on whether congestion at an intermediate node has been experienced. The EFCI bit is set when, for example, a buffer threshold has been exceeded.

explicit rate (ER) A field in the RM cell header specifying the cell rate a user should use for transmission over a virtual connection (VC), as it is dictated by the RM. *See* CCR.

explicit route (ER) In SNA, a series of one or more transmission groups that connect two subarea nodes. It is identified by an origin subarea address, a destination subarea address, an explicit route number, and a reverse explicit route number.

explicit route length The number of transmission groups in an explicit route.

explorer frame A frame sent out by a networked device in a SRB environment to determine the optimal route to another networked device.

explorer packet A packet generated by an end station trying to find its way through a SRB network. It gathers a hop-by-hop description of a path through the network by being marked (updated) by each bridge that it traverses, thereby creating a complete topological map. *See* local explorer packet.

export To format data in such a way that it can be used by another application. An application that can export data can create a file in a format that another application understands, enabling the two programs to share the same data.

expression In programming, an expression is any legal combination of symbols that represents a value.

extended ASCII A set of codes that extends the basic ASCII set. The basic ASCII set uses seven bits for each character, giving it a total of 128 unique symbols. The extended ASCII character set uses eight bits, which gives it an additional 128 characters. The extra characters represent characters from foreign languages and special symbols for drawing pictures.

Extended Binary-Coded Decimal Interchange Code (EBCDIC) IBM's basic character set, used to represent data within the SNA environment. It consists of 256 8-bit characters and control functions.

extended data output dynamic random access memory (EDO DRAM) A type of dynamic RAM (DRAM) that is faster than conventional DRAM. Unlike conventional DRAM, which can only access one block of data at a time, EDO RAM can start fetching the next block of memory at the same time that it sends the previous block to the CPU.

extended industry standard architecture (EISA) A 32-bit bus architecture designed for PCs; it uses an Intel 80386, 80486, or Pentium microprocessor, and can also be used for some UNIX workstations and servers. EISA buses are 32 bits wide and support multiprocessing. The EISA bus was designed by nine IBM competitors (sometimes called the *Gang of Nine*): AST Research, Compaq Computer, Epson, Hewlett-Packard, NEC, Olivetti, Tandy, WYSE, and Zenith Data Systems. They designed the architecture to compete with IBM's own high-speed bus architecture called *micro channel architecture (MCA)*.

extended network addressing (ENA) In IBM's traditional subarea networking, the

addressing system that splits addresses into an 8-bit subarea and a 15-bit element portion. The subarea portion of the address is used to address host processors or communication controllers. The element portion is used to permit processors or controllers to address resources.

extended recovery facility In SNA, a facility that provides an alternate subsystem to take over sessions from the failing subsystem.

extended subarea addressing A network addressing system used in a network with more than 255 subareas.

extended superframe format (ESF) A T1 framing standard, used for frame synchronization and to locate signaling bits. ESF consists of 24 bits instead of the previous standard 12 bits. ESF allows easy error data storage and retrieval, thus facilitating network maintenance and performance monitoring.

extended system configuration data (ESCD) A format for storing information about plug-and-play (PnP) devices in the BIOS. Windows and the BIOS access the ESCD area each time a user reboots the computer.

Exterior Gateway Protocol (EGP) A dynamic routing Internet protocol for exchanging routing information between autonomous systems. Documented in RFC 904. Not to be confused with the general term *exterior gateway protocol*. EGP is an obsolete protocol that has been replaced by Border Gateway Protocol (BGP). *See* BGP.

exterior router A router connected to an AURP tunnel, responsible for the encapsulation and unencapsulation of AppleTalk packets in a foreign protocol header (for example, IP). *See* AURP *and* AURP tunnel.

exterior routing Routing that occurs between autonomous systems. It is of concern to service providers and other large or complex networks. The basic routable element is the *autonomous system (AS)*, a collection of CIDR prefixes identified by an *autonomous system number*. Although there may be many different interior routing schemes, a single exterior routing system manages the global

Internet, based primarily on the BGP-4 exterior routing protocol.

external bus A bus that connects a computer to peripheral devices. Two examples are the *universal serial bus (USB)* and *IEEE 1394*.

e-zine Electronic magazine. A Web site that is modeled after a print magazine. Some e-zines are simply electronic versions of existing print magazines, whereas others exist only in their digital format.

F

FADU *See* file access data unit.

failure domain Area where a failure has occurred in a Token Ring nework, as defined by the information contained in the beacon frame.

fair information practices (FIP) A general term for a set of standards governing the collection and use of personal data and addressing issues of privacy and accuracy. Different organizations and countries have their own terms for these concerns. In the United Kingdom, the term is *data protection*; the European Union calls it *personal data privacy*.

fanout The degree of replication in a multicast tree or the number of copies of a call in a switch, associated with IP multicasting and ATM.

fan-out box In a local area network (LAN), a device that functions like a hub. It provides the capability for multiple connections to make a central connection.

FAQ (frequently asked questions) A document that answers questions about some technical topic. Frequently, FAQs are formatted as help files or hypertext documents. FAQs are usually written by people who have tired of answering the same question over and over.

FARNET A non-profit organization that seeks to facilitate research and education through the use of computer networks

Fast Ethernet 100Mbps version of IEEE 802.3. Fast Ethernet offers a speed increase 10 times that of the 10BaseT Ethernet specification, while preserving qualities such as frame format, MAC mechanisms, and MTU. These similarities allow the use of existing 10BaseT applications and network management tools on Fast Ethernet networks. Based on an extension to the IEEE802.3 specification. Compare with Ethernet. *See* 100BaseFX, 100BaseT, 100BaseT4, 100BaseTX, 100BaseX, and IEEE 802.3.

fast packet A data transmission technique where the packet is transmitted without any error checking at points along the route. The end-points are responsible for performing error checking.

fast page mode RAM (FPM RAM) A dynamic RAM (DRAM) that allows faster access to data in the same row or page.

fast resource management (FRM) A form of network management for allocating resources (buffers, bandwidth) dynamically.

fast switching A Cisco IOS feature where a route cache is used to speed up packet switching through a router.

FastCGI A programming interface to speed up Web applications using common gateway interface (CGI). FastCGI enables user requests to a Web site to be handled 3 to 30 times faster than CGI. As a plug-in to a Web server, FastCGI requires only small changes to existing server applications, usually developed in Perl or TCL scripts and C and C++ programs, to get the performance benefits.

fat client In a client/server architecture, a client that performs the bulk of data processing operations. The data itself is stored on the server. *See* thin client for contrast. Although the term usually refers to software, it can also apply to a network computer with relatively strong processing abilities.

Fat Mac An application program for the Macintosh compiled to run on either a Mac containing the Motorola 68000 series microprocessor or the PowerPC microprocessor. A fat Mac library is one that contains library routines (program code) that will run with either microprocessor.

FAT *See* file allocation table.

FAT32 A new version of the file allocation table (FAT) supported by Windows 95 and Windows 98. FAT32 increases the number of bits used to address clusters and also reduces the size of each cluster, enabling the support of larger hard disks (up to 2 terabytes), even though personal computer users are more likely to take advantage of FAT32 with 5 or 10 gigabyte drives. *See* file allocation table (FAT).

fatal error An error that causes a program to abort, or may return the user to the operating system. When a fatal error occurs, whatever data the program was currently processing may be lost. In Windows, fatal errors are called the *blue screen of death*.

fault management Fault management attempts to ensure that network faults are detected and controlled as soon as possible. One of the five categories of network management as defined by ISO for the management of OSI networks. *See* performance management *and* security management.

Favicon A *favorite icon*, a customized image that Microsoft Internet Explorer 5.x uses to mark user-specified bookmarked sites on the Links bar at the top of a Web browser window. Windows 98 enables users to add visible links to favorite Web sites by dragging the URL of the Web site to the optional Links bar near the top of the window. If a particular Web site has made available a small image of a specified size, the browser downloads it and put it next to the text for the favorite link on the Links bar. The favorite icon image must use the standard name of favicon.ico. If no favicon.ico has been provided, the default icon for your Internet browser is used.

fax modem A device attached to a personal computer that enables the user to transmit and receive electronic documents as faxes. A fax modem is like a regular modem except that it is designed to transmit documents to a fax machine or to another fax modem.

fax (*v.*) To send a document via a fax machine. (*n.*) (*a*) A document that has been sent, or is about to be sent, via a fax machine. (*b*) A facsimile machine.

FCC *See* Federal Communications Commission.

FCS *See* frame check sequence *and* first customer ship.

FDDI *See* Fiber Distributed Data Interface.

FDDI-II ANSI standard that enhances FDDI. FDDI II provides isochronous transmission for connectionless data circuits and connection-oriented voice and video circuits. *See* FDDI.

FDHD Floppy drive, high density.

fdisk A DOS utility, included in all versions of MS-DOS and Windows. fdisk prepares a hard disk for formatting by creating one or more partitions on the disk to hold data, specifying and naming major portions of it for different uses.

FDL *See* File Definition Language.

FDM *See* frequency division multiplexing.

FDMA *See* frequency division multiplexing analog.

FDR/DDR *See* frame delivery ratio/data delivery ratio.

FDX *See* full duplex.

fear, uncertainty, and doubt (FUD) The term for any strategy intended to make a company's customers insecure about future product plans, with the purpose of discouraging them from adopting competitors' products.

feature A notable property of a device or software application.

FEC *See* forward error correction.

FECN *See* forward explicit congestion notification.

FED *See* field emission display.

Federal Communications Commission (FCC) United States government agency that supervises, licenses, and controls electronic and electromagnetic transmission standards. Among other duties, the FCC is responsible for rating personal computers and other equipment as either Class A or Class B under FCC-Part 15.

Federal Information Processing Standard (FIPS) A set of standards describing document processing. It contains algorithms for searching, and other standards for use within government agencies.

Federal Networking Council (FNC) Group responsible for assessing and coordinating the United States federal agency networking policies and needs.

Federation of Telecommunications Engineers of the European Community (FITCE) An international association committed to affecting telecommunication developments in a positive and constructive manner throughout Europe and the rest of the world.

The FITCE Association informs and updates members and others engaged in the telecommunication industry. FITCE maintains a resource database for linking globally to telecommunication opportunities and contacts.

feed line In wireless communications or broadcasting antenna system, the connection of the antenna to the receiver, transmitter, or transceiver. The line transfers radio-frequency (RF) energy from a transmitter to an antenna, and/or from an antenna to a receiver, but, if operating properly, does not radiate or intercept energy itself. There are three types of antenna feed lines, also called *RF transmission lines*, commonly used in wireless systems.

femtosecond One millionth of a nanosecond or 10^{-15} of a second; a measurement sometimes used in laser technology.

FEP *See* front-end processor.

Ferret A program that searches through selected files, databases, or search engine indexes for information that meets specified search criteria. *See* spider.

ferroelectric random access memory (FRAM) A type of non-volatile memory combines the access speed of DRAM and SRAM with the non-volatility of ROM.

FET *See* field-effect transistor.

fetch The loading of an instruction or piece of data, measured in ticks, from a computer's memory into a CPU's register.

Fiber Channel A technology for serially transmitting data between computer devices at a data rate of up to 1 Gpbs (one billion bits per second). Fibre Channel is especially suited for connecting computer servers to shared storage devices and for interconnecting storage controllers and drives. The most prominent Fiber Channel standard is Fiber Channel Arbitrated Loop (FC-AL), designed for new mass storage devices and other peripheral devices that require very high bandwidth.

Fiber Distributed A set of ANSI/ISO standards defining a high-bandwidth (100 Mbps) Fiber Distributed Data Interface (FDDI). *See* Fiber Distributed Data Interface.

Fiber Distributed Data Interface (FDDI) *(Illustration)* A set of ANSI protocols for sending digital data over fiber optic cable. FDDI networks are token-passing networks, using dual-ring topology over fiber-optic transmission media.

Data rates of up to 100 Mbps (100 million bits) per second are supported. FDDI networks were typically used as backbones for campus and wide-area networks. FDDI networks are being replaced by asynchronous transfer mode (ATM), packet over Sonet (POS) and Gigabit-Ethernet.

In the WAN environment, the explosion of dense wave division multiplexing (DWDM) has all but eliminated the use of FDDI. FDDI is a link-layer protocol, which means that higher-layer protocols operate independently of the FDDI protocol. Applications pass packet-level data using higher-layer protocols down to the logical link control layer, in the same way as they do over Ethernet or token ring. But because FDDI uses a different physical layer protocol than Ethernet and token ring, traffic must be bridged or routed on and off an FDDI ring.

FDDI also allows for larger packet sizes than lower-speed LANs; for this reason, connections between FDDI and Ethernet or token ring LANs require the fragmentation and reassembly of frames. FDDI is defined by four separate logical components.

The *Media Access Control (MAC)* defines how the medium is accessed, including frame for-

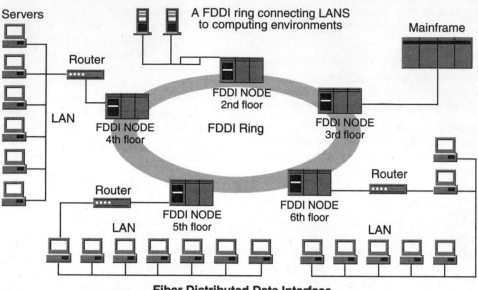

Fiber Distributed Data Interface

mat, token handling, addressing, algorithm for calculating a cyclic redundancy check value, and error recovery mechanisms.

The *Physical Layer Protocol (PHY)* defines data encoding/decoding procedures, clocking requirements, framing, and other functions.

The *Physical Layer Medium (PMD)* defines the characteristics of the transmission medium, including the fiber-optic link, power levels, bit error rates, optical components, and connectors.

The *Station Management (SMT)* defines the FDDI station configuration, ring configuration, and ring control features, including station insertion and removal, initialization, fault isolation and recovery, scheduling, and collection of statistics.

fiber exhaust Industry term defining the amount of network traffic that may exhaust the amount of collective bandwidth available through installed optical fiber lines.

fiber optic cable (*Illustration*) A thin, flexible (usually glass or plastic) physical medium capable of conducting modulated light for data transmission. A fiber optic cable consists of a

bundle of glass threads, each of which is capable of transmitting messages at close to the speed of light. Compared with other physical transmission media, fiber is not susceptible to electromagnetic interference (but it is susceptible to changes from radiation), capable of higher data rates, and occupies far less physical volume for an equivalent transmission capacity.

Fiber optic cable has several advantages over traditional metal communication media types:

- A greater bandwidth than metal cables.

- Less susceptibility than metal cables to interference.

- Much thinner and lighter than metal wires.

- Data can be transmitted digitally.

- Difficult (but not impossible) to tap as a secure media.

- Capacity to transmit extremely high data rates.

The main disadvantage of fiber optics is that the cables are expensive to install and fragile.

Fiber Optic Inter-Repeater Link (FOIRL) A vendor independent standard means for con-

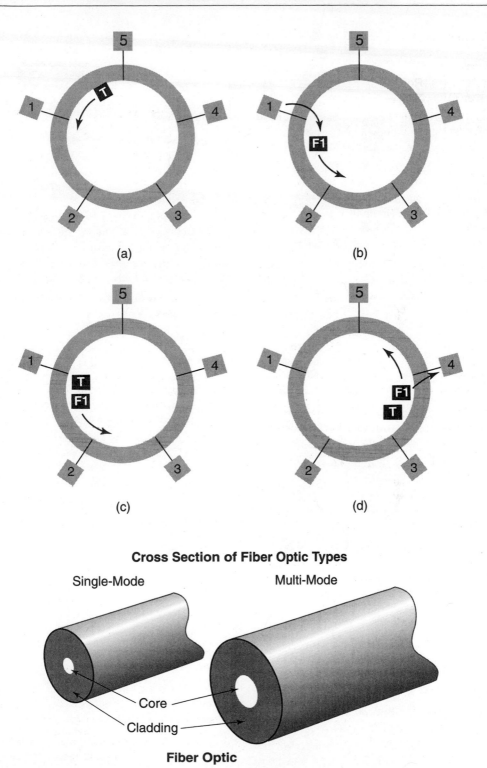

Cross Section of Fiber Optic Types

Single-Mode

Multi-Mode

Core

Cladding

Fiber Optic

necting only two repeater units based on the IEEE 802.3 fiber optic specification. FOIRL is a precursor of the 10BaseFL specification, which is designed to replace it. *See* 10BaseFL.

FID0 (format indicator 0) FID0 transmission header is used for communication between an SNA node and a non-SNA node. One of five formats that an SNA transmission header can use.

FID1 (format indicator 1) A FID1 transmission header encapsulates messages between two SNA subarea nodes that do not support virtual and explicit routes. One of five formats that an SNA transmission header can use.

FID2 (format indicator 2) A FID2 transmission header is used for transferring messages between a subarea node and a PU2, using local addresses. One of five formats that an SNA transmission header can use.

FID3 (format indicator 3) A FID3 transmission header is used for transferring messages between a subarea node and a PU1, using local addresses. One of five formats that an SNA transmission header can use.

FID4 (format indicator 4) A FID4 transmission header encapsulates messages between two SNA subarea nodes that are capable of supporting virtual and explicit routes. One of five formats that an SNA transmission header can use.

FidoNet A system using the UNIX-to-UNIX Copy Protocol (UUCP) for e-mail, discussion groups, and file sharing among users of over 30,000 bulletin board services (BBSs). Messages can travel over the Internet after being converted to TCP/IP format by computer servers that act as Internet gateways.

field emission display (FED) A flat-panel display in which electron emitters, arranged in a grid, are individually controlled by "cold" cathodes to generate colored light. This technique also makes possible the thin panel liquid crystal displays (LCDs).

field-effect transistor (FET) A type of transistor commonly used for weak digital or analog signal amplification, such as for amplifying

wireless signals. It can also switch DC or function as an oscillator.

field-formatted In SNA, requests or responses that are encoded into fields, each having a specified format such as binary code, bit-significant flags, and symbolic names.

field-programmable gate array (FPGA) A type of programmable logic chip.

FIF *See* Fractal Image Format.

FIFO *See* first-in, first-out.

file A collection of data or information, identified by a *filename*. Almost all information stored in a computer must be in a file. There are many different types of files: data files, text files, program files, directory files, etc.

file access data unit Used to specify a location on a file structure.

file allocation table (FAT) A table maintained by an operating system on a hard disk, which provides a map of the clusters in which a file has been stored. When files are written to a hard disk, they are stored in one or more clusters, which are not necessarily next to each other; they may be rather widely scattered over the disk. The operating system creates a FAT entry for the new file that records where each cluster is located and their sequential order. *See* FAT32.

file attributes The properties of a file that do not depend on an file transfer and management dialog.

File Definition Language (FDL) A special-purpose language used to write specifications for data files. These specifications are written in text files called *FDL files*; they are used by OpenVMS record management services utilities and library routines to create the actual data files.

file directory The OSI equivalent of a directory in a file system.

file extension A three-letter suffix, following a filename, which shows the type of file. DOS, UNIX, and Linux environments require extensions. Although the Macintosh does not normally require a filename extension, its applications have extensions that, when crossing the network (and the Internet), are used to identify the originating application.

file filter function An application-supplied function for determining which files the user can open through a standard file dialog box.

file format A format for encoding information in a file. Each different type of file has a different file format. The file format specifies first whether the file is a binary or ASCII file, then how the information is organized.

file handle A number temporarily assigned to an opened file by the operating system. The operating system uses the file handle internally when accessing the file. A special area of main memory is reserved for file handles, and the size of this area determines how many files can be open at once. In DOS and Windows, you can set the maximum number of open files with the FILES= statement in CONFIG.SYS.

file header A portion of code that contains information needed by the file system to find and use the file.

file ID (*a*) In the Apple environment, an unchanging number assigned by the file manager to identify a file on a volume. When it establishes a file ID, the file manager records the filename and parent directory ID of the file. (*b*) A 6-byte value used to uniquely identify a file on a Files-11 disk volume. The file number, file sequence number, and relative volume number are contained in the file identifier.

file management system The system used by an operating system or program to organize and keep track of files. In a *hierarchical* file system, directories are used to organize files into a tree structure.

file server A device which serves as a central location for files commonly used by everyone on a LAN. A computer whose primary task is to control the storage and retrieval of data from hard disks. Any number of other computers can be linked to the file server to use it to access data. Thus, less storage space is required on individual computers.

file sharing A technique that allows the file system of a remote host computer appear as if it were part of the local file system. File sharing is so common and important that servers implementing this function are given the name *file servers*.

file system *See* file management system.

File Transfer Access and Management (FTAM). In OSI, an application layer protocol developed for network file exchange and management between diverse types of computers. FTAM allows remote files to be transferred, accessed, and managed.

File Transfer Protocol (FTP) In TCP/IP, a very common method of moving files between two Internet sites. FTP is a way to log in to another Internet site to retrieve and/or send files between different machines across a network.

There are many Internet sites that have established publicly accessible repositories of material that can be obtained using *anonymous FTP*, i.e., by logging in using the account name "anonymous;" these sites are called *anonymous FTP servers*.

FTP consists of a client and a server. The FTP client is used to invoke the FTP program. The FTP server is used to serve the request of the client. In normal implementations, FTP uses ports 20 and 21.

file translator A generic term referring to a utility program that converts a file from one computer format to another, such as from Macintosh to DOS.

filename The name of a file. Different operating systems have special restrictions on filenames, from limiting the length of a filename to the type of extension it uses. Filenames must have unique names within a single directory.

fill In graphics applications, to paint the inside of an enclosed object. In spreadsheet applications, to copy (fill) the contents of one cell to an entire range of cells.

filter (*a*) A program that accepts a certain type of data as input, transforms it in some manner, and then outputs the transformed data in accordance with specified criteria. (*b*) A pattern through which data is passed. Only

F

data that matches the pattern is allowed to pass through the filter. (*c*) In paint programs and image editors, an effect that can be applied to a bit map. (*d*) Utilities that allow data to be imported and exported.

Finder Apple Macintosh desktop and file management system, used to manage files and disks, as well as the Clipboard, Scrapbook, and all desktop icons and windows.

finger A BSD UNIX program that identifies the name associated with an e-mail address. It may also identify whether the individual in question is logged on at their system, their most recent logon session, or other information, depending on the data maintained about users on that computer.

finite-state machine (FSM) The logical representation of a protocol layer/stack and how the protocol responds to stimuli.

FIP *See* fair information practices.

FIPS *See* Federal Information Processing Standard.

firewall A set of related programs, located at a network gateway server, which protects the resources of a private network from users of other networks. (The term also implies the security policy that is used with the programs.) An enterprise with an intranet that allows its workers access to the wider Internet installs a firewall to prevent outsiders from accessing its own private data resources and for controlling to which outside resources its own users have access. There are several types of firewall techniques.

filters Look at each packet entering or leaving the network and accepts or rejects it based on user-defined rules. Packet filtering is fairly effective and transparent to users, but it is difficult to configure. In addition, it is susceptible to IP address spoofing.

Application gateways apply security mechanisms to specific applications, such as FTP and Telnet servers. This is a very effective filtering method, but can cause performance degradation.

Circuit-level gateways apply security mechanisms when a TCP or UDP connection is established. Once the connection has been made, packets can flow between hosts without further checking.

Proxy servers intercept all messages entering and leaving the network. The proxy server effectively hides the true network addresses.

A *firewall* is considered a first line of defense in protecting private information. For greater security, data can be encrypted. *See* encryption.

FireWire Apple Computer's version of the IEEE 1394 High Performance Serial Bus standard, for connecting devices to personal computers. FireWire provides a single plug-and-socket connection on which up to 63 devices can be attached. It allows data transfer speeds up to 400 Mbps (megabits per second). The standard describes a serial bus or pathway between one or more peripheral devices and a computer's microprocessor.

firmware Programming inserted into programmable read-only memory (PROM), thus becoming a permanent part of a computing device. Firmware is created and tested like software (using microcode simulation). When ready, it is distributed like other software and, using a special user interface, installed in the programmable read-only memory by the user.

first customer ship (FCS) An initial release of any product to the general public.

First MOSPF Some portions of the Mbone support *MOSPF*. MOSPF uses the OSPF link-state metric to determine the least-cost path and calculate a *spanning tree* for routing multicast traffic with the multicast source at the root and the group members as leaves. *See* OSPF, SPT, *and* SFP algorithm.

first-in, first-out An approach of handling program work requests from queues or stacks so that the oldest request is handled first.

FITCE *See* Federation of Telecommunications Engineers of the European Community.

fixed length Having a set length that never varies. In database systems, a field can have a fixed or a variable length. A fixed-length record is one in which every field has a fixed length.

fixed pitch Fonts in which every character has the same width; also called *monospaced fonts*.

flame On the Internet, originally, to carry forth in a passionate manner in the spirit of honorable debate. Flames most often involved the use of flowery language, and flaming well was an art form. More recently, it has come to refer to any kind of derogatory comment no matter how witless or crude. *See* flame war.

flame war An online discussion that has degenerated into a series of personal attacks in a heated exchange against the debaters, rather than a discussion of their positions. *See* flame.

flapping A routing situation where an advertised route between two nodes flaps back and forth between two paths (routers). This situation is typically caused by intermittent interface failures (i.e., they go up and then down frequently).

flash memory Memory that does not lose its information when powered off. Developed by Intel and licensed to other semiconductor companies. Used like a small hard disk to store the router operating system (OS). Available as a SIMM or a PCMCIA card, depending on the router using it.

Many modern PCs have their BIOS stored on a flash memory chip so that it can easily be updated if necessary. Such a BIOS is sometimes called a *flash BIOS*. Flash memory is also popular in modems because it enables the modem manufacturer to support new protocols as they become standardized.

flash update When just a routing update is sent asynchronously, in response to a change in the network topology. *See* routing update.

FlashPix A format for storing digital images, especially digital photographs, developed by Eastman Kodak Company.

floating-point number A number that has no fixed number of digits before and after the decimal point; i.e., the decimal point "floats."

Fixed-point representations contain a set number of digits before and after the decimal point. In general, floating-point representations are slower and less accurate than fixed-point representations, but they can handle a larger range of numbers.

floating-point operations per second (FLOPS) A method of encoding real numbers within the limits of finite precision available on computers. This enables extremely long numbers to be handled relatively easily. A floating-point number is expressed as a basic number or *mantissa*, an exponent, and a number base or *radix*, which is often assumed.

floating-point unit (FPU) A specially designed chip that performs floating-point calculations. Computers equipped with an FPU perform certain types of applications much faster than computers that lack one. Floating-point units are also called *numeric coprocessors*, *math coprocessors*, and *floating-point processors*.

flooding Forwarding of a data packet by a router, switch, or bridge from any node to every other node attached to the device, except the node from which the packet arrived. Flooding distributes routing information updates quickly to every node in a large network. It is also sometimes used in multicasting and OSPF.

floppy disk A soft, magnetic portable disk.

floppy drive Short for floppy disk drive (FDD). A disk drive that can read and write to floppy disks. A high density floppy drive (FDHD) is a 3 1/2-inch disk drive for Macintosh computers that can accept double-density or high-density 3 1/2-inch floppy disks.

FLOPS *See* floating-point operations per second.

floptical A type of disk drive technology that uses a combination of magnetic and optical techniques to achieve greater storage capacity than normal floppy disks without sacrificing access speeds.

flow A stream of data traveling between two endpoints across a network (for example, from one LAN station to another). Multiple flows can be transmitted on a single circuit.

flow control In networking, a method used for congestion avoidance and traffic regulation. There are four techniques:

- *Window-based control*, where a sliding window is used to determine how many cells can be transmitted during a predefined period.

- *Credit-based control*, where a source can transmit a cell if there is a credit available. CAC is also part of the flow control.

- *Request/reply flow control* requires each data packet to be acknowledge by the remote host before the next packet is sent.

- *Sliding window algorithms*, used by TCP, permit multiple data packets to be in simultaneous transit, making more efficient use of network bandwidth.

flowchart A formalized graphic representation of a program's logic sequence, work or manufacturing process, organization chart, or similar formalized structure. In computer programming, flowcharts are used to describe each processing path in a program (the main program and various subroutines that may be branched to).

flush (*a*) Text that is aligned along a margin. (*b*) To copy data from a temporary storage area, such as RAM, to a more permanent storage medium, such as a disk.

flux The presence of a force field in a specified physical medium. The term also applies to electrostatic fields and magnetic fields, as "lines" in a plane that contains or intersects electric charge poles or magnetic poles.

FM *See* frequency modulation.

FNC *See* Federal Networking Council.

Fnord The space between the pixels on a display screen; also defined as the smallest number greater than zero.

FOD *See* foreign object damage.

FOIRL *See* Fiber Optic Inter-Repeater Link.

folder In graphical user interfaces such as Windows and Macintosh, an object that can contain multiple documents. Folders are used to organize information. In DOS and UNIX, folders are called *directories*.

font A set of printable or displayable text characters in a specific style and size. The type design for a set of fonts is the combination of typeface and other qualities, such as size, pitch, and spacing. For example, Helvetica is a typeface family, Helvetica italic is a typeface, and Helvetica italic 10-point is a font.

font cartridge A ROM cartridge containing one or more fonts. By inserting the cartridge into a laser printer, you give the printer the ability to print different fonts.

font family A set of fonts all with the same typeface, but with different sizes, weights, and slants.

font size The size of the *glyphs* in a font in points, measured from the baseline of one line of text to the baseline of the next line of single-spaced text.

font style How a font is represented.

footer One or more lines of text that appear at the bottom of every page of a document. Once the footer is specified by the user, the application automatically inserts the designated text.

footprint The amount of floor or desk space required by a device.

foreground (*a*) In multiprocessing systems, the process currently accepting input from the keyboard or other input device; i.e., the *foreground process*. (*b*) On display screens, the characters and pictures that appear on the screen; the *background* is the uniform canvas behind the characters and pictures.

foreign object damage (FOD) Used to describe damage from objects foreign to an aircraft, such as birds or screws.

form A formatted document containing blank fields that users fill in with data.

form factor The physical size and shape of a device; often used to describe the size of circuit boards.

form feed (*a*) In printers that use continuous paper, a button or command that advances the paper to the beginning of the next page. (*b*) A special character that causes the printer to advance one page length or to the top of the next page. In systems that use the ASCII character set, a form feed has a decimal value of 12.

format (*a*) To prepare a storage medium, usually a disk, for reading and writing. To format a disk, the operating system erases all bookkeeping information on the disk, tests the disk to make sure all sectors are reliable, marks bad sectors (i.e., those that are scratched), and creates internal address tables that it later uses to locate information. A disk must be formatted before it can be used. (*b*) To specify the properties, particularly visible properties, of an object. For example, word processing applications allow the user to format text, which involves specifying the font, alignment, margins, and other properties.

format indicator 0/1/2/3/4 *See* FID0/1/2/3/4.

formatted system services In IBM's SNA, a portion of VTAM that provides certain system services as a result of receiving a field-formatted command, such as an initiate or terminate command.

formula (*a*) An equation or expression. (*b*) In spreadsheet applications, an expression that defines how one cell relates to other cells.

FORTRAN Acronym for FORmula TRANslation, a third-generation (3GL) programming language, designed by John Backus for IBM in the late 1950s for use by engineers, mathematicians, and other users and creators of scientific algorithms. It has a very succinct and spartan syntax.

forum An online discussion group provided by online services, in which participants with common interests exchange open messages. Forums are sometimes called *conferences*.

forward channel Communications path carrying information from the call initiator to the called party.

forward delay interval Amount of time an interface spends listening for topology change information after that interface has been activated for bridging and before forwarding actually begins.

forward error correction (FEC) An error correction technique using no retransmissions. Therefore, the receiver is responsible for correcting any errors in the packets.

forward explicit congestion notification (FECN) Bit set by a frame relay network to inform DTE receiving the frame that congestion was experienced in the path from source to destination. DTE-receiving frames with the FECN bit set can request that higher-level protocols take flow-control action as appropriate. *See* BECN.

 For more information, see *http://www.frforum.com*.

forwarding The process of sending a frame toward its ultimate destination by way of an internetworking device.

Fourier transform Technique for evaluating the importance of various frequency cycles in a time series pattern.

four-part dotted notation *See* dot address.

FPGA *See* field-programmable gate array.

FPM RAM *See* fast page mode RAM.

fps *See* frames per second.

FPU *See* floating-point unit.

FR *See* frame relay.

fractal A word coined by Benoit Mandelbrot in 1975 to describe shapes that are "self-similar"—i.e., shapes that look the same at different magnifications. Structures possessing similar-looking forms of many different sizes. They can be used to create any real-world object, like a mountain or a cloud, provided it doesn't correspond to a simple geometric shape. To create a fractal, a simple shape is duplicated successively according to a set of fixed rules.

Oddly enough, such a simple formula for creating shapes can produce very complex structures, some of which have a striking resemblance to real-world objects. For example, graphics designers use fractals to generate images of mountainous landscapes, coastlines, and flowers. In fact, many computer-generated images appearing in science fiction films utilize fractals.

 Check out the following website for some cool fractals: *http://www. digitalblasphemy.com.*

Fractal Image Format (FIF) A graphics file format using fractal geometry to compress images, developed by Iterated Systems, Inc. Because the format can be expressed in mathematical terms, an image may be recorded as repeated patterns.

 For more information on Fractal Image Format (FIF), see *http://www.iterated.com.*

FRAD *See* frame relay assembler/disassembler.

fragment In TCP/IP network environments, one of the pieces that results when an IP router divides an IP datagram into smaller pieces for transmission across a network. Fragments use the same format as datagrams. Fields in the IP header declare whether a datagram is a fragment, and if so, whether it is the offset of the fragment in the original datagram. IP software at the receiving end must reassemble fragments into complete datagrams.

fragmentation (*a*) Process of breaking a packet into smaller units when transmitting over a network medium that cannot support a packet of the original size. (For example, TCP into IP, ATM SAR function, etc.) *See* reassembly. (*b*) A disk in which files are divided into pieces scattered around the disk. Fragmentation occurs naturally when you use a disk frequently, creating, deleting, and modifying files. (*c*) RAM with small, unused holes scattered throughout it. This is called *external fragmentation*. In modern operating systems that use a *paging scheme*, a more common type of RAM fragmentation is *internal fragmentation*. This occurs when memory is allocated in frames, and the frame size is larger than the amount of memory requested.

FRAM *See* ferroelectric random access memory.

frame (*Illustration*) (*a*) In telecommunications, a logical grouping of bits sent as a data link layer unit serially (one after another), which is transmitted between network points, complete with addressing and necessary protocol control information. Often refers to the header and trailer, used for synchronization and error control, which surround the user data contained in the unit. (*b*) In graphics and desktop publishing applications, a rectangular area in which text or graphics can appear. (*c*) In HTML, the browser display area divided into separate sections, each of which is really a different Web page. (*d*) In video and animation, a

A DS1 Frame

Each box represents an 8 bit sample for one of 24 channels.
The last box represents a timing bit.

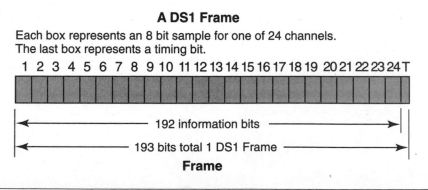

Frame

single image in a sequence of images. *See* frames per second (fps).

frame buffer The portion of memory reserved for holding the complete bit-mapped image that is sent to the monitor. Typically the frame buffer is stored in memory chips on the video adapter. In some instances, however, the video chipset is integrated into the motherboard design, and the frame buffer is stored in general main memory.

frame check sequence In a token-ring LAN, a 32-bit field which follows the data field in every token-ring frame.

frame delivery ratio/data delivery ratio (FDR/DDR) The two most common metrics used to measure data throughput.

frame relay (FR) A Layer 2 protocol defined by the CCITT and ANSI that identifies how data frames are switched in speeds higher than X.25, but in packet mode used across the interface between user devices (e.g., hosts, routers) and network equipment (e.g., switching nodes).

Frame relay is more efficient than the X.25 protocol and is generally considered its replacement. User devices are called *data ter-*

minal equipment (DTE), while network equipment that interfaces to DTE is called *data circuit-terminating equipment (DCE)*. The network providing the frame relay interface can be either a carrier-provided public network or a network of privately owned equipment serving a single enterprise.

Frame relay networks in the United States support data transfer rates at T-1 (1.544 Mbps) and T-3 (45 Mbps) speeds. Most telephone companies provide frame relay service for customers who want connections at 56 Kbps to T-1 speeds. In Europe, frame relay speeds vary from 64 Kbps to 2 Mbps.

For FR specifications go to: *http://www.frforum.com.*

For more information on frame relay, see *http://www.frforum.com.*

frame relay assembler/disassembler (FRAD) (*Illustration*) Also called a *frame relay access device*, a communications device that encapsulates (inserts header and trailer information) on outgoing data packets and decapsulates (removes frame relay headers

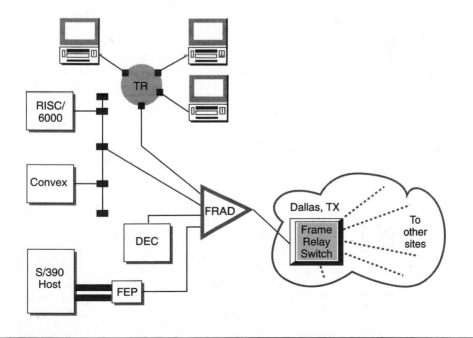

and trailers) from incoming packets during transmissions over a frame relay network and recreates a data stream from incoming frames.

frame relay bridging Bridging technique, described in RFC1490, that uses the same spanning-tree algorithm in LAN bridging functions, but allows packets to be encapsulated for transmission across a frame relay network.

frame relay frame handler (FRFH) A router function using the address field in a frame relay frame.

frame relay switching equipment (FRSE) subport set In frame relay technology, the set of primary and, optionally, substitute subports within an FRSE that represent those used for a given segment set.

frame relay switching equipment (FRSE) support An agreed-on set of NCP frame relay functions that include the frame relay frame handler (FRFH) functions, defined by American National Standards Institute (ANSI) Standards T1.617 and T1.618. A device capable of relaying frames to the next device in a frame relay network en route to a frame relay terminal equipment (FRTE) destination.

frame relay terminal equipment (FRTE) In FR-technology-based networks, a device capable of connecting to a frame relay network. An FRTE adds a frame header when sending data to the frame relay network and removes the frame header when receiving data from the frame relay network.

frame tagging Marking a packet with special VLAN identifiers. A packet that must forwarded to another switch via an interswitch link or must go through a router to another VLAN carries a unique VLAN identifier (VLAN ID) as it leaves its local switch. The VLAN ID allows the VLAN switches and routers to selectively forward the packet to ports with the same VLAN ID. It is the responsibility of the local switch (which receives the packet from the source station) to insert the VLAN ID in the packet header. Similarly, it is the responsibility of the destination switch (on whose port the destination end user is located) to remove the VLAN ID and forward the packet to the appropriate port.

frame-aware DSU A DSU with a specific set of diagnostic, monitoring and test features designed for use in frame relay networks. In enhanced frame relay SLA service, the frame aware DSU is bundled with the service and becomes a *Managed Demarc*.

frame-check sequence (FCS) Extra characters added to a frame for error control purposes. Used in HDLC, frame relay, and other data link layer protocols.

frames per second (fps) A measure of how much information is used to store and display motion video. The term applies equally to film video and digital video. Each frame is a still image; displaying frames in quick succession creates the illusion of motion. The more frames per second (fps), the smoother the motion appears.

FreeBSD A popular, free version of UNIX that runs on Intel microprocessors. FreeBSD is distributed in executable and source code form. The source code enables ambitious users to actually extend the operating system.

free-trade zone Part of an AppleTalk internetwork, accessible by two other parts of the internetwork, which are unable to directly access one another. (Not to be confused with a city or municipality that is free of international tariffs on trade.)

freeware Copyrighted software given away free by the author. Although it is available free, the author retains the copyright, which means that no-one can alter or distribute it without express permission from the author. Usually, the author allows people to use the software, but not sell it.

frequency The rate of signal oscillation in hertz (Hz), cycles per second.

frequency-division multiplexing (FDM) A method of multiplexing data on a carrier channel based on frequency.

frequency division multiplexing (FDM) A scheme in which numerous signals are combined for transmission on a single communications line or channel. This allows the channel bandwidth of a circuit to be subdivided into smaller subbands to provide each user with exclusive use of a subband. FDM assigns a discrete carrier frequency to each data stream and then combines many modulated carrier frequencies for transmission. *See* ATDM, statistical multiplexing, and TDM.

frequency division multiplexing analog (FDMA) A basic technology in the analog Advanced Mobile Phone Service (AMPS), the division of the frequency band allocated for wireless cellular communication. This band is divided into 30 channels, each of which can carry a voice conversation or, with digital service, digital data. The most widely-installed cellular phone system in North America.

frequency modulation (FM) Modulation technique in which signals of different frequencies represent different data values. *See* AM, modulation, PAM.

frequency-shift keying (FSK) A method of transmitting digital signals. The two binary states, logic 0 (low) and 1 (high), are represented by analog sine waves. Logic 0 is represented by a wave at a specific frequency, and logic 1 is represented by a wave at a different frequency. A modem converts the binary data from a computer to FSK for transmission over telephone lines, cables, optical fiber, or wireless media.

FRFH *See* frame relay frame handler.

FRM *See* fast resource management.

front-end processor (FEP) (*Illustration*) A dedicated device usually connected to host computers and mainframes, which provides data communications functions and offloads network processing work for the attached computers. A key computer component in network design in main frame-centric systems. A device for off-loading line control, message handling, code conversion, error control, and routing of data from the host computer. IBM's 3725 and 3745 are examples of front-end processors. Also known as a *communication controller*.

frontside bus The data path and physical interface between the processor and the main memory (RAM). In contrast, a *backside bus* is the data path and physical interface between the processor and the L2 cache memory. Both the frontside and backside bus can be in use at the same time, so that the processor gets more done in a given number of clock cycles. Current frontside bus speeds are in excess of 133 Mhz.

frozen No longer reacts to input due to a malfunction.

FRSE *See* frame relay switching equipment.

FRTE *See* frame relay terminal equipment.

FSK *See* frequency-shift keying.

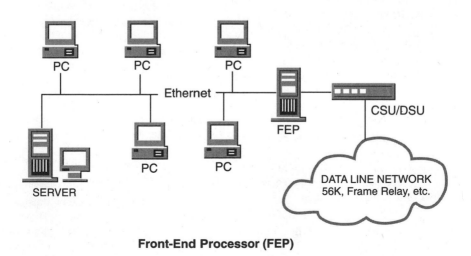

Front-End Processor (FEP)

FSM *See* finite-state machine.

FTAM *See* File Transfer Access and Management.

FTP *See* File Transfer Protocol.

FTS file A hidden index file ending in a .fts (full-text search) extension; created the first time a user selects the Find tab from a Help window in Windows 9x, Windows NT, and 2000 Help system. An FTS file can be deleted at any time. Each time Find is used, a new FTS file is created.

FUD *See* fear, uncertainty, and doubt.

full duplex (FDX) The transmission of data in two directions simultaneously. For example, a telephone is a full-duplex device because both parties can talk at once. In contrast, a walkie-talkie is a half-duplex device because only one party can transmit at a time. Most modems have a switch that lets the user choose between full- and half-duplex modes. The choice depends on which communications program is running. In full-duplex mode, data transmitted does not appear on screen until it has been received and sent back by the other party. This enables data to be validated as accurately transmitted. If the display screen shows two of each character, it probably means that the modem is set to half-duplex mode when it should be in full-duplex mode.

full mesh A network in which devices are organized in a *mesh topology*, with each network node having either a physical circuit or a virtual circuit connecting it to every other network node. A full mesh network provides a great deal of redundancy, but they can be prohibitively expensive to implement (both in monetary as well as network resources), full meshing is usually reserved for network backbones. *See* mesh *and* partial mesh.

full-screen mode The contents of an entire terminal screen is displayed at once. It can also be used when an application in Windows takes up the whole monitor screen versus a window on the terminal screen.

function keys Special keys on the keyboard that have different meanings depending on which program is running.

function (*a*) In programming, a named section of a program that performs a specific task; a type of procedure or routine. Some programming languages make a distinction between a *function*, which returns a value, and a *procedure*, which performs some operation but does not return a value. Most programming languages come with a prewritten set of functions that are kept in a *library*. Users can also write functions to perform specialized tasks. (*b*) Also used synonymously with *operation* and *command*. For example, the delete function is executed to erase a word.

functional address In IBM network adapters, a special kind of group address in which the address is *bit significant*, each "on" bit representing a function performed by the station (e.g., active monitor, ring-error monitor, LAN error monitor, or configuration report server).

functional programming A style of programming that emphasizes the evaluation of expressions rather than the execution of commands. *Erlang* is described as a functional programming language, because it avoids the use of global variables by multiple functions. These variables, when changed in one part of a program may have unexpected effects in another part.

functional specification A detailed formal document prepared for software developers to describe a product's intended capabilities, appearance, and interactions with users. The functional specification is a kind of guideline and continuing reference point as the developers write the programming code.

futzing Unstructured, playful, often experimental interaction between a human being and a computer, product, or any technology, sometimes but not always with a productive purpose in mind. Futzing can be pure play, learning by trying, or an attempt to achieve breakthrough insights.

Fuzzball Digital Equipment Corporation LSI-11 computer system running IP gateway software. The NSFnet used these systems as backbone packet switches.

fuzzy logic An approach to computing based on *degrees of truth* rather than the usual true-or-false (1 or 0) Boolean logic on which the modern computer is based. The idea of fuzzy logic was first advanced by Dr. Lotfi Zadeh of the University of California at Berkeley in the 1960s.

F

G

G.703/G.704 ITU-T electrical and mechanical specifications for connections between telephone company equipment and DTE devices using BNC connectors and operating at E1 data rates. *See* BNC connector *and* E1.

G.711 The international standard for encoding telephone audio on an 64 kbps channel. It is a pulse code modulation (PCM) scheme operating at a 8 kHz sample rate, with 8 bits per sample.

G.804 ITU-T framing standard that defines the standard mapping of ATM cells to the physical media.

G.Lite The informal name of an upcoming standard method to install Asymmetric Digital Subscriber Line (ADSL) service. Also known as *Universal ADSL*, G.Lite makes it possible to have Internet connections to home and business computers at up to 1.5 Mbps (millions of bits per second) over regular phone lines.

G *See* Giga *or* gigabyte.

GaAs Gallium arsenate; a semiconductor compound used in some diodes, field-effect transistors (FETs), and integrated circuits (ICs). The charge carriers, which are mostly electrons, move at high speed among the atoms, making GaAs components useful at ultra-high radio frequencies, and in fast electronic switching applications. GaAs devices generate less noise than most other types of semiconductor components—important in weak-signal amplification.

GaN Gallium nitride; a semiconductor compound expected to make possible miniaturized, high-power wireless transmitters. These transmitters will be combined with sensitive receivers into telephone sets capable of directly accessing communications satellites. The compound can also be used in light-emitting diodes (LEDs) and other semiconductor devices.

GateD A UNIX implementation maintained by the Merit Gated Consortium, of all routing protocols currently in common use, including RIP versions 1 and 2, OSPF 2, and BGP 2 through 4. The GateD Web site includes HTML pages describing the installation and configuration of the software. GateD it is available "upon request and at no charge for use as specified in the copyright and other restrictions contained in the GateD source files" (GateD Consortium Agreement).

gateway A network point that acts as an entrance to another network. On the Internet, in terms of routing, the network consists of gateway nodes and host nodes. The computers of network users and the computers that serve content (such as Web pages) are host nodes. The computers that control traffic within a company's network or at local Internet service providers (ISPs) are gateway nodes.

Gateway Discovery Protocol (GDP) Cisco Systems protocol, which allows hosts to dynamically detect the arrival of a new router on the network as well as detect when a router goes down. Based on UDP. *See* UDP.

gateway host In SNA, a host node that contains a gateway SSCP.

gateway NCP (GWNCP) An NCP that connects two or more SNA networks and performs address translation to allow cross-network session traffic.

Gateway-to-Gateway Protocol (GGP) MIL-NET protocol specifying how core routers (gateways) should exchange reachability and routing information. GGP uses a distributed shortest-path algorithm.

gauge (AWG) Wire diameter.

Gbits/s Gigabits per second; billions of bits per second. A measure of bandwidth on a digital data transmission medium like optical fiber, for high-speed networks such as Gigabit

Ethernet. With slower media and protocols, bandwidth may be in the Mbps (millions of bits or megabits per second) or the Kbps (thousands of bits or kilobits per second) range.

Gbyte *See* gigabit, gigabyte.

GCRA *See* generic cell rate algorithm.

GCS *See* group control system.

GD *See* general deployment.

GDI printer A printer with built-in support for Windows graphical device interface (GDI). GDI is used by most Windows applications to display images on a monitor, so when printing from a Windows application to a GDI printer, there is no need to convert the output to another format such as PostScript or PCL.

GDI *See* graphical device interface.

GDMO *See* Guidelines for the Definition of Managed Objects.

GDP *See* Gateway Discovery Protocol.

geek Short for computer geek, a person who is inordinately dedicated to and involved with technology to the point of appearing not to be normal. Depending on the context, it can be used in either a derogatory or affectionate manner, but being a geek also implies a capability with the technology.

GEN *See* generation.

general deployment (GD) Cisco designation of stable IOS releases.

General Packet Radio Service (GPRS) A packet-based wireless communication service that, when available in 2000, promises data rates from 56 up to 114 Kbps and continuous connection to the Internet for mobile phone and computer users. The higher data rates will allow users to take part in videoconferences and interact with multimedia Web sites and similar applications using mobile handheld devices as well as notebook computers.

general protection fault (GPS) A computer condition that causes a Windows application to crash. The most common cause of a GPF is two applications trying to use the same block of memory, or more specifically, one application trying to use memory assigned to another application. GPFs are often preceded by an invalid page fault. An error message used in personal computers to alert the user of an application (Microsoft Word, Netscape Web browser, etc.) that they are trying to access storage that is not designated for their use.

Generalized Markup Language (GML) An IBM document formatting language that describes a document in terms of its organization structure, content parts, and their relationship. GML markup or tags describe components like chapters, important sections and less important sections (by specifying heading levels), paragraphs, lists, tables, and so forth. GML frees document creators from specific document formatting concerns such as font specification, line spacing, and page layout required by IBM's printer formatting language, SCRIPT.

generalized trace facility (GTF) In SNA, an optional program that records significant system events, such as supervisor calls and start I/O operations, for the purpose of problem determination.

generation (GEN) In SNA, the process of assembling and link-editing definition statements so that resources can be identified to all the necessary programs in a network.

generic cell rate algorithm (GCRA) A reference model proposed by the ATM Forum for defining cell-rate conformance in terms of certain traffic parameters. It is usually referred as the *leaky bucket algorithm*. *See* traffic shaping *and* leaky bucket.

generic flow control (GFC) A 4-bit field in the ATM cell header used to support multiplexing functions. Its default value is '0000', when the GFC protocol is not enforced. The GFC mechanism is intended to support simple flow control in ATM connections.

generic routing encapsulation (GRE) Tunneling protocol developed by Cisco Systems that can encapsulate a wide variety of protocol packet types inside IP *tunnels*, creating a virtual point-to-point link between Cisco routers at remote points over an IP internetwork. By connecting multiprotocol subnetworks in a single-protocol backbone environment, IP tunneling using GRE allows network expansion across a single-protocol backbone environment.

generic unbind Synonym for *session deactivation request.*

geographic information system A system enabling the visualization of the geographic aspects of a body of data, letting users query or analyze a relational database and receive the results in the form of some kind of map. Because many kinds of data have important geographic aspects, a GIS can have many uses: weather forecasting, sales analysis, population forecasting, and land use planning, to name a few.

geostationary A satellite orbiting the earth directly over the equator, approximately, in a stationary orbit.

get nearest server (GNS) IPX request packet sent by a client on an IPX network to locate the nearest active server of a particular type. An IPX network client issues a GNS request to solicit either a direct response from a connected server or a response from a router that tells it where on the internetwork the service can be located. GNS is part of the IPX SAP. *See* IPX *and* SAP.

GFC *See* generic flow control.

GGP *See* Gateway-to-Gateway Protocol.

GHOST A product from Symantec, capable of cloning (copying) the entire contents of one hard disk to another while automatically formatting and partitioning the target disk. This product is especially useful in replicating systems.

For more information, see Symantec's web site: *http://www.symantec.com.*

GHz *See* gigahertz.

GID file A hidden Windows 95 configuration file, ending with a .gid extension, used by the Windows Help system.

GIF *See* Graphic Interchange Format.

GIF89a An image formatted according to Graphics Interchange Format (GIF) Version 89a. One of the chief advantages of the newer format is the ability to create an animated image that can be played after transmitting to a viewer, e.g., a twirling icon, a waving banner, or letters that change size. *See* Graphic Interchange Format.

giga (G) (*a*) In decimal notation, 10 to the 9th power. For example, a gigavolt is 1,000,000,000 volts. (*b*) In computers, which use the binary notation system, giga represents 2 to the 30th power, which is 1,073,741,824—a little more than 1 billion. A gigabyte, therefore, is about 1.073 billion bytes.

Gigabit Ethernet High-speed version of Ethernet (a billion bits per second) under development by the IEEE.

gigabit, gigabyte *See* giga.

gigahertz (GHz) A unit of alternating current (AC) or electromagnetic (EM) wave frequency equal to one billion hertz (1,000,000,000 Hz). The gigahertz is used primarily as an indicator of the frequency of ultra-high-frequency (UHF) and microwave EM signals. In some computers, the gigahertz is used to express microprocessor clock speed.

gigaPOP A network access point that supports data transfer rates of at least 1 Gbps. A gigaPOP can be either a single machine or a network of machines. Currently, only a few gigaPOPs exist, and they're used primarily for accessing the Internet-2 (I2) network. Each university that connects to I2 must do so through a gigaPOP, which connects the university's LANs and WANs to the I2 network. Originally, 12 gigaPOPs were planned so that each one would serve half a dozen I2 members, but the number of gigaPOPs is likely to grow. Whereas the POPs maintained by ISPs are designed to allow low-speed modems to connect to the Internet, gigaPOPs are designed for fast access to a high-speed network, such as I2.

GIS *See* geographic information system.

G

glitch A malfunction, a sudden break in function or continuity, sometimes of a transient nature, with a varying degree of seriousness. According to Eric Raymond, author of *The New Hacker's Dictionary*, glitch is from the German *glitschen*, meaning "to slip," via Yiddish *glitshen*, meaning "to slide or skid."

Global Positioning System (GPS) A "constellation" of 24 well-spaced satellites that orbit the Earth and make it possible for users with ground receivers to pinpoint their geographic location. The location accuracy is from 100 to 10 meters for most equipment. Accuracy can be pinpointed to within one (1) meter with special military-approved equipment. GPS equipment is widely used in science and is sufficiently low-cost so that almost anyone can own a GPS receiver.

global symbol An agreed-upon symbol defined in a module of a program potentially available for reference by another module. The linker resolves (matches references with definitions) global symbols.

global symbol table In a library, an index of defined global symbols used to access the modules defining the global symbols. The linker also puts global symbol tables into an image.

Global System for Mobile Communications (GSM) A digital mobile telephone system, widely used in Europe and other parts of the world. GSM uses a variation of *time division multiple access (TDMA)* and is the most widely used of the three digital wireless telephone technologies (TDMA, GSM, and CDMA). GSM digitizes and compresses data, then sends it down a channel with two other streams of user data, each in its own time slot. It operates at either the 900 MHz or 1800 MHz frequency band.

global unique identifier (GUID) A term used by Microsoft for a number generated by its programming to create a unique identity for an entity such as a Word document. GUIDs are widely used in Microsoft products to identify interfaces, replica sets, records, and other objects. Different kinds of objects have different kinds of GUIDs—for instance, a Microsoft Access database uses a 16-byte field to establish a unique identifier for replication.

Global/Regular Expression/Print (Grep) A UNIX command (also a utility available for Windows and other operating systems), used to search one or more files for a given character string or pattern and, if desired, replace the character string with another one.

glyph A distinct visual representation of a character that a display device, such as a monitor or printer, can display.

GML *See* Generalized Markup Language.

GNS *See* get nearest server.

GNU Gnu's Not UNIX. The Free Software Foundation's (FSF) GNU project, is a UNIX-like operating system that comes with source code which can be copied, modified, and redistributed. The philosophy behind GNU is to produce non-proprietary software that allows users to do whatever they want with the software they acquire, including making copies for friends and modifying the source code and repackaging it with a distribution charge.

The FSF uses a stipulation that it calls copyleft, which stipulates that anyone redistributing free software must also pass along the freedom to further copy and change the program, thereby ensuring that no one can claim ownership of future versions and place restrictions on users.

Linux systems rely heavily on GNU software; in the past, GNU systems used the Linux kernel. This close connection has led some people to mistakenly equate GNU with Linux. They are actually quite separate. In fact, the FSF is developing a new kernel called HURD to replace the Linux kernel in GNU systems.

gopher A widely successful method of information search and retrieval, documented in RFC 1436, which pre-dates the World Wide Web for organizing and displaying files on Internet servers. Gopher is a Client and Server style program, which requires that the user have a Gopher Client program. Although Gopher spread rapidly across the globe in only a couple of years, it has been largely supplanted by Hypertext, also known as WWW (World Wide Web).

A Gopher server presents its contents as a hierarchically structured list of files. With the ascendance of the Web, most Gopher databases are being converted to Web sites which can be more easily accessed via Web search engines. Gopher was developed at the University of Minnesota and named after the school's mascot. Two systems, *Veronica* and *Jughead*, let you search global indices of resources stored in Gopher systems. *See* client, server, WWW, hypertext.

GoS *See* grade of service.

GOSIP *See* government open-systems interconnection profile.

government open-systems interconnection profile (GOSIP) A federal information processing standard that specifies a well-defined set of OSI protocols for government communication systems procurement. GOSIP was intended to eliminate the use of TCP/IP protocols on government internets, but clarifications have specified that government agencies can continue to use TCP/IP. Originally based on the assumption that OSI standards and the associated protocols would be the dominant protocols used in networking equipment, pushing aside the use of SNA and TCP/IP. This did not happen and TCP/IP retained its dominance.

government OSI profile *See* GOSIP.

GPF *See* general protection fault.

gppm *See* graphics pages per minute.

GPRS *See* General Packet Radio Service.

grade of service (GoS) Measure of telephone service quality based on the probability that a call will encounter a busy signal during the busiest hours of the day.

granularity The relative size, scale, level of detail, or depth of penetration that characterizes an object. The more components in a system, or the greater the granularity, the more flexible it is.

Graphic Interchange Format (GIF) A common format for image files, especially suitable for images containing large areas of the same color. GIF supports color and various resolutions. It also includes data compression, making it specially effective for scanned photos. GIF format files of simple images are often smaller than the same file would be if stored in JPEG format, but GIF format does not store photographic images as well as JPEG. *See* GIF89a, JPEG.

graphical device interface (GDI) A Windows standard for representing graphical objects and transmitting them to output devices, such as monitors and printers. *See* GDI printer.

graphical user interface (GUI) Usually pronounced GOO-ee, a graphical (rather than purely textual) user interface to a computer. The first interactive user interfaces to computers were not graphical; they were text-and-keyboard oriented and usually consisted of commands that had to be memorized and computer responses that were infamously brief.

graphics Any computer device or program that makes a computer capable of displaying and manipulating pictures.

graphics accelerator A chipset attached to a video board that allows a computer program to offload the sending and refreshing of images to the display monitor and the computation of special effects common to 2-D and 3-D images. Graphics accelerators speed up the displaying of images on the monitor, making it possible to achieve effects not otherwise possible.

graphics coprocessor A microprocessor specially designed for handling graphics computations.

graphics pages per minute (gppm) The speed with which laser printers can print non-text pages.

graphics-based systems Software and hardware that treat objects on a display screen as bit maps or geometrical shapes rather than as characters. In contrast, *character-based systems* treat everything as ASCII or extended ASCII characters.

G

gray region In XWindow environments or Apple environments, that region defining the desktop, or the display area, of all active devices, excluding the menu bar on the main screen and the rounded corners on the outermost screens. It is the area in which windows can be moved.

gray scaling The use of many shades of gray to represent an image. Continuous-tone images, such as black-and-white photographs, use an almost unlimited number of shades of gray.

GRE *See* generic routing encapsulation.

Green Book The specification covering CD-I.

green PC A computer system especially designed to minimize power consumption. Green PCs shut off power to non-essential systems if no input has been detected for a specified amount of time.

Grep *See* Global/Regular Expression/Print.

ground station A collection of communications equipment designed to receive signals from (and usually transmit signals to) satellites. Also called a *downlink station*.

group Generically defined as a set of users in a system.

Group 3 protocol Protocol defined by the CCITT in RFC2301 for sending faxes.

Group 4 protocol A protocol defined by CCITT for sending faxes over ISDN networks.

group address In a LAN, a locally administered address assigned to two or more adapters to allow the adapters to copy the same frame. *See* multicast address.

group control system (GCS) A VM component that provides multiprogramming and shared memory support.

group delay *See* distortion delay.

group SAP A single address assigned to a group of service access points (SAPs).

groupware A class of software that helps groups of colleagues (workgroups) attached to a local area network organize their activities. Groupware may provide services for communicating (such as e-mail), group document development, scheduling, and tracking. Documents can include text, images, or other types of data. Groupware is sometimes called *workgroup productivity software*.

GSM *See* Global System for Mobile Communications.

GTF *See* generalized trace facility.

guard band Unused frequency band between two communications channels, which separates the channels in order to prevent mutual interference between the two.

GUI *See* graphical user interface.

GUID *See* global unique identifier.

Guideline RACE I project R1003.

Guidelines for the Definition of Managed Objects (GDMO) A standard for the consistent definition of objects in a network. With a consistent "language" for describing such objects as workstations, LAN servers, and switches, programs can be written to control or sense the status of network elements throughout a network. Basically, GDMO prescribes how a network product manufacturer must formally describe the product so that others can write programs that recognize and deal with the product. GDMO is used to describe the class or classes of the object, how the object behaves, its attributes, and classes that it may inherit.

gutter In desktop publishing, the space between columns in a multiple-column document.

GW-BASIC A dialect of the BASIC programming language that comes with many versions of the DOS operating system.

GWNCP *See* Gateway NCP.

H.323 A standard approved by the International Telecommunication Union (ITU) that defines how audiovisual conferencing data is transmitted across networks, in particular LAN networks. This is but one in a series of H.32X standards. In theory, H.323 should enable users to participate in the same conference even though they are using different videoconferencing applications.

H.324 A suite of standards approved by the International Telecommunications Union (ITU) that defines videoconferencing over analog (POTS) telephone wires. One of the main components of H.324 is the V.80 protocol that specifies how modems should handle streaming audio and video data.

hack To modify a program, often in an unauthorized manner, by changing the code itself. An inelegant and usually temporary solution to a problem.

hacker A term used by some to mean "a clever programmer" and by others, especially journalists or their editors, to mean "someone who tries to break into computer systems." Among professional programmers, the term implies a professional programmer; a *cracker* is someone who lacks formal training.

half duplex A method of data transmission where data can be transmitted in both directions on a signal carrier, but not at the same time. For example, on a local area network using a technology that has half-duplex transmission, one workstation can send data on the line and then immediately receive data on the line from the same direction in which data was just transmitted.

half-open connection A scenario in which one end connection is established but the other end connection is unreachable or has disposed of its connection information.

half-session A session-layer component consisting of the combination of data flow control and transmission control components comprising one end of a session.

halftone In printing, a continuous tone image, such as a photograph, that has been converted into a black-and-white image. Halftones are created through a process called *dithering*, in which the density and pattern of black and white dots are varied to simulate different shades of gray.

hand-held computer A computer that can conveniently be stored in a pocket (of sufficient size) and used while being held. Today's handheld computers, also called *personal digital assistants (PDAs)*, can be divided into those that accept handwriting as input and those with small keyboards.

Handheld Devices Markup Language (HDML) Also known as *Wireless Markup Language (WML)*, a language that allows the text portions of Web pages to be presented on cellular phones and personal digital assistants (PDAs) via wireless access. Developed by Unwired Planet, HDML (i.e., WML) is an open language offered royalty-free.

handle (*a*) In graphics applications, the small boxes that appear around a graphical object when it is selected; each box is a handle. By dragging the handles, shape and size of the object can be changed. (*b*) In programming, a token, typically a pointer, that enables the program to access a resource, such as a library function. (*c*) In communications, especially online services, the name used to identify an individual. It may be a real name, a nickname, or a completely fictitious name.

handler More of a "network engineer" definition as opposed to a hacker/cracker definition. This term refers to a compromised compuer that is responsible for running several agents or zombie computers. The implication of this definition is that these denial of service attacks are both distributed and layered in nature with all control going back to the hacker/cracker. *See* zombie computer.

handshake (*a*) Sequence of messages exchanged between two or more network devices to ensure transmission synchronization. A common attribute of connection oriented protocols. (*b*) The process by which two devices initiate communications. Handshaking begins when one device sends a message to another device indicating that it wants to establish a communications channel. The two devices then send several messages back and forth, which enables them to agree on a communications protocol. A very well known example of a handshake is the three-step TCP/IP handshake.

handwriting recognition The technique by which a computer system can recognize characters and other symbols written by hand. In theory, handwriting recognition should free us from our keyboards, allowing us to write and draw in a more natural way.

hang To crash in such a way that the computer does not respond to input from the keyboard or mouse. Usually corrected by rebooting.

haptics The science of applying touch (tactile) sensation and control to interaction with computer applications. By using special input/output devices (joysticks, data gloves, or other devices), users can receive feedback from computer applications in the form of felt sensations in the hand or other parts of the body.

hard Describes anything that is permanent or physically exists.

hard card A hard disk drive and controller on an expansion card. Unlike most disk drives that are either external to the computer or fit in one of the disk drive bays, a hard card slips into an expansion slot. Hard cards are often faster than conventional disk drives, and easier to install. Their storage capacities, however, are more limited.

hard copy Generally a printout.

hard disk drive (HDD) The mechanism that reads and writes data on a hard disk. Although the hard disk drive and the hard disk are not the same thing, they are packaged as a unit and so either term is sometimes used to refer to the whole unit. Hard disk drives (HDDs) for PCs generally have seek times of about 12 milliseconds or less.

Many disk drives improve their performance through a technique called *caching*. There are several interface standards for passing data between a hard disk and a computer. The most common are IDE and SCSI. Hard disk drives are sometimes called *Winchester drives*, the name of one of the first popular hard disk drive technologies developed by IBM in 1973.

hard disk (*a*) Part of a unit, often called a *disk drive, hard drive*, or *hard disk drive*, that stores and provides relatively quick access to large amounts of data on an electromagnetically charged surface or set of surfaces. (*b*) A magnetic disk on which you can store computer data. The term hard is used to distinguish it from a soft, or *floppy*, disk. Hard disks hold more data and are faster than floppy disks due to the extreme accuracy of the read-write heads in finding locations on the disk.

hard error An error condition on a network that requires the source of the error to be removed or that the network be reconfigured before the network can resume reliable operation.

hardware address Also called a *burned in* or *MAC address*. In Ethernet networks, the 48-bit address assigned to the Ethernet network interface card. In token ring, the 12-digit hex address assigned to the network interface card. *See* MAC address.

hardware monitor In SNA, a component of NetView. It is called the *network problem determination application*. It is used to identify network problems in hardware, software, and microcode.

hardware The physical aspect of computers, telecommunications, and other information technology devices. The term arose as a way to distinguish the "box" and the electronic circuitry and components of a computer from the programs put in it to make it perform. The programs came to be known as *software*.

hardwired Elements of a program or device that cannot be changed. Originally, the term was used to describe functionality which was built into the circuitry (i.e., the wires) of a device. Nowadays, however, the term is also used to describe constants built into software.

hashing The transformation of a string of characters into a usually shorter, fixed-length value or key that represents the original string. Hashing is used to index and retrieve items in a database because it is faster to find the item using the shorter hashed key than to find it using the original value. Consider, for example, a list of names:

Rebekah Thomas

Franny Kelly

Daniel Michael

To create an index, called a *hash table*, for these records, a formula is applied to each name to produce a unique numeric value. The results might be something like:

1345873 Rebekah Thomas

3097905 Franny Kelly

4060964 Daniel Michael

To search for the record containing Franny Kelly, the formula is reapplied and directly yields the index key to the record. This is much more efficient than searching through all the records till the matching record is found. CHAP uses a hashing function.

Hayes compatible Hayes Microcomputer Products, one of the leading manufacturers of modems, developed a language called the *AT command set* for controlling modems. This has become the de facto standard. Any modem that recognizes Hayes modem commands is said to be Hayes-compatible. This is very useful because most communications programs use Hayes modem commands. Virtually all modems manufactured today are Hayes-compatible.

HBD3 Line code type used on E1 circuits.

HDLC *See* High-Level Data Link Control.

HDML *See* Handheld Devices Markup Language.

HDSL *See* high bit-rate DSL.

HDTV *See* high-definition television.

head crash A serious disk drive malfunction. A head crash usually means that the head has scratched or burned the disk. In a hard disk drive, the head normally hovers a few microinches from the disk. If the head becomes misaligned or if dust particles come between it and the disk, it can touch the disk. Head crashes are less common for floppy disks because the head touches the disk under normal operation. Another term for head crash is *disk crash*.

head The mechanism that reads data from or writes data to a magnetic disk or tape. If the head becomes dirty, it will not work properly. It is one of the first things to check when a disk drive or tape drive begins to malfunction. The head is sometimes called a *read/write head*. Double-sided floppy disk drives have two heads, one for each side of the disk. Hard disk drives have many heads, usually two for each platter.

headend The end point of a broadband network. All stations transmit toward the headend; the headend then transmits toward the destination stations.

header (*Illustration*) (*a*) Control information that precedes user data in a frame or datagram that passes through networks. Specifically, this portion of a message contains control information. The portion of a message that contains control information for the message. Usually found at the beginning of a frame. (*b*) In word processing, one or more lines of text that appears at the top of each page of a document. Once specified, the text is automatically inserted by the word processor.

header error check or **header error control (HEC)** A 1-byte field in the cell header used for header error correction and detection. The information contained in the header is quite significant.

head-of-line (HOL) The head position of a buffer (i.e., inside a switch). A blocking phenomenon associated with the HOL, which requires cells in the queue to wait for the HOL cell to depart first.

H

Version	IML	Type of Service	Total Length
Identification		Flags	Fragment Offset
Time to Live		Protocol	Header Checksum
Source Address			
Destination Address			
Options			Padding

The components in the IP header and their meaning are presented in the following list.

VERSION — The version field is used to indicate the format of the IP header.

IHL — IHL stands for internet header length, which is the length of the internet header in 32-bit words and points to the beginning of data.

TYPE OF SERVICE — The type of service field specifies how the datagram is treated during its transmission through the network.

TOTAL LENGTH — This field indicates the total length of the datagram; this includes the IP header and data.

IDENTIFICATION — This is a 16-bit number which enables a target destination host to recognize fragments of datagrams that should be logically together.

FLAGS — The flag field has 3 bits which are used to indicate whether fragmentation is supported or not to fragment, and indicates more and last fragments.

FRAGMENT OFFSET — This indicates where in the datagram the fragment belongs (assuming that fragmentation has occurred).

TIME TO LIVE — This indicates the maximum time a datagram is permitted to stay in the internet system (whether this is a local internet or the Internet). When the value equals zero, the datagram is destroyed. Time is measured in units per second, and each entity that processes the datagram must decrease the value by one even if the process time is less than 1 s.

PROTOCOL — This field determines whether the data should be sent to TCP or UDP in the next layer in the network.

HEADER CHECKSUM — This is a header checksum only. Some header fields change and the header checksum is recomputed and verified wherever the header is processed.

SOURCE ADDRESS — This is the originator of the datagram. It consists of 32 bits.

DESTINATION ADDRESS — This is target for the header and data. It, too, is 32 bits.

heap sort A sorting algorithm that works by first organizing the data to be sorted into a special type of binary tree called a *heap*.

heap (*a*) In programming, an area of memory reserved for data created at runtime—that is, when the program actually executes. In contrast, the *stack* is an area of memory used for data whose size can be determined when the program is compiled. (*b*) A special type of binary tree in which the value of each node is greater than the values of its leaves. A *heap sort algorithm* works by first organizing a list of data into a heap.

heartbeat An interval of time, nominally measured in milliseconds, and a key parameter in transport state.

heat sink A component designed to lower the temperature of an electronic device by dissipating heat into the surrounding air. All modern CPUs require a heat sink. Some also require a fan. A heat sink without a fan is called a *passive heat sink*; a heat sink with a fan is called an *active heat sink*. Heat sinks are generally made of a zinc alloy and often have fins.

HEC *See* header error check *or* header error control.

hello packet Multicast packet used by routers for neighbor discovery and recovery. Hello packets also indicate that a client is still operating and network-ready. Hello packets are also used in ATM networks with the PNNI protocol to discover adjacent switches.

Hello protocol Protocol used by OSPF systems for establishing and maintaining neighbor relationships. Not to be confused with the *HELLO* routing protocol.

HELLO Interior routing protocol used principally by NSFnet nodes. HELLO allows particular packet switches to discover minimal delay routes. Not to be confused with the *Hello protocol* used by OSPF.

help balloon A rounded-type window containing explanatory information for the user when the pointer is positioned over that object.

help desk A department within a company that responds to user's technical questions.

Most large software companies have help desks to answer user questions. Questions and answers can be delivered by telephone, e-mail, BBS, or fax. There is even help desk software that makes it easier for the people running the help desk to quickly find answers to common questions.

help panel Also called a *help menu*. A display of information concerning a particular topic.

help Online documentation. Many programs come with the instruction manual, or a portion of the manual, integrated into the program. If a user encounters a problem or forgets a command while running the program, the documentation is summoned by pressing a designated Help key or entering a HELP command. In Windows, the Help key is function key F1.

helper address Address configured on an interface to which broadcasts received on that interface will be sent.

HEPnet *See* High-Energy Physics Network.

hertz A unit of frequency (of change in state or cycle in a sound wave, alternating current, or other cyclical waveform) equal to one cycle per second. It replaces the earlier term *cycle per second (cps)*.

heterogeneous network A network that includes computers and other devices from different manufacturers. For example, local-area networks (LANs) that connect PCs with Apple Macintosh computers are heterogeneous.

Hewlett-Packard (HP) One of the world's largest computer and electronics companies. Founded in 1939 by William Hewlett and David Packard, HP is best known today for its line of LaserJet and DeskJet printers.

Hewlett-Packard Graphics Language (HPGL) A set of commands for controlling plotters and printers. HPGL is part of Hewlett-Packard's PCL Level 5 page description language.

hexadecimal (*Illustration*) A base-16 number system; a numbering system containing 16 sequential numbers as base units (including 0) before adding a new position for the next num-

H

ber. (Note that we're using "16" here as a decimal number to explain a number that would be "10" in hexadecimal.) The hexadecimal numbers are 0-9 and then use the letters A-F. The equivalents of binary, decimal, and hexadecimal numbers are shown in the table below. To convert a value from hexadecimal to binary, you merely translate each hexadecimal digit into its 4-bit binary equivalent. Hexadecimal numbers have either and 0x prefix or an h suffix. For example, the hexadecimal number:

0x3F7A

translates to the following binary number:

011 1111 0111 1010

Letter/number	Binary	Hex value
A	01000001	41
a	01100001	61
E	01000101	45
2	00110010	32
3	00110011	33
7	00110111	37
T	01010100	54
k	01101011	6B
m	01101101	6D
z	01111010	7A

Table of Hexadecimal Values

Decimal	Hexadecimal	Binary
0	0	0000
1	1	0001
2	2	0010
3	3	0011
4	4	0100
5	5	0101
6	6	0110
7	7	0111
8	8	1000
9	9	1001
10	A	1010
11	B	1011
12	C	1100
13	D	1101
14	E	1110
15	F	1111

HFC *See* hybrid fiber coaxial cable.

hierarchical Systems organized in the shape of a pyramid, with each row of objects linked to objects directly beneath it. Hierarchical systems pervade everyday life. The army, for example, which has generals at the top of the pyramid and privates at the bottom, is a hierarchical system. Similarly, the system for classifying plants and animals according to species, family, genus, and so on, is also hierarchical.

hierarchical network A multi-segment network configuration providing only one path through intermediate segments between source segments and destination segments. One of the prime benefits in arranging a network in a hierarchical fashion is it greatly simplfies network address searches, because prefix addresses can be used to help accelerate the routing through the network to the destination address.

hierarchical routing In TCP/IP, routing based on a hierarchical addressing scheme. Most TCP/IP routing is based on a two- or three-level hierarchy in which an IP address is divided into a network portion until the datagram reaches a gateway that can deliver it directly. The concept of *subnets* introduces additional levels of hierarchical routing.

hierarchical storage management (HSM) A data storage system that automatically moves data between high- and low-cost storage media.

HiFD *See* high floppy disk.

high bit-rate DSL (HDSL) The earliest variation of DSL to be widely used, for wideband digital transmission within a corporate site and between the telephone company and a customer. The main characteristic of HDSL is that it is symmetrical: an equal amount of bandwidth is available in both directions. For this reason, the maximum data rate is lower than for ADSL. HDSL can carry as much on a single wire of twisted-pair as can be carried on a T1 line in North America or an E1 line in Europe (2,320 Kbps).

high-definition television (HDTV) Part of *Advanced TV (ATV)*, this is a new television technology that provides picture quality similar to 35 mm. movies with sound quality similar to compact disc. Some television stations have begun transmitting to users on limited channels. HDTV uses digital rather than analog signal transmission.

High-Energy Physics Network (HEPnet) Research network originated in the United States, but which has spread to most places involved in high-energy physics. Well-known sites include Argonne National Laboratory, Brookhaven National Laboratory, Lawrence Berkeley Laboratory, and the Stanford Linear Accelerator Center (SLAC).

high floppy disk (HiFD) A high-density floppy disk, developed by Sony, which holds 200 MB of data.

High-Level Data Link Control (HDLC) A group of protocols or rules for transmitting data between network points (sometimes called *nodes*). A method of WAN data encapsulation, where data is organized into a unit (called a *frame*) and sent across a network to a destination that verifies its successful arrival. The HDLC protocol also manages the flow or pacing at which data is sent and supports several modes of operation, including a simple sliding window mode for reliable delivery. HDLC is an ISO standard developed from the *Synchronous Data Link Control (SDLC)* standard proposed by IBM in the 1970s and documented in ISO 3309.

For any HDLC communications session, one station is designated primary and the other secondary. A session can use one of the following connection modes, which determine how the primary and secondary stations interact.

Normal unbalanced. The secondary station responds only to the primary station.

Asynchronous. The secondary station can initiate a message.

Asynchronous balanced. Both stations send and receive over its part of a duplex line.

This mode is used for X.25 packet-switching networks. The Link Access Procedure-Balanced (LAP-B) and Link Access Procedure D-channel (LAP-D) protocols are subsets of HDLC. Many variants of HDLC have been developed. Both PPP and SLIP use a subnet of HDLC's functionality. ISDN's D channel uses a slightly modified version of HDLC. Cisco routers' default serial link encapsulation is HDLC.

high-level language A programming language such as C, FORTRAN, or Pascal that enables a programmer to write programs that are more or less independent of a particular type of computer. Such languages are considered high-level because they are closer to human languages and further from machine languages. In contrast, *assembly languages* are considered low-level because they are very close to machine languages.

High-Level Language Application Program Interface (HLLAPI) An IBM API that allows a PC application to communicate with a mainframe computer. HLLAPI requires a PC to run 3270 emulation software and then defines an interface between a PC application and the emulation software. This API is also called *screen-scraping* because the approach uses characters that would otherwise be displayed on a terminal screen.

high memory In DOS-based systems, high memory refers to the memory area between the first 640K and 1 megabyte. It is also called the *upper memory area (UMA)*.

high-performance addressing (HPA) A passive-matrix display technology that provides better response rates and contrast than conventional LCD displays.

High-Performance Computing and Communications (HPCC) United States government-funded program advocating advances in computing, communications, and related fields. The HPCC is designed to ensure United States leadership in these fields through educa-

H

tion, research and development, industry collaboration, and implementation of high-performance technology. The five components of the HPCC are ASTA, BRHR, HPCS, IITA, and NREN.

High-Performance Computing Systems (HPCS) Component of the HPCC program designed to ensure United States technological leadership in high-performance computing through research and development of computing systems and related software. *See* HPCC.

high-performance option (HPO) An extension of VM/SP. The fundamental purpose of HPO is to provide performance and operation enhancements for large-system environments.

High-Performance Parallel Interface (HIPPI) A standard point-to-point protocol technology for transmitting large amounts of data at up to billions of bits per second over relatively short distances, mainly on local area networks (LANs).. HIPPI became an official ANSI standard in 1990, and its proponents believe that its use can make computers, interconnected storage devices, and other resources on a local area network function as though they were all within a single supercomputer.. The basic flavor of HIPPI transfers 32 bits in parallel for a data transfer speed of 0.8 Gbps. *Wide HIPPI* transfers 64 bits at a time to yield 1.6 Gbps. New HIPPI standards supporting rates of 6.4 Gbps are under development.

High-Performance Routing (HPR) Second-generation routing algorithm for APPN in SNA networks. HPR provides a connectionless layer with nondisruptive routing of sessions around link failures, and a connection-oriented layer with end-to-end flow control, error control, and sequencing. *See* APPN *and* ISR.

High-Speed Serial Interface (HSSI) High-speed WAN connection supporting speed up to 54Mbps.

highlight To make an object on a display screen stand out by displaying it in a different mode from other objects. Typical highlighted objects include menu options, command buttons, and selected blocks of text.

HIPPI *See* High-Performance Parallel Interface.

hit (*a*) The retrieval of any item, like a page or a graphic, from a Web server. For example, when a visitor calls up a Web page with four graphics, that's five hits, one for the page and four for the graphics. For this reason, hits often aren't a good indication of Web traffic. *See* page view. (*b*) A match between a a piece of data and selected criteria. For example, each of the matches from a search engine search is called a hit. (*c*) Any time information or data being searched matches that which is stored in a cache (memory).

HLLAPI *See* High-Level Language Application Program Interface.

HOL *See* head-of-line.

holddown State into which a route is placed so that routers will neither advertise the route nor accept advertisements about the route for a specific length of time (the holddown period). Holddown is used to flush bad information about a route from all routers in the network. A route is typically placed in holddown when a link in that route fails.

home page (*a*) The main page of a Web site. Typically, the home page serves as an index or table of contents to other documents stored at the site. (*b*) Originally, the Web page that your browser is set to use when it starts up. *See* browser, Web.

hop (*a*) The trip a data packet takes from one router or intermediate point to another in the network. On the Internet (or a network that uses TCP/IP), the number of hops a packet has taken toward its destination (called the *hop count*) is kept in the packet header. A packet with an exceedingly large hop count is discarded. (*b*) In token-ring networking, the connection between ring segments. The connection is usually made using bridges.

hop count (*a*) A measure of distance between two points in the Internet. Each hop count corresponds to one router separating a source from a destination (for example, a hop count of 3 indicates that three routers separate a source from a destination). (*b*) In TCP/IP networks, a measure of distance between two points in a network. A hop count of n means that *n* routers separate the source and the destination. (*c*) The number of ring segments spanned to establish a session between two workstations; in IBM token-ring networks the maximum is seven.

host (*a*) Any computer on a network that is a repository for services available to other computers on the network. It is quite common to have one host machine provide several services, such as WWW and USENET. (*b*) A computer system that is accessed by a user working at a remote location. Typically, the term is used when there are two computer systems connected by modems and telephone lines. The system that contains the data is called the host, while the computer at which the user sits is called the remote terminal. (*c*) A computer that is connected to a TCP/IP network, including the Internet. Each host has a unique IP address. *See* node *and* network.

host group All hosts belonging to a multicast session. The membership of a host group is dynamic: hosts can join and leave the group at any time. There can be any number of members in a host group and the members can be located anywhere on the local network or on the Internet. A host can be a member of more than one group at a time.

host master key In SNA, a deprecated term for *master cryptography key*.

host node (*a*) A node at which a host computer is situated. (*b*) In SNA, a subarea node that contains an SSCP.

host processor A processor that controls all or part of a user application network. Normally, the data communication access method resides on this host.

host system (*a*) A data processing system that is used to prepare programs and the operating environments for use on another computer or controller. (*b*) The data processing system to which a network is connected and with which the system can communicate.

hot key A user-defined key sequence that executes a command or causes the operating system to switch to another program. In DOS sys-

tems, hot keys are used to open *memory-resident programs* (TSRs). In Windows environments, hot keys execute common commands. For example, Ctrl +C usually copies the selected objects.

hot link A link between two applications allowing changes in one to affect the other.

hot plugging (*a*) The ability to add and remove devices to a computer while the computer is running and have the operating system automatically recognize the change. Two new external bus standards—*Universal Serial Bus (USB)* and *IEEE 1394*—support hot plugging. This is also a feature of PCMCIA.

Hot plugging is also called *hot swapping*. (*b*) Hot plugging in network devices allows one to add or remove components without the need to power cycle the network device. Hot plugging of a device component usually causes switched virtual connections (SVCs) to be lost.

hot spot The area of a graphics object, or a section of text, that activates a function when selected.

Hot Standby Router Protocol (HSRP) A protocol developed by Cisco Systems that provides high network availability and transparent network topology changes. HSRP creates a hot standby router group with a lead router that uses a virtual IP address, which services all packets sent to the hot standby (virtual) address. The lead router's operation is monitored by other routers in the group, and if it fails, one of these standby routers inherits the lead position and the hot standby (virtual) group address.

HotBot A World Wide Web search engine developed collaboratively by Inktomi Corporation and HotWired, Inc., the publisher of *Wired* magazine.

HotJava A set of products developed by Sun Microsystems that utilize Java technology. Currently, HotJava products include a set of libraries for building Java-aware applications, and a Java-enabled Web browser. Other Java-enabled Web browsers include the newest versions of Netscape Navigator and Microsoft

H

Internet Explorer.

hotlist A list of frequently accessed documents. The term is often used to describe a list of Web pages kept for easy access. In Netscape Navigator, the hotlist is called the *bookmark list*. In Internet Explorer, it's called the *Favorites* folder.

HP OpenView (Highest Potentiality OpenView) A network discovery engine developed by Hewlett-Packard. HP OpenView provides integrated network, system, application and database management for multivendor distributed computing environments. HP OpenView can probe IP-, IPX-, or SMS-based networks.

HP *See* Hewlett-Packard.

HPA *See* high-performance addressing.

HPCC *See* High Performance Computing and Communications.

HPCS *See* High Performance Computing Systems.

HPGL *See* Hewlett-Packard Graphics Language.

HPR *See* High-Performance Routing.

HSM *See* hierarchical storage management.

HSRP *See* Hot Standby Router Protocol.

HSSI *See* High-Speed Serial Interface.

HTML *See* HyperText Markup Language.

HTTP *See* Hypertext Transfer Protocol.

hub (*Illustration*) A common connection point or hardware device that connects multiple Ethernet devices together on the same physical network. The term hub is also liberally used to describe a device with multiple connections.

hybrid fiber coaxial cable (HFC) A telecommunication technology in which fiber optic cable and coaxial cable are used in different portions of a network to carry broadband content (such as video, data, and voice).

HyperCard A hypertext programming environment for the Macintosh, introduced by Apple in 1987. The HyperCard model consists of cards, and collections of cards, called *stacks*.

hyperlink An element in an electronic document that links to another place in the same document or to an entirely different document. Typically, a hyperlink is clicked on to follow the link. Hyperlinks are the essential ingredient of all hypertext systems, including the World Wide Web.

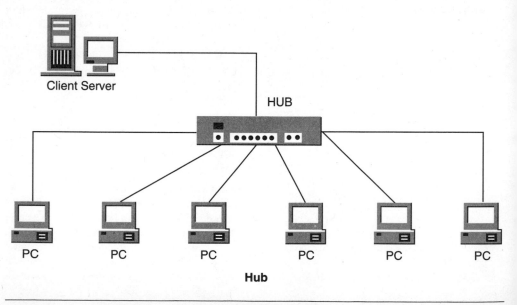

Hub

hypermedia An extension to hypertext that supports linking graphics, sound, and video elements in addition to text elements. The World Wide Web is a partial hypermedia system, because it supports graphical hyperlinks and links to sound and video files. New hypermedia systems under development will allow objects in computer videos to be hyperlinked.

HyperText Markup Language (HTML) Coding language used to create hypertext documents for use on the World Wide Web. HTML resembles typesetting code, where a block of text is surrounded with codes that indicate how it should appear.

Using HTML, a word or block of text may be linked to another file on the Internet. HTML files are meant to be viewed using a World Wide Web Client Program, such as Netscape or Mosaic. *See* client *and* server.

For more information about HTML, also see books by Laura Lamay.

hypertext Made famous by the World Wide Web; a way of constructing documents that reference other documents.

Within a hypertext document, a block of text can be tagged as a hypertext link pointing to another document. When viewed with a hypertext browser, the link can be activated to view the other document. The original idea of hypertext was to take advantage of electronic data processing to organize large quantities of information that would otherwise overwhelm a reader.

Two hundred years ago, the printing press made possible a similar innovation—the encyclopedia. Hypertext's older cousin combined topical articles with an indexing system to afford the researcher one or perhaps two orders of magnitude increase in the volume of accessible information. Early experience with hypertext suggests that it may ultimately yield an additional order of magnitude increase, by making directly accessible information that would otherwise be relegated to a bibliography.

Hypertext's limiting factor appears not to be the physical size of some books, but rather the ability of the reader to navigate increasingly complex search structures. Currently, additional increases in human information processing ability seem tied to developing more sophisticated automated search tools, although the present technology presents possibilities that remain far from fully explored.

Hypertext Transfer Protocol (HTTP) The protocol for moving hypertext files across the Internet. Requires an HTTP client program on one end, and an HTTP server program on the other end. HTTP is the most important protocol used in the World Wide Web (WWW). *See* client, server, *and* WWW.

Hz *See* Hertz.

H

I.430 *See* Integrated Services Digital Network (ISDN).

I/O *See* input/output.

I2 Internet2. A new global network being developed cooperatively by about 100 universities. The goal of I2 is to develop the technologies necessary to support the high bandwidths required by applications such as live video. I2 is expected to be 100 to 1,000 times faster than the current Internet. In addition to being fast, I2 will also support quality-of-service (QoS). This allows two hosts to establish a connection with a guaranteed bandwidth.

For more information, see
http://www.internet2.edu.

I2C *See* Inter-IC.

I2O A new I/O architecture in development; designed to eliminate I/O bottlenecks by utilizing special processors.

IAB *See* Internet Architecture Board.

IAC *See* Internet Access Coalition.

IAHC *See* Internet International Ad Hoc Committee.

IANA *See* Internet Assigned Numbers Authority.

IAP *See* Internet access provider.

IBM International Business Machines. The largest computer company in the world. IBM was founded in 1911 by Thomas J. Watson Sr., as a producer of punch-card tabulating machines. In 1953, it introduced its first computer, the 701. During the '60s and '70s, it began to offer mainframe (System-360 and System-370) and minicomputers (System-36 and AS400). In 1981, IBM launched its first personal computer, called the IBM PC, which quickly became the standard. However, IBM underestimated the market for PCs and lost market share to vendors of PC compatibles, such as Compaq, Dell, and Gateway

IBM PC A family of personal computers produced by IBM. The term can also refer to PC-like computers (also known as *IBM clones, IBM compatibles,* or simply *compatibles*).

ICA *See* integrated communication adapter.

ICD *See* international code designator.

ICM *See* integrated communication management.

ICMP *See* Internet Control Message Protocol.

icon A small, graphic representation of an object on the root window. Icons are found in Apple hosts as well as the X window system. *See* GUI.

icon family In the Apple Computer family of products, the set of icons that represent an object, such as an application or document, on the desktop.

ICQ An easy-to-use online instant messaging program developed by Mirabilis Ltd. It is used as a conferencing tool by individuals on the Net to chat, e-mail, perform file transfers, play computer games, and more. Once ICQ is downloaded and installed onto a PC, a user can create a list of friends, family, business associates, etc. (who also have ICQ on their PCs). ICQ uses this list to find friends, and notifies the user once they have signed onto the Net. A user can then send messages, chat in real time, play games, etc.

ICR *See* initial cell rate.

IDF *See* intermediate distribution frame.

IDI *See* initial domain identifier.

IDP *See* initial domain part.

IDPR *See* interdomain policy routing *and* IS-IS Interdomain Routing Protocol.

IEC *See* interexchange carrier.

IEEE *See* Institute of Electrical and Electronics Engineers.

IEEE 802 The IEEE committee overseeing standards for local area networks (LAN).

IEEE 802.1 The IEEE specification that describes an algorithm that prevents bridging loops by creating a *spanning tree*. The algorithm was invented by Digital Equipment Corporation. The Digital algorithm and the IEEE 802.1 algorithm are not exactly the same, nor are they compatible. *See* spanning tree, spanning-tree algorithm, *and* Spanning-Tree Protocol.

IEEE 802.2 The IEEE LAN protocol that specifies an implementation of the LLC sublayer of the data-link layer. IEEE 802.2 handles errors, framing, flow control, and the network-layer (Layer 3) service interface. Used in IEEE802.3 and IEEE802.5 LANs. *See* IEEE 802.3 *and* IEEE 802.5.

IEEE 802.3 The IEEE LAN protocol defining an implementation of the physical layer and MAC sublayer of the data-link layer. IEEE 802.3 uses CSMA/CD access method at a variety of speeds over several different media transmission types, such as unshielded twisted pair. IEEE 802.3 is the basis of the Ethernet standard. Extensions to the IEEE 802.3 standard specify implementations for *Fast Ethernet*. Physical variations of the original IEEE 802.3 specification include *10Base-2, 10Base-5, 10Base-F, 10Base-T*, and *10Broad36*. Physical variations for Fast Ethernet include *100Base-T, 100Base-T4*, 100BaseX, and *802.3Z Gigabit.*

IEEE 802.3Z The IEEE 802.3z standard created to extend the 802.3 protocol to an operating speed of 1,000 Mb/s in order to provide a significant increase in bandwidth, while maintaining maximum compatibility with the installed base of CSMA/CD nodes, previous investment in research and development, and principles of network operation and management. It defines *carrier sense multiple access with collision detection (CSMA/CD), media access control (MAC)* parameters, and minimal augmentation of its operation, physical-layer

characteristics, repeater functions, and management parameters for transfer of 802.3 and Ethernet format frames at 1,000 Mb/s.

IEEE 802.4 The IEEE physical layer standard specifying a LAN with a token-passing access method on a bus topology. Used with *manufacturing automation protocol (MAP)* LANs. Typical transmission speed is 10 Mbps.

IEEE 802.5 The IEEE LAN protocol defining an implementation of the physical layer and MAC sublayer of the link layer. 802.5 uses the token-passing access method at 4 or 16 Mbps, over shielded twisted pair (STP) cabling. *See* token ring.

IEEE 802.6 The IEEE *metropolitan area network (MAN)* specification based on DQDB technology. IEEE 802.6 supports data rates of 1.5to 155Mbps. *See* DQDB.

IEEE 802.12 The IEEE LAN standard that specifies the physical layer and the MAC sublayer of the data-link layer. IEEE802.12 uses the demand priority media-access scheme at 100-Mbps over a variety of physical media. *See* 100VG-AnyLAN.

IEEE 802.12VG 100 Base VG AnyLAN standard approved by the IEEE. 100 VG AnyLAN is a 100 Megabit/sec high speed networking standard that was originally developed to transmit Ethernet or token ring packets on existing wiring. The VG in 100 VG AnyLAN stands for *voice grade*, meaning that the 100 VG technology will run standard Ethernet frames at 100 Megabits/sec, utilizing voice grade category 3, 4, and 5 *unshielded twisted pair (UTP)* wire. Data packets are transferred from node to node by a hub, based on the address of the data packet. This ensures an orderly transmission and eliminates collisions. Because of this managed transfer of data, 100 VG AnyLAN can transmit data at peak speeds of 96 Megabits/sec, compared to 4 to 6 Megabits/sec on Ethernet. 100 VG AnyLAN is easily implemented either stand alone or in existing Ethernet networks. Additionally, 100 VG AnyLAN provides a high-speed migration path for token ring users and can be bridged to *asynchronous transfer mode (ATM)* backbones when necessary.

IEEE 1394 External bus standard that supports data transfer rates of up to 400 Mbps (400 million bits per second). Products supporting the 1394 standard go under different names, depending on their manufacturer. Apple, which originally developed the technology, uses the trademarked name *FireWire*. Other companies use other names, such as *I-link* and *Lynx*, to describe their 1394 products. A single 1394 port can be used to connect up 63 external devices. In addition to its high speed, 1394 also supports isochronous data—delivering data at a guaranteed rate. This makes it ideal for devices that need to transfer high levels of data in real time, such as video devices.

IESG *See* Internet Engineering Steering Group.

IETF *See* Internet Engineering Task Force.

IFC *See* internet foundation classes.

IGMP *See* Internet Group Management Protocol.

IGP *See* Interior Gateway Protocol.

IGRP *See* Interior Gateway Routing Protocol.

IIH *See* IS-IS Hello.

IIOP *See* Internet Inter-ORB Protocol.

IIS *See* Internet Information Server.

IISP *See* Interim Interswitch Signaling Protocol.

IITA *See* information infrastructure technology and applications.

ILMI *See* integrated local management interface.

ILU *See* independent logical unit.

iMac An Apple computer intended for home, school, and small offices, and promoted by Apple as an easy-to-use, stylish computer that outperforms other low-cost options. The computer comes equipped with a 233MHz G3 processor.

image The procedures and data bound together by a linker to form an executable program. This executable program is executed by the process. There are three types of images: *executable, sharable*, and *system*.

image map A single graphic image containing more than one *hot spot*. Image maps are used extensively on the World Wide Web. Each hot spot in a Web image map takes you to a different Web page. Sometimes spelled *imagemap*.

image mode The default screen mode using multiple image planes for a single screen. The number of image planes determines the variety of colors that are available to the screen.

image name The name of the file in which an image is stored.

IMAP *See* Internet Message Access Protocol.

IMHO In My Humble Opinion. A shorthand comment used in messages in an online forum. IMHO indicates that the writer is aware that they are expressing a debatable view, probably on a subject already under discussion. One of many such shorthand expressions in common use online, especially in discussion forums.

IMP *See* Interface Message Processor.

impact printer A class of printers that works by striking a head or needle against an ink ribbon to make a mark on the paper. *Dot-matrix printers, daisy-wheel printers*, and *line printers* are impact printers. In contrast, *laser* and *ink-jet printers* are *nonimpact printers*. The distinction is important because impact printers tend to be considerably noisier than nonimpact printers but are useful for multipart forms such as invoices.

impedance The combined effect of resistance, inductance, and capacitance on a signal at a particular frequency.

import To use data produced by another application. The ability to import data is very important in software applications because it means that one application can complement another. *See* export.

impression An advertisement's appearance on an accessed Web page. For example, if a page shows three ads, that counts as three impressions. Advertisers use impressions to

I

measure the number of views their ads receive, and publishers often sell ad space according to impressions. Impressions are tracked in a log maintained by a site server and are often sold on a cost per thousand (CPM) basis.

IMR *See* intensive mode recording.

inactive Not operational.

in-band Call information sent through the same channel as the call itself. When a voice call is placed on a POTS line, the tones or clicks used to indicate the number you are dialing are carried on the same line as the call itself. Although in-band is a more efficient use of network resources, it can be less reliable for management and call setup signaling.

in-band signaling Transmission within a frequency range normally used for information transmission. Compare with *out-of-band signaling*.

incoming call packet A call supervision packet transmitted by a data circuit-terminating equipment (DCE) to inform a called data terminal equipment (DTE) that another DTE has requested a call.

incremental backup A backup procedure that backs up only those files that have been modified since the previous backup. This is in contrast to *archival backup*, in which all files are backed up regardless of whether they have been modified since the last backup.

Indeo A type of codec (compression/decompression technology) for computer video developed by Intel Corporation.

independent logical unit (ILU) In SNA, a logical unit that does not require assistance from an SSCP to establish an LU-LU session.

index A structure that permits the retrieval of records from a file based on key values.

index path A logical ordering of records in a Btrieve file, based on the values of an index. An index path for each index in a file must exist. A file may have up to 24 separate index paths.

indexed file organization A DEC-type file organization in which a file contains records

and a primary key index used to process the records, either sequentially by index or randomly by index.

indexed sequential access method (ISAM) A method for managing how a computer accesses records and files stored on a hard disk. While storing data sequentially, ISAM provides direct access to specific records through an index. This combination results in quick data access regardless of whether records are being accessed sequentially or randomly.

indexed sequential file A record file in which each record has one or more data keys embedded in it. Records in the file are individually accessible by specifying a key associated with the record.

Industry-Standard Architecture (ISA) 16-bit bus used for Intel-based personal computers; a motherboard connector type. *See* EISA *and* PCI.

Inetd On UNIX systems, a program for maintaining passive sockets on a variety of well-known ports. Many Internet services are identified using a standard port number, the so-called well-known port numbers. For example, remote logins with Telnet are established using port 23. Mail delivery uses port 25. FTP file transfers are done with ports 20 and 21. Any TCP connection request targeted at one of these well-known port numbers is understood to be for a particular service. When a new connection is created, Inetd starts a program to handle the connection, based upon a configuration table. In this way, one program can handle incoming connections for a variety of services. Inetd only runs server programs as they are needed, and will spawn multiple server programs to service multiple network connections.

information infrastructure technology and applications (IITA) Component of the HPCC program intended to ensure United States leadership in the development of advanced information technologies. *See* HPCC.

Information Management System/Virtual Storage (IMS/VS) A software subsystem offering by IBM. It is a database/data communication system that can manage complex databases and networks.

information systems or **information services (IS)** In many corporations, the department responsible for computers, networking, and data management. This same department may be called the Information Technology (IT) or Management Information Services (MIS) department.

information technology (IT) The broad subject concerned with all aspects of managing and processing information, especially within a large organization or company.

Information/Management A feature of the Information/System that provides interactive systems management applications for problem, change, and configuration management.

Informix One of the fastest growing DBMS software companies, founded in 1980. Although still much smaller than its chief rival, Oracle, Informix has been able to make large market-share gains recently due to its innovative technology.

Infoseek A World Wide Web search engine developed by Infoseek Corporation. In addition to providing a full-text search engine, Infoseek also provides categorized lists of Web sites.

infrared (IR) Electromagnetic waves whose frequency range is above that of microwaves, but below that of the visible spectrum. LAN systems based on this technology represent an emerging technology.

init *See* initialize *or* initialization.

initial cell rate (ICR) The rate at which a source is allowed to start up following an idle period. It is established at connection setup and is between the MCR and the PCR.

initial domain identifier (IDI) In OSI, the portion of the NSAP that specifies the domain.

initial domain part (IDP) The part of a CLNS address that contains an authority and format identifier and a domain identifier.

initialize or **initialization (init)** (*a*) On Apple Macintosh computers, to format a disk.

(*b*) In programming, to assign a starting value to a variable. (*c*) The process of starting up a program or system.

initiator In OSI, a file service user which requests an FTAM establishment.

INN *See* intermediate network node.

inoperative The condition of a resource that has been, but is no longer, active. The resource may have failed, have received an INOP request, or be suspended while a reactivate command is being processed.

input device Any machine that feeds data into a computer. For example, a keyboard is an input device, whereas a display monitor is an output device. Input devices other than the keyboard are sometimes called *alternate input devices*. *Mice, trackballs*, and *light pens* are alternate input devices.

input/output (I/O) Devices or processes through which data is entered into or taken out from a computer.

input/output channel (*a*) In a data-processing system, a functional unit that handles transfer of data between internal and peripheral equipment. (*b*) In a computing system, a functional unit, controlled by a processor, that handles transfer of data between processor storage and local peripheral devices. (*c*) In IBM terminology, it refers to a specific type of path, either parallel or serial.

insert To place an object between two other objects. Inserting characters, words, paragraphs and documents is common in word processing. Insert differs from *append*, which means to add at the end. Most computer keyboards have an Insert key, which turns insert mode on and off.

installation exit Modifications to an IBM software product, made by a customer's system programmers to change or extend the functions of the IBM software product. Such modifications consist of *exit routines* written to replace one or more existing modules of an IBM software product.

installation exit routine A routine written by a user to take control at an installation exit of an IBM software product.

Institute of Electrical and Electronics Engineers (IEEE) Pronounced I-triple-E. Founded in 1884, the IEEE is an organization composed of engineers, scientists, and students. The IEEE is best known for developing standards for the computer and electronics industry. In particular, the IEEE 802 standards for local-area networks are widely followed.

 For more information, see *http://www.ieee.org*.

instruction A basic command. The term is often used to describe the most rudimentary programming commands.

instruction set The basic set of commands, or instructions, that a microprocessor understands. One of the principal characteristics that separates *reduced instruction set computer (RISC)* from *complex instruction set (CISC)* microprocessors is the size of the instruction set—RISC microprocessors have relatively small instruction sets whereas CISC processors have relatively large instruction sets.

insured rate The long-term data throughput, in bits or cells per second, that an ATM network commits to support under normal network conditions. The insured rate is 100-percent allocated; the entire amount is deducted from the total trunk bandwidth along the path of the circuit. Compare with excess rate and maximum rate.

insured traffic Traffic within the insured rate specified for the permanent virtual circuit (PVC). This traffic should not be dropped by the network under normal network conditions. *See* CLP *and* insured rate.

integer A whole number.

integrated (*a*) A popular computer buzzword that refers to two or more components merged together into a single system. For example, any software product that performs more than one task can be described as integrated. (*b*) Increasingly, the term *integrated software* is reserved for applications that combine word processing, database management, spreadsheet functions, and communications into a single package.

integrated circuit (IC) A microchip; a small electronic device made out of a semiconductor material. The first integrated circuit was developed in the 1950s by Jack Kilby of Texas Instruments and Robert Noyce of Fairchild Semiconductor. Integrated circuits are used for a variety of devices, including microprocessors, audio and video equipment, and automobiles. Integrated circuits are often classified by the number of transistors and other electronic components they contain:

SI (small-scale integration): Up to 100 electronic components per chip

MSI (medium-scale integration): From 100 to 3,000 electronic components per chip

LSI (large-scale integration): From 3,000 to100,000 electronic components per chip

VLSI (very large-scale integration): From 100,000 to 1,000,000 electronic components per chip

ULSI (ultra large-scale integration): More than 1 million electronic components per chip.

integrated communication adapter (ICA) A communication adapter that is an integral part of the host processor.

integrated communication management (ICM) The RACE II project R2059.

Integrated IS-IS Routing protocol based on the OSI routing protocol IS-IS, but with support for IP and other protocols. Integrated IS-IS implementations send only one set of routing updates, making it more efficient than two separate implementations. Formerly referred to as *Dual IS-IS*. *See* IS-IS.

integrated local management interface (ILMI) An ATM Forum-defined network management system (NMS) based on SNMP. It provides configuration, performance, and fault-management information concerning virtual circuit (VC) connections available at its user-to-network interface (UNI) (public and private). It operates over AAL3/4 and AAL5 and will be replaced once it becomes standardized by ITU-T. Initially, the ATM Forum called this interface the *Interim Local Management Interface*.

Integrated Services Digital Network (ISDN) (*Illustration*) ISDN An international communications standard developed within ANSI, ISO, and CCITT for sending voice, video, and data over digital telephone lines. ISDN requires special metal wires and supports data transfer rates of 64 Kbps (64,000 bits per second).

Most ISDN lines offered by telephone companies supply two lines at once, called *B channels*.

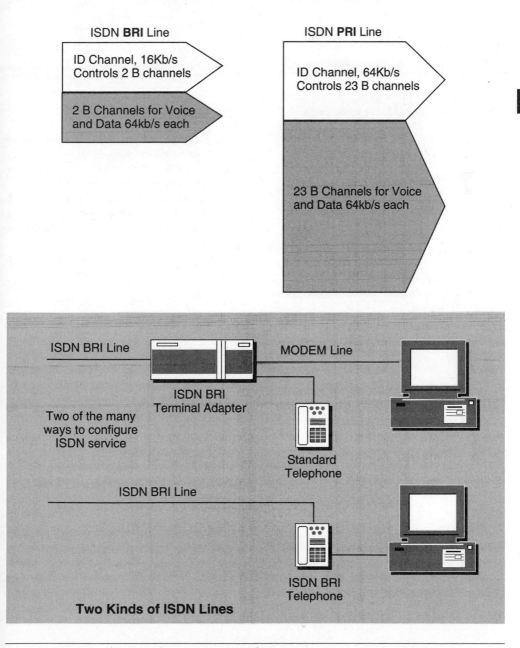

ISDN **BRI** Line

ID Channel, 16Kb/s
Controls 2 B channels

2 B Channels for Voice
and Data 64kb/s each

ISDN **PRI** Line

ID Channel, 64Kb/s
Controls 23 B channels

23 B Channels for Voice
and Data 64kb/s each

ISDN BRI Line

MODEM Line

ISDN BRI
Terminal Adapter

Two of the many
ways to configure
ISDN service

Standard
Telephone

ISDN BRI Line

ISDN BRI
Telephone

Two Kinds of ISDN Lines

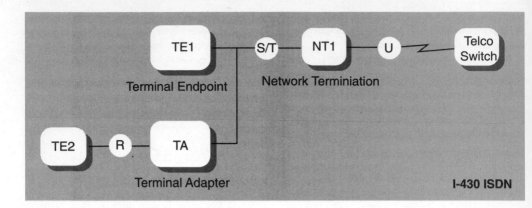

TE1 — S/T — NT1 — U — Telco Switch

Terminal Endpoint   Network Terminiation

TE2 — R — TA

Terminal Adapter

I-430 ISDN

One line may be used for voice and the other for data, or both lines can be used for data to obtain data rates of 128 Kbps—three times the data rate provided by today's fastest modems.

The two primary variants of ISDN are *basic rate interface (BRI)* and *primary rate interface (PRI)*. BRI, sometimes referred to as 2B+D, provides two 64 kbps B channels and a 16 kbps D channel over a single 192 kbps circuit (the remaining bandwidth is used for framing). BRI is the ISDN equivalent of a single phone line, though it can handle two calls simultaneously over its two B channels. PRI, essentially ISDN over T1, is referred to as 23B+D and provides 23 B channels and a 64 kbps D channel. PRI is intended for use by an Internet Service Provider, for example, multiplexing almost two dozen calls over a single pair of wires.

The international standard for the digital telephone network is *Signaling System 7 (SS-7)*, a protocol suite in its own right, roughly comparable to TCP/IP. End users never see SS-7, since it is only used between telephone switches. ISDN provides a fully digital user interface to the SS-7 network, capable of transporting either voice or data. BISDN (Broadband ISDN) uses ATM instead of SS-7 as the underlying networking technology.

ITU standard I.430 documents the physical layer and lower data-link layers of the ISDN BRI interface. The specification defines a number of reference points between the telco switch and the end system. The most important of these are S/T and U. The *U interface* is the local loop

between the telephone company and the customer premises. At the customer site, the 2-wire U interface is converted to a 4-wire S/T interface by an NT-1. Originally, the T interface was point-to-point and could be converted to a point-to-multipoint S interface by an NT-2. However, the electrical specification of the S and T interfaces were almost identical, so most modern NT-1s include built-in NT-2 functionality and can support either single or multiple ISDN devices on what is now called the *S/T interface*. The rarely used *R interface* is a normal serial connection, which allows non-ISDN devices to be connected via a Terminal Adapter.

In Europe and Japan, the telco owns the NT-1 and provides the S/T interface to the customer. In North America, however, largely due to the United States government's unwillingness to allow telephone companies to own customer premises equipment (such as the NT-1), the U interface is provided to the customer, who owns the NT-1.

integrity control According to Novell documentation, the method used to ensure the completeness of files. Specifically, Btrieve uses preimaging and NetWare's transaction tracking system to guarantee integrity.

Intel The world's largest manufacturer of computer chips. Although it has been challenged in recent years by newcomers AMD and Cyrix, Intel still dominates the market for PC microprocessors. Nearly all PCs are based on Intel's x86 architecture. Intel was founded in 1968 by Bob Noyce and Gordon Moore. Strategically, they are closely allied with Microsoft because the Windows 3.x and 95 operating systems are designed for x86 microprocessors.

intensive mode recording (IMR) An NCP function that forces the recording of temporary errors for a specified resource.

interactive Accepting input from a human. Interactive computer systems are programs that allow users to enter data or commands. Most popular programs, such as word processors and spreadsheet applications, are interactive.

interactive problem control system (IPCS) A component of virtual memory that permits online problem management, interactive problem diagnosis, online debugging for disk-resident CP a bend dumps, problem tracking, and problem reporting.

Interactive System Productivity Facility (ISPF) An IBM licensed program that serves as a full-screen editor and dialog manager. Used for writing application programs, it provides a means of generating standard screen panels and interactive dialogs between the application programmer and the terminal user.

interapplication communication In Apple terminology, a collection of features, provided by the edition manager, Apple event manager, event manager, and PPC toolbox, that help applications work together.

interarea routing Routing between two or more logical areas. Compare with intra-area routing.

Intercast A protocol created by Intel in 1996 for broadcasting information, such as Web pages and programs, along with television signals to a PC. With Intercast, a user can watch television on one portion of a PC monitor while receiving relevant information, often about the broadcast, from the Web on another. To browse the Web for information not being broadcast or not stored on the PC, however, the user must have Internet access through an Internet Service Provider; Intercast transmits in only one direction.

interchange node A new type of node supported by VTAM beginning in Version 4

Release 1. It acts as both an APPN network node and a subarea type 5 node to transform APPN protocols to subarea protocols and vice versa.

interdomain policy routing (IDPR) A routing protocol that dynamically exchanges policies between autonomous systems. IDPR encapsulates interautonomous system traffic and routes it according to the policies of each autonomous system along the path. IDPR is currently an IETF proposal. *See* policy routing.

interexchange carrier (IEC or IXC) A public switching network carrier that provides connectivity across and between LATAs.

interface A system's attachment point to a link. It is possible for a system to have more than one interface to the same link. Interfaces are uniquely identified by IP unicast addresses; a single interface may have more than one such address. An interface can be a connection between a router and one of its attached networks. A single IP address, domain name, or interface name can specify a physical interface (unless the network is an unnumbered point-to-point network).

Interface Message Processor (IMP) Archaic name for ARPANET packet switches. An IMP is now referred to as a packet-switch node (PSN). *See* packet-switch node (PSN).

Inter-IC (I2C) A type of bus which connects integrated circuits (ICs).

Interim Interswitch Signaling Protocol (IISP) A protocol that uses UNI-based signaling for switch-to-switch communication. *See* NNI.

Interior Gateway Protocol (IGP) Internet protocol used to exchange routing information within an autonomous system. Examples of common Internet IGPs include IGRP, OSPF, and RIP. *See* IGRP, OSPF, *and* RIP.

Interior Gateway Routing Protocol (IGRP) A proprietary dynamic routing protocol developed by Cisco to address the problems associated with routing in large, heterogeneous networks. *See* Enhanced IGRP, IGP, OSPF, *and* RIP.

interior routing A type of routing that occurs within an autonomous system. Most common routing protocols, such as RIP and OSPF, are interior routing protocols. The basic routable element is the IP network or subnetwork, or CIDR prefix for newer protocols.

inter-LATA Any phone service that occurs between local area transport areas (LATAs).

interleave To arrange data in a noncontiguous way to increase performance. When used to describe disk drives, it refers to the way sectors on a disk are organized. In one-to-one interleaving, the sectors are placed sequentially around each track. In two-to-one interleaving, sectors are staggered so that consecutively numbered sectors are separated by an intervening sector.

intermediate distribution frame (IDF) A structure where phone lines are terminated. Similar to a main distribution frame (MDF), an IDF is usually a phone line termination point for a floor's wiring domain, and usually connects to a central MDF somewhere else in the building. For example, a typical office building may have IDFs located on each floor, all cabled back to the MDF in the basement.

intermediate network node (INN) A node located at the end of more than one branch.

intermediate routing node (IRN) In SNA, a subarea node with intermediate routing capability. A node containing intermediate routing function.

intermediate session routing In APPN, a type of routing function within an APPN network node that provides session-level flow control and outage reporting for all sessions that pass through the node but whose endpoints are elsewhere.

Intermediate System-to-Intermediate System (IS-IS) OSI link-state hierarchical routing protocol based on DECnet Phase V routing. Routers exchange routing information based on a single metric to determine network topology. Compare with Integrated IS-IS. See ES-IS *and* OSPF.

internal command In DOS systems, any command that resides in the COMMAND.COM file.

international code designator (ICD) One of two ATM address formats developed by the ATM Forum for use by private networks for mapping network layer addresses to ATM addresses. See DCC.

international data number See X.121.

International Organization for Standardization (ISO) An organization of national standards-making bodies from various countries established to promote development of standards to facilitate international exchange of goods and services, and develop cooperation in intellectual, scientific, technological, and economic activity. One such standard is *Open Systems Interconnection (OSI)*.

International Standardization for Organization (ISO) A special agency of the United Nations, charged with the development of communication standards for computers. Membership in the ISO consists of representatives from international standards organizations throughout the world. Note that ISO is not an acronym; instead, the name derives from the Greek word *iso*, which means equal.

International Telecommunication Union (ITU) An intergovernmental organization through which public and private organizations develop telecommunications. The ITU was founded in 1865 and became a United Nations agency in 1947. It is responsible for adopting international treaties, regulations and standards governing telecommunications. The standardization functions were formerly performed by a group within the ITU called CCITT, but after a 1992 reorganization the CCITT no longer exists as a separate body.

International Telecommunications Union-Telecommunications Standards Sector (ITU-T) A formal international standards, specifications, and recommendations body, formerly known as CCITT–ITU-T is part of the International Telecommunications Union (ITU) founded in 1948 and sponsored by the United Nations to promote telephone and telegraphy issues.

Internet A collection of networks, routers, gateways, and other networking devices that use the TCP/IP protocol suite and function as a single, cooperative virtual network. The Internet provides universal connectivity and three levels of network services: unreliable, connectionless packet delivery; reliable, full-duplex stream delivery; and application-level services such as electronic mail that build on the first two. The Internet reaches many universities, government research labs, and military installations. As of 1998, the Internet had more than 100 million users worldwide, and that number is growing rapidly. More than 100 countries are linked into exchanges of data, news and opinions.

Unlike online services, which are centrally controlled, the Internet is decentralized by design. Each Internet computer, called a *host*, is independent. Its operators can choose which Internet services to use and which local services to make available to the global Internet community. Remarkably, this anarchy-by-design works exceedingly well. There are a variety of ways to access the Internet. Most online services, such as America Online, offer access to some Internet services. It is also pos-sible to gain access through a commercial *Internet service provider (ISP)*.

internet Any two or more networks connect-ed together. *See* Internet, network.

Internet Access Coalition (IAC) A consortium of companies whose goal is to make access to the Internet inexpensive and easily available.

Internet access provider (IAP) (*Illustration*) A company that provides access to the Internet. IAPs generally provide dial-up access through a modem and PPP connection. IAPs are not the same as *Internet Service Providers (ISPs)*. IAPs only offer Internet access; ISPs may also provide Web development or leased lines.

Internet address A 32-bit address assigned to the host. It is a software address that on local networks is locally managed, but on the central Internet is dictated to the user (entity desiring access to the Internet). The current Internet addressing scheme follows what is called IPV4. Over the past few years there has been work underway to increase the Internet address space. This effort is called *IPv6*. *See* IP address.

I

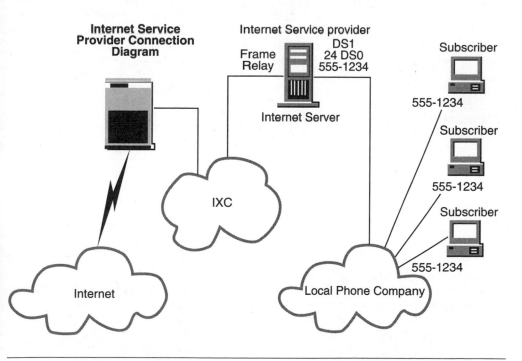

Internet Service Provider Connection Diagram

Internet Service provider

Frame Relay

DS1
24 DS0
555-1234

Internet Server

Subscriber
555-1234

Subscriber
555-1234

Subscriber
555-1234

IXC

Internet

Local Phone Company

Internet Architecture Board (IAB) A group overseeing the TCP/IP protocol, which sets policy and reviews standards for TCP/IP and the Internet. The IAB was reorganized in 1989; technically oriented individuals moved to research and engineering subgroups. The board is responsible for appointing a variety of Internet-related groups such as the IANA, IESG, and IRSG. As a technical advisory group of the ISOC, the IAB is chartered to provide oversight of the architecture of the Internet and its protocols, and to serve, in the context of the Internet standards process, as a body to which the decisions of the IESG may be appealed. The IAB is responsible for approving appointments to the IESG from among the nominees submitted by the IETF nominations committee (RFC 1718). *See* IANA, IESG, IRSG, ISOC, IRTF, *and* IETF.

For more information, the IAB can be contacted at *iab-contact@ isi.edu*. For more information, go to *http://www.ietf.org*.

Internet Assigned Number Authority (IANA) Many protocol specifications include numbers, keywords, and other parameters that must be uniquely assigned. Examples include version numbers, protocol numbers, port numbers, and MIB numbers. The IAB has delegated to the Internet Assigned Numbers Authority (IANA) the task of assigning such protocol parameters for the Internet. The IANA publishes tables of all currently assigned numbers and parameters in RFCs titled "Assigned Numbers" (RFC 1602). *See* IAB, ISOC, *and* NIC.

For more information, The IANA maintains a web page at *http://www.isi.edu/iana/* and can be contacted at *iana@isi.edu*.

Internet Control Message Protocol (ICMP) An extension to the *Internet Protocol (IP)*, defined by RFC 792 and specific to the TCP/IP protocol suite. It is an integral part of the Internet protocol. ICMP supports packets containing error, control, and informational messages. The *Ping* command, for example, uses ICMP to test an Internet connection. ICMP messages, delivered in IP packets, are used for out-of-band messages related to network operation or mis-operation. Of course, since ICMP uses IP, ICMP packet delivery is unreliable, so hosts can't count on receiving ICMP packets for any network problem. Some of ICMP's functions are to:

Announce network errors, such as a host or entire portion of the network being unreachable, due to some type of failure. A TCP or UDP packet directed at a port number with no receiver attached is also reported via ICMP.

Announce network congestion. When a router begins buffering too many packets, due to an inability to transmit them as fast as they are being received, it will generate ICMP *source quench* messages. Directed at the sender, these messages should cause the rate of packet transmission to be slowed. Of course, generating too many source quench messages would cause even more network congestion, so they are used sparingly.

Assist Troubleshooting. ICMP supports an *echo* function, which just sends a packet on a round-trip between two hosts. Ping, a common network management tool, is based on this feature. Ping transmits a series of packets, measuring average round—trip times and computing loss percentages.

Announce Time-outs. If an IP packet's TTL field drops to zero, the router discarding the packet will often generate an ICMP packet announcing this fact. *TraceRoute* is a tool which maps network routes by sending packets with small TTL values and watching the ICMP time-out announcements.

Internet datagram The unit of data exchanged between an Internet module and the higher level protocol together with the Internet header.

Internet Engineering Steering Group (IESG) The organization responsible for technical management of IETF activities and the Internet standards process. As part of the

ISOC, it administers the process according to the rules and procedures which have been ratified by the ISOC Trustees. The IESG is directly responsible for the actions associated with entry into and movement along the Internet "standards track," including final approval of specifications as Internet Standards. The IESG can be contacted at iesg@cnri.reston.va.us. *See* IAB and IETF.

Internet Engineering Task Force (IETF) The main standards organization of the Internet. A loosely self-organized group of network designers, operators, vendors, and researchers who make technical and other contributions to the engineering and evolution of the Internet and its technologies. It is the principal body engaged in the development of new Internet standard specifications.

Its mission includes identifying, and proposing solutions to, pressing operational and technical problems in the Internet; specifying the development or usage of protocols and the near-term architecture to solve such technical problems for the Internet; making recommendations to the Internet Engineering Steering Group (IESG) regarding the standardization of protocols and protocol usage in the Internet; facilitating technology transfer from the Internet Research Task Force (IRTF) to the wider Internet community; and providing a forum for the exchange of information within the Internet community between vendors, users, researchers, agency contractors and network managers.

The IETF is divided into eight functional areas: Applications, Internet, Network Management, Operational Requirements, Routing, Security, Transport, and User Services. Each area has one or two area directors. The area directors, along with the IETF/IESG Chair, form the IESG. Each area has several *working groups*.

The individuals belonging to the working group work under a charter to achieve a certain goal. That goal may be the creation of an informational document, the creation of a protocol specification, or the resolution of problems in the Internet. Most working groups have a finite lifetime. That is, once a working group has achieved its goal, it disbands. As in the IETF, there is no official membership for a working group. Unofficially, a working group member is somebody who is on that working group's mailing list; however, anyone may attend a working group meeting (RFC 1718).

The IETF and its various working groups maintain numerous mailing lists. To join the IETF announcement list, send a request to *ietf-announce-request@cnri.reston.va.us*. To join the IETF discussion list, send a request to *ietf-request@cnri.reston.va.us*.

 For more information, see *http://www.ietf.org*.

Internet Explorer Microsoft's Web browser. Like Netscape Navigator, Internet Explorer enables the user to view Web pages. Both browsers support Java and JavaScript. Internet Explorer also supports ActiveX.

internet foundation classes (IFC) A set of Java classes developed by Netscape, which enables programmers to easily add GUI elements, such as windows, menus, and buttons.

Internet Gateway Routing Protocol (IGRP) A proprietary protocol designed for Cisco routers.

Internet group Multicast routers use this protocol to learn the existence of host group

Internet Group Management Protocol (IGMP) A protocol, documented in Appendix I of RFC 1112, which allows Internet hosts to participate in multicasting. RFC 1112 describes the basics of multicasting IP traffic, including the format of multicast IP addresses, multicast Ethernet encapsulation, and the concept of a *host group*, which is the set of hosts interested in traffic for a particular multicast address. Important multicast addresses are documented in the most recent Assigned Numbers RFC, currently RFC 1700. IGMP allows a router to determine which host groups have members on a given network segment. The exchange of multicast packets between routers is not addressed by IGMP.

Internet Information Server (IIS)
Microsoft's Web server that runs on Windows NT platforms. IIS comes bundled with Windows NT 4.0. Because IIS is tightly integrated with the operating system, it is relatively easy to administer. Currently, IIS is available only for the Windows NT platform, whereas Netscape's Web servers run on all major platforms, including Windows NT, OS/2, and UNIX.

Internet International Ad Hoc Committee (IAHC) The organization which managed the Internet's Domain Name System (DNS). The Committee was dissolved on May 1, 1997.

Internet Inter-ORB Protocol (IIOP) A protocol developed by the *Object Management Group (OMG)* to implement CORBA solutions over the World Wide Web. IIOP enables browsers and servers to exchange integers, arrays, and more complex objects—unlike *Hypertext Transfer Protocol (HTTP)*, which only supports transmission of text.

Internet Message Access Protocol (IMAP) A protocol for retrieving e-mail messages, documented in RFC 2060. It represents an improvement over *Post Office Protocol (POP)*. The latest version, IMAP4, is similar to POP3 but supports some additional features. For example, with IMAP4, a user can search through e-mail messages for keywords while the messages are still on the mail server. Messages can be chosen to download to the user's machine. Like POP, IMAP uses *simple mail transfer protocol (SMTP)* for communication between the e-mail client and server. IMAP was developed at Stanford University in 1986.

Internet organization The Internet; a loosely-organized international collaboration of autonomous, interconnected networks, supports host-to-host communication through voluntary adherence to open protocols and procedures defined by Internet standards. There are also many isolated internets, i.e., sets of interconnected networks, which are not connected to the Internet but use the Internet Standards (RFC 1602). The Internet is neither owned nor controlled by any one group. Rather, participation in the Internet derives from voluntary participation in Internet standards. Many Internet providers not only adhere to these standards, but make access to their networks available to the public. It is the voluntary interconnection and cooperation of these providers that forms the global Internet.

Internet packet exchange (IPX) A Novell protocol that operates at OSI layer 3. It is used in the NetWare protocols; it is similar to IP in TCP/IP.

Internet Printing Protocol (IPP) A protocol that defines for end users' use most common printing situations over the Internet. First drafted between Novell and Xerox with necessary support from Internet Engineering Task Force (IETF).

Internet protocol (IP) A protocol used to route data from its source to its destination. A part of TCP/IP protocol.

Internet Protocol Control Protocol (IPCP) Part of the PPP protocol negotiation.

Internet Relay Chat (IRC) A chat system developed by Jarkko Oikarinen in Finland in the late 1980s. IRC has become very popular as more people get connected to the Internet because it enables people connected anywhere on the Internet to join in live discussions. Unlike older chat systems, IRC is not limited to just two participants. To join an IRC discussion, a user needs an IRC client and Internet access. The IRC client is a program that runs on a computer and sends and receives messages to and from an IRC server. The IRC server, in turn, is responsible for making sure that all messages are broadcast to everyone participating in a discussion. There can be many discussions going on at once; each one is assigned a unique channel.

Internet Research Steering Group (IRSG) A committee consisting of the IRTF research group chairpersons plus the IRTF chairperson, who direct and coordinate research related to TCP/IP and the connected Internet.

Internet Research Task Force (IRTF) A group of people working on research problems related to TCP/IP and the connected Internet.

Internet Server API (ISAPI) An API for Microsoft's Internet Information Server (IIS) Web server. ISAPI enables programmers to develop Web-based applications that run much faster than conventional CGI programs because they're more tightly integrated with the Web server. In addition to IIS, several Web servers from companies other than Microsoft support ISAPI.

Internet service A business that provides subscription services, such as online information.

Internet service provider (ISP) A company that provides access to the Internet. For a monthly fee, the service provider gives a subscriber a software package, username, password, and access phone number. Equipped with a modem, the user may log on to the Internet and browse the World Wide Web and USENET, and send and receive e-mail. In addition to serving individuals, ISPs also serve large companies, providing a direct connection from the company's networks to the Internet. ISPs themselves are connected to one another through *network access points (NAPs)*. ISPs are also called *Internet access providers (IAPs)*.

Internet Society (ISOC) A professional society that is concerned with the growth and evolution of the worldwide Internet; with the way in which the Internet is and can be used; and with the social, political, and technical issues which arise as a result. The ISOC Trustees are responsible for approving appointments to the IAB from among the nominees submitted by the IETF nominating committee (RFC 1718).

 For more information, ISOC maintains a web page at *http://www.isoc.org*. The ISOC Executive Directory can be contacted at *amr@isoc.org*.

Internetwork Packet Exchange (IPX) A networking protocol used by the Novell NetWare operating systems. Like UDP/IP, IPX is a datagram protocol used for connectionless communications. Higher-level protocols, such as SPX and NCP, are used for additional error

recovery services. The successor to IPX is the *NetWare Link Services Protocol (NLSP)*.

Internetwork Packet Exchange/ Sequenced Packet Exchange (IPX/SPX) (*Illustration*) Network protocol used by Novell NetWare.

Service type	Value
User	1
User group	2
Print queue	3
File server	4
Job server	5
Gateway	6
Print server	7
Archive server	9
Archive queue	8
Job queue	A
Administration	B
SNA gateway	21
NAS gateway	29
TCP/IP gateway	27
Time synchronization server	2D
Print queue user	53
Network access server	98
Portable NetWare	9E
Wildcard	FFFF
NNS domain	133
NetWare 386 print server	137
NetWare 386	107
Communication execution	130
Advertising print server	47

Internetworking Operating System (IOS) The Operating System of most Cisco devices.

 For more information, see *http://www.cisco.com*.

InterNIC A collaborative project between AT&T and Network Solutions, Inc. (NSI) supported by the National Science Foundation. The Internet Network Information Center, has two major components. AT&T provides Directory and Database Services, most importantly the *Internet White Pages*, used by the *Whois* program to locate people, networks, and domains. Network Solutions, Inc. provides

Registration Services, including domain name registration. Originally funded by NSF, InterNIC is becoming self-sufficient.

InterNIC currently offers the following services:

InterNIC Directory and Database Services: Online white pages directory and directory of publicly accessible databases managed by AT&T.

Registration Services: Domain name and IP address assignment managed by NSI.

Support Services: Outreach, education, and information services for the Internet community managed by NSI.

Net Scout Services: Online publications that summarize recent happenings of interest to Internet users (managed by NSI).

 For more information, InterNIC maintains a web page at *http://www.internic.net/*.

interpersonal message (IPM) In OSI-related documents, it is defined as a type of message used for human-to-human communication in MHS.

interpersonal messaging system (IPMS) An MHS system supporting the communication of interpersonal messages.

InterPoll Apple software that helps administrators monitor the network and diagnose the source of problems that arise.

interpreter A program that executes instructions written in a high-level language. There are two ways to run programs written in a high-level language. The most common is to compile the program; the other method is to pass the program through an interpreter.

interrupt (*n*) A signal informing a program that an event has occurred. When a program receives an interrupt signal, it takes a specified action (which can be to ignore the signal). Interrupt signals can cause a program to suspend itself temporarily to service the interrupt. Interrupt signals can come from a variety of sources. For example, every keystroke gen-erates an interrupt signal. Interrupts can also be generated by other devices, such as a printer, to indicate that some event has occurred. These are called *hardware interrupts*. Interrupt signals initiated by programs are called *software interrupts, traps* or *exceptions*. PCs support 256 types of software interrupts and 15 hardware interrupts. Each type of software interrupt is associated with an *interrupt handler*—a routine that takes control when the interrupt occurs. For example, when you press a key on your keyboard, this triggers a specific interrupt handler. The complete list of interrupts and associated interrupt handlers is stored in a table called the *interrupt vector table*, which resides in the first 1 K of addressable memory. (*v*) To send an interrupt signal.

interrupt request line (IRQ) Hardware lines over which devices can send interrupt signals to the microprocessor. When a new device is added to a PC, its IRQ number is set with a DIP switch. This specifies which interrupt line the device may use. IRQ conflicts used to be a common problem when adding expansion boards, but the plug-and-play specification has removed this headache in most cases. *See* interrupt request.

interuser communication vehicle (IUCV) According to IBM documentation, a virtual machine facility for passing data between virtual machines and VM components.

intra-area routing Routing within a logical area. Compare with interarea routing.

Intra-LATA Any phone service that happens within a LATA.

intranet A private network based on TCP/IP protocols (an internet) belonging to an organization, usually a corporation, accessible only by the organization's members, employees, or others with authorization. An intranet's Web sites look and act just like any other Web sites, but the firewall surrounding an intranet fends off unauthorized access. Like the Internet itself, intranets are used to share information. Secure intranets are the fastest-growing segment of the Internet because they are much less expensive to build and manage than private networks based on proprietary protocols. *See* internet, Internet, *and* network.

Inverse Address Resolution Protocol A method of building dynamic routes in a network. This allows an access server to discover the network address of a device associated with a virtual circuit.

invocation The execution of a program or function.

invoke To activate. One usually speaks of invoking a function or routine in a program. In this sense, the term invoke is synonymous with call.

IOS *See* Internetworking Operating System.

IP *See* Internet Protocol.

IP address The 32-bit dotted-decimal address assigned to hosts as an identifier for a computer or device on a TCP/IP network that wants to participate in a local TCP/IP internet or the central (connected) Internet. IP addresses are software addresses. An IP address consists of a network portion and a host portion. The partition makes routing efficient. Networks using the TCP/IP protocol route messages based on the IP address of the destination.

The format of an IP address is a 32-bit numeric address written as four numbers separated by periods. Each number can be zero to 255. For example, 1.160.10.240 is an IP address. These numbers are placed in the IP packet header and are used to route packets to their destination. Within an isolated network, you can assign IP addresses at random as long as each one is unique. However, connecting a private network to the Internet requires using registered IP addresses (called *Internet addresses*) to avoid duplication. The four numbers in an IP address are used in different ways to identify a particular network and a host on that network.

An IP address has five classes, three of which (A, B, and C) are primary. The InterNIC Registration Service assigns Internet addresses from the following three classes:

Class A: Supports 16 million hosts on each of 127 networks.

Class B: Supports 65,000 hosts on each of 16,000 networks.

Class C: Supports 254 hosts on each of 2 million networks.

The number of unassigned Internet addresses is running out, so a new classless scheme called *classless interdomain routing (CIDR)* is gradually replacing the system based on classes A, B, and C and is tied to adoption of IPv6. *See* domain name, Internet, *and* TCP/IP.

IP datagram In TCP/IP networks, a basic unit of information passed across a TCP/IP internet. An IP datagram is to an internet as a hardware packet is to a physical network. It contains a source address and a destination address along with data.

IP Multicast A one-to-many transmission described in RFC 1112. The RFC describes IP multicasting as: "the transmission of an IP datagram to a *host group*, a set of zero or more hosts identified by a single IP destination address. A multicast datagram is delivered to all members of its destination host group with the same best-efforts reliability as regular unicast IP datagrams. The membership of a host group is dynamic; that is, hosts may join and leave groups at any time. There is no restriction on the location or number of members in a host group. A host may be a member of more than one group at a time."

IPCP *See* Internet Protocol Control Protocol.

IPCS *See* interactive problem control system.

IPM *See* interpersonal message.

IPMS *See* interpersonal messaging system.

IPng Internet Protocol next generation. A new version of the Internet Protocol (IP) currently being reviewed in IETF standards committees. The official name of IPng is IPv6, or Internet Protocol version 6. The current version of IP is version 4 (IPv4). IPng is designed as an evolutionary upgrade to the Internet Protocol and will, in fact, coexist with the older IPv4 for some time. IPng is designed to allow the Internet to grow steadily, both in terms of the number of hosts connected and the total amount of data traffic transmitted.

IPP *See* Internet Printing Protocol.

IPsec IP Security. A set of protocols being developed by the IETF to support secure exchange of packets at the IP layer. Once it's completed, IPsec is expected to be deployed widely to implement *virtual private networks (VPNs)*. IPsec supports two encryption modes: *transport* and *tunnel*. Transport mode encrypts only the data portion (payload) of each packet, but leaves the header untouched. The more secure tunnel mode encrypts both the header and the payload. On the receiving side, an IPSec-compliant device decrypts each packet. For IPsec to work, the sending and receiving devices must share a public key. This is accomplished through a protocol known as *Internet Security Association and Key Management Protocol/Oakley (ISAKMP/Oakley)*, which allows the receiver to obtain a public key and authenticate the sender using digital certificates.

IPv6 *See* IPng.

IPX *See* Internetwork Packet Exchange.

IPX/SPX *See* Internetwork Packet Exchange/Sequenced Packet Exchange.

IPXWAN A protocol that negotiates end-to-end options for new WAN links, defined by RFC-1362. When a link comes up, the first IPX packets sent across are IPXWAN packets negotiating the options for the link. When the IPXWAN options have been successfully determined, normal IPX transmission begins.

IR *See* infrared.

IRC *See* Internet Relay Chat.

IRMA board A popular expansion board for PCs and Macintoshes that enables these personal computers to emulate IBM 3278 and 3279 mainframe terminals. Personal computers with IRMA boards can function as both stand-alone computers and as terminals connected to a mainframe computer. IRMA boards are manufactured by DCA.

IRN *See* intermediate routing node.

IRQ *See* interrupt request line.

IRSG *See* Internet Research Steering Group.

IRTF *See* Internet Research Task Force.

IS *See* information systems *or* information services.

ISA *See* Industry-Standard Architecture.

ISAM *See* indexed sequential access method.

ISAPI *See* Internet Server API.

ISDN *See* Integrated Services Digital Network

IS-IS *See* Intermediate System-to-Intermediate System.

IS-IS Hello (IIH) Message sent by all IS-IS systems to maintain adjacencies. *See* IS-IS.

IS-IS Interdomain Routing Protocol (IDRP) An OSI protocol that specifies how routers communicate with routers in different domains.

IS-IS routing Routing between intermediate systems (IS) within a routing domain.

ISO *See* International Standardization for Organization *and* International Organizaton for Standardization.

ISO 3309 ISO 3309:1979 specifies the HDLC frame structure for use in synchronous environments. ISO3309:1984 specifies proposed modifications to allow the use of HDLC in asynchronous environments as well.

ISO 9000 A family of standards (ISO 900X) approved by the International Standards Organization (ISO) that define a quality assurance program. Companies that conform to these standards can receive ISO 9000 certification. This doesn't necessarily mean that the company's products have a high quality; only that the company follows well-defined procedures for ensuring quality products. Increasingly, software buyers are requiring ISO 9000 certification from their suppliers.

ISO Development Environment (ISODE) A set of public-domain software subroutines that provide an interface between the GOSIP-specified session layer (ISO) and the DoD-specified transport layer (TCP/IP). This allows the development of applications that will execute over both OSI and TCP/IP protocol stacks as a migration path from TCP/IP networks to GOSIP networks.

ISOC *See* Internet Society.

isochronous A time slot divided into equal-size minislots and allocated to different channels for synchronous transmission of information (used in DQDB). For example, multimedia streams require an isochronous transport mechanism to ensure that data is delivered as fast as it is displayed and to ensure that the audio is synchronized with the video. Isochronous can be contrasted with *asynchronous*, which refers to processes in which data streams can be broken by random intervals, and *synchronous* processes, in which data streams can be delivered only at specific intervals. Isochronous service is not as rigid as synchronous service, but not as lenient as asynchronous service. Certain types of networks, such as ATM, are said to be isochronous because they can guarantee a specified throughput. Likewise, new bus architectures, such as IEEE 1394, support isochronous delivery.

ISODE *See* ISO Development Environment.

ISP *See* Internet service provider.

ISPF *See* Interactive System Productivity Facility.

ISR *See* intermediate session routing.

IT *See* information technology.

iteration A single pass through a group of instructions. Most programs contain loops of instructions that are executed over and over again. The computer iterates through the loop, which means that it repeatedly executes the loop.

ITU *See* International Telecommunication Union.

ITU-T *See* International Telecommunications Union-Telecommunications Standards Sector.

IUCV *See* interuser communication vehicle.

IXC *See* interexchange carrier.

I

J

jabber Used to describe an error caused by a network device that is continuously transmitting on the network. Jabber is especially harmful in contention-based networks such as Ethernet, because its transmissions adversely affects network performance.

JANET *See* Joint Academic Network.

Japan UNIX Network (JUNET) A nationwide network that is designed between researchers within Japan and elsewhere.

JAR *See* Java archive.

Java A network-oriented programming language, originally called Oak, invented by Sun Microsystems that is specifically designed for writing programs that can be safely downloaded to a computer through the Internet and immediately run without fear of viruses or other harm to your computer or files. Using small Java programs (called *applets*), Web pages can include functions such as animations, calculators, and other fancy tricks. A huge variety of features can be added to the Web using Java, because a Java program can be written to do almost anything a regular computer program can do. That program is then included in a Web page. *See* applet.

For Cut-N-Paste JavaScript, go to *http://www.infohiway.com/ javascript/indexf.htm*.

Java archive (JAR) A file format used to bundle all components (.class files, images, sounds, etc.) required by a Java applet in order to simplify downloading.

Java database connectivity (JDBC) A Java API that enables Java programs to execute SQL statements

Java Development Kit (JDK) A software development package from Sun Microsystems that implements the basic set of tools needed to write, test, and debug Java applications and applets. *See* applet *and* Java.

JavaBeans A specification developed by Sun Microsystems that defines how Java objects interact with each other. This specification allows applications to be run in the JavaBeans format and then run on any platform.

JavaScript An open scripting language developed by Netscape (not with Sun, the creators of Java) to enable Web authors to interact with HTML source code, enabling Web authors to spice up their sites with dynamic content.

JavaSoft The business unit within Sun Microsystems that is responsible for Java technology.

JCL *See* job control language.

JDBC *See* Java database connectivity.

JDK *See* Java Development Kit.

JET *See* joint engine technology.

Jini Pronounced GEE-nee; the name is loosely derived from the Arabic word for magician. Software from Sun Microsystems that seeks to simplify the connection and sharing of devices, such as printers and disk drives, on a network. Currently, adding a new device to a computer or network requires installation and a reboot, but a device that incorporates Jini will announce itself to the network, provide some details about its capabilities, and immediately become accessible to other devices on the network, thus creating distributed computing, whereby capabilities are shared among the machines on a common network.

jitter (*a*) Flickering on a display screen. (*b*) Distortion of a signal or image caused by poor synchronization. (*c*) Delay variation of a signal.

job A task performed by a computer system such as printing a file.

job control language (JCL) A language used in IBM's MVS operating system environment to identify a job and its requirements to the operating system

job controller The system process that establishes a job's process context, starts a process running the login image for the job, maintains the accounting record for the job, manages symbionts, and terminates a process and its subprocesses.

job information block A data structure associated with a job that contains the quotas pooled by all processes in the job.

John von Neumann Computer Network (JvNCnet) A network, found in the Northeastern United States, which provides mid-level networking.

join In relational databases, a join operation matches records in two tables when they share at least one common field.

Joint Academic Network (JANET) The name of the WAN network that connects research and universities computers in the United Kingdom.

joint engine technology (JET) A database engine used by Microsoft Office and Visual Basic.

Joint Photographic Experts Group (JPEG) A standard developed for encoding, transmitting, and decoding still images. JPEG is most commonly mentioned as a format for image files. JPEG format is preferred to the GIF format for photographic images as opposed to line art or simple logo art. *See* GIF.

Joint Technical Committee (JTC) A committee developed to define IT standards to meet business needs.

 For more information, see *www.jtc1.org*.

JPEG *See* Joint Photographic Experts Group.

JScript Microsoft's version of JavaScript, which is built into Internet Explorer (IE) browsers. Unfortunately, Netscape's JavaScript and JScript are not entirely compatible, so Web pages containing JavaScript/JScript code may run properly in a Navigator browser, but not in an IE browser, or vice versa.

JTC *See* Joint Technical Committee.

Jughead A search engine for Gopher sites; similar to Veronica but with fewer options and resources.

jukebox A device that stores numerous CD-ROMs and uses a mechanical arm or some other physical method to load additional CD-ROMs.

jumper A metal bridge, typically covered in plastic that encloses an pair of pins, thus completing a electrical circuit.

JUNET *See* Japan UNIX Network.

Just a Bunch of Disks A term used to describe hard disks that configured with RAID.

JvNCnet *See* John von Neumann Computer Network.

K *See* kilo-.

K56flex Modem technology developed by Rockwell International Corporation and Lucent Technologies for receiving data at a rate of 56Kbps over phone lines. K56flex chips in modems achieve higher speeds than 33.6 Kbps on plain old telephone services (POTS) or twisted-pair phone lines by utilizing the phone company's high-speed digital network. An ISP connects directly to the central office's digital network and bypasses the digital-to-analog conversion. Modems can then accept and decode the digital downstream traffic (data that is sent to a computer); however, the upstream traffic (data sent by a computer) still undergoes the digital-to-analog conversion and therefore is transmitted at 33.6Kbps. K56flex technology, along with X2 technology from US Robotics (now part of 3COM), gave way to the V.90 technology standard, which was approved by the International Telecommunications Union (ITU) and provided as a software upgrade by many vendors.

K6 A microprocessor from AMD, which is completely compatible with Intel's Pentium processors and supports the MMX instruction set.

KB *See* kilobyte.

kbits *See* kilobits.

Kbps *See* kilobits per second.

kbyte *See* kilobyte.

keepalive interval A value for the time between keepalive messages.

keepalive message A message to inform a network device that the established connection is still active.

Kerberos A secured authentication system developed at the Massachusetts Institute of Technology (MIT), designed for an open network such as the Internet. The Kerberos system uses an encrypted "ticket" or key, which is embedded in the message. No password information is sent across the network.

Kermit A communications protocol used with modem connections. Also a set of associated software utilities to transfer files or for terminal emulation, developed at Columbia University.

kernel The central module that loads first in an operating system and stays in memory. It provides all the essential services required by other parts of the operating system and by applications.

key (*a*) A button on a keyboard. (*b*) In database management systems, a key is a field used to sort data. (*c*) A password or table needed to decipher encoded data.

keyboard binding An association of a special keypress with a window manager function. For example, pressing the key combination of Shift-Esc displays the system menu of the active window.

keyboard A device that enables the user to enter data into a computer, laid out similar to an electric-typewriter but containing additional keys. The alphanumeric keys of a keyboard represent letters and numbers. The punctuation keys represent the comma, period, semicolon, and more. Special keys on a computer keyboard include the *function keys*, which control certain computer operations; *control* and *alt keys*, which allow the user to alter the response of other keystrokes; and *arrow keys*, which allow navigation across the display screen.

keystroke The pressing of a key. The efficiency of software programs can sometimes be measured by the number of keystrokes it requires to perform a specific function.

keyword (*a*) In text editing and database management systems, an index entry that identifies a specific record or document. (*b*) In programming, a word that is reserved by a program because the word has a special meaning.

kHz *See* kilohertz.

kilo- (K) A unit of measure equaling 1,000 in the metric system. Often seen as an abbreviation for kilobyte (KB). *See* kilobyte.

kilobits (kbits) One thousand bits. The measurement of kilobits per second (kbits/s) is used to designate a data transfer rate of one thousand bits per second.

kilobits per second (Kbps) A measure of data transfer speed.

kilobyte (KB) In the metric system, 1,000 bytes. However, KB can also represent 1,024 bytes when used to describe data storage because the binary value closest to 1,000 bytes is 1,024.

kilohertz (kHz) One thousand hertz. KHz is used to measure signal bandwidth.

kilometer (km) A metric measure of distance, meaning 1,000 meters. In large networks that span large areas, the physical distance between network nodes may affect network design, configuration, and performance.

kludge Derogatory term used to describe a poor solution or design.

km *See* kilometer.

L

L1 cache Level-1 cache memory. Usually built onto the microprocessor chip itself, such as with the Intel MMX microprocessor, which comes with 32,000 bytes of L1. If the computer processor can find the data it needs for its next operation in cache memory, it will save time over having to get it from random access memory.

L2 cache Level-2 cache memory, or *secondary cache*. Usually built on a separate chip or an expansion card, which can be accessed more quickly than the larger "main" memory. A popular L2 cache memory size is 1,024 kilobytes (one megabyte).

L2F *See* Layer 2 Forwarding Protocol.

L2TP *See* Layer Two Tunneling Protocol.

LAA *See* locally administered address.

label swapping Routing algorithm used by APPN in which each router along the route when a message passes on its way to its destination independently determines the best path to the next router. An identifier in the header (i.e., a label) is swapped for the outgoing identifier. The packet is then sent out on the appropriate port to the next router.

LAG *See* logical address group.

lamer Used on interactive Web sites to describe an irritating or immature participant. Among users of Internet Relay Chat (IRC), a lamer is someone who irritates other users by typing in all caps or randomly mixed-case letters (iN pART cAPS), by insulting and flaming other users, by typing abbreviations for almost every word, or by performing other annoying acts in chat rooms.

LAN *See* local area network.

LAN adapter A circuit board installed in workstations that connects the workstation with the LAN media.

LAN emulation (LANE) A technique that specifies the interfaces and protocols needed to provide LAN-supported functionality and connectivity in an ATM environment. This allows legacy LAN protocols to be interoperable with the ATM protocols, interfaces, and devices.

LAN emulation ARP (LE-ARP) A type of ARP used in LAN emulation to bind a requested ATM address to a MAC address.

LAN emulation configuration server (LECS) A server whose main function is to provide configuration information to an LEC (such as the ELAN to which it belongs, or to its LES).

LAN emulation network node interface (LENNI or LNNI) Specifies the NNI operation between the LANE servers (LES, LECS, BUS).

LAN emulation server (LES) A server which provides support for the *LAN emulation Address Resolution Protocol (LE-ARP)*. The LAN emulation clients (LECs) register their own ATM and MAC addresses with the LES. A LES is uniquely identified by an ATM address.

LAN emulation service An ATM Forum-appointed technical workgroup to address the standards and specifications for LAN emulation (LANE).

LAN emulation user network interface (LUNI) Specifies the UNI between an LEC and the network providing the LAN emulation.

LAN Manager A distributed network operating system (NOS), developed by Microsoft, which supports a variety of protocols and platforms.

LAN Server A local area network (LAN) server-based NOS developed by IBM and derived from LNM. *See* LAN Network Manager.

LAN switch A high-speed switch that forwards packets between data-link segments. Most LAN switches forward traffic based on MAC addresses. This type of LAN switch is sometimes called a *frame switch*. LAN switches are often categorized according to the method they use to forward traffic: *cut-through packet switches* or *store-and-forward packet switches*. *Multilayer switches* are an intelligent subset of LAN switches. *See* cut-through packet switching *and* store-and-forward packet switching.

LANDesk Client Manager (LDCM) A software product from Intel that lets a system administrator for a LAN see the configurations and monitor the status of PCs on the LAN. The product is an implementation of the *desktop management interface (DMI)* standard established by the Desktop Management Task Force, an industry group. To take advantage of DMI, product components must provide a management information format (MIF) file.

LANE *See* LAN emulation.

language Any system used in communication. A natural language includes the spoken and written word, understandable by humans. A machine language is a coded form of communication, decipherable only by computers. Computer programming languages can be based upon either natural or machine languages, or both.

LAP manager A set of operating system utilities that provide a standard interface between the AppleTalk protocols and the various link-access protocols, such as LocalTalk (LLAP), EtherTalk (ELAP), and TokenTalk (TLAP).

LAP *See* Link-Access Procedure or Protocol.

LAPB *See* link-access procedure balanced.

LAPD *See* link-access procedure D-channel.

laptop computer Also called a *notebook computer*. A battery-powered personal computer, generally smaller than a briefcase, that can easily be transported and conveniently used in temporary spaces such as on airplanes, in libraries, temporary offices, and at meetings. A laptop typically weighs less than five pounds and is three inches or less in thickness. Among the best-known makers of laptop computers are IBM, NEC, Dell, Toshiba, and Hewlett-Packard.

laser diode Also called an *injection laser* or *diode laser*. A semiconductor device that produces coherent radiation in the visible or infrared (IR) spectrum when current passes through it. Laser diodes are used in fiber optic systems, compact disc (CD) players, laser printers, remote-control devices, and intrusion detection systems.

laser printer A type of printer that utilizes a laser beam to produce an image on a drum. The light of the laser alters the electrical charge on the drum wherever it strikes the surface of the drum. The drum is then rolled through a reservoir of toner, which is picked up by the charged portions of the drum. Finally, the toner is transferred to the paper through a combination of heat and pressure.

laserdisc A type of CD-ROM used to store and provide programmed access to a large database of text, pictures, and other objects, including motion video and full multimedia presentations.

last-mile technology Any telecommunications technology, such as wireless radio, that carries signals from the broad telecommunication infrastructure along the relatively short distance (hence, the "last mile") to and from the home or business. This is also sometimes referred to as the *local loop*.

LAT *See* local area transport.

LATA *See* local access and transport area.

latency One of three basic service-level agreement parameters. A synonym for *delay*, latency is an expression of how much time it takes for a packet of data to get from one designated point to another. Together, latency and bandwidth define the speed and capacity of a network. *See* bandwidth *and* latency.

launch To start a program or process

layer In networking architectures, a collection of network processing functions that together comprise a set of rules and standards for successful data communication.

Layer 1 VLAN Layer 1 (port-based) VLANs are documented by the IEEE 802.1Q VLAN committee, and have been approved as of the writing of this book. In this type of port-centric virtual LAN, VLAN members are switch ports, and all end-stations attached to a switch port inherit the VLAN number assigned to that port. Note that a port can be in more than one VLAN if needed.

Layer 2 Forwarding Protocol (L2F) The underlying link-level technology for both Multichassis MP and virtual private networks (VPNs), which provides a virtual dial-up service functionality based on the L2F protocol. The L2F protocol is documented in the Internet Engineering Task Force (IETF) draft request for comments (RFC)1. L2F focuses on providing a standards-based tunneling mechanism for transporting the link-layer frames (for example, high-level data-link control (HDLC), async PPP, SLIP, or PPP ISDN) of higher-layer protocols.

Layer 2 VLAN MAC address-based VLANs that permit users on the same link to belong to different VLANs. Although this type of VLAN is more complicated than the port-based VLAN, it is also more flexible. When Layer 2 VLANs are used, each switch has to examine every arriving packet for its VLAN membership. This process involves more complicated processing than the port-based VLAN uses. However, this type of VLAN provides a greater flexibility in defining VLAN membership, because members of a VLAN can be located anywhere in the network.

Layer 3 VLAN Layer 3 (protocol-based) VLANs operate at layer 3 of the OSI reference model, and thus are defined according to layer 3 protocols, such as IP, IPX, AppleTalk, and DECnet. They are usually referred as *virtual subnets*. These virtual subnets are essentially implemented with proprietary vendor-specific protocols because they are not covered by the IEEE 802.1Q specification. The argument against their inclusion in the specification is that the IEEE 802 LAN specifications deal only with layer 2 issues, not layer 3.

Layer Two Tunneling Protocol (L2TP) An extension to the PPP protocol that enables ISPs to operate virtual private networks (VPNs). L2TP merges the best features of two other tunneling protocols: *Point-to-Point Tunneling Protocol (PPTP)* from Microsoft and *Layer 2 Forwarding* from Cisco Systems.

Like PPTP, L2TP requires that the ISP's routers support the protocol to operate properly.

LB *See* leaky bucket entry *and* load balancing.

LBA *See* logical block addressing.

LCD *See* liquid crystal display.

LCP *See* Link Control Protocol.

LDAP *See* Lightweight Directory Access Protocol.

LDCM *See* LANDesk Client Manager.

leaf Items at the top of a hierarchical tree structure.

leaf internetwork In a star topology, an internetwork whose sole access to other internetworks in the star is through a core router.

leaky bucket entry (LB) An analogy for a specialized algorithm used in flow control, where cells are monitored to check whether they comply with the connection parameters. Nonconforming cells are either tagged (as violators) or dropped from the network. The analogy is taken from a bucket (memory buffer) with a hole in its bottom that allows the fluid (cells) to leak out. *See* GCRA, traffic contract, *and* UPC.

learn mode A specialized mode, such as that defined in a macro, in which a program learns to perform certain actions.

learning bridge A specialized type of bridge that performs MAC address learning to reduce traffic on the network. Learning bridges manage a database of MAC addresses and the interfaces associated with each address. *See* MAC address learning.

LE-ARP *See* LAN emulation ARP.

leased line (*Illustration*) Transmission line reserved by a communications carrier for the private use of a customer. A leased line is a type of *dedicated line*. A leased line is usually contrasted with a *switched line* or *dial-up line*. Typically, leased lines are used by businesses to connect geographically distant offices. The fee for the connection is a fixed monthly rate. The primary factors affecting the

L

56K Analog Leased Line/ Private Line application

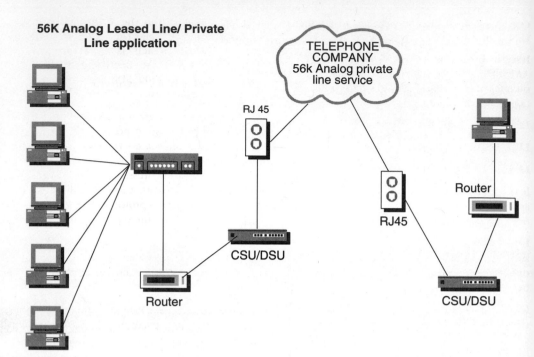

monthly fee are distance between end points and the speed of the circuit. Because the connection doesn't carry anybody else's communications, the carrier can assure a given level of quality. For example, a T-1 channel is a type of leased line that provides a maximum transmission speed of 1.544 Mbps.

You can divide the connection into different lines for data and voice communication or use the channel for one high-speed data circuit. Dividing the connection is called *multiplexing*.

Increasingly, companies and individuals, are using leased lines for Internet access because the lines afford faster data transfer rates and are cost-effective if the Internet is used heavily. Typically the highest speed data connections require a leased line; with the advent of such new technologies as DSL and cable modems, however, this might not be true for much longer. *See* T-1 *and* T-3.

LEC *See* local exchange carrier.

LECS *See* LAN emulation configuration server.

LED *See* light emitting diode.

legacy application An application in which a company or organization has already invested considerable time and money. Typically, legacy applications are database management systems (DBMSs) running on mainframes or minicomputers. An important feature of new software products is the ability to work with a company's legacy applications, or at least be able to import data from them. This is sometimes called *backward compatibility.*

Lempel-Zif-Welsh (LZW) compression A popular data compression technique developed in 1977 by J. Zif and A. Lempel, and later refined by T. Welsh. It is the compression algorithm used in the GIF graphics file format.

LEN connection A link over which LEN protocols are used.

LEN node A term used in APPN. According to IBM documentation, a node that supports independent LU protocols but does not support CP-CP sessions. It may be a peripheral node attached to a boundary node in a subarea network, an end node attached to an APPN network node in an APPN network, or a peer-connected node directly attached to another LEN node or APPN end node.

length indicator (LI) A 6-bit field in the AAL3/4 SAR-PDU trailer that indicates the number of bytes in the SAR-PDU that will contain CPCS information.

LENNI *See* LNNI.

LEO *See* low-earth orbit satellite.

LES *See* LAN emulation server.

level 1 router A DECnet node that can send and receive packets, and route packets from one node to another node within a single area.

level 2 router A DECnet node that can send and receive packets, and route packets from one node to another within its own area and between areas.

lexical function A command language construct that the Digital Command Language command interpreter evaluates and substitutes before it parses a command string.

LI *See* length indicator.

library (*a*) A collection of files. (*b*) In programming, a collection of precompiled routines that a program can use.

LIDB *See* line information database.

light amplification by stimulated emission of radiation *See* laser.

light emitting diode (LED) (*Illustration*) An electronic device that lights up when electricity is passed through it.

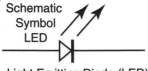

Light Emitting Diode (LED)

light pen An input device that utilizes a light-sensitive detector to select objects on a display screen.

Lightweight Directory Access Protocol (LDAP) A set of protocols for accessing information directories. LDAP is based on the stan-dards contained within the X.500 standard, but is significantly simpler. Unlike X.500, LDAP supports TCP/IP, which is necessary for Internet access and use. Because LDAP is a simpler version of X.500, LDAP is sometimes referred to as X.500-lite.

Although not yet widely implemented, LDAP should eventually make it possible for almost any application running on virtually any computer platform to obtain directory information, such as e-mail addresses and public keys through an internetwork. Because LDAP is an *open standard-based* protocol, applications need not worry about the type of server hosting the directory.

LIMDOW A technology that speeds the copying of information from main memory to CD-ROM.

limited resource link Resource defined by a device operator to remain active only when being used.

limited-route explorer packet *See* spanning explorer packet.

line (*a*) A physical circuit connecting two devices. (*b*) In programming, a single program statement. (*c*) In caches, a single data entry.

line code type One of a number of coding schemes used on serial lines to maintain data integrity and reliability. The carrier service provider determines the line code type used. *See* AMI *and* HBD3.

line conditioning Use of specialized equipment on leased voice-grade channels to improve analog signal characteristics, thereby allowing higher transmission rates.

line control *See* data-link-control protocol.

line control discipline *See* link protocol.

line driver A typically inexpensive amplifier and signal converter that conditions digital signals to ensure their reliable transmission over extended distances.

line group One or more telecommunication lines of the same type that can be activated and deactivated as a group.

line information database (LIDB) A database maintained by the local telephone company that contains subscriber information, such as a service profile, name and address, and credit card validation information.

line print terminal (LPT) The usual designation for a parallel port connection to a printer or other device on a personal computer. Most PCs come with one or two LPT connections designated as LPT1 and LPT2. Some systems support a third, LPT3.

line speed The number of binary digits that can be sent over a telecommunication line in one second, normally expressed in bits per second.

line switching *See* circuit switching.

line-of-sight Operational characteristic of certain transmission systems, such as laser, microwave, and infrared systems, that requires no obstructions in a direct path between transmitter and receiver can exist.

link (*a*) To bind together. (*b*) In programming, to execute a linker. (*c*) To paste a copy of an object into a document in such a way that it retains its connection with the original object. Updates to the original object can be reflected in the duplicate by updating the link. (*d*) The ability of a worksheet within a spreadsheet to take data for particular cell or cells from another worksheet. (*e*) In communications, a physical line or logical channel over which data is transmitted. (*f*) In data management systems, a pointer to another record. One or more records can be connected by inserting links into them. (*g*) In some operating systems (UNIX, for example), a pointer to a file. Links make it possible to reference a file by several different names and to access a file without specifying a full path. (*h*) In hypertext systems, such as those found on the World Wide Web, a reference to another document.

link A connection point provided by a system. It may be a dedicated hardware interface (such as an asynchronous interface) or a channel on a multi-channel hardware interface (such as a PRI or BRI). A medium over which nodes can communicate using a link-layer protocol.

link-access procedure balanced (LAPB) Balanced mode, bit-oriented protocols; an enhanced version of HDLC. A method of WAN data encapsulation used in X.25 packet-switching networks.

link-access procedure D-Channel (LAPD) A ISDN protocol that operates at the data-link layer (level 2) of OSI 7 layer model. LAPD was derived from the LAPB protocol and is designed primarily to satisfy the signaling requirements of ISDN basic access (ISDN BRI). The D channel carries signaling information for circuit switching. ITU-T Recommendations Q.920 and Q.921 define LAPD.

link connection The physical equipment providing two-way communication between one device and one or more other devices; for example, a telecommunication line and data circuit-terminating equipment (DCE).

link connection segment A part of the link that is located between two resources listed consecutively in the service point command service (SPCS) query link configuration request list.

Link Control Protocol (LPP) A part of the Point-to-Point Protocol (PPP) protocol negotiation scheme.

link level The physical connection between two nodes and/or the protocols used to govern that connection.

link problem determination aid (LPDA) A series of procedures used to test the status of and to control DCEs, the communication line, and the remote device interface within a network. These procedures are implemented by specialized host programs (such as the NetView program and VTAM), or communication controller programs, and IBM LPDA DCEs.

link protocol A set of rules for sending and receiving data over a physical link.

link-services layer The layer of network services that routes packets between LAN boards with their MLIDs and protocol stacks. The link-services layer maintains LAN board, protocol stack, and packet buffer information.

Link State Routing Algorithm A type of routing algorithm used in link state protocols, such as OSPF. The router running the link state routing protocol uses the link state routing algorithm broadcast or multicast link (routing) information regarding the cost of reaching each of its neighbors in relation to all other devices in the internetwork.

Link-State Routing Protocols Routing protocol that requires each router to maintain at least a partial map of the "links" within a network. When a network link changes state (up to down, or vice versa), a notification, called a *link-state advertisement (LSA)* is flooded throughout the network. All the routers note the change, and recompute their routes accordingly. This method is more reliable, easier to debug and less bandwidth-intensive than a *Distance-Vector Routing Protocol*. It is also more complex and more processor and memory intensive. OSPF and IS-IS are examples of link state routing protocols. *See* Open Shortest Path First (OSPF) *and* Intermediate-System-to-Intermediate System (IS-IS) *for additional information.*

link station The hardware and software components within a node that represent a connection to an adjacent node. In VTAM, a named resource within an APPN or a subarea node that represents the connection to another APPN or subarea node that is attached by an APPN or a subarea link. In the resource hierarchy in a subarea network, the link station is subordinate to the subarea link.

link type In Hyper-G and other hypertext systems, the specification of the nature of the information object being linked to. A single link can have any number of defined link types. For example, for any word from which one might link to another information object, that object could be an example of that word, or a graphic illustration of it, or a definition of it, or it might be associated with one person's comments on that subject.

Link-Access Procedure or **Protocol) (LAP)** According to DEC documentation, a set of procedures used for link control on a packet-switching data network; X.25 defines two sets of procedures:

LAP: The DTE-DCE interface, defined as operating in two-way simultaneous asynchronous response mode with the DTE and DCE containing both a primary and secondary function.

LAPB: The DTE/DCE interface, defined as operating in two-way asynchronous balanced mode. (*b*) According to Apple documentation, an AppleTalk protocol that controls the access of a node to the network hardware. A link access protocol makes it possible for many nodes to share the same communication hardware.

link attached Pertaining to devices that are connected to a controlling unit by a data link.

linkrot The tendency of hypertext links between sites on the World Wide Web to become useless as other sites cease to exist or remove or reorganize their Web pages.

Linux A freely-distributable implementation of UNIX that runs on a number of hardware platforms, including Intel and Motorola microprocessors. It was developed mainly by Linus Torvalds. Because it's free, and because it runs on many platforms, including PCs, Macintoshes, and Amigas, Linux has become extremely popular over the last several years. Another popular, free version of UNIX that runs on Intel microprocessors is FreeBSD.

 Some excellent resources can be found at *http://www.netcerts.com/linux.asp* and *http://www.redhat.com*.

liquid crystal display (LCD) The technology used for displays in notebook and other smaller computers. Like *light-emitting diode (LED)* and *gas-plasma* technologies, LCD displays utilize two sheets of polarizing material with a liquid crystal solution between them. An electric current passed through the liquid causes the crystals to align so that light cannot pass through them.

LIS *See* logical IP subnet.

LISP List Processor. A high-level programming language especially popular for artificial intelligence applications. LISP was developed in the early 1960s by John McCarthy at MIT.

L

Listserv The most common kind of maillist, "Listserv" is a registered trademark of L-Soft International, Inc. Listservs originated on BIT-NET but they are now common on the Internet. *See* BITNET, e-mail, *and* Maillist.

literal A value written exactly as it's meant to be interpreted.

Litestep An alternative user interface (shell) for use with any Windows operating system (Windows 9x/NT). It replaces the Windows shell. (A *shell* is a program that interfaces directly with the user on one side and with underlying operating system functions on the other side.) Like Windows, the Litestep shell lets you create your own personal user environment on the display screen, but offers many more options for creativity and personalization.

liteware Software that is distributed freely, in a version having less capability than the full for-sale version. It's usually designed to provide a potential customer with a sample of the "look-and-feel" of a product and a subset of its full capability. Liteware can be considered a type of *shareware* (shareware also includes products distributed freely, usually on a trial basis; however these distributions usually have full capability).

little endian A storage format or transmission of binary data in which the least significant byte comes first. *See* big-endian.

live cam A video camera, usually attached directly to a computer, whose current or latest image is requestable from a Web site. A live cam is one that is continually providing new images that are transmitted in rapid succession or, in some cases, in streaming video.

LL2 *See* link level 2.

LLC *See* logical link control.

LLC2 *See* Logical Link Control, type 2.

LMDS *See* local multipoint distribution system.

LMI *See* local management interface.

LNNI *See* LAN emulation network node interface.

LNP *See* local number portability.

load (*a*) In networking, the amount of data (traffic) being carried by the network. (*b*) In programming, to copy data from main memory into a data register. (*c*) To install. For example, to load a disk means to mount it in a disk drive.

load balancing In routing, the ability of a router to distribute traffic over all its network ports that are the same distance from the destination address. Good load-balancing algorithms use both line speed and reliability information.

Loader An operating system utility that copies programs from a storage device, such as a hard drive, to main memory, where they can be executed.

lobe The connection from a workstation to a token-ring concentrator such as a *multistation access unit (MAU)*. When the workstation's adapter signals the MAU, the lobe is added as another section of the ring.

local In networks, files, devices, and other resources at your workstation. Pertaining to a device accessed directly without use of a telecommunication line. Resources located at other nodes on the networks are remote.

local access The ability to execute a program on the computer to which you are attached.

local access and transport area (LATA) In the United States, a geographic area covered by one or more local telephone companies, which are legally referred to as *local exchange carriers (LECs)*. Within this area, a local carrier can provide communications services. A connection between two local exchanges within the LATA is referred to as *intraLATA*. A connection between a carrier in one LATA and a carrier in another LATA is referred to as *interLATA*. InterLATA is long-distance service. LATAs were formed by the breakup of AT&T. *See* LEC *and* IXC.

local acknowledgment Method whereby an intermediate network node, such as a router, responds to acknowledgments for a remote end host.

local address In SNA, an address used in a peripheral node in place of a network address and transformed to or from a network address by the boundary function in a subarea node.

local area network (LAN) (*Illustration*) A data communication network of interconnected workstations, PCs, terminals, servers, printers, and other peripherals, operating at a high speed over short distances (usually within the same floor or building) and sharing the resources of a single processor or server within a relatively small geographic area. Various LAN standards have been developed:

Ethernet is the most widely used LAN standard.

Fiber distributed data interface (FDDI) extends a local area network over a much wider area.

Usually, the server has applications and data storage that are shared in common by multiple workstation users.

The following briefly lists the characteristics that differentiate one LAN from another:

Topology: The physical arrangement of devices on the network.

Protocols: The rules and encoding specifications for sending data; these vary from LAN to LAN. Examples of protocols are Ethernet or *token ring*.

Physical media types: Devices that can be connected by twisted-pair wire (UTP, STP), coaxial cables, or fiber optic cables. Some networks, known as *wireless networks*, use radio waves instead of cables.

See campus area network (CAN), metropolitan area network (MAN), *and* wide area network (WAN).

local area transport (LAT) (*a*) A DECNet remote terminal protocol. (*b*) A routed communications protocol that an operating system uses within a local area network to communicate with terminal servers.

local area VAXcluster system A type of VAXcluster configuration in which cluster communication is carried out over the Ethernet by software that emulates certain computer interconnect (CI) port functions. A VAXcluster node can be a VAX or a micro VAX processor; hierarchical storage controllers (HSCs) are not used.

local bridge A bridge that directly connects two distinct, but physically close, LAN segments into a unified network.

local bus A data bus that connects directly, or almost directly, to the microprocessor. Although local buses can support only a few devices, they provide very fast throughput. Modern PCs include both a PCI local bus and a more general ISA expansion bus for

L

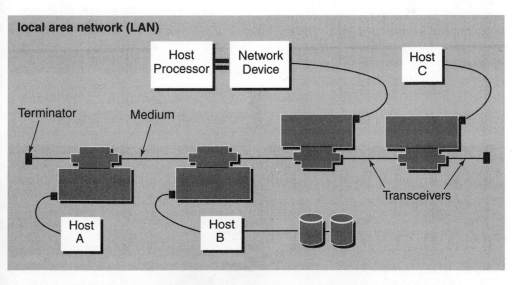

local area network (LAN)

Host Processor — Network Device — Host C

Terminator — Medium — Transceivers

Host A — Host B

devices that do not require such fast data throughput.

local client A program that is running in an Xwindows environment, on your local computer.

local exchange carrier (LEC) A public telephone company in the United States that provides local service. Some of the largest LECs are the *Bell operating companies (BOCs)*, which were grouped into holding companies known collectively as the *regional Bell operating companies (RBOCs)* when the Bell System was broken up by a 1983 consent decree. In addition to the Bell companies, there are a number of independent LECs, such as GTE.

local explorer packet A specialized packet generated by an end system in an source route-bridged network to assist the end system in finding a host connected to the local token ring. If the local explorer packet fails to find a local host, the end system produces either a spanning explorer packet or an all-routes explorer packet. *See* all-routes explorer packet, explorer packet, *and* spanning explorer.

local loop The wired connection from a telephone company's central office (CO) in a locality to its customers' telephones at homes and businesses. This connection is usually on a pair of copper wires called *twisted pair*. The system was originally designed for voice transmission only, using analog transmission technology on a single voice channel.

local management interface (LMI) (*a*) A specification for frame relay networking that defines a method of exchanging status information between FR network ports and customer premises devices such as routers, FRADs, or frame aware DSUs. (*b*) An ITU-T-defined interface to provide an ATM end-system user with network management information.

local multipoint distribution system (LMDS) A system for broadband microwave wireless transmission direct from a local antenna to homes and businesses within a line-of-sight radius. This provides a solution to the so-called *last mile problem* of economically bringing high-bandwidth services to

users. LMDS is an alternative to installing optical fiber all the way to the user or to adapting cable TV for broadband Internet service.

local number portability (LNP) The ability of a telephone customer in the United States to retain a local phone number when switching to another local telephone service provider. The Telecommunications Act of 1996 required that the Local Exchange Carriers (LECs) in the 100 largest metropolitan markets provide this capability by the end of 1998.

local termination (LT) *See* local acknowledgment.

local traffic filtering Filtering process by which a bridge filters out (drops) frames whose source and destination MAC addresses are located on the same interface on the bridge. this filter prevents unnecessary traffic from being forwarded through the bridge. Defined in the IEEE-802.1 standard. *See* IEEE 802.1.

localization The process of adapting software for a particular country or region. Software companies that wish to sell their software internationally must invest considerable money and energy in localization efforts. There are also companies that specialize in localizing software for third parties.

locally administered address (LAA) An adapter address that the user can assign to override the universally administered address (UAA).

LocalTalk The cabling scheme supported by the AppleTalk network protocol for Macintosh computers. Most local-area networks that use AppleTalk, such as TOPS, also conform to the LocalTalk cable system. Such networks are sometimes called LocalTalk networks. Although LocalTalk networks are relatively slow, they are popular because they are easy and inexpensive to install and maintain.

location name An identifier for the network location of the computer on which a port resides.

location routing number (LRN) In the United States, a 10-digit number in a database called a *service control point (SCP)* that identifies a switching port for a local telephone exchange. LRN is a technique for providing local number portability (LNP).

LOCKD Lock manager daemon.

log file A file that lists actions that have occurred. In networking a router can log events to its internal buffer or it can send them to a syslog server that will record all the events in a log file for later use. In addition, Web servers maintain log files listing every request (hit or page view) made to the server. With log file analysis tools, it's possible to get an idea of where visitors are coming from, how often they return, and how they navigate through a site.

log off To request that a session be terminated.

log on (*a*) To make a computer system or network recognize a user so that a session can begin. (*b*) In SNA products, to initiate a session between an application program and a logical unit (LU).

log out To end a session at the computer.

logical address *See* network address.

logical address group (LAG) Similar to an LIS, except that the decision to establish a direct SVC is made on a traffic and QoS requirement rather than the destination IP address.

logical block addressing (LBA) A technique used with SCSI and IDE disk drives that allows a computer to address a hard disk larger than 528 megabytes by translating the cylinder, head, and sector specifications of the drive into addresses that can be used by an enhanced BIOS. A logical block address is a 28-bit value that maps to a specific cylinder-head-sector address on the disk. Twenty-eight bits allows sufficient variation to specify addresses on a hard disk of up to 8.4 gigabytes in data storage capacity. Logical block addressing is one of the defining features of *enhanced IDE (EIDE)*, a hard-disk interface to the computer bus or data paths

logical channel In packet-mode operation, a sending channel and a receiving channel that are used to send and receive data over a data link at the same time.

logical channel identifier A bit string in the header of a packet that associates the packet with a specific switched virtual circuit or permanent virtual circuit. *See* VCN.

logical connection In a network, a device that can communicate or work with another device because they share the same protocol.

logical IP subnet (LIS) A group of ATM-attached devices that share a common address prefix. LIS members can communicate using direct virtual connections.

logical link A temporary connection between source and destination nodes, or between two processes on the same node for direct communications. Several logical links may be able to utilize the same physical hardware.

Logical Link Control (LLC) A protocol developed by the IEEE 802 committee, common to all of its LAN standards, for data-link-level transmission control that governs the transmission of frames between data stations independently of how the transmission medium is shared. The upper sublayer of the IEEE layer 2 (OSI) protocol that further defines the media access control (MAC) protocol; IEEE standard 802.2.

The Logical Link Control (LLC) layer provides the basis for an unacknowledged connectionless service or connection-oriented service on the local area network such as error control, broadcasting, multiplexing, and flow control functions. *See* MAC.

Logical Link Control, type 2 (LLC2) Connection-oriented OSI LLC-sublayer protocol. *See* logical link control (LLC).

logical name A unique user-specified name for a file within a computer system. For example, the logical name NetCerts can be assigned to a terminal device from which a program reads data entered by a user. Logical name assignments are maintained in logical name tables for each process, each group, and the system. Logical names can be assigned translation attributes, such as terminal and concealed.

logical name table A table that contains a set of logical names and their equivalent names

L

for a particular process, a particular group, or the system.

logical protocol Protocols are formal sets of rules governing how network devices exchange information. Logical protocols generally define data-link details, such as packet-switching technology in X.25 or frame relay frames.

logical record A group of related fields treated as a single record or unit.

logical topologies The view of the network as seen by the network's components, access methods, or rules of operation.

logical unit (LU) An access port for users to gain access to the services of a network. In IBM's Systems Network Architecture (SNA), a logical unit identifies an end-user in an SNA network. By end-user, IBM means either a human being interacting with the network or an application program that is indirectly representing such an end-user.

Logical unit 6.2 (LU6.2) Those protocols and the type of logical unit which supports advanced program-to-program communication (APPC).

log-in directory The default directory a user is assigned to on log-on into a system, commonly used in FTP or TFTP to assign the starting or default directory for a user.

loop (*a*) A situation that occurs when network devices have multiple circular paths to a destination, when in fact no path ever reaches the destination. (*b*) In programming, a series of instructions that is repeated until a certain condition is met. Each pass through the loop is called an *iteration*. Loops constitute one of the most basic and powerful programming concepts.

loopback address An address used for communications between clients and servers that reside on the same host. For example, the address 127.0.0.1, is a commonly acknowledged loopback address. When the Ping command is issued, this address will always return the name of the computer from which the Ping command was issued.

lossless compression A data compression technique in which no data is lost.

lossy compression A data compression technique in which some amount of data is lost.

low memory In DOS systems, the first 640K of memory. This portion of memory is reserved for applications, device drivers, and memory-resident programs (TSRs). Low memory is also called *conventional memory*.

low-voltage differential signaling (LVDS) A low-noise, low-power, low-amplitude method for high-speed (gigabits per second) data transmission over copper wire.

low-earth orbit satellite (LEO) A satellite with a specialized wireless receiver/transmitter that is launched by a rocket and placed in orbit around the earth, usually at an altitude of a few hundred miles. There are hundreds of these satellites currently in operation. They are used for such diverse purposes as weather forecasting, television broadcast, amateur radio communications, Internet communications, and the Global Positioning System (GPS).

low-level language A machine or assembly language. Low-level languages are closer to the hardware than are high-level programming languages, which are closer to human languages.

LPDA *See* link problem determination application.

LPT *See* line print terminal.

LRN *See* location routing number.

LS *See* link station.

LT *See* local termination.

LU6.2 session A logical connection utilizing LU6.2 protocols.

LU-LU session A logical connection created between two logical units in an SNA network that provides communication between two different end users.

LUNI *See* LAN emulation user network interface.

lurk To eavesdrop on a chat room, mailing list, or conference.

LVDS *See* low-voltage differential signaling.

Lycos A popular World Wide Web search engine and directory.

 For more information, see *www.lycos.com*.

Lynx A keyboard-oriented text-only Web browser that was developed at the University of Kansas primarily for students who used UNIX workstations. It has also been rewritten to run on VMS operating systems for users of VT100 terminals.

LZW *See* Lempel-Zif-Welsh compression.

L

M

Mac Short for Macintosh computer.

MAC *See* media access control.

MAC address Also known as an *Ethernet address, hardware address, station address, burned-in address*, or *physical address*. It uniquely identifies each node in a network. A set of 6 two-digit hexadecimal numbers burned into an Ethernet product by its manufacturer.

This is a data-link layer address associated with a particular network device; it is often called a hardware address or physical address because of its device association. This is in contrast to an IP protocol address, which is a network-layer address that defines a network connection.

In IEEE 802 networks, the data-link control (DLC) layer of the OSI Reference Model is divided into two sublayers: the *logical-link control (LLC)* layer and the *media-access control (MAC)* layer. The MAC layer interfaces directly with the network media. Consequently, each different type of network media requires a different MAC layer.

On networks that do not conform to the IEEE 802 standards, but do conform to the OSI Reference Model, the node address is called the data-link control (DLC) address. *See* network address.

MAC address learning A service that characterizes a learning bridge, in which the source MAC address of each received packet is stored so that future packets destined for that address can be forwarded only to the bridge interface on which that address is located. Packets destined for unrecognized addresses are forwarded out every bridge interface. This helps minimize traffic on the attached LANs. MAC address learning is defined in the IEEE802.1 standard. *See* learning bridge *and* MAC address.

MAC frame Frames used to carry information to maintain the ring protocol and to exchange management information.

Mac OS The computer operating system for Apple Computer's Macintosh line of personal computers and workstations. A popular feature of its latest version, Mac OS 8.5, is *Sherlock*, a search facility similar to a "find a file" command.

MAC protocol The data-link control (DLC) sublayer protocol that includes functions for recognizing adapter addresses, copying message units from the physical network, and message-unit format recognition, error detection, and routing within the processor.

machine address *See* absolute address.

machine code The elemental language of computers, consisting of a stream of 0s and 1s. Ultimately, the output of any programming language analysis and processing is machine code. After a user writes a program, the source language statements are compiled or (in the case of assembler language) assembled into output that is machine code.

machine language The lowest-level programming language (except for computers that utilize programmable microcode). Machine languages are the only languages understood by computers. While easily understood by computers, machine languages are almost impossible for humans to use because they consist entirely of numbers.

machine readable When a file is written in a form that a computer can accept. Machine-readable data includes files stored on disk or tape, or data that comes from a device connected to a computer.

machine vision The ability of a computer to "see." A machine-vision system employs one or more video cameras, analog-to-digital conversion (ADC), and digital signal processing (DSP). The resulting data goes to a computer or robot controller. Machine vision is similar in complexity to voice recognition.

Macintosh (Mac) Introduced in 1984 by Apple Computer, this was the first widely sold personal computer with a graphical user interface (GUI). The Mac was designed to provide users with a natural, intuitively understandable, and, in general, "user-friendly" computer interface.

MacIP Network layer protocol that encapsulates IP packets in DDS or transmission over AppleTalk. MacIP also provides proxy ARP services.

macro A symbol, name, or key that represents a list of commands, actions, or keystrokes.

MAE *See* Metropolitan Area Ethernet.

Magellan A Web directory published by the McKinley Group, now owned by Excite, Inc. Magellan takes its name from Ferdinand Magellan, a Portuguese explorer who navigated the Strait of Magellan in 1520.

magnetic field Generated when electric-charge carriers such as electrons move through space or within an electrical conductor. The geometric shapes of the magnetic flux lines produced by moving charge carriers (electric current) are similar to the shapes of the flux lines in an electrostatic field, although there are differences in the ways electrostatic and magnetic fields interact with the environment.

magneto-optical disk drive A magneto-optical (MO) device that employs both magnetic and optical technologies to obtain ultra-high data density. It is used to backup computer data. A typical MO cartridge is slightly larger than a conventional 3.5-inch magnetic diskette, and looks similar.

mail bomb An e-mail message sent with the intent to crash the recipient's mailserver or mailreader. Mail bombing is a form of electronic harassment and can, on many systems, result in the cancellation of the bomber's account.

mail filter A program that allows you to sort e-mail according to information in the header.

mail software Communication software generally divided into two categories: *mail transfer*

agents (MTAs) and *mail user agents (MUAs)* An MTA is a program that relays messages between machines. An MUA is a client program responsible for interacting with the user.

mailbox An area in memory or on a storage device where e-mail is placed. In e-mail systems, each user has a private mailbox. When the user receives e-mail, the mail system automatically puts it in the mailbox.

main distribution frame (MDF) A structure where phone lines are terminated. For example, a typical office building may have a single MDF located in the basement, where all office phone lines terminate. Some large companies may employ multiple MDFs for redundancy; this is especially true in investment firms.

main memory Physical memory that is internal to the computer.

main storage The main area in a computer in which data is stored for quick access by the computer's processor. This term originated in the days of the mainframe computer to distinguish the more immediately accessible data storage from *auxiliary storage*. On today's computers, especially personal computers and workstations, the term random access memory (RAM) is usually used instead of main storage, and the hard disk, diskettes, and CD-ROMs collectively describe auxiliary storage

mainframe A large computer, typically manufactured by a large company such as IBM, for commercial applications and other large-scale computing purposes. Historically, a mainframe is associated with centralized rather than distributed computing

Maintenance Operation Protocol (MOP) A Digital Equipment Corporation network file transfer protocol that allows basic maintenance operations on DECnet systems. For example, MOP can be used to download a system image to a diskless station.

Majordomo From Latin "master of the house." A small program that automatically redistributes e-mail to names on a mailing list. Users can subscribe to a mailing list by sending an e-mail note to a mailing list they learn about; Majordomo will automatically add the name and distribute future e-mail postings to every subscriber.

man page Short for manual page, a page of on-line documentation in UNIX systems. Every UNIX command, utility, and library function has an associated man page that you can view by entering the command:

> man command name>

For example, to find out about the man command itself, you would enter:

> man man

MAN *See* metropolitan area network.

managed object In network management, when a network device is managed by a network management protocol such as SNMP.

management information base (MIB) A collection of managed objects. A term used with the concept of SNMP-based network management. A database of objects for referencing variables such as integers and strings. In general, it contains information regarding a network's management and performance, i.e., traffic parameters that can be monitored by a network management system. Both SNMP and RMON use standardized MIB formats that allow any SNMP and RMON tools to monitor any device defined by a MIB. An individual equipment manufacturer may develop an MIB extension to the standard to uniquely define variables that apply to its implementation (that cannot be defined by the variables already in the base MIB standard). *See* SNMP.

management information format (MIF) A format used to describe a hardware or software component. MIF files are used by DMI to report system configuration information.

management information system (MIS) A class of software that provides managers with tools for organizing and evaluating their department. Typically, MIS systems are written in COBOL and run on mainframes or mini-computers. Within companies and large organizations, the department responsible for computer systems is sometimes called the MIS department. Other names for MIS include information services (IS) and information technology (IT).

management information tree (MIT) A tree structure of the management information base.

Manufacturing Automation Protocol (MAP) Network architecture created by General Motors to satisfy the specific needs of the factory floor. MAP specifies a token-passing LAN similar to IEEE802.4. *See* IEEE 802.4.

manufacturing messaging service (MMS) According to OSI documentation, a messaging service between programmable devices,

MAP *See* Manufacturing Automation Protocol.

map (*a*) A file showing the structure of a program after it has been compiled. (*b*) To make logical connections between two entities. (*c*) To copy a set of objects from one place to another while preserving the objects' organization.

MAPI *See* messaging application programming interface.

Mapuccino A Java applet, or small program, that can show a visual map of how a Web site is organized. For example, if the user wants a map view of a site, Mapuccino quickly assesses the Web files and creates map views of the site that can be viewed or saved. Mapuccino lets the use alternate between a horizontal map view, a vertical map view, a regular Table of Contents (that looks like a Windows directory/file hierarchy), and a goldfish view.

margins In word processing, the strips of white space around the edge of the paper, where text is not printed.

MARS *See* multicast address resolution server.

marshalling The process of gathering data from one or more applications or non-contiguous sources in computer storage, putting the data pieces into a message buffer, and organizing or converting the data into a format that is prescribed for a particular receiver or programming interface.

mask A means of subdividing networks using address modification. A mask is a dotted quad specifying which bits of the destination are

M

significant. See IP address, address mask, *and* subnet mask.

massively parallel processing (MPP) The coordinated processing of a program by multiple processors that work on different parts of the program, using their own operating systems and memory. Typically, MPP processors communicate using some messaging interface

master boot record (MBR) A small program that is executed when a computer boots up. The MBR usually resides on the first sector of the hard disk or diskette.

MAU *See* media access unit *and* multistation access unit.

maximize In graphical user interfaces, to enlarge a window to its maximum size.

maximum burst Specifies the largest possible burst of data allowed above the insured rate that will be allowed temporarily on an ATM PVC, but will not be dropped by the traffic policing function, even if it exceeds the maximum rate. This amount of traffic will be allowed only temporarily; on average, the traffic source needs to be within the maximum rate. Specified in bytes or cells. *See* maximum rate.

maximum burst size (MBS) A traffic parameter that specifies the maximum number of cells that can be transmitted at the peak rate.

maximum cell delay variation (MCDV) The maximum cell delay variation (CDV) over a given QoS class.

maximum cell loss ratio (MCLR) The maximum CTD over a given QoS class, defined for CBR and VBR traffic and for cells with CLP=0.

maximum cell transfer delay (MCTD) The maximum CTD over a given QoS class.

maximum rate Maximum rate of total data throughput allowed on a given virtual ATM circuit, equal to the sum of the insured and uninsured traffic from the traffic source. The uninsured data might be dropped if the network becomes congested. The maximum rate, which cannot exceed the media rate, represents the highest data throughput the virtual circuit will

ever deliver, measured in bits or cells per second. Compare with excess rate and insured rate. *See* maximum burst.

maximum transmission unit (MTU) The largest physical packet size, measured in bytes, that a network can transmit. Any messages larger than the MTU are divided into smaller packets before being sent. For long-haul networks that use serial lines to interconnect packet switches, the MTU is determined by software. Every network has a different MTU, which is set by the network administrator.

On Windows 95, the user can also set the MTU of your machine. This defines the maximum size of the packets sent from a computer onto the network. Ideally, the user wants the MTU to be the same as the smallest MTU of all the networks between his machine and a message's final destination. Otherwise, if the messages are larger than one of the intervening MTUs, they will get broken up (fragmented), which slows down transmission speeds.

Trial and error is the only sure way of finding the optimal MTU, but there are some guidelines that can help. For example, the MTU of many PPP connections is 576, so if you connect to the Internet via PPP, you might want to set your machine's MTU to 576 too. Most Ethernet networks, on the other hand, have an MTU of 1,500, which is the default MTU setting for Windows 95.

MB *See* megabyte.

Mbits/s *See* megabits per second.

Mbits *See* megabits.

Mbone *See* Multicast Backbone on the Internet.

Mbps *See* megabits per second.

MBR *See* master boot record.

MBS *See* maximum burst size.

Mbyte *See* megabyte.

Mbytes/s *See* megabytes per second.

MCA *See* micro channel architecture.

MCDV *See* maximum cell delay variation.

MCI *See* media control interface *and* multi-port communications interface.

MCI, Inc. A large telecommunications company that used to be named Microwave Communications, Inc. Recently purchased by WorldCom, Inc.

MCLR *See* maximum cell loss ratio.

MCR *See* minimum cell rate.

MCSE *See* Microsoft Certified Systems Engineer.

MCTD *See* maximum cell transfer delay.

MD5 An algorithm created in 1991 by Prof. Ronald Rivest that is used to create digital signatures. It is intended for use with 32-bit machines and is safer than the MD4 algorithm, which has been broken. MD5 is a one-way hash function, meaning that it takes a message and converts it into a fixed string of digits, also called a *message digest*. When using a one-way hash function, one can compare a calculated message digest against the message digest that is decrypted with a public key to verify that the message hasn't been tampered with. This comparison is called a *hashcheck*.

MDF *See* main distribution frame.

MDI *See* multiple document interface.

MDRAM *See* multibank DRAM.

mean cell transfer delay The average of the processing, queuing, and propagation delays.

mean time between failures (MTBF) A measure of the reliability of a hardware product. For most components, the measure is typically in thousands or even tens of thousands of hours between failures.

media (*a*) Physical carriers of electrons or photons. The medium may be hard, as in a type of cable, or soft, in the sense of microwaves, for example. (*b*) Objects on which data can be stored. These include hard disks, floppy disks, CD-ROMs, and tapes. (*c*) In computer networks, the cables linking workstations together. There are many different types of transmission media, the most popular being twisted-pair wire (normal electrical wire), coaxial cable (the type of cable used for cable television), and fiber optic cable (cables made out of glass). (*d*) The form and technology used to communicate information. *Multimedia* presentations, for example, combine sound, pictures, and videos, all of which are different types of media.

media access control (MAC) (*Illustration*) (*a*) Lower of the two sublayers of the data-link layer defined by the IEEE. The MAC sublayer handles access to shared media, such as whether token passing or contention will be

M

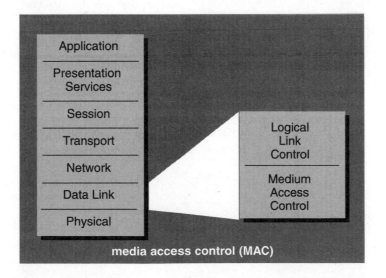

media access control (MAC)

used. (*b*) According to OSI nomenclature, a sublayer in the data-link layer, which controls access to the physical medium of a network. The MAC sublayer that supports topology-dependent functions and uses services of the physical layer to provide services to the logical-link control (LLC) sublayer. *See* data-link layer, MAC address, *and* LLC.

media access unit (MAU) An Ethernet transceiver.

media control interface (MCI) A high-level API developed by Microsoft and IBM for controlling multimedia devices, such as CD-ROM players and audio controllers. Both OS/2 and Windows support MCI.

Media Access Control (MAC) protocol Protocol that governs access to the transmission medium to enable the exchange of data between nodes.

Media Gateway Control Protocol (MGCP) Developed by Nortel Networks, MGCP is one of a few proposed control and signal standards to compete with the older H.323 standard for the conversion of audio signals carried on telephone circuits (PSTN) to data packets carried over the Internet or other packet networks. New standards are being developed because of the growing popularity of *Voice-over-IP (VoIP)*. Regular phones are relatively inexpensive because they don't need to be complex; they are fixed to a specific switch at a central switching location. IP phones and devices, on the other hand, are not fixed to a specific switch, so they must contain processors that enable them to function and be intelligent on their own, independent of a central switching location. This makes the terminal (phone or device) more complex, and therefore, more expensive. The MGCP is meant to simplify standards for this new technology by eliminating the need for complex, processor-intense IP telephony devices, thus simplifying and lowering the cost of these terminals.

media initialization Data type/codec specific initialization. This includes such things as clock rates, color tables, etc. Any transport-independent information required by a client

for playback of a media stream that occurs in the media initialization phase of stream setup.

media interface connector (MIC) The mating interface at the bulkhead receptacle. The MIC interfaces to the cable plant.

media menu The menu that contains the transmission media choices available using NetSuite Advanced Professional Design. Media choices include unshielded twisted pair, shielded twisted pair, fiber optic, analog, T1, and so on.

media parameter Parameter specific to a media type that may be changed before or during stream playback.

media rate Maximum traffic throughput for a particular media type.

megabit (Mbits) (*a*) When used to describe data storage, 1,048,576 (2 to the 20th power) bytes. (*b*) When used to described data transfer rates, it refers to one million bits. Networks are often measured in megabits per second, abbreviated as Mbps.

megabits per second (Mbits/s) Transmission speed or rate of one million bits per second.

megabyte (MB) One million (actually 1,048,576) bytes.

megabytes per second (Mbytes/s) Transmission speed or rate of one million bytes per second.

megaflop A measure of a computer's speed that can be expressed as a million floating point operations per second.

megahertz (MHz) One million cycles per second. The speed of microprocessors, called the *clock speed*, is measured in megahertz. For example, a microprocessor that runs at 200 MHz executes 200 million cycles per second. Each computer instruction requires a fixed number of cycles, so the clock speed determines how many instructions per second the microprocessor can execute.

Melissa A fast-spreading macro virus. It is distributed as an e-mail attachment that, when opened, disables a number of safeguards in

Word 97/98 or Word 2000. If the user has the Microsoft Outlook e-mail program, the virus is transmitted to the first 50 people in each of the user's address books.

memory leak The gradual loss of available computer memory when a program repeatedly fails to return memory that it has obtained for temporary use. As a result, the available memory for that application or that part of the operating system becomes exhausted and the program can no longer function.

memory management unit (MMU) The hardware component that manages virtual memory systems. Typically, the MMU is part of the CPU, although in some designs it is a separate chip. The MMU includes a small amount of memory that holds a table matching virtual addresses to physical addresses.

MEMS *See* micro-electromechanical systems.

menu A list of selections from which to make a choice.

Merced The code name for the 64-bit microprocessor from Intel, the first of Intel's IA-64 series. Because of its greatly increased I/O bandwidth relative to today's 32-bit microprocessors, it will make possible visual computing or the ability to interact dynamically with visual images as models of work objects.

mesh network A multisegment network configuration providing more than one path through intermediate LAN segments between source and destination LAN segments.

mesh In network topology, where devices are organized in a manageable, segmented manner with many, often redundant connections. The connections between devices are strategically placed between network nodes. *See* full mesh and partial mesh.

message Generically, a reference to meaningful data passed from one end-user to another. The end-user may be a human or a program.

Message Digest5 *See* MD5.

message handling service (MHS) The service provided by the CCITT X.400 series of standards, consisting of a user agent to allow users to

create and read electronic mail; a message transfer agent to provide addressing, sending, and receiving services; and a reliable transfer agent to provide routing and delivery services.

Message Queuing Interface (MQI) International standard API that provides functionality similar to that of the RPC interface. In contrast to RPC, MQI is implemented strictly at the application layer. *See* RPC.

message store (MS) In a TCP/IP environment, an entity acting as an intermediary between a user agent and its local message transfer agent.

message switching Switching technique involving transmission of messages from node to node through a network. The message is stored at each node until such time as a forwarding path is available. Contrast with circuit switching and packet switching.

message transfer agent (MTA) In TCP/IP, a subpart of the electronic mail component known as simple mail transfer protocol (SMTP). It is an object in the message transfer system. MTAs use a store-and-forward method to relay messages from an originator to a recipient. They interact with user agents when a message is submitted, and on delivery.

message unit In SNA, the unit of data processed by any layer; for example, a basic information unit (BIU), a path information unit (PIU), or a request (or response) unit (RU). A unit of data processed by any network layer.

messaging application programming interface (MAPI) A system built into Microsoft Windows that enables different e-mail applications to work together to distribute mail. As long as both applications are MAPI-enabled, they can share mail messages with each other.

meta In computer science, a common prefix that means "about". So, for example, *metadata* is data that describes other data (data about data). A *metalanguage* is a language used to describe other languages. A *metafile* is a file that contains other files. The HTML meta tag is used to describe the contents of a Web page.

M

meta tag A special HTML tag that provides information about a Web page. Unlike normal HTML tags, meta tags do not affect how the page is displayed. Instead, they provide information such as who created the page, how often it is updated, what the page is about, and which keywords represent the page's content. Many search engines use this information when building their indices.

metafile A file containing information that describes or specifies another file.

meta language A definition or description of a language.

meta-signaling Process running at the ATM layer that manages signaling types and virtual circuits.

metering *See* traffic shaping.

method A programmed procedure that is defined as part of a class and included in any object of that class. A class (and thus an object) can have more than one method. A method in an object can only have access to the data known to that object, which ensures data integrity among the set of objects in an application. A method can be re-used in multiple objects metadata.

metric The measurement of a particular characteristic of a program's performance or efficiency.

Metropolitan Area Ethernet (MAE) A *network access point (NAP)*, where Internet Service Providers (ISPs) can connect with each other. The original MAE was set up by a company called MFS and is based in Washington, D.C. Later, MFS built another one in Silicon Valley, dubbed MAE-West. In addition to the MAEs from MFS, there are many other NAPs. Although MAE refers really only to the NAPs from MFS, the two terms are often used interchangeably.

metropolitan area network (MAN) (*Illustrations*) A data network that extends to 50-kilometer range, spanning an entire metropolitan area such as a city or town. Generally, MANs span a larger geographic area than LANs, but a smaller area than WANs. They are essentially somewhere in between them both. MANs operate at speeds from 1 Mbps up to the gigabit level; these high-speed connections are common characteristics.

SONET transmission systems are often deployed in MAN rings. Layered on top of (or within) SONET payload envelopes is LAN traffic; 4, 10, 16, 100 Mbps plus traditional analog

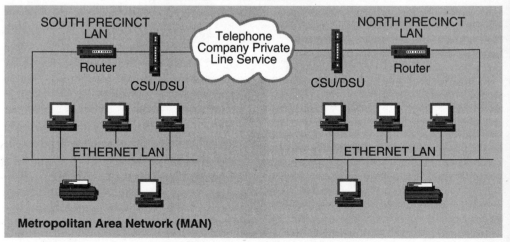

A MAN NETWORK USING TELEPHONE COMPANY PRIVATE LINES

SOUTH PRECINCT LAN
Router
CSU/DSU
Telephone Company Private Line Service
NORTH PRECINCT LAN
Router
CSU/DSU
ETHERNET LAN
ETHERNET LAN

Metropolitan Area Network (MAN)

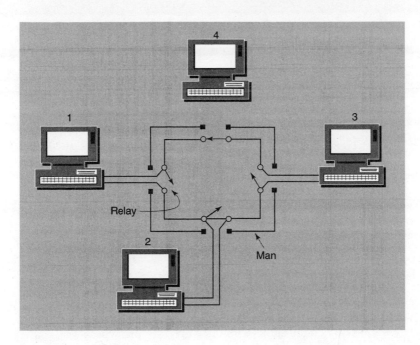

and digital services such as 1200, 2400, 4800, 9600, 19.2 Kbps and so on.

MANs also provide an integrated set of services for real-time data, voice, and image transmission including 56k, 64K, and other fractional T1 rates as well as full T1, T3, and SONET OC-N capabilities.

MFC *See* Microsoft Foundation Classes.

MFM *See* modified frequency modulation.

MFP *See* multifunction peripheral.

MGCP *See* Media Gateway Control Protocol.

MHS *See* message handling service.

MHz *See* megahertz.

MIB *See* management information base.

MIC *See* media interface connector.

MICA *See* Modem ISDN Channel Aggregation.

micro channel architecture (MCA) Bus interface commonly used in PCs and some UNIX workstations and servers.

microcode Resides in ROM and is a translation layer that allows the addition of new machine instructions without requiring that they be designed into electronic circuits when new instructions are needed.

Microcom Networking Protocol (MNP) A communications protocol developed by Microcom, Inc., that is used by many high-speed modems. MNP supports several different classes of communication, each higher class providing additional features. Modems can support one or more classes.

Class 4 provides error detection and automatically varies the transmission speed based on the quality of the line.

Class 5 provides data compression.

Class 6 attempts to detect the highest transmission speed of the modem at the other end of the connect and transmit at that speed.

The most common levels of MNP support are Class 4 and Class 5, frequently called MNP-4 and MNP-5. Using the data compression techniques provided by MNP-5, devices can double normal transmission speeds. Because MNP is usually built into the modem hardware, it affects all data transmission. In contrast, software protocols, such as Xmodem and Kermit, affect only file transfer operations.

microcontroller A highly integrated chip that contains all the components comprising a controller. A microcontroller can be compared to a microprocessor in that the microcontroller only performs a specific task or limit scope of operations where the microprocessor is more generalized in functional operations.

micro-electromechanical systems (MEMS) A technology that combines computers with tiny mechanical devices such as sensors, valves, gears, mirrors, and actuators embedded in semiconductor chips.

microprocessor A silicon chip that contains a CPU. In the world of personal computers, the terms microprocessor and CPU are used interchangeably. At the heart of all personal computers and most workstations sits a microprocessor. Microprocessors also control the logic of almost all digital devices, from clock radios to fuel-injection systems for automobiles.

microsegmentation The division of a network into smaller segments, usually with the intention of increasing available bandwidth to network devices.

Microsoft Founded in 1975 by Paul Allen and Bill Gates, Microsoft Corporation is the largest and most influential company in the personal computer industry. In addition to developing the de facto standard operating systems—DOS and Windows—Microsoft has a strong presence in almost every area of computer software, from programming tools to end-user applications.

In recent years, Microsoft has broadened its product categories to include different types of media, such as CD-ROMs and its TV news network (together with NBC) called MSNBC. In the mid-90s, Microsoft was caught somewhat by surprise by the sudden explosion of the Internet, but it quickly re-created itself to make the Internet the core element of its product line.

Many people have criticized Microsoft for monopolistic policies and it has been investigated several times by the United States Justice Department. Currently, it is in a fierce battle with Netscape Communications and other companies for control of the corporate desktop. Microsoft wants Windows to retain its role as the standard operating system for PCs, whereas Netscape and some of its allies, such as Sun Microsystems, would like to see Windows give way to a new model of computing in which PCs run small Java applets locally, with the bulk of the operating system functionality performed by Internet servers.

In 1999 Microsoft was found to be a monopoly, which is illegal in the United States. As of this printing the future of Microsoft is being decided.

 For more information, see Microsoft's site at *http://www.microsoft.com*

Microsoft CD-ROM Extension (MSCDEX) A driver that enables DOS and Windows 3.x systems to recognize and control CD-ROM players. The driver is located in a file called MSCDEX.EXE. Windows 95 replaces MSCDEX with a 32-bit, dynamically loadable driver called CDFS.

Microsoft Certified Systems Engineer (MCSE) A person who has passed exams about the Microsoft Windows NT operating system, related desktop systems, networking, and Microsoft's BackOffice server products. To prepare for the exams, an individual can take courses at a certified training company location, certified courses in a high school or college, through self-study at Microsoft's self-study Web site, or through certified training materials.

Microsoft cluster server (MSCS) A clustering technology built into Windows NT 4.0 and later versions. MSCS supports clustering of two NT servers to provide a single fault-tolerant server.

Microsoft Foundation Classes (MFC) A large library of C++ classes developed by Microsoft.

Microsoft Network Microsoft's online service. Like competing services such as America

Online, MSN offers e-mail, topic-related forums, and full access to the World Wide Web.

Microsoft SMS The Systems Management Server™ network discovery engine developed by Microsoft Corporation for Windows NT.

Microsoft Windows A family of operating systems for personal computers. Windows provides a graphical user interface (GUI), virtual memory management, multitasking, and support for many peripheral devices.

microwave Broadcast electromagnetic waves in the range 1 to 30 GHz. Microwave-based networks are an evolving technology gaining favor due to high bandwidth and relatively low cost.

MID *See* multiplex identification.

midband A communication channel with a bandwidth range of 28.8 to 56 Kbps.

middleware Software that connects two otherwise separate applications. For example, there are a number of middleware products that link a database system to a Web server. This allows users to request data from the database using forms displayed on a Web browser, and it enables the Web server to return dynamic Web pages based on the user's requests and profile. Middleware is sometimes very hard to define because it maybe integrated into another software product and there is no clear interface between the application and the middleware function.

MIDI *See* musical instrument digital interface.

midsplit A type of broadband cable system in which the available frequencies transmission are split into two groups: one for transmission and one for reception.

MIF *See* management information format.

Military Network (MILNET) Originally part of the ARPANET. In 1984 it was segmented for military installation usage. Unclassified portion of the DDN. Operated and maintained by the DISA. *See* DDN *and* DISA.

Millennium A Microsoft research project that seeks to build distributed computing—networks that share resources.

million instructions per second (mips) A general measure of computing performance and, by implication, the amount of work a larger computer can do; used by some computer manufacturers (including IBM).

millisecond (ms) One thousandth of a second. Access times of hard disk drives are measured in milliseconds.

MILNET *See* Military Network.

MIME *See* Multipurpose Internet Mail Extensions.

MIN *See* multistage interconnection network.

minicomputer A midsized computer. In size and power, minicomputers lie between workstations and mainframes. In the past decade, the distinction between large minicomputers and small mainframes has blurred. There has been a similar problem in the distinction between small minicomputers and workstations. In general, a minicomputer is a multiprocessing system capable of supporting from 4 to about 200 users simultaneously.

minimize To turn a window into an icon.

minimum cell rate (MCR) A parameter that gives the minimum rate that cells can be transmitted by a source over a virtual connection (VC). *See* available bit rate (ABR), ACR, *and* PCR.

mips *See* million instructions per second.

mirror (*a*) To maintain an exact copy of something. Probably the most common use of the term on the Internet refers to *mirror sites*, which are Web or FTP sites, which maintain exact copies of material originated at another location, usually in order to provide more widespread access to the resource. (*b*) An arrangement where information is written to more than one hard disk simultaneously, so that if one disk fails, the computer keeps on working without losing anything. *See* FTP *and* Web.

MIS *See* management information system.

MIT *See* management information tree.

MME A file in multi-purpose Internet mail extensions (MIME) format that is created by

M

some e-mail programs, including that of America Online (AOL), to encapsulate e-mail that contains image or program attachments.

MMF *See* multimode fiber.

MMP *See* Multichassis Multilink Point-to-Point Protocol.

MMS *See* manufacturing messaging service.

MMU *See* memory management unit.

MMX A set of 57 multimedia instructions built into Intel's newest microprocessors and other x86-compatible microprocessors. MMX-enabled microprocessors can handle many common multimedia operations, such as digital signal processing (DSP), that are normally handled by a separate sound or video card. However, only software especially written to call MMX instructions—so-called MMX-enabled software—can take advantage of the MMX instruction set. The first generation of computers with MMX chips was released to the public in January, 1997.

MNP *See* Microcom Networking Protocol.

mobo Motherboard. Sometimes used in Usenet newsgroups and Web forum discussions.

mode name In SNA, a name used by the initiator of a session to designate the characteristics desired for the session.

modeling Generally, the process of representing a real-world object or phenomenon as a set of mathematical equations. More specifically, the term is often used to describe the process of representing 3-dimensional objects in a computer. All 3-D applications, including CAD/CAM and animation software, perform modeling.

modem A modulator/demodulator. A modem converts the serial digital data from a transmitting device into a form suitable for transmission over the analog telephone channel and vice versa for the purpose of using computer devices in remote locations. Computer information is stored digitally, whereas information transmitted over telephone lines is transmitted in the form of analog waves. A modem con-

verts between these two forms. Basically, modems do for computers what a telephone does for humans.

Fortunately, there is one standard interface for connecting external modems to computers, called RS-232. Consequently, any external modem can be attached to any computer that has an RS-232 port, which almost all personal computers have. There are also modems that come as expansion boards that the user can insert into vacant expansion slots. These are sometimes called *onboard* or *internal* modems.

Although the modem interfaces are standardized, a number of different protocols for formatting data to be transmitted over telephone lines exist. Some, like CCITT V.34, are official standards, while others have been developed by private companies.

Most modems have built-in support for the more common protocols—at slow data transmission speeds at least, most modems can communicate with each other. At high transmission speeds, however, the protocols are less standardized. Aside from the transmission protocols that they support, the following characteristics distinguish one modem from another—the *bits per second (bps)* rate, which determines how fast the modem can transmit and receive data. At slow rates, modems are measured in terms of *baud rates*. The slowest rate is 300 baud (about 25 cps). At higher speeds, modems are measured in terms of bits per second (bps). The fastest modems run at 57,600 bps, although they can achieve even higher data-transfer rates by compressing the data.

Obviously, the faster the transmission rate, the faster you can send and receive data. Note, however, that a modem cannot receive data any faster than it is being sent. If, for example, the device sending data to a computer is sending it at 2,400 bps, the modem must receive it at 2,400 bps. It does not always pay, therefore, to have a very fast modem. In addition, some telephone lines are unable to transmit data reliably at very high rates.

Many modems support a *voice/data* switch to change between voice and data modes. In data mode, the modem acts like a regular modem.

In voice mode, the modem acts like a regular telephone. A modem that supports a voice/data switch has a built-in loudspeaker and microphone for voice communication.

An *auto-answer* modem enables your computer to receive calls in your absence. This is only necessary if you are offering some type of computer service that people can call in to use.

Some modems perform *data compression*, which enables them to send data at faster rates. However, the modem at the receiving end must be able to decompress the data using the same compression technique.

Some modems come with *flash memory* rather than conventional ROM, which means that the communications protocols can be easily updated if necessary.

Most modern modems are *fax modems*, which means that they can send and receive faxes. To get the most out of a modem, you should have a communications software package, a program that simplifies the task of transferring data.

Modems are also being used to modulate and demodulate digital signals over broadband cable networks *cable modems*).

modem eliminator Device that connects two DTE devices together without modems.

Modem ISDN Channel Aggregation (MICA) Cisco trademarked modem/ISDN integration technology.

modified frequency modulation (MFM) An encoding scheme used by PC floppy disk drives and older hard drives.

Modula-2 A programming language designed by Niklaus Wirth, the author of Pascal. Wirth created Modula-2 in the late 1970s to answer many of the criticisms leveled at Pascal, which he had created ten years earlier. In particular, Modula-2 addresses Pascal's lack of support for separate compilation of modules and multitasking. Although Modula-2 found support in academia, it is not often used for applications.

modular architecture The design of any system composed of separate components that can be connected together. The beauty of modular architecture is that components or modules can be replaced or added without affecting the rest of the system. The opposite of a modular architecture is an *integrated architecture*, in which no clear divisions exist between components. The term modular can apply to both hardware and software. Modular software design, for example, refers to a design strategy in which a system is composed of relatively small and autonomous routines that fit together.

modulate To blend data into a carrier signal. At the receiving side, a device demodulates the signals by separating the constant carrier signals from the variable data signals. For example, radio uses two types of modulation— *amplitude modulation (AM)* and *frequency modulation (FM)*—to mix audio signals with an AM or FM carrier signal. A modem modulates data by converting it to audible tones that can be transmitted on a telephone wire, and demodulates received signals to get the data.

modulation The process in which the characteristics of one wave or signal are varied in accordance with another wave or signal. Modulation can alter frequency, phase, or amplitude characteristics.

modulator-demodulator *See* modem.

module (*a*) In software, a module is a part of a program. Programs are composed of one or more independently developed modules that are not combined until the program is linked. A single module can contain one or several routines. (*b*) In hardware, a module is a self-contained component.

monitor (*v.*) To watch or observe a task, program execution, or the like. (*n.*) A display screen; or, more usually, the entire display unit.

monochrome One color. Monitors, for example, can be monochrome, grayscale, or color. Monochrome monitors actually use two colors, one for the display image (the foreground) and one for the background. Graphic images can also be monochrome, grayscale, or color.

monomode fiber *See* single-mode fiber.

monospacing Refers to fonts in which each character has the same width. The opposite of

M

monospacing is *proportional spacing*, in which different characters have different widths. For example, in a proportionally spaced font, the letter o would be wider than the letter i. Proportionally spaced fonts look more professional, but monospaced fonts are often superior for tabular data because the uniform width of each character makes alignment of columns easier. Most printed matter, including this book, uses proportional spacing.

MOO *See* Mud, Object Oriented.

Moore's Law The observation made in 1965 by Gordon Moore, co-founder of Intel, that the number of transistors per square inch on integrated circuits had doubled every year since the integrated circuit was invented. Moore predicted that this trend would continue for the foreseeable future. In subsequent years, the pace slowed, but data density has doubled approximately every 18 months; this is the current definition of Moore's Law, which Moore himself has blessed. Most experts, including Moore, expect Moore's Law to hold for at least another two decades.

MOP *See* Maintenance Operation Protocol.

Mosaic The first WWW browser that was available for the Macintosh, Windows, and UNIX all with the same interface. Mosaic really started the popularity of the Web. Originally produced by the National Center for Supercomputing Applications (NCSA), Mosaic has always been distributed as freeware. In 1994, however, the NCSA turned over commercial development of the program to a company called Spyglass. There are now several varieties of Mosaic, some free and some for sale. The source code to Mosaic has been licensed by several companies and there are several other pieces of software as good as or better than Mosaic, most notably, Netscape. *See* browser, client, *and* WWW.

MOSPF *See* multicast OSPF.

motherboard The main circuit board of a microcomputer. The motherboard contains the connectors for attaching additional boards. Typically, the motherboard contains the CPU, BIOS, memory, mass storage interfaces, serial and parallel ports, expansion slots,

and all the controllers required to control standard peripheral devices, such as the display screen, keyboard, and disk drive. Collectively, all these chips that reside on the motherboard are known as the motherboard's *chipset*.

On most PCs, it is possible to add memory chips directly to the motherboard. You may also be able to upgrade to a faster CP by replacing the CPU chip. To add additional core features, you may need to replace the motherboard entirely.

Motif A set of user interface guidelines created by the Open Software Foundation that specify how an application should look and feel, covering issues like the placement of title bars and menus. It is used on more than 200 hardware and software platforms and has become the standard graphical user interface (GUI) for UNIX.

 For more information, see the Open Software Foundation site at *www.opengroup.org*.

mount (*a*) To make a mass storage device available. (*b*) To install a device, such as a disk drive or expansion board.

mouse A device that controls the movement of the cursor or pointer on a display screen. A mouse is a small object that the user can roll along a hard, flat surface.

Its name is derived from its shape, which looks a bit like a mouse, its connecting wire that one can imagine to be the mouse's tail, and the fact that one must make it scurry along a surface. As the user moves the mouse, the pointer on the display screen moves in the same direction. Mice contain at least one button and sometimes as many as three, which have different functions depending on what program is running. Some newer mice also include a scroll wheel for scrolling through long documents.

The mouse was invented by Douglas Engelbart of Stanford Research Center in 1963, and pioneered by Xerox in the 1970s, the mouse is one of the great breakthroughs in computer ergonomics because it frees the user, to a large extent from using the keyboard. In particular, the mouse is important for graphical user interfaces because the user can simply point to options and objects and click a mouse button. Such applications are often called *point-and-click* programs. The mouse is also useful for graphics programs that allow users to draw pictures by using the mouse like a pen, pencil, or paintbrush.

mouseover A JavaScript element that triggers a change on an item (usually a graphic) in a Web page when the mouse passes over it. The change usually signifies that the item is a link to related or additional information. Mouseovers are widely used in Navigation Bars, pop-up boxes, and/or form submissions.

Mouseovers require JavaScript in two places of an HTML document. At the beginning of a document and before the body tag, JavaScript defines the event to take place. After the body tag, HTML code contains the actual mouseover element in the place on the Web page where the user wants the action to take place. When the mouse passes over the HTML code containing the mouseover element, it signals the JavaScript event to take place.

Moving Picture Experts Group (MPEG) A working group of ISO. The term also refers to the family of digital video compression standards and file formats developed by the group. MPEG generally produces better-quality video than competing formats, such as Video for Windows, Indeo, and QuickTime. MPEG files can be decoded by special hardware or by software.

Mozilla The original name for Netscape's browser, now called Navigator. Some people claim that the term is a contraction of Mosaic Godzilla (e.g., Mosaic killer), because Mosaic was the primary Web browser at the time Netscape began developing its product. The term Mozilla is still used by many Web developers and appears in server log files that identify the browsers being used. In 1998, Netscape decided to make the source code for Navigator freely available to the public. The

Netscape group responsible for releasing the code is called mozilla.org.

 For more information, see Mozilla's site at *www.mozilla.org*.

MP Multilink Point-to-Point Protocol.

MP3 *See* MPEG, audio layer 3.

MPEG *See* Moving Picture Experts Group.

MPEG, audio layer 3 (MP3) Layer 3 is one of three coding schemes (layer 1, layer 2, and layer 3) for the compression of audio signals. Layer 3 uses perceptual audio coding and psychoacoustic compression to remove all superfluous information (more specifically, the redundant and irrelevant parts of a sound signal, which the human ear doesn't hear anyway). It also adds a modified discrete cosine transform (MDCT) that implements a filter bank, increasing the frequency resolution 18 times higher than that of layer 2.

The result in real terms is that layer 3 shrinks the original sound data from a CD (with a bit rate of 1411.2 kilobits per one second of stereo music) by a factor of 12 (down to 112–128 Kbps) without sacrificing sound quality. (Bit rate denotes the average number of bits that one second of audio data will consume.) Because MP3 files are small, they can easily be transferred across the Internet.

Controversy arises when copyrighted songs are sold and distributed illegally from Web sites. On the other hand, musicians may be able to use this technology to distribute their own songs from their own Web sites to their listeners, thus eliminating the need for record companies. Costs to the consumer would decrease, and profits for the musicians would increase.

MPOA *See* Multiprotocol over ATM.

MPP *See* massively parallel processing.

MPPP *See* multi-link PPP.

MQI *See* Message Queuing Interface.

MR Mean rate. *See* average cell rate.

M

ms *See* millisecond.

MSCDEX *See* Microsoft CD-ROM Extension.

MSCS *See* Microsoft cluster server.

MS-Windows *See* Microsoft Windows.

MTA *See* message transfer agent.

MTBF *See* mean time between failures.

MTU *See* maximum transmission unit.

MUCK *See* Multi-User Chat Kingdom.

MUD *See* Multi-User Dungeon (or Multi-User Dimension).

MUD, Object Oriented (MOO) A specific implementation of a MUD system developed by Stephen White. MOO is in the public domain and can be freely downloaded and executed.

multiaccess A physical network that supports the attachment of more than two routers.

multibank DRAM (MDRAM) A relatively new memory technology developed by MoSys Inc.

multicast Method of transmitting messages from a host using a singe transmission to a selected subset of all the hosts that can receive the messages; also a message that is sent out to multiple devices on the network by a host. A simple example of multicasting is sending an e-mail message to a mailing list. Teleconferencing and videoconferencing also use multicasting, but require more robust protocols and networks. Standards are being developed to support multicasting over a TCP/IP network such as the Internet. These standards, IP Multicast and Mbone, will allow users to easily join multicast groups. *See* anycast, unicast, broadcast, *and* IP.

multicast address resolution server (MARS) A program used to support IP Multicast over ATM. It contains tables of IP multicast addresses and associated ATM addresses.

Multicast Backbone on the Internet (Mbone) An extension to the Internet to sup-

port IP multicasting, or the two-way transmission of data between multiple sites. The TCP/IP protocol used by the Internet divides messages into packets and sends each packet independently. Packets can travel different routes to their destination which means that they can arrive in any order and with sizable delays between the first and last packets. In addition, each recipient of the data requires that separate packets be sent from the source to the destination.

This works well for static information, such as text and graphics, but not for real-time audio and video. With Mbone, a single packet can have multiple destinations and isn't split up until the last possible moment. This means that it can pass through several routers before it needs to be divided to reach its final destinations. This leads to much more efficient transmission and also ensures that packets reach multiple destinations at roughly the same time.

MBone is an experiment to upgrade the Internet to handle live multimedia messages. MBone servers have special Class D IP addresses. As of March 1997, there were more than 3,000 MBone servers on the Internet. The Mbone was developed by Steve Deering at Xerox PARC and adopted by the Internet Engineering Task Force (IETF) in March 1992.

multicast group A group set up to receive messages from a source. These groups can be established based on frame relay or IP in the TCP/IP protocol suite, as well as in other networks.

multicast interface An interface to a to a link over which IP multicast or IP broadcast service is supported.

multicast link A link over which IP multicast or IP broadcast service is supported. This includes broadcast media such as LANs and satellite channels, single point-to-point links, and some store-and-forward networks such as SMDS networks.

multicast OSPF (MOSPF) A series of extensions applied to the OSPF intradomain routing protocol for all OSPF to support IP multicast routing.

multicast router Router running a multicast enabled routing protocol, like MOSPF, used to route IGMP query messages on their attached local networks.

multicast server A specialized server that establishes a one-to-many connection to each device in a VLAN, thus establishing a broadcast domain for each VLAN segment. The multicast server forwards incoming broadcasts only to the multicast address that maps to the broadcast address.

multicasting A directory service agent uses this mode to chain a request to many other directory service agents.

Multichassis Multilink Point-to-Point Protocol (MMP) A Cisco protocol that allows multiple connections from a single site to terminate in multiple access servers while still looking like one single larger connection.

Multics Multiplexed Information and Computing Service was a mainframe time-sharing operating system that was developed in the 1963–1969 period through the collaboration of the Massachusetts Institute of Technology (MIT), General Electric (GE), and Bell Labs. Multics was the first or one of the first operating systems that used page-segmented storage. The operating system was written in PL/I and run on GE hardware. By 1970, Bell Labs had withdrawn from the project, and Honeywell, which had bought GE's computer division, continued as the hardware provider.

multidrop line A communications line having multiple cable access points. Sometimes called a *multipoint line*.

multifunction peripheral (MFP) A single device that serves several functions, including printing. Typically, multifunction printers can act as a printer, a scanner, a fax machine, and a photocopier. These devices are becoming a popular option for SOHO users because they're less expensive than buying three or four separate devices.

multihomed host (*a*) Host attached to multiple physical network segments in an OSI CLNS network. (*b*) A TCP/IP host connected to two or more physical networks; thus they have more than one address. They can serve as router-type devices.

multihoming Addressing scheme in IS-IS routing that supports assignment of multiple area addresses.

multilayer switch Switch that filters and forwards packets based on MAC addresses and network addresses. A subset of LAN switch. Compare with LAN switch.

Multilink Point-to-Point Protocol (MP) An extension to the PPP protocol that allows multiple physical connections between two points to be combined into a single logical connection. The combined connections, called a bundle, provide greater bandwidth than a single connection. Unlike *channel bonding*, which usually combines two channels for the duration of a connection, MP supports dynamic bandwidth allocation, which means that physical links can be added or removed from the bundle as needed. MP works with a number of technologies, including ISDN, X.25, and frame relay. It is an open standard, specified in RFC 1990.

multi-link PPP (MPPP) Method of extending PPP so that multiple connections can be added together for higher bandwidth and lower latency. Must be supported at both ends of the connection.

multilink transmission group According to IBM documentation, a transmission group containing two or more links.

multimedia A way of presenting to the user a combination of different forms of information such as text, data, images, video, audio, and graphics (i.e., videoconference). Nearly all PCs are capable of displaying video, although the resolution available depends on the power of the computer's video adapter and CPU. Because of the storage demands of multimedia applications, the most effective media are CD-ROMs.

multimode The transmission of multiple modes of light.

multimode fiber (MMF) A type of fiber mostly used for short distances such as those found in a campus LAN. It can carry 100 Mbs/sec for

M

typical campus distances, the actual maximum speed (given the right electronics) depending upon the actual distance. It is easier to connect to than single-mode fiber, but its limit on speed x distance is lower.

multiple access A situation where each station waits for an idle channel before transmitting.

multiple document interface (MDI) A Microsoft Windows programming interface for creating an application that enables users to work with multiple documents at the same time. Each document is in a separate space with its own controls for scrolling. The user can see and work with different documents such as a spreadsheet, a text document, or a drawing space by simply moving the cursor from one space to another.

multiple virtual storage (MVS) The operating system for older IBM mainframes. MVS was first introduced in 1974 and continues to be used, though it has been largely superseded by IBM's newer operating system, OS/390.

multiple virtual storage/extended architecture (MVS/XA) An IBM operating system.

multiple-domain network In SNA, a network with more than one SSCP. In APPN, a network with more than one network node.

multiplex (*Illustration*) To combine multiple signals (analog or digital) for transmission over a single line or media. A common type of multiplexing combines several low-speed signals for transmission over a single high-speed connection. The following are examples of different multiplexing methods: *frequency division multiplexing (FDM)*, where each signal is assigned a different frequency; *time division multiplexing (TDM)*, where each signal is assigned a fixed time slot in a fixed rotation (a common example of this in the telecommunication industry is the SONET ADM (add drop multiplexer) used to selectively combine or remove multiple digital channels); *statistical time division multiplexing (STDM)*, where time slots are assigned to signals dynamically to make better use of bandwidth; *wavelength division multiplexing (WDM)*, where each signal is assigned a particular wavelength; used on optical fiber.

multiplex identification (MID) A 10-bit field in the AAL3/4 SAR-PDU header for identifying the different CPCS-PDUs multiplexed over the same VCC.

multiplexer A device that allows several users to share a single circuit and funnels different data streams into a single stream. At the other end of the communications link, another

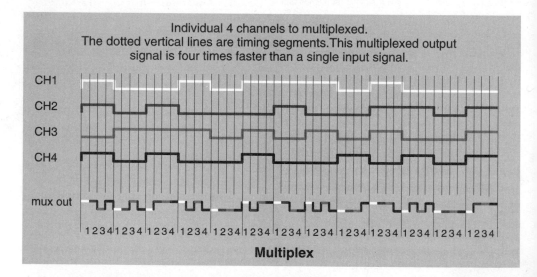

Individual 4 channels to multiplexed.
The dotted vertical lines are timing segments. This multiplexed output signal is four times faster than a single input signal.

Multiplex

multiplexer reverses the process by splitting the data stream back into the original streams. A MUX is a networking local device where multiple streams of information are combined so they can share a common physical medium.

multipoint line A telecommunication line or circuit that connects two or more stations.

multiport communications interface (MCI) A card on the AGS+ that provides two Ethernet interfaces and up to two synchronous serial interfaces. The MCI processes packets rapidly, without the typical interframe delays common in other Ethernet interfaces.

multiprotocol encapsulation Provides for higher protocols, such as IP, to perform bridging and routing functions over an ATM network.

Multiprotocol over ATM (MPOA) A set of standards to support, other than IP, (distributed) routing protocols. Developed on top of LANE and NHRP, it will support switches, route servers, and hosts, all attached to an ATM network. The goal of MPOA is to allow different LANs to send packets to each other via an ATM backbone. Unlike other techniques, such as LAN Emulation (LANE), which operates at level 2 of the OSI Reference Model, MPOA operates at level 3.

For more detail see:
http://www.atmforum.com.

Multipurpose Internet Mail Extensions (MIME) Defined in 1992 by the Internet Engineering Task Force (IETF) for formatting non-ASCII (text) messages so that they can be sent over the Internet. It is documented in RFC 1521 and RFC 1522, which define the standard representation for "complex" message bodies. A "complex" message body doesn't conform to the default of a single, human-readable, ASCII mail message. Examples of "complex" message bodies include messages with embedded graphics or audio clips, messages with file attachments, messages in Japanese or Russian, or signed messages.

MIME defines several new header fields: *Mime-Version* (identifying a MIME document),

Content-Type, and *Content-Transfer-Encoding*. The most interesting of these is Content-Type, which defines the content of the document, and comes in seven predefined types, each of which has subtypes. An extension mechanism exists for defining new types and subtypes. The Content-Transfer-Encoding defines several encoding mechanisms for binary data that may otherwise be difficult to transport.

An e-mail program is said to be *MIME compliant* if it can both send and receive files using the MIME standard. When non-text files are sent using the MIME standard they are converted (encoded) into text—although the resulting text is not really readable.

The MIME standard is also universally used by Web Servers to identify the files they are sending to Web clients; in this way new file formats can be accommodated simply by updating the browsers' list of pairs of MIME-Types and appropriate software for handling each type. This enables the browser to display or output files that are not in HTML format.

There are many predefined MIME types, such as GIF graphics files and PostScript files. It is also possible to define your own MIME types. A new version, *secure MIME (S/MIME)*, supports encrypted messages. *See* browser, client, server, binhex, *and* UUENCODE.

MultiRead A new specification for CD-ROM and compact disc players that enables them to read discs created by CD-RW drives.

Multi-Router Traffic Grapher (MRTG) A free program that graphs statistics taken from routers.

The MRTG is available at
http://www.ee.ethz.ch/~oetiker/ webtools/mrtg.

multistage interconnection network (MIN) A switch fabric built from switching elements organized in series and/or in parallel, for providing physical connections between the inputs and the outputs of a switch.

multistation access unit (MAU/MSAU) Wiring concentrators to which token ring sta-

M

tions attach. Patch cables are used to connect MAUs to adjacent MAUs, and network adapter/lobe cables are used to connect eight or more stations to a MAU. Up to 12 MAUs can be interconnected. MAUs include bypass relays for removing powered-down or failed stations from the ring in order to preserve the integrity of the ring. MAUs come in various types (passive or active) from various manufacturers. When operating in passive mode, the MAU does not perform any regeneration of the signal. The actual station NIC generates the signal and drives it around the ring. When operating in active mode the MAU drives the signal to the device(s) and between any MAUs that are interconnected. Unfortunately there are no standards for active products and there can be problems when operating at 16 Mbps.

In a token-ring network, the MAU is a device that physically connects network computers in a star topology while retaining the logical ring structure. One of the problems with the token-ring topology is that a single non-operating node can break the ring. The MAU solves this problem because it has the ability to short out non-operating nodes and maintain the ring structure. A MAU is a special type of hub.

multitasking The ability to execute more than one task/program at the same time. The terms multitasking and multiprocessing are often used interchangeably, although multiprocessing sometimes implies that more than one CPU is involved.

Multi-User Chat Kingdom (MUCK) A text-based MUD system. MUCK is similar to MUSH, although it uses different software. *See* MUD.

Multi-User Dungeon (or **Multi-User Dimension**) **(MUD)** A cyberspace where users can take on an identity in the form of an *avatar* and interact with one another. Originally, MUDs tended to be adventure

games played within enormous old castles with hidden rooms, trap-doors, exotic beasts, and magical items. Nowadays, the term is used more generically to refer to any cyberspace.

MUDs are also known as 3-D worlds and chat worlds. Some are purely for fun and flirting, others are used for serious software development, or education purposes, and all that lies in between. A significant feature of most MUDs is that users can create things that stay after they leave which other users can interact with in their absence, thus allowing a world to be built gradually and collectively.

multi-user shared hallucination (MUSH) A text-based MUD system. There are many MUSH worlds that have been evolving for years.

multivendor network Network that uses equipment from more than one vendor, posing more compatibility problems than single-vendor networks.

MUMPs A program that assists companies and academic researchers with ideas for microelectromechanical systems (MEMS) to manufacture prototypes. Because the manufacture of silicon chips in which MEMS are embedded is costly, MUMPs provides special manufacturing "runs" that qualified enterprises can be part of. MUMPs is administered by the MEMS Technology Application Center (MCNC).

MUSH *See* multi-user shared hallucination.

musical instrument digital interface (MIDI) A standard adopted by the electronic music industry for controlling devices, such as synthesizers and sound cards, that emit music.

MUX *See* multiplexer.

MVS *See* multiple virtual storage.

MVS/XA *See* multiple virtual storage/extended architecture.

Nagle's algorithm The Nagle algorithm was introduced in TCP to reduce the number of small TCP segments by delaying their transmission, in hopes of further data becoming available, as commonly occurs in Telnet or rlogin traffic. It's actually two separate congestion control algorithms, which can be used in TCP-based networks. One algorithm reduces the sending window; the other limits small datagrams. For example, when someone types in a Telnet session, one character is sent in as packet. (The transmission of a single-character message originating at a keyboard typically results in a 41-byte packet [one byte of data, plus 40 bytes of header] being transmitted for each byte). This is very wasteful of bandwidth. Instead, if the source waits some finite time before sending another short packet, then a couple of characters accumulate in the next packet. The ratio of overhead to real data goes down and network efficiency goes up.

NAK *See* negative-acknowledge character.

name A sequence of one or more characters that uniquely identifies a file, variable, account, or other entity. Names are sometimes called *identifiers*.

Name Binding Protocol (NBP) A protocol in the AppleTalk protocol suite that maps user-designated names into appropriate network addresses and network services.

name caching A method by which remotely discovered host names are stored by a router for use in future packet-forwarding decisions. This allows quick access.

name resolution The process of locating an entry by sequentially matching each relative distinguished name in a purported name to a vertex of the directory information tree. Accessing a resource, once given its name, requires the following two steps: (1) finding a name-to-location mapping service that knows locations for the name in question;

and (2) querying that service to obtain a list of locations.

name server A server, connected to a network, which resolves network names into network addresses.

names information socket (NIS) Another name given to socket 2 of Mac computers.

naming context In OSI networks, this refers to a substructure of the directory information tree. It starts at a vertex (top) and extends downward to a leaf and/or nonleaf structure.

nanometer Common unit of length in optical measurements, such as wavelengths. Equivalent to 1/1,000,000,000 (one-billionth) meter.

nanosecond (ns) One billionth of a second. Used to measure the speed of memory access; (e.g.) the speed of memory chips is measured in nanoseconds. Many microprocessors operate at hundreds of megahertz, which is equivalent to a tenth of a nanosecond per clock cycle.

NAP *See* network access point.

narrowband A transmission medium or channel with a single voice channel with a carrier wave of a certain modulated frequency. A low-capacity, voice-grade communication channel with a bandwidth of less than 28.8 Kbps. It usually implies a speed of 56Kbps or less. *See* broadband; wideband.

Narrowband Integrated Services Digital Network (N-ISDN) Predecessor to Broadband ISDN (B-ISDN), N-ISDN, encompasses the original standards for ISDN. Communication standards developed by the ITU-T for baseband networks. Based on 64-kbps B channels and 16- or 64-kbps D channels. *See* OSI standards Q.921 and Q.931 standards for a more detailed definition.

narrowcast To send data to a specific list of recipients. Cable television is an example of a narrowcasting, because the cable TV signals are sent only to homes that have subscribed to the cable service—the signals are said to be a "narrowcast". In contrast, television reception through an antenna uses a broadcast model, in which the signals are transmitted everywhere and anyone with an antenna can receive them.

NASDAQ National Association of Security/ Securities Dealers Automated Quotations. The National Association of Securities Dealers (NASD) is the largest self-regulatory organization for the securities industry in the United States. NASD is responsible for the operation and regulation of Nasdaq and the over-the-counter securities markets; it is the parent company of NASD Regulation, Inc., and The Nasdaq Stock Market, Inc., which is home to many emerging high-tech companies.

National Bureau of Standards *See* National Institute of Standards and Technology (NIST).

National Electrical Code (NEC) A set of standards controlling the installation, use, and applications of all electrical devices and components (e.g.) wire, cable, fixtures, and electrical and optical communications cables. The NEC was developed by the fire-prevention and insurance industry's NEC Committee of the American National Standards Institute (ANSI), was sponsored by the National Fire Protection Association (NFPA), and is identified by the description ANSI/NFPA 70-XXXX, the last four digits representing the year of the NEC revision.

National Institute of Standards and Technology (NIST) A federal agency under the Department of Commerce, originally established by an act of Congress on March 3, 1901 as the National Bureau of Standards. The Institute's overall goal is to strengthen and advance the Nation's science and technology and facilitate their effective application for public benefit. The National Computer Systems Laboratory conducts research and provides, among other things, the technical foundation for computer-related policies of the Federal Government.

National Research and Education Network (NREN) An interconnected gigabit computer network system devoted to High Performance Computing and Communications (HPCC), designed to ensure the United States' technical leadership in computer communications through research and development efforts in state-of-the-art telecommunications and networking technologies. *See* High Performance Computing *and* Communications (HPCC).

National Science Foundation (NSF) An independent United States government agency responsible for promoting science and engineering through programs that invest over $4.4 billion per year in almost 30,000 research and education projects in science and engineering. The now-defunct National Science Foundation Network (NSFNET) was funded by the NSF. *See* National Science Foundation Network (NSFNET).

National Science Foundation Network (NSFNET) A National Science Foundation (NSF) network or "backbone" that connected six United States supercomputing centers together. To expand access to the Internet, the National Science Foundation (NSF) also supported the development of regional networks, which were then connected to the NSFNET backbone. In addition, the NSF supported institutions, such as universities, in their efforts to connect to the regional networks. *See* National Science Foundation (NSF).

National Television Standards Committee (NTSC) An agency responsible for setting television and video standards in the United States (in Europe and the rest of the world, the dominant television standards are *PAL* and *SECAM*). The NTSC standard for television defines a composite video signal with a refresh rate of 60 half-frames (interlaced) per second. Each frame contains 525 lines and can contain 16 million different colors.

native Referring to an original form.

NAUN *See* nearest active upstream neighbor.

Navigator Netscape Communication's popular Web browser. There are many versions of Navigator, which run on all major platforms (e.g.) Windows, Macintosh, UNIX.

NBMA *See* nonbroadcast multi-access (NBMA).

NBP *See* Name Binding Protocol.

NBS *See* National Bureau of Standards.

NC *See* network control.

NCB *See* node control block.

NCCF *See* Network Communications Control Facility.

NCE *See* network connection endpoint.

NCP/EP Definition Facility (NDF) Network control emulation program definition facility or network control program echo protocol definition facility.

NCP *See* Network control program.

NCS *See* network computing system.

NCTE *See* network channel-terminating equipment.

NDF *See* NCP/EP Definition Facility.

NDIS *See* Network Device Interface Specification.

NDS *See* Novell Directory Services.

NE *See* network element.

nearest active upstream neighbor (NAUN) In Token Ring or IEEE802.5 networks, the closest upstream network device from any given device that is still actively participating on the ring. A token ring algorithm called *beaconing* detects and tries to repair certain network faults. Whenever a station detects a serious problem with the network (such as a cable break), it sends a beacon frame. The beacon frame defines a *failure domain*, which includes the station reporting the failure, its nearest active upstream neighbor (NAUN), and everything in between. Beaconing initiates a process called *autoreconfiguration*, where nodes within the failure domain automatically perform diagnostics in an attempt to reconfigure the network around the failed areas. Physically, the MSAU can accomplish this through electrical reconfiguration.

NEC Technologies A Japanese company; one of the world's largest computer and electron-ics manufacturers, and the second largest producers of semiconductors (Intel is first). Its line of monitors has set the standard for many years. It also produces PCs and notebook computers, and controls half the PC market in Japan.

NEC *See* National Electrical Code.

NEF *See* Network Element Function.

negative response (NR) A response indicating that a request did not arrive successfully or was not processed successfully by the receiver. In SNA, a response (also -RSP) that indicates that a request has not arrived successfully or was not processed successfully by the receiver.

negative-acknowledge character (NAK) A transmission control character is sent by a station as a negative response to the station with which the connection has been set up. In a binary synchronous communication protocol, the NAK is used to indicate that an error was detected in the previously received block, and that the receiver is ready to accept retransmission of that block. In a multipoint systems, the NAK is used as the not-ready reply to a poll.

negotiable BIND The capability that allows two half-sessions to negotiate the parameters of a session when that session is being activated. I.e., it is the ability of two LU-LU half sessions to determine the parameters of a session during session activation. Each half session can negotiate for the LU's desired session parameters.

neighboring routers In a routing protocol like OSPF, two routers that have interfaces to a common network. On multi-access networks, neighbors are dynamically discovered by the OSPF Hello protocol.

NEL *See* Network Element Layer.

NEM *See* Network Element Management.

NEMESYS RACE I Project R 1005. RACE projects are European community (EC) funded projects to investigate advanced computing and IT (information technology) ideas.

Net PC A Windows-based type of network computer designed cooperatively by Microsoft and Intel. Net PC is seen as a significant cost savings, because it may have a small hard disk (or none at all), with programs downloaded from the network.

NetBEUI (NetBIOS Enhanced User Interface) An enhanced version of the NetBIOS protocol used by Windows-based operating systems such as Windows 95, 98, 2000 and Windows NT. NetBEUI adds additional functions and features to NetBIOS and communicates to the network adapter via NDIS. NetBEUI was originally designed by IBM for their LAN Manager server and later extended by Microsoft and Novell.

NetBIOS (Network Basic Input Output System) A commonly used network protocol for local area networks. NetBIOS provides session and transport services (layers 4 and 5 of the OSI model). Because NetBIOS does not provide a standard frame format for transmission over networks, various implementations of NetBIOS have been created. Almost all LANs for PCs are based on NetBIOS. Some LAN manufacturers have even extended it, adding additional network capabilities. With a TCP/IP network, NetBIOS refers to a set of guidelines that describe how to map NetBIOS operations into equivalent TCP/IP operations. NetBIOS relies on a message format called Server Message Block (SMB). *See* NetBEUI.

NETID *See* network identifier.

netiquette Correct usage or etiquette on the Internet. *See* Internet.

netizen Derived from the term *citizen*; refers to a citizen of the Internet, or someone who uses networked resources.

NetMeeting A product developed by Microsoft Corporation that enables groups to teleconference using a network connection. It has become popular wherever a network is extended beyond an intranet to the extranet (i.e.), by using the Internet as the transmission medium. NetMeeting supports Voice on the Net, chat sessions, a whiteboard, and application sharing. It is built into Microsoft's Internet Explorer Web browser.

Netscape A Web browser and the name of its parent company, officially called Netscape Communications Corporation. The Netscape browser was originally based on the Mosaic program, developed at the National Center for Supercomputing Applications (NCSA). The author of Netscape, Mark Andreessen, was hired away from the NCSA by Jim H. Clark, and, in 1994, they founded a company called Mosaic Communications, which soon changed to Netscape Communications Corporation. Netscape revolutionized the computer software market by giving away free copies of its popular Navigator Web browser until it had acquired an overwhelming market share for this category of software. In addition to its browsers, Netscape also produces Web servers and tools for building intranets. Netscape provided major improvements in speed and interface over other browsers, and has also engendered debate by creating new elements for the HTML language used by Web pages. (Netscape extensions to HTML are not universally supported.) Netscape's headquarters are located in Mountain View, California. *See* browser, Mosaic, server, *and* World Wide Web.

NetShow A specification developed by Microsoft for streaming multimedia content over the World Wide Web. Client and server software from Microsoft for streaming audio and video multimedia content over the Internet. RTSP is a competing specification backed by Netscape.

NetView performance monitor An IBM network management program that can run on many IBM platforms, created by IBM to monitor and manage a network and diagnose network problems. It is based on HP OpenView. It consolidates three primary modules (NCCF, NPDA, and NLDM) and two secondary modules (VTAM Node Control Application [VNCA] and Network Management Productivity Facility [NMPF]). Originally announced with ACF/VTAM 3.1.1 and ACF/NCP 4.2.

NetWare A popular local-area network (LAN) operating system developed by Novell Corporation. NetWare runs on a variety of different types of LANs, from Ethernets to IBM token-ring networks. It provides users and programmers with a consistent interface, independent of the actual hardware used to transmit messages.

NetWare Link Services Protocol (NLSP) A link-state routing protocol similar to Open Shortest Path First (OSPF), the link-state routing protocol used in TCP/IP environments. A link-state router maintains a map of the entire network and knows the route from one network to another. In addition, if a link-state router is congested, it can assume a less important role in exchanging link information.

NetWare Link Services Protocol (NLSP) Link-state routing protocol based on IS-IS. *See* IS-IS.

NetWare Loadable Module (NLM) A program that is part of a file server memory with NetWare. An NLM can be loaded or unloaded while the file server is running, become part of the operating system, and access NetWare directly.

network An interconnection of three or more communicating entities. i.e., an interconnection of usually passive electronic components that perform a specific functions (which are usually limited in scope), to simulate a transmission line or to perform a mathematical function such as integration or differentiation. network may be part of a larger circuit. In *local-area networks (LANs)* the devices are geographically close together (that is, in the same building). In *wide-area networks (WANs)*, the devices are geographically separate and are connected by telephone lines or radio waves. The usual connection rates are T1, E1, BRI-ISDN, and T3. In *campus-area networks (CANs)*, the computers and network elements are located within a contiguous assortment of buildings. In *metropolitan area networks (MANs)*, the computers or network elements are located within a metropolitan area (for example New York City). Networks are further categorized by *topology, protocol,* and *architecture*. A topology is the geometric arrangement of a computer system. Common topologies include a bus, star, and ring. A protocol defines a common set of rules and signals that computers on the network use to communicate. One of the most ubiquitous protocols for LANs is called Ethernet. Another popular LAN protocol for PCs is the IBM token-ring network. An architecture is the definition of the processes and logical interrelationships of the network elements that compose the network system being described. Examples of network architecture are a document that explains directory services, routing service. The architecture of a network can be broadly classified as being either peer-to-peer or client/server. Computers on a network are sometimes called *nodes*. Computers and devices that allocate resources for a network are called servers. *See* Internet *and* intranet.

network access point (NAP) In the United States, a network access point—sometimes called a *network access provider*—is one of several major Internet interconnection points that tie all the Internet access providers together. For example, an AT&T user in Portland, Oregon can reach the Web site of a Bell South customer in Miami, Florida using a NAP. Originally, four NAPs—in New York, Washington, D.C., Chicago, and San Francisco—were created and supported by the National Science Foundation as part of the transition from the original United States government-financed Internet to a commercially operated Internet. Since that time, several new NAPs have been created, including WorldCom's "MAE West" site in San Jose, California and ICS Network Systems' "Big East." NAPs provide major switching facilities to serve the general public. Using companies apply to use NAP facilities and make their own intercompany peering arrangements. A lot of Internet traffic is handled without involving NAPs, through peering arrangements and interconnections within geographic regions. The vBNS network, a separate network supported by the National Science Foundation for research purposes, also makes use of the NAPs.

network address In general, each participating entity on a network has an address to identify it when exchanging data. An SNA network address consists of the combination of the subarea and element fields. Other examples of network addressing schemes are NSAP, E.164. The

N

network addressing scheme usually is constructed in a hierarchical manner to expedite searches or routing schemes. The hierarchy structure also allows summarization of many addresses by a shorter prefix, thus reducing the entries in a routing table. *See* IP address.

network address translation (NAT) An IETF Internet standard (RFC 1631) that enables a local-area network (LAN) to hide multiple machines behind a single IP address—one set of IP addresses for internal traffic and a second set of addresses for external traffic. A NAT box located where the LAN meets the Internet makes all necessary IP address translations. NAT provides a type of firewall by hiding internal IP addresses and enabling a company to use more internal IP addresses. Because the addresses are used internally only, there's no possibility of conflict with IP addresses used by other companies and organizations. This allows a company to combine multiple ISDN connections into a single Internet connection. Because NAT allows an organization's IP network to appear to use an IP address space different from what it is actually using, private IP addresses (always at a premium) may be conserved. Public addresses are used within the intranet, while private addresses are used for the Internet. NAT also allows some protection by masking the internal network and provides a more graceful renumbering strategy for organizations that are changing service providers or voluntarily renumbering into classless interdomain routing (CIDR) blocks.

network addressable unit (NAU) In the SNA protocol, *network addressable unit*. An SSCP, CP, PU, or LU SNA resource, which contains a unique network address and network name. Each NAU contains a unique network address used to represent it to the path control network. LUs may contain multiple addresses to support parallel sessions. An SNA network is the aggregation of all NAUs and the path control network.

network architecture The logical and physical structure of a computer network. It is the design principles, physical configuration, functional organization, operational procedures, and data formats used as the basis for the design, construction, modification, and operation of a communications network. It is also the structure of an existing communications network, including the physical configuration, facilities, operational structure, operational procedures, and the data formats in use.

Network Basic Input/Output System *See* NetBIOS.

network channel-terminating equipment (NCTE) Customer premises equipment used with US West's Switched Digital Service.

Network Communications Control Facility (NCCF) A VTAM network management program. NCCF monitors, controls, and modifies the operation of a physical SNA network. A component of NetView.

network computing system (NCS) A computer system designed to deliver networked information and applications to the user.

network connect block (NCB) A user-generated data structure used in a nontransparent task to identify a remote task and optionally send user data in calls to request, accept, or reject a logical link connection.

network connection endpoint (NCE) NCEs identify CPs, LUs, Boundary Functions (BFs), and Route Setup (RS) components.

network control (NC) (*a*) A type of network computer designed to execute Java programs locally. (*b*) The lowest of the three Transmission Control (Layer 4) sublayers. Designated as an RU category within an RH that is utilized for activating and deactivating explicit and virtual routes, and for sending load modules to adjacent peripheral nodes. A request or response unit (RU) category used for request and responses exchanged between physical units (PUs).

network control program (NCP) An interactive utility program that allows a manager to control and monitor a network. Also a switch or network node; software designed to store and forward frames between nodes. An NCP may be used in local area networks or larger networks. In IBM systems, the main software component in a 37xx communication controller. NCP is generated from a library of IBM-supplied modules and controls communication controller operations.

Network Device Interface Specification (NDIS) A hardware-independent Windows-based generic device driver for network interface cards. They allow NICs to support multiple network protocols, such as TCP/IP and IPX, at the same time. NDIS was originally developed by Microsoft and 3Com.

network element (NE) In integrated services digital networks, a piece of telecommunications equipment that provides support or services to the user. An example of a network element is a router, switch, or hub in the network.

Network Element Function (NEF) A function within an ATM entity that supports the ATM-based network transport services, (e.g., multiplexing, cross-connection).

Network Element Layer (NEL) A network layer representing data of network elements and the operations that can be performed on those elements.

Network Element Management (NEM) A network-layer element (NM-layer) that offers functions for management of a network as a whole. In this layer, separate NEs are visible as are the relationships between the different NEs. This layer offers a network-view to the network manager. This can, for example, be a group of network elements (NEs) from the same manufacturer, or a group of NEs located in the same region, etc. This layer handles the transformation of manufacturer-specific characteristics to general characteristics of NEs.

Network File System (NFS) (*a*) A proprietary distributed file system widely used by TCP/IP vendors. NFS allows different computer systems to share files, and uses user datagram protocol (UDP) for data transfer. (*b*) An open operating system, designed by Sun Microsystems, which allows network users to access shared files stored on a variety of computer platforms. NFS provides access to shared files through an interface called the *Virtual File System (VFS)*, which uses TCP/IP to make shared files appear, and be manipulated, as if they are local to a user's hard drive. NFS conceals differences between local and remote files by placing them in the same name space. Originally designed for UNIX systems, it is now implemented on many other systems, including PCs and Apple computers. With NFS, computers connected to a network operate as clients when accessing remote files, and as servers when providing remote user access to local shared files. The NFS standards are publicly available and widely used. NFS is implemented using the RPC Protocol, designed to support remote procedure calls. All NFS operations are implemented as RPC procedures. A summary of NFS procedures is shown below:

Procedure 0: NULL—Do nothing

Procedure 1: GETATTR—Get file attributes

Procedure 2: SETATTR—Set file attributes

Procedure 3: LOOKUP—Look up filename

Procedure 4: ACCESS—Check access permission

Procedure 5: READLINK—Read from symbolic link

Procedure 6: READ—Read from file

Procedure 7: WRITE—Write to file

Procedure 8: CREATE—Create a file

Procedure 9: MKDIR—Create a directory

Procedure 10: SYMLINK—Create a symbolic link

Procedure 11: MKNOD—Create a special device

Procedure 12: REMOVE—Remove a file

Procedure 13: RMDIR—Remove a directory

Procedure 14: RENAME—Rename a file or directory

Procedure 15: LINK—Create link to an object

Procedure 16: READDIR—Read from directory

Procedure 17: READDIRPLUS—Extended read from directory

Procedure 18: FSSTAT—Get dynamic file system information

N

Procedure 19: FSINFO—Get static file system information

Procedure 20: PATHCONF—Retrieve POSIX information

Procedure 21: COMMIT—Commit cached data on a server to stable storage

network identifier (NetID) A network name defined to NCPs and VTAMs to indicate the name of the network within which they reside. Net ID is unique across all communicating SNA networks.

network information center (NIC) An organization that provides information, assistance, and administrative services to users of a network. The NIC also oversees network names and addresses, and it is often a repository of requests for comment (RFCs).

network information file Files designed from the beginning to facilitate indexing, archiving, and distribution of electronic information. Design is integrated from the beginning and throughout the information file creation, as contrasted to cataloging and redesigning the completed subject document.

network information service (NIS) A distributed database used to manage a network of computers. Sun Microsystem's Solaris operating system introduced NIS+, and enhanced version of NIS.

network interface card (NIC) A network interface device (NID) in the form of a circuit card that is installed in an expansion slot of a computer to provide network access. Examples of NICs are cards that interface a computer with an Ethernet LAN and cards that interface a computer with an FDDI ring network.

network job entry (NJE) The NJE uses any number of TCP/IP software products for transport, and typically uses Ethernet or IEEE 802.3 local area networks and IP routers for physical connections. These communications facilities can be shared with other applications, such as Telnet terminal emulation.

Network Layer Layer 3 of the seven-layer Open Systems Interconnection (OSI) stack. It is responsible for data transfer across the network. It functions independently of network media and topology. There are seven network layers in the Open Systems Interconnection Reference Model (OSI-RM), which is an abstract description of the digital communications between application processes running in distinct systems. The model employs a hierarchical structure. Each layer performs value-added service at the request of the adjacent higher layer and, in turn, requests more basic services from the adjacent lower layer:

The *Physical Layer (Layer 1)*, is the lowest of the seven hierarchical layers. The Physical layer performs services requested by the Data Link Layer. The major functions and services performed by the physical layer are: (*a*) establishment and termination of a connection to a communications medium; (*b*) participation in the process whereby the communication resources are effectively shared among multiple users, e.g., contention resolution and flow control; and (*c*) conversion between the representation of digital data in user equipment and the corresponding signals transmitted over a communications channel.

The *Data Link Layer (Layer 2)* responds to service requests from the Network Layer and issues service requests to the Physical Layer. The Data Link Layer provides the functional and procedural means to transfer data between network entities and to detect and possibly correct errors that may occur in the Physical Layer. Examples of data link protocols are HDLC and ADCCP for point-to-point or packet-switched networks and LLC for local area networks.

The *Network Layer (Layer 3)* responds to service requests from the Transport Layer and issues service requests to the Data Link Layer. The Network Layer provides the functional and procedural means of transferring variable length data sequences from a source to a destination via one or more networks while maintaining the quality of service requested by the Transport Layer. The Network Layer performs network routing, flow control, segmentation/desegmentation, and error control functions.

The *Transport Layer (Layer 4)* responds to service requests from the Session Layer and issues service requests to the Network Layer. The Transport Layer provides transparent transfer of data between end users, thus relieving the upper layers from any concern with providing reliable and cost-effective data transfer.

The *Session Layer (Layer 5)* responds to service requests from the Presentation Layer and issues service requests to the Transport Layer. The Session Layer provides the mechanism for managing the dialogue between end-user application processes. It provides for either duplex or half-duplex operation and establishes checkpointing, adjournment, termination, and restart procedures.

The *Presentation Layer (Layer 6)* responds to service requests from the Application Layer and issues service requests to the Session Layer. The Presentation Layer relieves the Application Layer of concern regarding syntactical differences in data representation within end-user systems. An example of a presentation service would be the conversion of an EBCDIC-coded text file to an ASCII-coded file.

The *Application Layer (Layer 7)* is the highest layer; it interfaces directly to and performs common application services for application processes; it also issues requests to the Presentation Layer. The common application services provide semantic conversion between associated application processes. Examples of common application services of general interest include the virtual file, virtual terminal, and job transfer and manipulation protocols.

network logical data manager (NLDM) A NCCF program that collects and correlates LU-LU session-related data and monitors the SNA network for logical errors through session trace. A component of NetView.

Network Management Forum (NMF) A forum which evaluates and critiques systems and network management products. The NMF insists that product offerings are designed to cover a diversity of management protocols prevalent in IT, and have the flexibility to move towards applications management in the future. This insistence on design independence is crucial as the industry moves towards measuring 'service availability' against Service Level Agreements, rather than simply measuring at an element level.

network management processor (NMP) A processor module on the Cisco Catalyst 5000 switch that is used to control and monitor the switch.

network management system (NMS) (*a*) The execution of the set of functions required for controlling, planning, allocating, deploying, coordinating, and monitoring the resources of a telecommunications network, including performing functions such as initial network planning, frequency allocation, predetermined traffic routing to support load balancing, cryptographic key distribution authorization, configuration management, fault management, security management, performance management, and accounting management. Network management does not include user terminal equipment. (*b*) A product that helps manage a network (e.g., HP OpenView, Cableton's Spectrum, Bay/Nortel's Optivity, etc.). An NMS program generally is hosted on a reasonably powerful and well-equipped computer such as an engineering workstation. NMSs communicate with agents to help keep track of network statistics and resources.

network management vector transport (NMVT) An SNA message consisting of a series of vectors that convey network management-specific information. NMVT RUs provide alert, problem determination statistics, and other network management data. NMVT is specified within SNA Management Services (SNA/MS), also Network Management Architecture (NMA). The NMVT vectorizes and sub-vectorizes network management data.

network management A network engineer's ability to manipulate his resources from a central location, using the network itself as a communication and configuration medium. Because hosts, routers, and other networking devices often require maintenance operations, and the network is a communications medium, it is possible to use the network itself to perform the maintenance. The oldest and simplest form of network management is the *remote login*, because many routers support Telnet access to some sort of command

N

prompt, and many operations can be performed in no other way. Remote logins are designed for human interaction; the command style and syntax may vary between different hardware and software platforms. A more specialized and standardized approach allows automated software tools to easily perform management operations on a variety of platforms. Also useful is a standard method of reporting network failures and error conditions to a centralized location. For Internet engineers, the Simple Network Management Protocol (SNMP) is currently the most popular vehicle for network management.

network module (NM) Type of plug-in module used in Cisco® 2600 and 3600 routers.

Network News Transport Protocol (NNTP) The protocol used by client and server software to carry USENET postings back and forth over a TCP/IP network. If you are using any of the more common software such as Netscape, Nuntius, Internet Explorer, etc. to participate in newsgroups then you are benefiting from an NNTP connection. The official specification is RFC 977. *See* newsgroup, TCP/IP, *and* USENET.

network node (NN) An SNA intermediate node that provides connectivity, directory services, route selection, intermediate session routing, data transport, and network management services to LEN nodes and ENs. The machine at the intersection of two or more links on an APPN network. Provides session-level intermediate routing as well as directory and route selection services for Type 2.1 nodes. An extension of LEN that supports peer communications between non-adjacent Type 2.1 nodes. Outside of the SNA architecture, a basic building block of the network cloud; e.g., SONET ADM's are network nodes, as are ATM switches and routers in an ATM cloud. *See* network node interface (NNI).

network node interface (NNI) ITU-T-specified standard interface between nodes within the same network. The ATM Forum distinguishes between two standards: one for private networks called P-NNI and one for public networks known as public-NNI.

network number A 16-bit number that provides a unique identifier for a network in an AppleTalk network.

network operating system (NOS) A generic term used to define what are actually distributed file systems. Examples of NOSs include LAN Manager, NetWare, NFS, VINEs, Windows NT4.0, SCO UNIX, Solaris by Sun Systems, Linux, etc.

network operator A person who performs a variety of functions on a network, some of which are control functions.

Network Packet-Switching Interface (NPSI) IBM software that lets SNA data be carried over an X.25 network to another SNA environment.

network parameter control (NPC) Traffic management/engineering mechanism (performed at the NNI) and exercised by a network for traffic received by another network.

network performance (NP) The measurement of a network's ability to meet user needs. Many people in your organization can benefit day-to-day by having network performance information available to them. People outside your organization, such as local LAN administrators, financial planners, or even users, also benefit by performing network performance tasks like planning, budget support, confirmation of network upgrades, monitoring service level agreements, communications with internal clients, quality control, and baselining of network performance.

network performance parameter (NPP) Values usually derived from quality of service (QoS) parameter values.

network problem determination application (NPDA) A program product, presently a component of NetView, used to assist in the identification of physical network problems. Provides event, alert data, and statistical data.

network processor module (NPM) A plug-in module used in Cisco 4000 series routers.

network protocol control information (NPCI) As defined in the RFC941, NPCI is responsible for carrying a network address in a network protocol data unit (NPDU).

network protocol data unit (NPDU) Sometimes called the *protocol data unit (PDU)*, at Layer 3 or the Network Layer. In OSI terminology, a packet. A logical block of control symbols and data transmitted by the network-layer protocol.

network range A unique range of contiguous network numbers used to identify each Ethernet and token-ring network on an AppleTalk network.

network routing facility (NRF) A system that allows an enterprise network to make call routing decisions for calls within the toll-free carrier network before they get to the enterprise. It also allows a customer to decide whether route interactions are based upon real-time statistics, agent skills, customer-stored data, or customer defined business rules and situations.

network service data unit (NSDU) The parameters of the following N.UNITDATA_ request and N.UNITDATA_indication are collectively referred to as Network Service Data Unit (NSDUs). An N.UNITDATA_request consists of NS Source_Address, NS_Destination_ Address, NS_Quality_of_Service, and NS_Userdata. The N.UNITDATA_indication consists of NS_ Source_Address, NS_Destination_Address, NS_ Quality_of_Service, and NS_Userdata).

network service NAU service which controls network operation through SSCP-SSCP, SSCP-PU, and SSCP-LU (control) sessions. Network service includes configuration services, maintenance services, management services, and sessions services.

network service provider (NSP) A company that provides Internet access connectivity to Internet Service Providers (ISPs). Sometimes called *backbone providers*, NSPs offer direct access to the Internet backbone through network access points (NAPs). AT&T, Sprint, and MCI are examples of NSPs.

network services access point (NSAP) In the OSI environment, the *service access point (SAP)* between the network and the transport layers, which identifies data terminal equipment (DTE) by a unique address.

Network Services Protocol (NSP) DECnet transport layer protocol.

Network Terminal One (NT-1) A type of digital modem for ISDN service. The telephone company supplies this everywhere in the world except North America. It is the physical box on site that converts U-loop into S/T-loop.

network terminal option (NTO) An NCP-resident program product that supports certain non-SNA devices on a communications controller. For example, start-stop (3101 emulating) devices are converted within NTO to appear to NCP as a PU 1, LU 1 flow.

network terminating unit (NTU) A device placed at the final interconnect point between the Public Service Telephone Network (PSTN) and the customer-owned equipment. Generally, NTUs are used by government-controlled Post, Telephone, and Telegraph (PTT) entities to terminate various data services, including frame relay.

Network Time Protocol (NTP) A protocol used to synchronize date and time for computers and routers.

Network Voice Protocol (NVP) A TCP/IP protocol for handling voice information.

network-qualified name A name that uniquely identifies a specific resource within a specific network. It consists of a network identifier and a resource name, each of which is a 1- to 8-byte symbol string.

network-to-network interface (NNI) A powerful new diagnostic tool developed for use by frame relay service providers to effectively monitor and manage their networks.

newsgroup Same as *forum*, an on-line discussion group. On the Internet, there are literally thousands of newsgroups covering every conceivable interest. To view and post messages to a newsgroup, you need a *news reader*, a program that runs on your computer and connects you to a news server on the Internet. Also, the name for discussion groups on *USENET*. *See* USENET.

Next Hop Resolution Protocol (NHRP) A protocol used by routers to dynamically dis-

N

cover the MAC address of other routers and hosts connected to a NBMA network. These systems directly communicate without requiring traffic to use an intermediate hop, increasing performance in ATM, frame relay, SMDS, and X.25 environments. *See* RFC 2333.

NEXTSTEP An object-oriented operating system developed by Next Inc., a company started in 1985 by Steven Jobs, one of the cofounders of Apple Computer. In 1997, Apple Computer acquired Next, with idea of making NextStep the foundation of its new Macintosh operating system.

NFS *See* Network File System.

NHRP *See* Next Hop Resolution Protocol.

nibble Half a byte or 4 bits. Nibbles are important in hexadecimal and BCD representations. *See* bit, byte, *and* BCD.

NIC *See* network interface card.

NIF *See* network information file.

NIS *See* names information socket.

N-ISDN *See* Narrowband Integrated Services Digital Network.

NIST *See* National Institute of Standards and Technology.

NIUF *See* North American ISDN Users' Forum.

NJE *See* network job entry.

NL *See* Network Layer.

NLDM *See* network logical data manager.

NLSP *See* NetWare Link Services Protocol.

NM *See* network module.

NMF *See* Network Management Forum.

NMP *See* network management processor.

NMS *See* network management system.

NMVT *See* network management vector transport.

NN *See* network node.

NNI *See* network node interface *and* network-to-network interface.

NNTP *See* Network News Transport Protocol.

node A device that joins one or more links in an SNA network such as processors, communication controllers, and cluster controllers. (*a*) In networks, a processing location. Any single computer connected to a network. A node can be a computer or some other device, such as a printer, terminal servers, and host computers. Every node has a unique network address, sometimes called a Data Link Control (DLC) address or Media Access Control (MAC) address. (*b*) In tree structures, a point where two or more lines meet. *See* network, Internet, intranet.

node control block (NCB) A structure that represents a network control block, which contains information about the command to perform, an optional post routine, an optional event handle, and a pointer to a buffer that is used for messages or other data. A pointer to this structure is passed to the NetBIOS function.

node number A unique number used to identify each node on a network.

node operator facility (NOF) A manager request for Node Type 2.1 Control Point database updates and queries; it activates and deactivates LUs and links.

node type The classification of a network device based on the protocols it supports and the network addressable unit it can contain.

NOF *See* node operator facility.

noise A disturbance that affects a signal and may distort the information carried by the signal. (*a*) An undesired disturbance within the frequency band of interest; the summation of unwanted or disturbing energy introduced into a communications system from man-made and natural sources. (*b*) Random variations of one or more characteristics of any entity such as voltage, current, or data. (*c*) A random signal of known statistical properties of amplitude, distribution, and spectral density. (*d*) Loosely, any disturbance tending to interfere with the normal operation of a device or system.

nonbroadcast frame A frame containing a specific destination address that may contain routing information specifying which bridges are to forward it. A bridge will forward a non-broadcast frame only if that bridge is included in the frame's routing information.

nonbroadcast multi access (NBMA) One of the new wide area network (WAN) technologies, a type of network broacast services found in frame relay and asynchronous transfer mode (ATM).

nonreturn-to-zero (NRZ) A code in which 1s are represented by one significant condition and 0s are represented by another, with no neutral or rest condition, such as a zero amplitude in amplitude modulation (AM), zero phase shift in phase-shift keying (PSK), or mid-frequency in frequency-shift keying (FSK). (*a*) Contrast with return-to-zero. (*b*) For a given data signaling rate, i.e., bit rate, the NRZ code requires only half the bandwidth required by the Manchester code.

nonreturn-to-zero inverted (NRZI) A code in which 1s are represented by a change in a significant condition and 0s are represented by no change. A method for transmitting and recording data so that it keeps the sending and receiving clocks synchronized.

nonseed router In AppleTalk, a router that must first obtain and then verify its configuration with a seed router before it can begin operation. *See* seed router.

non-stub area Resource-intensive OSPF area that carries a default route, static routes, intra-area routes, interarea routes, and external routes. Nonstub areas are the only OSPF areas that can have virtual links configured across them and are the only areas that can contain an ASBR. Compare with stub area. *See* ASBR *and* OSPF.

nonvolatile RAM (NVRAM) Like flash RAM, a memory type that keeps its information after power is removed. On Cisco routers, NVRAM is used to store configuration information.

nonvolatile random access memory (NVRAM) A form of static RAM, the contents of which are saved when a computer is turned off or loses its external power source. NVRAM can be implemented by providing static RAM

with backup battery power or by saving its contents and restoring them from an electrically erasable programmable ROM (EEPROM).

normal response mode (NRM) Also known as *high level data link control (HDLC)*; the basis for the ISO standard data link protocol.

North American ISDN Users' Forum (NIUF) A NIST/industry collaboration, begun in 1988. A Cooperative Research and Development Agreement (CRADA) with industry was established in 1991 to govern the management of the forum. NIST's Information Technology Laboratory (ITL) serves as chair of the forum and hosts the NIUF Secretariat. Through support of the forum, ITL advances new uses of computer and telecommunications technology in government and industry. The purpose of the NIUF is to create a strong user voice in the implementation of ISDN applications. The NIUF provides users of ISDN technology with the opportunity to work with implementers that assure that users' needs are met in the ISDN design process. Through the NIUF, users and manufacturers concur on ISDN applications, the selection of options from standards, and conformance tests, enhancing the strength of the United States telecommunications industry in the world marketplace.

Northwest Net NSF-funded regional network serving the Northwestern United States, Alaska, Montana, and North Dakota. Northwest Net connects all major universities in the region, as well as many leading industrial concerns.

NOS *See* network operating system.

notification An indication that something in the network requires the operator's attention.

Novell Directory Services (NDS) The directory services for Novell Netware networks. NDS complies with the OSI X.500 standard and provides a logical tree-structure view of all resources on the network so that users can access them. NDS also interoperates with other types of networks.

Novell IPX A NetWare network layer (Layer 3) protocol used for transferring data from servers to workstations. IPX is similar to IP and XNS. *See* IPX.

N

NP *See* network performance.

NPA *See* numbering plan area.

NPC *See* network parameter control.

NPCI *See* network protocol control information.

NPDA *See* network problem determination application.

NPDU *See* network protocol data unit.

NPM *See* network processor module.

NPP *See* network performance parameter.

NPSI *See* Network Packet-Switching Interface.

NR *See* negative response.

NREN *See* National Research and Education Network.

NRF *See* network routing facility.

NRM *See* normal response mode.

NRZ *See* nonreturn-to-zero.

NRZI *See* nonreturn-to-zero inverted.

ns *See* nanosecond.

NSAP *See* network services access point.

NSDU *See* network service data unit.

NSF *See* National Science Foundation.

NSFnet A wide-area network developed under the auspices of the National Science Foundation (NSF) and no longer in service. NSFnet replaced ARPANET as the main government network linking universities and research facilities. In 1995, however, the NSF dismantled NSFnet and replaced it with a commercial Internet backbone. At the same time, the NSF implemented a new backbone called *very high-speed Backbone Network Service (vBNS)*, which serves as a testing ground for the next generation of Internet technologies.

NSP *See* network service provider.

NT File System (NTFS) One of several file systems used in Windows NT operating system. Windows NT also supports the FAT file system. NTFS has features to improve reliability, such as transaction logs to help recover from disk failures.

NT-1 *See* Network Terminal One.

NTFS *See* NT File System.

NTO *See* network terminal option.

NTP *See* Network Time Protocol.

NTSC *See* National Television Standards Committee.

NTU *See* network terminating unit.

NuBus The expansion bus for versions of the Macintosh computers starting with the Macintosh II and ending with the Performa. Current Macs use the PCI bus.

null-modem cable (*Illustration*) A specially designed cable that allows two computers to connect directly to each other via their communications ports (RS-232 ports). A null modem cable connects to both computers' serial ports and crosses the sending wire on one end to the receiving wire on the other. Null modems are particularly useful with portable computers because they enable the portable computer to exchange data with a larger system. The null modem flips the lines to accomplish this, making a DTE look like a DCE to the other side and visa versa. This is sometimes called a *crossover cable* for serial connections.

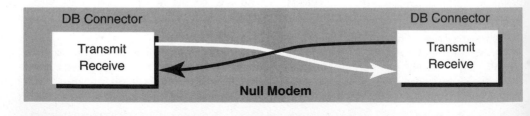

DB Connector

Transmit
Receive

DB Connector

Transmit
Receive

Null Modem

number of sends The number of times that a button must be activated to operate an infrared-controlled device. Most infrared-controlled equipment requires that commands be sent more than once to operate; if you briefly tap a button on your controller, it will send a signal but won't operate the equipment. You have to hold your finger on the button long enough for the code to be sent two or more times. The exact number of times required can vary.

numbering plan area (NPA) North American telecommunications area codes, composed of three digits: 2 to 9, 0 or 1, and 0 to 9. The middle digit is expected to expand soon.

 See *http://www.nanpa.com* for a list of numbering plans.

NVP *See* Network Voice Protocol.

NVRAM *See* nonvolatile RAM.

N

O/R *See* originator/recipient.

OAF *See* origination address field.

OAM *See* operations, administration, and maintenance.

OAM&P *See* operations, administration, maintenance, *and* provisioning.

object Generally, any item that can be individually selected and manipulated. This can include shapes and pictures that appear on a display screen as well as less tangible software entities. In *object-oriented programming*, an object is a self-contained entity that consists of both data and procedures to manipulate the data.

object code The code produced by a compiler. Programmers write programs in a form called *source code*, which consists of instructions in a particular language, like C or FORTRAN. Computers, however, can only execute instructions written in a low-level language called *machine language*. To get from source code to machine language, programs must be transformed by a compiler. The compiler produces an intermediary form called *object code*.

object identifier tree (OIT) Used to promote directory infrastructure and consistency among corporate directories. To promote such a directory schema, an object identifier tree is defined and used to allocate information in a structured (tree) way.

object identifier type In OSI and other environments that implement ASN.1, an ASN.1 type whose values are the pathnames of the nodes of the object identifier tree.

object identifier-based name Names based on the object identifier type.

object instance In network management, an instance of an object type that has been bound to a value.

object linking and embedding (OLE) A technique that allows users to create objects with one application and then link or embed them in a second application. Embedded objects retain their original format but are linked to the application that created them.

object management (OM) A series of specifications which provide a common framework for application development. Conformance to these specifications makes it possible to develop a heterogeneous computing environment across all major hardware platforms and operating systems.

Object Management Group (OMG) A consortium with a membership of more than 700 companies. The organization's goal is to provide a common framework for developing applications using object-oriented programming techniques. OMG is responsible for the CORBA specification.

object oriented A system dealing primarily with different types of objects.

object oriented design (OOD) A software development technique in which a system or component is expressed in terms of objects and connections between those objects.

OCA *See* open communication architectures.

OCC *See* other common carrier.

OC-n *See* optical carrier level n.

octal The base-8 number system, which uses just eight unique symbols (0, 1, 2, 3, 4, 5, 6, and 7). Programs often display data in octal format because it is relatively easy for humans to read and can easily be translated into binary format, which is the most important format for computers. By contrast, decimal format is the easiest format for humans to read because it is the one we use in everyday life; translating between decimal and binary formats is relatively difficult. In octal format, each digit represents three binary digits, as shown:

Octal and Binary Equivalents

Octal	Binary
0	000
1	001
2	010
3	011
4	100
5	101
6	110
7	111

octothorpe The proper name for the symbol "#".

OCX *See* OLE Custom Control.

ODA *See* Open Document Architecture.

ODBC *See* Open DataBase Connectivity.

ODI *See* Open Data-link Interface.

ODI NSIS support (ODINSUP) A shim used to run NDIS over ODI. A *shim* is software that runs on top of one set of drivers to provide an interface equivalent to another set. This is useful, for example, if you want to run software requiring an NDIS driver (such as Chameleon NFS) alongside software requiring a packet driver interface (such as KA9Q, Gopher, Popmail, NCSA Telnet, etc.), or run software intended for, say, a packet driver over an NDIS driver instead.

ODIF *See* Office Document Interchange Format.

ODINSUP *See* ODI NSIS support.

ODP *See* open distributed processing.

Office Document Interchange Format (ODIF) A standard for the actual encoding of the Open Document Architecture (ODA) format, which is a markup code standard devised by the ISO.

offline (*a*) Not connected. (*b*) Used in a more general sense to describe events that occur outside of a standard procedure. (*c*) A resource not being available.

OIM *See* OSI Internet Management.

OIT *See* object identifier tree.

OIW *See* OSI Implementation Workshop.

OLAP *See* online analytical processing.

OLE *See* object linking and embedding.

OLE Custom Control (OCX) An independent program module that can be accessed by other programs in a Windows environment.

OLRT *See* online real time.

OLTP *See* online transaction processing.

OLU *See* originating logical unit.

OM *See* object management.

OMG *See* Object Management Group.

ONA *See* Open Network Architecture.

ONC *See* Open Network Computing.

ones density Scheme that allows a CSU/DSU to recover the data clock reliably. The CSU/DSU derives the data clock from the data that passes through it. To recover the clock, the CSU/DSU hardware must receive at least one 1 bit value for every 8 bits of data that pass through it. Also called *pulse density*.

on-line Turned on and connected. Users are considered on-line when they are connected to a computer service through a modem. That is, they are actually "on the line."

online analytical processing (OLAP) A category of software tools that provides analysis of data stored in a database.

online real time (OLRT) Computer systems capable of executing online transactions in real time, as in electronic money applications such as cybercash.

online transaction processing (OLTP) Transaction processing.

on-the-fly packet switching Packet-switching method in which the switching device begins to forward an incoming data packet as soon as the first portion of the packet (containing the destination address) is completely received and the outgoing port is determined. *See* cut-through packet switching.

OO *See* object oriented.

OOD *See* object-oriented design.

open architecture Architecture with which third-party developers can legally develop products and for which public domain specifications exist.

open circuit Broken path along a transmission medium. Open circuits will usually prevent network communication.

open communication architectures (OCA) Computer systems that do not depend upon proprietary components. There are many more-or-less open communications architectures, for example: IBM's Systems Network Architecture, DEC's Digital Network Architecture, and the set of standards associated with the US DARPA network. Other examples of open architectures are ISDN, ATM, and X.25.

Open DataBase Connectivity (ODBC) A standard database access method developed by Microsoft Corporation. The goal of ODBC is to make it possible to access any data from any application, regardless of which database management system (DBMS) is handling the data.

Open Data-link Interface (ODI) An application programming interface (API) developed by Novell for writing network drivers. ODI separates the physical network layer (the data-link layer in the OSI model) from the network protocol layer (the transport layer). As a result, the same network interface card (NIC) can be used to carry data for different protocols. For example, ODI allows a computer with just one NIC to be simultaneously connected to both an IPX/SPX network and a TCP/IP network.

open destination (OPNDST) Occurring when a destination host opens a connection that is accessible to users.

open distributed processing (ODP) Systems that support heterogeneous distributed processing both within and between organizations through the use of a common interaction model.

Open Document Architecture (ODA) ISO standard that specifies how documents are represented and transmitted electronically.

Open Network Architecture (ONA) In the context of the FCC's Computer Inquiry III, the overall design of a communication carrier's basic network facilities and services to permit all users of the basic network to interconnect to specific basic network functions and interfaces on an unbundled, equal-access basis. The ONA concept consists of three integral components: (*a*) basic serving arrangements (BSAs), (*b*) basic service elements (BSEs), and (*c*) complementary network services.

Open Network Computing (ONC) The distributed applications architecture designed by Sun Microsystems and currently controlled by a consortium led by Sun. The NFS protocols are part of ONC. *See* NFS.

Open Shortest Path First (OSPF) A routing protocol developed for IP networks based on the shortest path first or *link-state algorithm*. OSPF uses the *Djikstra* or Shortest Path Algorithm to calculate the shortest path between routers in an internetwork. Each router running OSPF will send the "links" it is aware of and their status to its neighboring routers. From this link-state database, a routing table is calculated using the shortest path first algorithm. Routers use link-state algorithms to send routing information to all nodes in an internetwork by calculating the shortest path to each node based on a topography of the Internet constructed by each node. Each router sends that portion of the routing table (keeps track of routes to particular network destinations) that describes the state of its own links, and it also sends the complete routing structure (topography). The advantage of shortest path first algorithms is that they result in smaller, more frequent updates everywhere. They converge quickly, thus preventing such problems as *routing loops* and *count-to-infinity* (when routers continuously increment the hop count to a particular network). This makes for a stable network. The disadvantage of shortest path first algorithms is that they require a lot of CPU power and memory. In the end, the advantages out weigh the disadvantages. OSPF Version 2 is defined in RFC 1583.

Open Software Foundation (OSF) Now part of *The Open Group*. A consortium formed by Digital, IBM, and Hewlett-Packard for the promotion of open architectures and systems.

O

Open System Interconnection (OSI) Also known as the *OSI Reference Model* or *OSI Model*. In the 1980s, the International Standards Organization (ISO), began to develop the Open Systems Interconnection (OSI) networking suite. The result was an ISO standard for worldwide communications that defines a networking framework for implementing protocols in seven layers.

Open Systems Interconnection (OSI) (*Illustration*) The only internationally accepted framework for communication between two systems made by different vendors. It is a seven-layer architecture developed by the ISO.

Instructions are passed from one layer to the next, starting at the application layer in one end station, proceeding to the bottom layer, over to the next station and back up the layers. OSI has two major components: an abstract model of networking (the Basic Reference Model, or seven-layer model), and a set of concrete protocols. The standard documents that describe OSI are for sale and not currently available online. The seven layers of the OSI Basic Reference Model are (from bottom to top):

1. The *Physical layer*, which describes the physical properties of the various communications media, as well as the electrical properties and interpretation of the exchanged signals. For example, this layer defines the size of Ethernet coaxial cable, the type of BNC connector used, and the termination method.

2. The *Data Link layer* describes the logical organization of data bits transmitted on a particular medium; this layer defines the framing, addressing and check summing of Ethernet packets.

3. The *Network layer* describes how a series of exchanges over various data links can deliver data between any two nodes in a network; this layer defines the addressing and routing structure of the Internet.

4. The *Transport layer* describes the quality and nature of the data delivery. It defines if and how retransmissions will be used to ensure data delivery.

5. The *Session layer* describes the organization of data sequences larger than the packets handled by lower layers. This layer describes how request and reply packets are paired in a remote procedure call.

6. The *Presentation layer* describes the syntax of data being transferred. For example, this

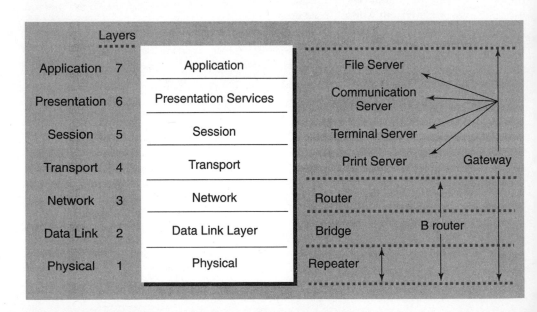

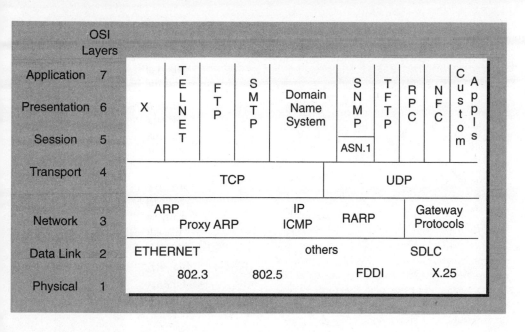

OSI Layers											
Application 7		TELNET	FTP	SMTP	Domain Name System	SNMP	TFTP	RPC	NFC	Custom	Appls
Presentation 6	X										
Session 5						ASN.1					
Transport 4		TCP				UDP					
Network 3		ARP / Proxy ARP		IP / ICMP		RARP	Gateway Protocols				
Data Link 2	ETHERNET		others		SDLC						
Physical 1		802.3	802.5		FDDI	X.25					

layer describes how floating point numbers can be exchanged between hosts with different math formats.

7. The *Application layer* describes how real work actually gets done. This layer implements file system operations.

open-systems environment (OSE) An operating system environment in which the souce code and kernel are open for changes; a nonproprietary system.

open-systems interconnection lower layers (OSILL) The lower layers of the OSI model, which are concerned with physical interconnection.

open-systems interconnection upper layers (OSIUL) The upper layers of the OSI model, which handle the transfer of sematical application information.

open-systems network services (OSNS) Typically, a group that provide technical expertise for network services and open systems. The basic purpose of this group is to keep the computers systems operational and efficient.

operand In SNA, an entity on which an operation is performed. That which is operated on.

An operand is usually identified by an address part of an instruction.

operating environment The environment in which users run programs on a computer.

operating system A software program which manages the basic operation of a computer system.

operations, administration, and maintenance (OAM) Set of administrative and supervisory actions regarding network performance monitoring, failure detection, and system protection. Special-type cells are used to carry OAM-related information.

operations, administration, maintenance, and provisioning (OAM&P) A set of network management functions and services that interact to provide the necessary network management tools and control.

operations system function A functional block that controls, monitors, coordinates management activities, and is also responsible for maintaining the Management Information Base (MIB), which is a collection of objects that can be accessed via a management protocol.

O

operator (*a*) A symbol that represents a specific action. (*b*) An individual who is responsible for ensuring that a computer runs properly.

OPNDST *See* open destination.

optical carrier level n (OC-n) (*Illustration*) The fundamental unit in the Sonet (Synchronous Optical Network) hierarchy. OC indicates an optical signal and *n* represents increments of 51.84 Mbit/s. Thus, OC-1, -3, and -12 equal optical signals of 51, 155, and 622 Mbit/s.

optical disk An optical storage medium that uses lasers to write and read data with a capacity of up to 6 gigabytes. Data is read from and written to by lasers. Optical disks can store much more data—up to 6 gigabytes (6 billion bytes)—than most portable magnetic media, such as floppies. There are Read-only optical disks and Read/Write disks. The Read-only versions have a much greater retention time for data stored.

optical network A network that uses light pulses or photons instead of electronic pulses to transmit data, usually over fiber optic cables or through infrared transmissions. *See* SONET.

optical scanner A device that can read text or illustrations printed on paper and translate the information into an electronic format that a computer can use.

optical spectrum analyzer (OSA) A device used to obtain the absolute accuracy of the wavelength across the entire temperature range.

Oracle Corporation The largest vendor of database products in the software arena, headquartered in Redwood City, California.

Orange Book The specification covering writable CDs, including CD-R and CD-W.

organizational unique identifier (OUI) The threeoctets assigned by the IEEE in a block of 48-bit LAN addresses.

originating logical unit (OLU) An SNA term used to identify the initiating entity or LU in a session or transmission.

origination address field (OAF) A field which gives the address of the origination network addressable unit (NAU).

originator/recipient (O/R) A collection of at least one MTA, zero or more UAs, zero or more MSs, and zero or more AUs operated by an organisation, which constitutes a Management Domain(MD). For instance, in country codes, either a two-character code from ISO 3166 or an X.121 Data Country.

orphan file A file that no longer has a purpose.

OS *See* operating system.

Name/Acronym	Bandwidth	Equivalent DS0	Equivalent DS1	Equivalent DS3	comments
DS0	64Kb/s	1	*	*	one phone line
DS1/T1	1.544Mb/s	24	1	*	popular service
DS1C	3.152Mb/s	48	2	*	equipment
E1/CEPT1	2.048Mb/s	32	1	*	European
DS2	6.312Mb/s	96	4	*	equipment
E2	8.448Mb/s	96	4	*	European
DS3/T3	44.736Mb/s	672	28	1	popular service
E3	34.368Mb/s	512	16	1	European
DS4	139.264Mb/s	2016	80	6	long haul radio
STS-1	51.84Mb/s	672	28	1	electrical OC1
OC-1	51.84Mb/s	672	28	1	SONET
OC-3	155.520Mb/s	2,016	84	3	SONET
OC-12	622.080Mb/s	8,064	336	12	SONET
OC-48	2.488Gb/s	32,256	1,344	48	SONET
OC-192	9.953Gb/s	129,024	5,376	192	SONET

OS/2 An operating system for PCs developed originally by Microsoft Corporation and IBM, but sold and managed solely by IBM.

OS/400 Operating System/400 for the AS/400 computer, IBM's mid-range operating system.

OS/9 A real-time, multi-user, multitasking operating system developed by Microware Systems Corporation.

OSA *See* optical spectrum analyzer.

oscillation The periodic movement between two values.

OSE *See* open-systems environment.

OSF *See* Open Software Foundation.

OSI Implementation Workshop (OIW) A series of OSI workshops hosted by the National Institute of Standards and Technology (NIST), which specifies the details of an OSI configuration for use in the government so that interoperable OSI products can be procured from commercial vendors.

OSI Internet Management (OIM) The group assigned to define how OSI network management protocols can be used to manage TCP/IP networks.

OSI Management Information Service (OSIMIS) A package from UCL that uses object-oriented design and implementation in the creation of managed objects.

OSILL *See* open-systems interconnection lower layers.

OSIMIS *See* OSI Management Information Service.

OSINET International association designed to promote OSI in vendor architectures.

OSIRM *See* Open Systems Interconnection (OSI).

OSIUL *See* open-systems interconnection upper layers.

OSNS *See* open systems network services.

OSPF *See* Open Shortest Path First.

other common carrier (OCC) A communications common carrier—usually an interexchange carrier—that offers communications services in competition with AT&T and/or the established United States telephone local exchange carriers.

OUI *See* organizational unique identifier.

outframe Maximum number of outstanding frames allowed in an SNA PU2 server at any time.

out-of-band Call detail information that is not sent through the same channel as the call itself (i.e., a voice call is carried on an ISDN-B channel, but the call setup information—the number to dial, type of call, duration, etc.—is carried on the D channel).

output device Any machine capable of accepting and representing information from a computer. This includes display screens, printers, plotters, and synthesizers.

overclock To run a microprocessor faster than the speed for which it has been tested and approved.

overflow error An error that occurs when the computer attempts to handle a number that is too large for it.

overhead Use of computer resources for performing a specific feature.

O

P

P/F *See* poll/final bit.

P1 Protocol 1 (message transfer protocol/ MHS/X.400).

P2 Protocol 2 (interpersonal messaging MHS/ X.400).

P3 Protocol 3 (submission and delivery protocol/ MHS/X.400).

P5 Protocol 5 (teletext access protocol).

P7 Protocol 7 (message store access protocol in X.400).

PABX *See* private automatic branch exchange.

pacing A technique by which a receiving component controls the rate of transmission of a sending component to prevent overrun or congestion. *See* flow control.

pacing response According to IBM documentation, in SNA, an indicator that signifies the readiness of a receiving component to accept another pacing group. The indicator is carried in a response header for session-level pacing and in a transmission header for virtual route pacing.

pacing window According to IBM documentation, the path information units (PIUs) that can be transmitted on a virtual route before a virtual-route pacing response is received, indicating that the virtual route receiver is ready to receive more PIUs on the route.

packet A series of bits logically grouped together and found at the network layer of the OSI model. A packet contains data and control information, including the source and destination addresses formatted with a header, to ready it for transmission from one end station (host) to another. The terms *datagram, frame, message*, and *segment* are also used to describe logical information groupings at various layers of the OSI reference model and in various technology circles. *See* PDU.

packet assembler/disassembler (PAD) A functional unit that enables data terminal equipment (DTE), not equipped for packet switching, to access a packet-switched network. In packet-switching technology, a device at a packet-switching network permitting access from an asynchronous terminal. Terminals connect to a PAD, and a PAD puts the terminal's input data into packets, then takes the terminal's output data out of packets. This is a key component of an X.25 network.

packet handler or **packet handling (PH)** The ET/PCX.25 level 3 driver; a state machine implementation of the X.25 packet layer protocol compatible with the widely accepted CCITT recommendations. Functionally, the driver retrieves frames from the communication board and passes them to the level 3 packet handler. The packet handler performs the required functions and passes user data and event indications to the user interface. Control packets pertinent to protocol processing are transmitted automatically, without user intervention.

All variable management, state changes, data buffering and error control is handled by the driver without user intervention. The Application Interface (API) utilizes system work areas (dynamically allocated at installation time), which provide the user with the necessary interface for monitoring and controlling driver activity. The packet handler is completely interrupt driven, producing real-time background performance while maintaining the ability to process user commands in a multi-user, multi-tasking environment.

packet Internet groper Erroneous definition of the word *ping*, which has become something of an urban legend. *See* ping.

packet-level protocol Network-layer protocol in the X.25 protocol stack. Sometimes called *X.25 Level 3* or *X.25 Protocol*.

packet switch WAN device that routes packets along the most efficient path and allows a communications channel to be shared by multiple connections.

packet-switched data network (PSDN) Network that uses packet-switching technology for data transfer.

packet switching Wide area network transmission method where a network device shares a single synchronous serial point-to-point link to transport packets from source to destination. Examples of a packet, switched network include frame relay and X.25. Packets within this type of network can vary in length, whereas cell switching uses fixed-length packets.

packet-by-packet An implementation of Layer 3 switching that uses industry-wide, standard routing protocols to examine all packets and forward them to their destination entirely within Layer 3.

Packet-layer (also level) Protocol (PLP) Network-layer protocol in the X.25 protocol stack. Sometimes called *X.25 Level 3* or *X.25 Protocol*.

packets per second (PPS) A measure of router processing speed.

Packet-Switched Interface (PSI) DEC software that lets a VAX participate in an X.25 network.

packet-switched network (PSN) A network in which data is transmitted in units called *packets*. The packets can be routed individually over the best available network connection and reassembled to form a complete message at the destination.

packet-switched public data network (PSPDN) Packet-oriented public network usually based on X.25.

PAD *See* packet assembler/disassembler.

padding Units used to fill in unused space.

page fault An invalid page fault or a page fault error occurs when the operating system cannot find the requested data in its virtual memory.

page table base register On AXP systems, the processor register or its equivalent, in a hardware privileged context block, which contains the page frame number of the process' first-level page table.

page view The accessing of a Web page. Often used by sites to give advertisers a sense of traffic, a page view differs from a *hit* by counting only the number of times a page has been accessed, whereas a hit counts the number of times that all the elements in a page, including graphics, have been accessed. Page views, however, have become more difficult to gauge, because pages can include frames that divide them into separate parts.

page (*a*) A fixed amount of data. (*b*) In word processing, a page of text. (*c*) In virtual memory systems, a fixed number of bytes recognized by the operating system. (*d*) Short for Web page.

pagelet A 512-byte unit of memory in an AXP environment. On AXP systems, certain DCLs and utilities use pagelets to accept as input or provide as output memory requirements and quotas for commands, system services, and system routines.

paging A technique used by virtual memory operating systems to help ensure that needed data need is available as quickly as possible. The operating system copies a certain number of pages from a storage device to main memory. When a program needs a page that is not in main memory, the operating system copies the required page into memory and copies another page back to the disk.

PAL *See* phase alternating line *and* programmable array logic.

palette (*a*) In computer graphics, the set of available colors. (*b*) In paint and illustration programs, a collection of symbols that represent drawing tools.

Palo Alto Research Center (PARC) Research and development center operated by Xerox. A number of widely used technologies were originally conceived at PARC, including the first personal computers and LANs.

PAM *See* pulse amplitude modulation.

PAP *See* Password Authentication Protocol.

paperless office An idealized vision of an office in which paper is absent because all information is stored and transferred electronically. .

parallel (*Illustration*) (*a*) A device capable of receiving more than one bit at a time. (*b*) Processes are occurring simultaneously.

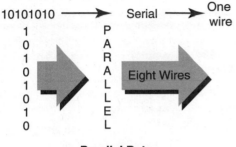

Parallel Data

parallel bridge One of the two or more bridges that connect the same two LAN segments in a network.

parallel channel Channel that uses bus and tag cables as a transmission medium.

parallel links Two or more links between adjacent subarea nodes.

parallel sessions Two or more concurrently active sessions between the same two network-accessible units (NAUs) using different pairs of network addresses or local-form session identifiers. Each session can have independent session parameters.

parallel transmission groups Multiple transmission groups (TGs) connecting two adjacent nodes.

parallelism Indicates that multiple paths exist between two points in a network. Parallelism is often a network design goal. Thus, if one path fails, redundancy in the network ensures that a duplicate path to the same point exists.

parameter (*a*) A characteristic that helps define something. (*b*) An adjustable item used to customize a computer program. (*c*) In programming, a value passed to a routine.

parameterized executable test suite (PETS) A selected executable test suite in which all test cases have been made parameterized for the appropriate PICS and PIXIT, and correspond to a parameterized abstract test suite.

PARC *See* Palo Alto Research Center.

parent window In windowing environments, a window that causes another window to appear.

parity check Process for checking the integrity of a character through appending a bit that makes the total number of binary 1 digits in a character or word (excluding the parity bit) either odd (for odd parity) or even (for even parity).

partial mesh A partially meshed network does not provide the level of redundancy of a *full-mesh* topology, and is less expensive to implement. *See* full mesh *and* mesh.

partition To divide a network, memory, or mass storage into isolated sections. This usually occurs where a single network device or link, which is the only connection between two sections, fails, thereby splitting the network. In DOS, a hard disk is partition so that each partition behaves like a separate disk drive, enabling a user to run more than one operating system—one partition might be reserved for Windows and another for Linux.

partitioned data set A data set that is divided into partitions, called *members*. (It contains a list of its members, called a *directory*. The system uses the directory to locate a program in the library.)

partitioned emulation program (PEP) An ACF/NCP extension that enables a single communication controller to operate certain lines in NCP (SNA) mode and others in Emulation Program (EP, non-SNA) mode.

Pascal High-level programming language known for its affinity to structured programming techniques, developed by Niklaus Wirth in the late 1960s. The language is named after Blaise Pascal, a seventeenth-century French mathematician who constructed one of the first mechanical adding machines.

password A secret series of characters that enables a user to access a file, computer, or program. Good passwords contain letters and non-letters or special characters and are not simple combinations such as cisco4U. *See* login.

Password Authentication Protocol (PAP) The most basic form of authentication used in PPP, in which a user's name and password are transmitted in clear (unencrypted) text. *See* CHAP.

paste To copy an object from a buffer (or clipboard) to a file.

path (*a*) In a network, any route between two or more nodes, or the route in a network from a source to the destination address. (*b*) A directory list used by many operating systems to look for executable files if the file is not found in the working directory. (*c*) Another name for *pathname*.

path control A function that routes message units between network-accessible units in the network and provides the paths between them. It is depicted in traditional SNA layers.

path control layer Layer 3 in the SNA that performs sequencing services related to data reassembly. The path control layer is also responsible for routing. Corresponds roughly with the network layer of the OSI model.

path cost An arbitrary value, typically based on hop count, media bandwidth, or other measures, that is assigned by a network administrator and used to compare various paths through an internetwork environment. Cost values are used by routing protocols to determine the most favorable path to a particular destination: the lower the cost, the better the path.

path information unit (PIU) An SNA message unit consisting either of a transmission header (TH) in isolation or a TH followed by a basic information unit (BIU).

Pause key A key used to temporarily halt the display of data.

payload Portion of a frame that contains upper-layer information (data).

payload type or **payload type identifier (PT** or **PTI)** A 3-bit cell-header field for encoding information regarding the AAL and EFCI.

PBX *See* private branch exchange.

PC (*a*) Short for personal computer or IBM PC. The first personal computer produced by IBM was called the PC; increasingly, the term PC came to mean IBM or IBM-compatible personal computers. (*b*) Printed circuit. (*c*) Path control. (*d*) Priority control. A congestion control function that uses the CLP bit to perform priority queuing and scheduling actions in ATM networks.

PC card A computer device which conforms to the PCMCIA standard.

PC-DOS The name IBM uses to market its version of the DOS operating system.

C/TV A combination of a personal computer and television.

PCI *See* peripheral component interconnect *and* protocol control information.

PCL *See* Printer Control Language.

PCM *See* pulse code modulation.

PCMCIA *See* Personal Computer Memory Card International Association.

PCR *See* peak cell rate.

PCS *See* Personal Communications Service.

PDA *See* personal digital assistant.

PDF *See* Portable Document Format.

PDH *See* plesiochronous digital hierarchy.

PDN *See* public data network.

PDP *See* programmable data processor.

PDS *See* partitioned data set.

PDU *See* protocol data unit.

peak cell rate (PCR) A traffic parameter that characterizes the source and gives the maximum rate at which cells can be transmitted. It is calculated as the reciprocal of the minimum

intercell interval (time between two cells) over a given virtual connection (VC).

peak rate Maximum rate, in kilobits per second, at which a virtual circuit can transmit.

peering A relationship between two or more ISPs in which the ISPs create a direct link between themselves and agree to forward each other's packets directly across this link instead of using the standard Internet backbone. Peering can also involve more than two ISPs, in which case all traffic destined for any of the ISPs is first routed to a central exchange, called a *peering point*, and then forwarded to the final destination.

peer-to-peer The arrangement of communication functions and services in layers so that the network layer in one network device communicates to the same network layer in another network element.

PELS *See* picture elements.

pending active session In VTAM, the state of an LU-LU session recorded by the SSCP when it finds both LUs available and has sent a CINIT request to the primary logical unit (PLU) of the requested session.

Pentium III Type of CPU, launched in January 1999. The primary difference between the Pentium III and its predecessor, the Pentium II, is the 70 *Katmai New Instructions (KNI)*. These instructions are now called the *Streaming SIMD (Single Instruction Multiple Data) Extensions*. SIMD can tell a single program instruction to perform the same operation on two or more pieces of data. SIMD floating-point operations are very useful for graphics, polygons, lighting effects, physics models, and 3D games.

PEP *See* partitioned emulation program.

performance management One of five categories of network management defined by ISO for management of OSI networks. Performance management subsystems are responsible for analyzing and controlling network performance including network throughput and error rates. *See* fault management *and* security management.

peripheral component interconnect (PCI) A local bus standard developed by Intel Corporation.

peripheral device Any external device attached to a computer, such as a printer, disk drive, display monitor, keyboard, or mouse.

peripheral logical unit (PLU) A logical unit in a peripheral node found in SNA networks. It should not be confused with a *primary logical unit*, also known as a PLU.

Perl Practical Extraction Report Language. An interpretive programming language, written by Larry Wall, combining syntax from several UNIX utilities and languages. It has since been adapted to other operating systems. Perl is the only programming language with built-in Internet networking support. Because of its strong text processing abilities, Perl has become one of the most popular languages for writing CGI scripts.

 For more information on Perl, see the following websites:

http://language.perl.com/index.html

http://www.perl.com/perl/

http://www.yahoo.com/Computers Internet/Languages/ Perl/.

P

permanent (or provisioned) virtual connection (PVC) A virtual connection provisioned for indefinite use in an ATM network, established by the network management system (NMS). *See* SVC.

permanent virtual circuit A virtual connection, established by network management between an origin and a destination, which can be left up permanently (used in X.25, frame relay, and ATM protocols). Generally, it is a permanent logical association between two DTEs, analogous to a leased line. Packets are routed directly by the network from one DTE to the other.

This is in contrast to *switched virtual circuits (SVCs)*, which are initiated by the calling party and are torn down at the end of the call or session.

permit processing Process used to measure the actual traffic flow across a given connection and compare it to the total admissible traffic flow for that connection. Traffic outside of the agreed-upon flow can be tagged (where the CLP bit is set to 1) and can be discarded en route if congestion develops. Traffic policing is used in ATM, frame relay, and other types of networks. Also known as *admission control, permit processing, rate enforcement,* and *UPC.*

Personal Communications Service (PCS) The United States Federal Communications Commission (FCC) term used to describe a set of digital cellular technologies being deployed in the United States. PCS includes CDMA (also called IS-95), GSM, and North American TDMA (also called IS-136).

Personal Computer Memory Card International Association (PCMCIA) A standard for PC cards for notebook and laptop computers as well as certain routers. Also, People Can't Memorize Computer Industry Acronyms.

personal digital assistant (PDA) A handheld device that combines either computing, telephone/fax, or networking features.

petabyte 1,125,899,906,842,624 bytes. A petabyte is equal to 1,024 terabytes.

PETS *See* parameterized executable test suite.

PGA *See* pin grid array *and* professional graphics adapter.

PGP *See* pretty good privacy.

PH *See* packet handler.

phase The place of a wave in an oscillation cycle.

phase alternating line (PAL) The dominant television standard in Europe. PAL delivers 625 lines at 50 half-frames per second.

phase modulation (PM) (*Illustration*) Angle modulation in which the phase angle of a carrier is departs from its reference value by an amount proportional to the instantaneous value of the modulating signal. A technique that changes the characteristics of a generated sine wave or signal so that it will carry information.

phase shift Phenomenon occurring when the relative position in time between the clock and data signals of a transmission becomes unsynchronized. In systems using long cables at higher transmission speeds, slight variances in cable construction, temperature, impedance, and other factors can cause a phase shift, resulting in high error rates.

phase-shift keying (PSK) (*a*) In digital transmission, angle modulation in which the phase of the carrier is discretely varied in relation either to a reference phase or to the phase of the immediately preceding signal element, in accordance with data being transmitted. (*b*) In a communications system, the representing of characters, such as bits or quaternary digits, by a shift in the phase of an electromagnetic carrier wave with respect to a reference, by an amount corresponding to the symbol being encoded.

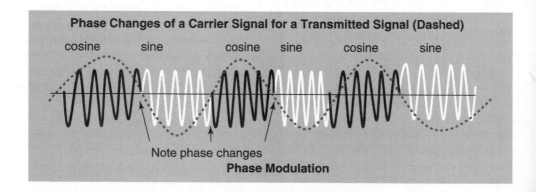

Phase Changes of a Carrier Signal for a Transmitted Signal (Dashed)

cosine   sine   cosine   sine   cosine   sine

Note phase changes
Phase Modulation

For example, when bits are encoded, the phase shift could be 0° for encoding a 0, and 180° for encoding a 1, or the phase shift could be –90 for 0 and +90° for a 1, thus making the representations for 0 and 1 a total of 180° apart. In PSK systems designed so that the carrier can assume only two different *phase angle.* Each change of phase carries one bit of information, i.e., the bit rate equals the modulation rate. If the number of recognizable phase angles is increased to 4, then 2 bits of information can be encoded into each signal element; likewise, 8 phase angles can encode 3 bits in each signal element. Synonyms are *biphase modulation* and *phase-shift signaling.*

PhL *See* Physical layer.

Phoenix BIOS Phoenix Corporation is one of the largest producers of BIOS firmware for IBM PC clones.

phreaking Using a computer or other device to trick a phone system, usually to make free calls or to have calls charged to a different telephone number. *See* hacking.

PHY *See* Physical layer.

PHY-SAP *See* Physical layer service access point.

physical address Standardized data-link layer address required for every port or device that connects to a LAN. Other devices in the network use these addresses to locate specific ports in the network and to create and update routing tables and data structures. MAC addresses are 6 bytes long and are controlled by the IEEE. Also known as a *hardware address, MAC-layer address,* and *physical address. See* MAC address.

physical connection A link that makes transmission of data possible. Generally agreed as a tangible link; it may support electron, photon, or other data type representation transfer.

Physical layer Layer 1 of the OSI model, the lowest of seven hierarchical layers. The physical layer performs services requested by the data-link layer. The major functions and services performed by the physical layer are: (*a*) establishment and termination of a connec-

tion to a communications medium; (*b*) participation in the process whereby the communication resources are effectively shared among multiple users, e.g., contention resolution and flow control; and (*c*) conversion between the representation of digital data in user equipment and the corresponding signals transmitted over a communications channel.

As the first layer of the ATM protocol reference model, it is subdivided into two sublayers, the *transmission convergence (TC)* and the *physical medium (PM)* sublayers. It provides to ATM cells transmission over the physical interfaces that interconnect ATM devices. It is also one of the first two sublayers of the FDDI physical layer. *See* PMD.

Physical Layer Convergence Protocol (PLCP) A protocol that specifies a TC mapping of ATM cells to DS-3 frames.

Physical layer service access point (PHY-SAP) The physical interface at the boundary between the Physical and ATM layers. *See* SAP, ATM-SAP.

physical media (*a*) Various physical environments through which transmission signals pass. Common network media include twisted-pair, coaxial, and fiber optic cable, and the atmosphere (through which microwave, laser, and infrared transmission occurs). (*b*) One of the two physical layer sublayers, which provides bit timing and performs the actual transmission of the bits over the physical medium. *See* media.

physical medium dependent (PMD) Sublayer of the FDDI Physical layer that interfaces directly with the physical medium and performs the most basic bit-transmission functions of the network.

physical protocol Formal sets of rules governing how network devices exchange information. Physical protocols generally define the Physical layer, or Layer 1 of the OSI reference model.

physical topologies (*Illustration*) A local area network (LAN) of computers connected for communication. The three different types of physical topologies are *ring, star,* and *bus.*

P

physical unit (PU) The component that manages and monitors the resources of a node. The type PU, indicated by number, is typically either 5, 4, 2.0, or 2.1. The type PU dictates what supporting services are available. Each node in an SNA subarea network contains a PU.

picoJava A cheap RISC microprocessor dedicated to executing Java -based byte codes without the need for an interpreter or JIT compiler. This chip is used in network computers, cellular telephones and pagers, handheld PCs, and enterprise peripherals.

picture elements (PELS) In a facsimile system, the smallest discrete scanning line sample containing only monochrome information, i.e., not containing gray-scale information.

pie chart A presentation graphic in which percentage values are represented as proportionally-sized slices of a pie.

PIF file Program InFormation file; a type of file that holds information about how Windows should run a non-Windows application.

piggybacking Process of carrying acknowledgments within a data packet to save network bandwidth.

PIM *See* protocol independent multicast.

PIM dense mode A protocol that operates in an environment where group members are relatively densely packed. Sometimes called dense mode PIM or PIM DM. Contrast with PIM sparse mode. *See* PIM and PIM sparse mode.

PIM sparse mode A protocol that tries to constrain data distribution so that a minimal number of routers in the network receive it. Packets are sent only if they are explicitly requested at the rendezvous point (RP). In sparse mode, receivers are widely distributed, and the assumption is that downstream networks will not necessarily use the datagrams sent to them.

pin (*a*) In dot-matrix printers, the devices that press on the ink ribbon to make dots on the paper. (*b*) A male lead on a connector.

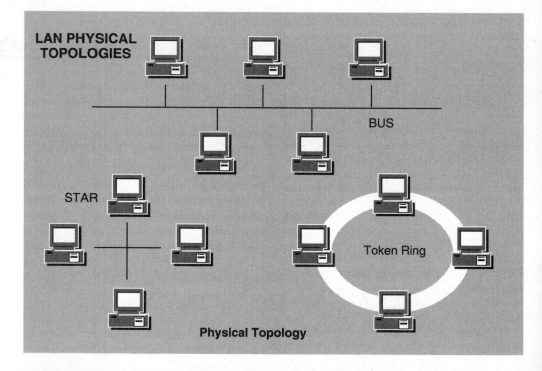

LAN PHYSICAL TOPOLOGIES

BUS

STAR

Token Ring

Physical Topology

PIN *See* Positive-intrinsic negative photo-diode.

pin grid array (PGA) A chip package in which the connecting pins are located on the bottom in concentric squares. They are particularly good for chips that have many pins, such as modern microprocessors. *See* DIP *and* SIP.

ping A TCP/IP utility based upon ICMP. It takes its name from a sonar search—a short sound burst is sent out and an echo or "ping" is received. The ping utility works by sending an ICMP echo request packet to the specified address and waiting for a reply. Ping is implemented using the required ICMP Echo function, as documented in RFC 792.

Ping places a unique sequence number on each packet it transmits, and reports which sequence numbers it receives back. Thus, it can be determined if packets have been dropped, duplicated, or reordered. Ping checksums each packet it exchanges, so that damaged packets may be detected. Ping also places a timestamp in each packet, which is echoed back and can easily be used to compute how long each packet exchange took—known as the round trip time (RTT).

Ping reports other ICMP messages that might otherwise get buried in the system software. It reports, for example, if a router is declaring the target host unreachable. Some routers may silently discard undeliverable packets. Others may believe a packet has been transmitted successfully when it has not been. Ping cannot tell why a packet was damaged, delayed, or duplicated, nor where this happened, although the causes may be deduced.

ping-ponging Phrase used to describe the actions of a packet in a two-node routing loop.

pinout A diagram or table that describes the purpose of each pin in a cable, chip, or connector.

pipeline burst cache A type of memory cache built into many modern DRAM controller and chipset designs. Pipeline burst caches use two techniques—a burst mode and pipelining.

pitch The number of characters printed per inch.

PIU *See* path information unit.

pixel Picture element; a single point in a graphic image. On color monitors, each pixel is actually composed of three dots—a red, a blue, and a green.

PIXIT *See* Protocol Implementation eXtra Information for Testing.

PKCS *See* public key cryptosystems.

PKZIP One of the most widely used file compression methods developed by PKWARE, Inc. in 1989 and distributed as shareware.

 For more information on PKZIP, see *http://www.winzip.com*.

plain old telephone service (POTS) The standard analog telephone service used in most homes. Data transmission over a POTS system is usually accomplished via a modulator/demodulator (modem). POTS is restricted to about 52 Kbps (52,000 bits per second) and is also known as the *public switched telephone network (PSTN)*.

plain text (*a*) Text in ASCII format. Plain text is the most portable format; it is also known as *clear text* because it is widely supported. (*b*) In cryptography, any message that is not encrypted.

platform The underlying hardware or software for a system.

platter A round magnetic plate that constitutes part of a hard disk.

PLC *See* programmable logic controller.

PLCP *See* Physical Layer Convergence Protocol.

PLD *See* programmable logic device.

plesiochronous digital hierarchy (PDH) A hierarchy that refers to the DS-0, DS-1, DS-2, and DS-3 interfaces for digital and voice transmission. Originally developed to efficiently carry digitized voice over twisted pair.

P

plotter A drawing device that plots pictures on paper based on commands from a computer using a pen.

PLP *See* Packet-layer (also level) Protocol.

PLS *See* primary link station.

PLU *See* primary (also peripheral) logical unit.

plug A physical connector used to link devices together.

Plug and Play (PnP) A technology developed by Microsoft and Intel that supports plug-and-play installation.

plug-in Typically, a small hardware or software module that adds a specific feature or service to a larger system or program. The idea behind plug-ins is that a small piece of software is loaded into memory by the larger program, adding a new feature. Common examples are plug-ins for the Netscape browser, Web server, and Adobe Photoshop.

PM *See* protocol machine.

PMD *See* physical medium dependent.

PN *See* private network.

PNG Portable Network Graphics.

PNNI *See* private network node interface.

PnP *See* Plug and Play

PNP *See* private numbering plan.

point-of-presence (POP) A physical access point to a long distance carrier's network, typically found in a city or location where customers can connect to it, often with dial up phone lines.

point-to-multipoint optical network (PON) A high-bandwidth fiber network based on the asynchronous transfer mode protocol (ATM).

Point-to-Point Protocol (PPP) The successor to SLIP is documented in RFC 1661, PPP is currently the best solution for dial-up Internet connections, including ISDN.

PPP is a layered protocol, starting with a *Link Control Protocol (LCP)* for link establishment,

configuration and testing. Once the LCP is initialized, one or more of several *Network Control Protocols (NCPs)* can be used to transport traffic for a particular protocol suite. Each NCP is documented in its own RFC.

The *IP Control Protocol (IPCP)*, documented in RFC 1332, permits the transport of IP packets over a PPP link.

Other NCPs exist for AppleTalk (RFC 1378), OSI (RFC 1377), DECnet Phase IV (RFC 1762), Vines (RFC 1763), XNS (RFC 1764), and transparent Ethernet bridging (RFC 1638).

Point-to-Point Tunneling Protocol (PPTP) A protocol used to ensure transmission between virtual private network (VPN) nodes. Developed jointly by Microsoft Corporation, U.S. Robotics, and several remote-access vendor companies, known collectively as the PPTP Forum.

poison reverse updates Routing updates that explicitly indicate a network or subnet is unreachable, rather than implying that a network is unreachable by not including it in updates. Poison reverse is a technique used to prevent routing loops.

policy routing, policy-based routing Routing scheme that forwards packets to specific interfaces based on user-configured policies. Such policies might specify, for example, that traffic sent from a particular network should be forwarded out one interface, while all other traffic should be forwarded out another interface. These decisions are usually based on source and/or destination network addresses.

poll/final (P/F) bit Bit in bit-synchronous data-link layer protocols that indicates the function of a frame depending on its type. If the frame is a command, a 1 bit indicates a poll. If the frame is a response, a 1 bit indicates that the current frame is the last frame in the response.

polling The process in which data stations transmit on a multipoint or point-to-point connection.

polyline A continuous line composed of one or more line segments.

PON *See* point-to-multipoint optical network.

POP *See* point-of-presence *and* Post Office Protocol.

port (*a*) An interface on a computer to which you can connect a device. (*b*) In TCP/IP and UDP networks, an end-point to a logical connection. The *port number* identifies the type of port; i.e., port 80 is used for HTTP traffic. (*c*) To move a program from one type of computer to another. (*d*) To recompile the source code of one platform on another. *See* domain name, server, *and* URL.

Portable Document Format (PDF) A file format developed by Adobe Systems. PDF files are created, through the use of the program known as *Adobe Acrobat*, by capturing formatting information from a variety of desktop publishing applications such as MS Office or Visio.

For more information on Adobe, see *http://www.adobe.com*.

Portable Network Graphics (PNG) A bit-mapped graphics format.

Portable Operating System Interface (POSIX) For UNIX; a set of IEEE and ISO standards that define an interface between programs and operating systems.

portal A marketing term to describe a Web site that is or is intended to be the first place people see when using the Web. Typically, a portal site has a catalog of Web sites, a search engine, or both. A portal site may also offer e-mail and other services to entice people to use that site as their main point of entry to the Internet.

www.netcerts.com is a networking portal site.

portrait A sheet of paper oriented vertically for on-screen viewing or printing.

positive-intrinsic negative photodiode (PIN) A photodiode with a large, neutrally doped intrinsic region sandwiched between p-doped and n-doped semiconducting regions. A PIN diode exhibits an increase in its electrical conductivity as a function of the intensity, wavelength, and modulation rate of the incident radiation.

POSIX *See* Portable Operating System Interface.

POST *See* power-on self test.

Post Office Protocol (POP-3) Documented in RFC 1725; a protocol designed for user-to-mailbox access. Refers to the way e-mail software such as MS Outlook gets mail from a mail server. There are two versions of POP. The first, POP2, became a standard in the 80s and requires SMTP to send messages. The newer version, POP3, can be used with or without SMTP. *See* SLIP *and* PPP.

posting A single message posted to a newsgroup or message board. *See* newsgroup.

PostScript A page description language (PDL) developed by Adobe Systems, which is the standard for desktop publishing.

POTS *See* plain old telephone service.

POTS splitter A passive filter that separates voice traffic from data traffic.

power down/up To turn a machine off/on.

power user A user with considerable experience in computers who utilizes the most advanced features of applications.

power-on self test (POST) A series of diagnostic tests that run automatically when a computer is turned on.

PPDU *See* presentation protocol data unit.

PPO *See* primary program operator.

PPP *See* Point-to-Point Protocol.

PPS *See* packets per second.

PPTP *See* Point-to-Point Tunneling Protocol.

programmed input/output (PIO) A method of transferring data between two devices, using a computer's CPU.

PR/SM *See* Processor Resource/Systems Manager.

P

presentation A set of one or more streams presented to the client as a complete media feed, using a presentation description. In the RTSP context, this implies aggregate control of those streams.

Presentation layer Layer 6 of the OSI reference model. This layer ensures that information sent by the application layer of one system will be readable by the application layer of another. The presentation layer is also concerned with the data structures used by programs and, therefore, negotiates data transfer syntax for the application layer. Syntax of data such as ASCII or EBCDIC is determined at this layer.

This layer corresponds roughly with the presentation services layer of the SNA model. *See* application layer, data-link layer, network layer, physical layer, session layer, transport layer, *and* OSI model.

presentation protocol data unit (PPDU) In OSI terminology, a term referring to logical blocks of control symbols and data transmitted at the presentation-layer protocol.

presentation services (PS) A set of facilities used to manage a connection between two application-entities. The fundamental responsibility of the presentation service is to maintain transfer syntaxes, which are used to serialize application protocol data units for transmission on the network and subsequent de-serialization for reception.

pretty good privacy (PGP) Both a protocol and the name of the program that most widely implements that protocol. The PGP protocol, documented in RFC 1991, is a presentation-layer protocol that defines a standard for cryptographically secure e-mail messages. RFC 2015 describes how various kinds of PGP messages should be encapsulated using MIME. There is some controversy over the development and use of this application, in part due to United States national security concerns.

PRI *See* primary rate interface.

primary (also **peripheral**) **logical unit (PLU)** The LU containing the primary half-session, which is the half-session that sends the BIND. The primary LU is also responsible for error recovery and control.

primary application program An application program acting as the primary end of a LU-LU session.

primary link station (PLS) The link station responsible for control of the link. A link has only one primary link station. All traffic over the link is between the primary and secondary link stations.

primary program operator (PPO) A program which captures all VTAM messages.

primary rate interface (PRI) A high-speed ISDN service that consists of 23 B-channels (30 in Europe) and one D-Channel. PRI service is generally transmitted through a T-1 line (or an E1 line in Europe).

primary ring One of the two rings that make up an FDDI or CDDI ring. The primary ring is the default path for data transmissions. *See* secondary ring.

primary station In bit-synchronous data-link layer protocols such as HDLC and SDLC, a station that controls the transmission activity of secondary stations and performs other management functions, such as error control, through polling or other means. Primary stations send commands to secondary stations and receive responses.

print server In networking, generally, a computer that controls spooling and other printer operations.

Printer Control Language (PCL) The page description language (PDL) developed by Hewlett-Packard and used in many HP printers.

private automatic branch exchange (PABX) (*Illustration*) (*a*) A subscriber-owned telecommunications exchange that usually includes access to the public switched network. (*b*) A switch that serves a selected group of users and that is subordinate to a switch at a higher level military establishment. (*c*) A private telephone switchboard that provides on-premises dial service and may provide connections to local and trunked communications networks.

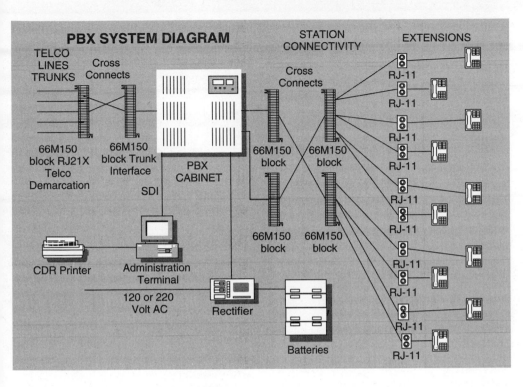

PBX SYSTEM DIAGRAM

A PBX operates with only a manual switch-board; a private automatic exchange (PAX) does not have a switchboard, a private automatic branch exchange (PABX) may or may not have a switchboard. Use of the term *PBX* is far more common than PABX, regardless of automation.

private branch exchange (PBX) A private telephone network, used within an enterprise, which relays telephones, terminals, or other equipment, and provides access to the public telephone system.

private line (*Illustration*) Also called a *leased line* or *leased circuit*. A leased line is a telephone service that is permanently connected from one point to another.

private management domain (PRMD) A message-handling system management domain managed by a private organization.

private network (PN) A network, usually over dedicated, leased lines of a public communications system, with access (use) restricted to those authorized by the network owner.

private network node interface (PNNI) ATM Forum specification that describes an ATM virtual circuit routing protocol, as well as a signaling protocol between ATM switches

private numbering plan (PNP) The capability for calls to be made within and between geographically separate locations. The numbering plan may also be used to reserve codes for specialized functions, such as public network (off-net) dialing.

private user network interface (P-UNI) The UNI used between a user and a private network.

private virtual network (PVN) A private data network that makes use of the public telecommunication infrastructure, maintaining privacy through the use of Windows NT security procedures. A virtual private network can be contrasted with a system of owned or leased lines that can only be used by one company. The idea of the VPN is to give the company the same capabilities at much lower cost

P

56K Analog Leased Line/ Private Line application

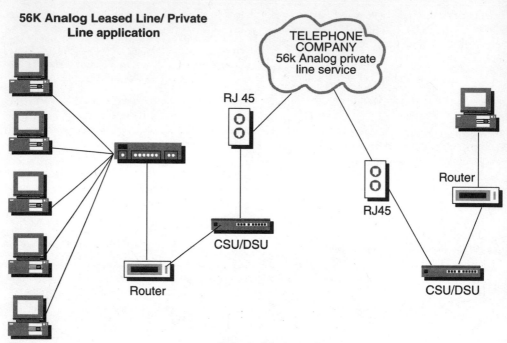

Private Line

by sharing the public infrastructure. Phone companies have provided secure shared resources for voice messages.

A virtual private network makes it possible to have the same secure sharing of public resources for data. Companies may use a private virtual network for both extranets and wide-area intranets. Using a virtual private network involves encrypting data before sending it through the public network and decrypting it at the receiving end.

PRMD *See* private management domain.

procedure (*a*) A section of a program that performs a specific task. (*b*) An ordered set of tasks for performing some action.

process (*n*) An executing program. The term is used loosely as a synonym of *task*. (*v*) To perform some useful operations on data.

process switching An operation that provides full route evaluation and per-packet load balancing across parallel WAN links.

processor The component within a computer that interprets and executes instructions.

Processor Resource/Systems Manager (PR/SM) A trademarked processor used to create a logical partition (LPAR).

professional graphics adapter (PGA) A video standard, developed by IBM, which supports 640 x 480 resolution.

Professional Office System (PROFS) A program developed by IBM. Similar to DISOSS, but running under the VM operating system, PROFS provides electronic mail, calendaring, and document preparation capabilities.

program An organized list of instructions that, when executed, causes the computer to behave in a predetermined or programmed manner.

program operator In SNA and according to IBM documentation, a VTAM application program that is authorized to issue VTAM operator commands and receive VTAM operator awareness messages.

program status word (PSW) A coding word, 32 bits in length, that contains the information required for proper program execution. The PSW includes the instruction address, condition code, and other fields. In general, the PSW is used to control instruction sequencing and to hold and indicate the status of the system in relation to the program currently being executed. The active or controlling PSW is called the *current PSW*. By storing the current PSW during an interruption, the status of the CPU can be preserved for subsequent inspection. By loading a new PSW or part of a PSW, the state of the CPU can be initialized or changed.

program temporary fix (PTF) Software used to distribute upgrades to customers between releases. Such between-release upgrades allow software to perform better right away without waiting for the next version of the product. Each PTF is actually a collection of files. For example, the www120002 PTF actually contains three files: www120002.savf, www120002r.savf, and www120002.txt.

The first file, with the PTF number and "savf" extension, is the PTF for IMPI machines; the second file, with the character "r", is for RISC machines. Some PTFs are only available for either RISC or IMPI, but not both; if a PTF is not available for a particular platform, it is not necessary. The ".txt" file is a detailed description of how to obtain and install the PTF and describes its exact function.

program update tape (PUT) A type of FTP transaction that provides multiple I-stream, as well as a more dynamic logical unit support.

programmable array logic (PAL) A type of programmable logic device (PLD).

programmable data processor (PDP) minicomputer on which the VAX was originally based. The introduction of virtual memory is mainly due to the PDP.

programmable logic controller (PLC) Industrial controllers used to automate equipment from rocket fuel plants to bakery ovens. They are highly intelligent compact control modules which feature easy programming using software for ladder diagram or statement list programs, and pre-built C or assembler modules for popular PC-based formats.

programmable logic device (PLD) An integrated circuit that can be programmed in a laboratory to perform complex functions.

programmable read-only memory (PROM) A memory chip on which data can be written only once. Once a program has been written onto a PROM, it remains there even if power is removed. PROM programming can be done during the manufacture of the semiconductor chip or programmed after manufacturing by using an electrical signal. *See* EEPROM.

programmer (*a*) An individual who writes programs. (*b*) A device that writes a program onto a PROM chip.

programming language A set of grammatical rules used to instruct a computer to perform specific tasks. The term programming language usually refers to high-level languages, such as BASIC, C, C++, COBOL, FORTRAN, Ada, and Pascal. Each language has a unique set of keywords and a special syntax for organizing program instructions.

Prolog Programming Logic. A high-level programming language based on formal logic.

PROM *See* programmable read-only memory.

prompt A symbol on a display screen indicating that the computer is waiting for input.

propagation delay Time required for data to travel over a network, from its source to its ultimate destination.

property Characteristic or attribute of an object.

proportional spacing Using different widths for different characters. In a proportionally spaced font, the letter **I** is narrower than the letter **q** and the letter **m** wider still. This book uses a proportionally spaced font, as do most books, magazines, and newspapers.

proprietary Privately owned and controlled.

protocol Douglas Comer defines a protocol as "a formal description of message formats and the rules two or more machines must fol-

P

low to exchange those messages." An agreed-upon format for transmitting data between two devices. The majority of Internet protocols are distributed as RFCs, which can be read to understand the protocols' design and operation. Protocols exist as programming code for computers to understand.

protocol address An SNA network address consisting of the combination of the subarea and element fields. *See* network address.

protocol control information (PCI) Control information added to user data to comprise an OSI packet. The OSI equivalent of the term *header*. Data exchanged among communications equipment, used for determining the capabilities of each end of the communications link.

protocol converter A device that enables equipment with different data formats to communicate by translating the data transmission code of one device to the data transmission code of another device.

protocol data unit (PDU) A general term used to refer to that which is exchanged between peer-layer entities. Originally used in the OSI model to describe what passed across two adjoining layers. It contains header, data, and trailer information.

Protocol Implementation eXtra Information for Testing (PIXIT) The information supplied, pro forma or through a questionnaire, beyond that required for strict conformance. Supplied by the PICS and needed to repeat the test environment for the implementation under test.

protocol independent multicast (PIM) Multicast routing architecture that allows the addition of IP multicast routing on existing IP networks. PIM is unicast routing protocol independent and can be operated in dense or sparse mode. *See* PIM dense mode *and* PIM sparse mode.

protocol layering A common technique to simplify networking designs by dividing them into functional layers, and assigning protocols to perform each layer's task. For example, it is common to separate the functions of data delivery and connection management into

separate layers, and therefore separate protocols. Thus, one protocol is designed to perform data delivery, and another protocol, layered above the first, performs connection management. The data delivery protocol is fairly simple and knows nothing of connection management. The connection management protocol is also fairly simple, because it doesn't concern itself with data delivery.

protocol machine (PM) Consisting of six classes: General, Class 0, Class 1, Class 2, Class 3, and Class 4. The General PM is instantiated when a connection request is received from a transport user or when a CR TPDU is received from a remote peer entity. This PM is replaced by a class-specific PM when the connect response is received from the responding user or when the CC TPDU is received from the responding peer entity.

protocol stack Set of related communications protocols such as TCP/IP that operate together and, as a group and address communication at some or all of the seven layers of the OSI reference model.

protocol translator Network device or software that converts one protocol into another similar protocol.

proxy ARP In TCP/IP networks, a technique where one router answers ARP requests intended for another by supplying its own physical address.

proxy polling Technique replaced by SDLC transport, alleviates the load across an SDLC network by allowing routers to act as proxies for primary and secondary nodes. Proxy polling has been replaced by SDLC Transport.

proxy Entity that stands in for another entity.

PS *See* presentation services.

PS/2 Personal System/2 (IBM). A personal computer manufactured by IBM.

PS/2 port A type of port developed by IBM for connecting a mouse or keyboard to a PC. The PS/2 port supports a mini-DIN plug containing just 6 pins. Most PCs have a PS/2 port so that the serial port can be used by another device, such as a modem. The PS/2 port is often called the *mouse port*.

PSAP *See* public safety answering point.

PSDN *See* packet-switched data network.

pseudocode An outline of a program, written in a form that can easily be converted into real programming statements.

PSI *See* Packet-Switched Interface.

PSK *See* phase-shift keying.

PSN *See* packet-switched network.

PSPDN *See* packet-switched public data network.

PSW *See* program status word.

PT *See* payload type.

PTF *See* program temporary fix.

PTI *See* payload type identifier.

PU *See* physical unit.

public data network (PDN) A network established and operated by a telecommunications administration, or a recognized private operating agency, for the specific purpose of providing data transmission services for the public.

public key cryptosystems (PKCS) A cryptography system in which the encryption process is publicly available and unprotected, but in which a part of the decryption key is protected so that only a party with knowledge of both parts of the decryption process can decrypt the cipher text. Commonly called *non-secret encryption* in professional cryptologic circles. FIREFLY is an application of public key cryptosystems.

public network A communications network where users have shared access to the network resources. Network services are usually provided by common carriers (i.e., telephone companies and the Internet). *See* private network.

public safety answering point (PSAP) A 24-hour local jurisdiction communications facility that receives enhanced 911 service calls and directly dispatches emergency response services or relays calls to the appropriate public or private safety agency.

Public Utility Commission (PUC) In the United States, a state regulatory body charged with regulating intrastate utilities, including telecommunications systems. In some states this regulatory function is performed by public service commissions or state corporation commissions.

PUC *See* Public Utility Commission.

pulse amplitude modulation (PAM) (*Illustration*) A modulation scheme where the waveform is caused to modulate in direct relation to the amplitude of a pulse stream.

pulse code modulation (PCM) A sampling technique for digitizing analog signals. Pulse code modulation samples the signal 8,000 times a second; each sample is represented by 8 bits for a total of 64 Kbps. Pulse code modulation can be used for any number of bits per sample—some popular ones are 8, 16, 20, and 24 bits per sample. The sample rate is also variable. There are two standards for coding the sample level. The *Mu-Law standard* is used in North America and Japan, while the *A-Law standard* is use in most other countries. PCM is used with T-1 and T-3 carrier systems.

pulse dispersion The spreading of pulses as they traverse an optical fiber.

P-UNI *See* private user network interface.

PU-PU flow In SNA and according to IBM documentation, the exchange between physical units (PUs) of network control requests and responses.

purge To systematically and permanently remove old and unneeded data.

PUT Program update tape or type of FTP transaction.

PVC *See* permanent (or provisioned) virtual connection.

PVN private virtual network.

P

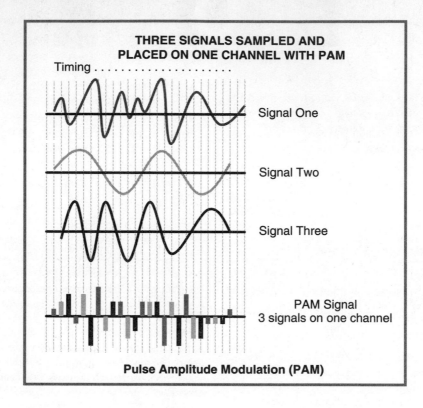

**THREE SIGNALS SAMPLED AND
PLACED ON ONE CHANNEL WITH PAM**

Timing . . . .

Signal One

Signal Two

Signal Three

PAM Signal
3 signals on one channel

Pulse Amplitude Modulation (PAM)

Q.2110 ITU-T recommendation for specifying the UNI SSCOP.

Q.2130 ITU-T recommendation for specifying the UNI SSCF.

Q.2931 ITU-T recommendation derived from both Q.931 and Q.933 to provide SVC specifications and standards. An ATM signaling specification.

Q.920/Q.921 ITU-T specifications for the ISDN UNI data link layer. *See* UNI.

Q.921 Also referred to as *Link Access Protocol-D Channel (LAPD)* and a close cousin of HDLC, this is the Data Link protocol used over ISDN's D channel.

Q.922A ITU-T specification for frame relay encapsulation.

Q.931 ITU-T recommendation for specifying the UNI signaling protocol in N-ISDN. ISDN's connection control protocol, roughly comparable to TCP in the Internet protocol stack. Q.931 doesn't provide flow control or perform retransmission, because the underlying layers are assumed to be reliable and the circuit-oriented nature of ISDN allocates bandwidth in fixed increments of 64 kbps. Q.931 manages connection setup and breakdown. Like TCP, Q.931 documents both the protocol itself and a protocol state machine. In accordance with the conventions of ITU standards, bits are numbered from least significant bit (LSB) to most significant bit (MSB), 1 to 8 (Internet standards use MSB to LSB, 0 to 7).

The general format of a Q.931 message includes a single-byte protocol discriminator (8 for Q.931 messages), a call reference value to distinguish between different calls being managed over the same D channel, a message type, and various information elements (IEs) as required by the message type in question.

Q.933 ITU-T recommendation for specifying the UNI signaling protocol in frame relay.

Q.93B Currently called Q.2931.

QBASIC An advanced interpreter for the BASIC programming language provided by Microsoft with the DOS and Windows 95 operating systems.

QCIF *See* Quarter Common Intermediate Format.

QLLC *See* qualified logical link control.

QMF *See* query management facility.

QoS *See* quality of service.

QoS classes *See* quality of service classes.

quadrature A bandwidth conservation process routinely used in modems. *See* QAM.

qualified logical link control (QLLC) Data link layer protocol, defined by IBM, which allows SNA data to be transported across X.25 networks.

quality of service (QoS) A guaranteed throughput level for critical network applications, such as voice over IP. One of the biggest advantages of ATM over competing technologies such as frame relay and Fast Ethernet, is that it supports QoS levels. This allows ATM providers to guarantee to their customers that end-to-end latency will not exceed a specified level. These parameters include the CLR, CER, CMR, CDV, CTD, and the average cell transfer delay. Simply stated, QoS parameters are used in traffic engineering to state the level of loss (inverse of throughput), latency, and jitter that a traffic stream will be guaranteed in a network.

 For more information, see *http://www.ietf.org/html.charters/qosr-charter.html*.

quality of service classes (QoS classes) Five service classes defined by the ATM Forum in terms of the QoS parameters:

Class 0: Refers to best-effort service.

Class 1: Specifies the parameters for circuit emulation, CBR (uncompressed) video and for VPN. AAL1 supports this kind of connection-oriented service.

Class 2: Specifies the parameters for VBR audio and video. AAL2 supports this delay-dependent, connection-oriented class.

Class 3: Specifies the parameters for connection-oriented data transfer. AAL3/4 and mostly AAL5 support this delay-independent class of service.

Quarter Common Intermediate Format (QCIF) A videoconferencing format that specifies data rates of 30 frames per second (fps), with each frame containing 144 lines and 176 pixels per line.

quartet signaling Signaling technique used in 100VG-AnyLAN networks, which allows data transmission at 100 Mbps over four pairs of UTP cabling at the same frequencies used in 10BaseT networks. *See* 100VG-AnyLAN.

query (*a*) A request for information from a database. (*b*) Message used to inquire about the value of some variable or set of variables.

query management facility (QMF) Software which provides interactive database functionality to end users. Also used as a database software development tool.

queue (*a*) To line up. (*b*) A group of jobs waiting to be executed. (*c*) In programming, a data structure in which elements are removed in the same order they were entered.

queued session In VTAM, a requested LU-LU session that cannot be started because one of the LUs is not available. If the session-initiation request specifies queuing, the system services control points (SSCPs) record the request and later continue with the session establishment procedure when both LUs become available.

queuing delay Amount of time that data must wait before it can be transmitted onto a statistically multiplexed physical circuit.

queuing theory Scientific principles governing the formation or lack of formation of congestion on a network or at an interface.

QuickTime A video and animation system developed by Apple Computer. QuickTime is built into the Macintosh operating system and is used by most Mac applications that include video or animation.

quit To exit a program.

R

RAB *See* record access block.

RACE *See* Research in Advanced Communications for Europe.

RACF *See* resource access control facility.

radio buttons In graphical user interfaces, groups of buttons, of which only one can be on at a time. When you select one button, all the others are automatically deselected. Compare with *check box*, which allows you to select any combination of options.

RADIUS *See* Remote Authentication Dial-In User Service.

RAID *See* redundant array of independent disks.

RAM *See* random access memory.

Rambus DRAM (RDRAM) A type of memory developed by Rambus, Inc. Whereas the fastest current memory technologies used by PCs (SDRAM) can deliver data at a maximum speed of about 100 MHz, RDRAM transfers data at up to 600 MHz.

random access The ability to access data at random. The opposite of random access is *sequential access*. Random access is sometimes called *direct access*.

random access memory (RAM) A type of computer memory that can be accessed randomly; that is, any byte of memory can be accessed without touching the preceding bytes. RAM is the most common type of memory found in computers and other devices, such as printers. There are two basic types of RAM, *dynamic RAM (DRAM)* and *static RAM (SRAM)*.

random delay The random amount of time a transmission is delayed to prevent multiple nodes from transmitting at exactly the same time, or to prevent long-range periodic transmissions from synchronizing with each other.

range In spreadsheet applications, one or more contiguous cells. For example, a range could be an entire row or column, or multiple rows or columns.

Rapid Transport Protocol (RTP) Provides pacing and error recovery for APPN data. With RTP, error recovery and flow control are done end-to-end rather than at every node. RTP prevents congestion rather than reacts to it.

RARP *See* Reverse Address Resolution Protocol.

RAS *See* Remote Access Services.

raster The rectangular area of a display screen actually being used to display images. The raster is slightly smaller than the physical dimensions of the display screen. The raster varies for different resolutions.

rate decrease factor (RDF) A factor by which a source should decrease its transmission rate if there is congestion. *See* RIF..

rate increase factor (RIF) A factor by which a source can increase its transmission rate if the RM cell indicates no congestion. This can result in an additive cell rate (ACR). *See* RDF.

rate queue Value associated with one or more virtual circuits that defines the speed at which an individual virtual circuit will transmit data.

raw data Information that has not been organized, formatted, or analyzed.

RBHC *See* Regional Bell Holding Company.

RBOC *See* Regional Bell Operating Company.

RBW *See* required bandwidth.

RCP Remote Copy Protocol.

RDBMS Relational database management system.

RDF *See* rate decrease factor.

RDI *See* remote defect indication.

RDN *See* relative distinguished name.

RDRAM *See* Rambus DRAM.

RDT *See* resource definition table.

reachability Whether or not the one-way forward path to a neighbor is functioning properly. For neighboring routers, reachability means that packets sent by a node's IP layer are delivered to the router's IP layer, and the router is indeed forwarding packets. This means the node is configured as a router, not a host. For hosts, reachability means that packets sent by a node's IP layer are delivered to the neighbor host's IP layer.

read/write Capable of being displayed (read) and modified (written to). Most objects (disks, files, directories) are read/write, but operating systems also allow you to protect objects with a *read-only* attribute that prevents other users from modifying the object.

read-only Capable of being displayed, but not modified or deleted. All operating systems allow you to protect objects (disks, files, directories) with a read-only attribute that prevents other users from modifying the object.

read-only memory (ROM) Computer memory (chip) on which data has been prerecorded. Once written onto a ROM chip, data cannot be removed and can only be read. Unlike main memory (RAM), ROM retains its contents even when the computer is turned off. ROM is *nonvolatile*, whereas RAM is *volatile* memory. Memory in which stored data cannot be modified except under special conditions.

real resource In VTAM, a resource identified by its real name and its real network identifier.

real time Occurring immediately. The term is used to describe a number of different computer features. For example, real-time operating systems are systems that respond to input immediately.

Real-Time An application-level protocol providing control for the delivery of data

Real-Time Streaming Protocol (RTSP) A proposed standard for controlling streaming data over the World Wide Web. A session involves the complete RTSP "transaction", e.g., the viewing of a movie. A session typically consists of a client setting up a transport mechanism for the continuous media stream, starting the stream with Play or Record, and closing the stream with a tear down.

Real-Time Transport Protocol (RTP) An Internet protocol for transmitting real-time data such as audio and video. RTP itself does not guarantee real-time delivery of data, but it does provide mechanisms for sending and receiving applications to support streaming data. Typically, RTP runs on top of the UDP protocol, although the specification is general enough to support other transport protocols.

RealAudio The de facto standard for streaming audio data over the World Wide Web.

For more infomation, see *www.realaudio.com*.

RealVideo A streaming technology developed by RealNetworks for transmitting live video over the Internet. RealVideo uses a variety of data compression techniques and works with both normal IP connections as well as IP multicast connections.

reassembly The putting back together of an IP datagram at the destination after it has been fragmented either at the source or at an intermediate node. *See* fragmentation.

reboot To restart a computer.

recognized private operating agency (RPOA) A service that allows a user, at a call setup time, to select a private X.25 to control the X.25 traffic.

record (*a*) In database management systems, a complete set of information. Records are composed of fields, each of which contains one item of information. A set of records constitutes a file. In relational database management systems, records are called *tuples*. (*b*) In some programming languages, a special data structure, usually user-defined. Generally, a record is a combination of other data objects.

record access block (RAB) The method by which records are processed.

Red Book The standard for audio CDs, developed by Phillips and Sony. The specification is formally known as *Compact Disc-Digital Audio (CD-DA)*. It specifies up to 74 minutes of digital audio transferred at 150 Kbps. The first CD-ROM players also transmitted data at this rate, so they came to be called *single-speed drives*.

redirect Part of the ICMP and ES-IS protocols that allows a router to tell a host that using another router would be more effective.

redistribution Process that allows routing information to be discovered by one routing protocol to be distributed in a routing update message of another (different) routing protocol. Sometimes called *route redistribution*.

reduced instruction set computer (RISC) A type of microprocessor that recognizes a relatively limited number of instructions.

redundancy In networking, the duplication of devices, services, or connections so that, in the event of a failure, the redundant devices, services, or connections can perform the work of those that failed. *See* redundant system.

redundant array of independent disks (RAID) A category of disk drives that employ two or more drives in combination for fault tolerance and performance.

redundant power supply (RPS) The ability to add additional power supplies to a router, making it more resilient with regard to power problems.

redundant system Computer, router, switch, or other computer system that contains two or more of each of the most important subsystems, such as two disk drives, two CPUs, or two power supplies.

refresh (*a*) To update something with new data. For example, some Web browsers include a refresh button that updates the currently displayed Web pages. This feature is also called *reload*. (*b*) To recharge a device with power or information.

region code A number used to indicate a particular localized version of Macintosh system software.

Regional Bell A telecommunication company formed as a result of the divestiture of AT&T.

Regional Bell Holding Company (RBHC) One of seven telephone companies created by the AT&T divestiture in 1984.

Regional Bell Operating Company (RBOC) Local or regional telephone company that owns and operates telephone lines and switches in one of seven United States regions. The RBOCs were created by the divestiture of AT&T. Also called *Bell Operating Company (BOC)*.

register (*a*) A special, high-speed storage area within the CPU. All data must be represented in a register before being processed. For example, if two numbers are to be multiplied, both numbers must be in registers, and the result is also placed in a register. (*b*) To notify a manufacturer that you have purchased its product. Registering a product is often a prerequisite to receiving customer support, and it is one of the ways that software producers control software piracy.

registered jack connector *See* RJ connector.

Registry A database used by the Windows operating system to store configuration information. The windows Registry consists of the following major sections:

■ HKEY_Classes_Root—File associations and OLE information

■ HKEY_Current_User—All preferences set for current user

■ HKEY_User—All the current user information for each user of the system

■ HKEY_Local_Machine—Settings for hardware, operating system, and installed applications

■ HKEY_Current_Configuration—Settings for the display and printers

■ HKEY_Dyn_Data—Performance data

Most Windows applications write data to the Registry, at least during installation. You can

R

edit the Registry directly by using the *Registry Editor (regedit.exe)* provided with the operating system. However, you must take great care because errors in the Registry could disable your computer.

reject (REJ) To delete or not allow applied updates from becoming permanent parts of the product.

relational database management system (RDBMS) A type of database management system (DBMS) that stores data in the form of related tables. Relational databases are powerful because they require few assumptions about how data is related or will be extracted from the database. As a result, the same database can be viewed in many different ways. An important feature of relational systems is that a single database can be spread across several tables. This differs from *flat-file databases*, in which each database is self contained in a single table.

Almost all full-scale database systems are RDBMSs. Small database systems, however, use other designs that provide less flexibility in posing queries.

relative address An address specified by indicating its distance from another address, called the *base address*.

relative distinguished name (RDN) A set of Attribute Value Assertions relating to the distinguished values of a certain entry.

relative path The path through a volume's (disk's) hierarchy from one file or directory to another.

relay A device that interconnects LANs. Different kinds of relays include repeaters, bridges, routers, and gateways.

release A distribution of a new product or new function.

reliable multicast Protocols that provide for reliable transmission of datagrams.

reliable transfer service element (RTSE) A dependable way of transferring a message, by verifying delivery or informing of any possible errors.

remote In networks, files, devices, and other resources that are not connected directly to a workstation. Resources at a particular workstation are considered local.

Remote Access Services (RAS) A feature built into Windows NT that enables users to log into an NT-based LAN using a modem, X.25 connection, or WAN link. RAS works with several major network protocols, including TCP/IP, IPX, and NetBEUI. To use RAS from a remote node, a user needs a RAS client program, which is built into most versions of Windows, or any PPP client software. For example, most remote control programs work with RAS.

Remote Authentication Dial-In User Service (RADIUS) A protocol invented by Livingston Enterprises (recently acquired by Lucent) for authenticating dial-in users across multiple dial-in servers. Used by many Internet Service Providers (ISPs). When a user dials in to the ISP, they enter a username and password. This information is passed to a RADIUS server, which checks that the information is correct, and then authorizes access to the ISP system.

Though not an official standard, the RADIUS specification is maintained by a working group of the IETF.

remote client In an XWindow environment, an X program running on a remote system, through the output of the program can be viewed locally.

Remote Copy Protocol (RCP) Protocol that allows users to copy files to and from a file system residing on a remote host or server on the network. The RCP protocol uses TCP to ensure the reliable delivery of data. An RCP server is a router or other device that acts as a server for RCP.

Remote Copy Protocol server Router or other device that acts as a server for RCP.

remote defect indication (RDI) One of the OAM function types used for fault management.

remote job entry (RJE) Using an input unit with access to a computer to submit a job through a data link.

remote login Occurring when a user connects to an Internet host to use its native user interface. In the 1970s and early 1980s, text-oriented terminals were the predominant tools for computer users. Protocols such as Telnet and rlogin were developed for terminal users to use their terminals as if they were directly connected to a remote system. UNIX systems, with their predominantly terminal-oriented interface, still make heavy use of these protocols.

Remote Method Invocation (RMI) A set of protocols being developed by Sun's JavaSoft division that enables Java objects to communicate remotely with other Java objects.

Remote Network Monitoring (RMON) A standards-based network management protocol that allows network information to be gathered at a single workstation. Whereas SNMP gathers network data from a single type of Management Information Base (MIB), RMON 1 defines nine additional MIBs that provide a much richer set of data about network usage. For RMON to work, network devices, such as hubs and switches, must be designed to support it.

The newest version of RMON, RMON 2, provides data about traffic at the network layer in addition to the physical layer. This allows administrators to analyze traffic by protocol.

remote office (RO) Medium-sized office that has a WAN or MAN connection back to a larger corporate network.

remote operations service element (ROSE) In open networking environments, an application support service element that provides the basis for remote requests.

remote procedure call (RPC) A type of protocol (documented in RFC 1831) that allows a program on one computer to execute a program on a server computer. RPC was designed to augment IP in a different way from TCP. While TCP is targeted at the transfer of large data streams (such as a file download), RPC is designed for network programming, allowing a program to make a subroutine call on a remote machine. The most important application of RPC is the *NFS file sharing protocol.* The key features of RPC are:

Request-reply. RPC is a request-reply protocol.

UDP or TCP transport. RPC actually operates over UDP or TCP. RPC/UDP is a connection-less, stateless protocol. RPC/TCP is slower, but provides a reliable, stateful connection.

Standardized data representation. RPC encodes its data using the eXternal Data Representation (XDR) protocol, documented in RFC 1832, which standardizes the format of integers, floating point numbers, and strings, permitting different types of computers to enhance information seamlessly.

Authentication. RPC provides support for authenticating the calling program on one machine to the target subroutine on the other. Authentication can operate in several different modes. During NFS operations, authentication usually takes the form of relaying UNIX user and group IDs to the file server for permission checking.

remote spooling communication system (RSCS) A program that allows VM users to transfer spooled files, commands, and messages.

removable hard disk A type of disk drive system in which hard disks are enclosed in plastic or metal cartridges so that they can be removed like floppy disks.

render The process of adding realism to computer graphics by adding three-dimensional qualities such as shadows and variations in color and shade.

repeater A network device used to regenerate or replicate a signal. Repeaters are used in transmission systems to regenerate analog or digital signals distorted by transmission loss. Analog repeaters frequently can only amplify the signal, although digital repeaters can reconstruct a signal to near its original quality. In a data network, a repeater can relay messages between subnetworks that use different protocols or cable types. Hubs can operate as repeaters by relaying messages to all connected computers. A repeater cannot do the intel-

R

ligent routing performed by bridges and routers.

repeaters (100Base-TX) The Fast Ethernet standard specifies two classes of repeaters: Class I and Class II.

A *Class I repeater* has larger timing delays and operates by translating line signals on an incoming port to a digital form, and then retranslating them to line signals when sending them out on other ports. Because of this it is possible to repeat signals between media segments that use different signaling techniques, such as 100Base-TX/FX segments, and 100Base-T4 segments, further allowing these segment types to be mixed within a single repeater hub. This translation process uses a number of bit times; therefore only one Class I repeater can be used in a given collision domain.

A *Class II repeater* is restricted to smaller timing delays, and immediately repeats the incoming signal to all ports without the translation process. To achieve smaller timing delays, Class II repeaters connect only to segment types that use the same signaling technique, such as 100Base-TX, and 100Base-FX segments. A maximum of two Class II repeater/hubs can be used in a collision domain. Segment types of different signaling techniques (e.g., 100Base-TX/FX and 100Base-T4) cannot be mixed in a Class II repeater/hub.

replication The process of creating and managing duplicate versions of a database. Replication not only copies a database but also synchronizes a set of replicas so that changes made to one replica are reflected in all the others.

report writer Also called a *report generator*, a program, usually part of a database management system, that extracts information from one or more files and presents the information in a specified format.

REQ *See* request.

request (REQ) A command that signals the initiation of an action or protocol.

request (or response) header (RH) The header which precedes a request/response

unit (RU). It also contain control information about the RU.

request (or response) unit (RU) Request and response messages exchanged between NAUs in an SNA network.

request for a price quotation (RFQ) A document created by an end user and sent to a vendor asking for a price quote on specific products or services.

request for comments (RFC) A series of notes about the Internet, started in 1969 (when the Internet was the ARPANET). An RFC can be submitted by anyone to the IETF. The Internet Engineering Task Force is a consensus-building body that facilitates discussion, and eventually establishes new standards. The reference number/name for the standard retains the acronym RFC, e.g. the official standard for e-mail is RFC 822. Each RFC is designated by an RFC number. Once published, an RFC never changes. Modifications to an original RFC are assigned a new RFC number.

request parameter list (RPL) A list of supplied parameter values.

request/reply Protocols using request/reply behavior send a single block of data (usually a single packet), and wait for a reply before sending another. Sometimes referred to as *ping-pong* behavior, request/reply is simple to understand and implement, but not very efficient. In LAN topologies with fast links, this isn't much of a concern, but WAN links will spend most of their time idle, especially if several hops are required.

required bandwidth (RBW) The amount of bandwidth necessary for workstation(s) to operate effectively, without using excessive bandwidth, because of high cost.

Research in Advanced Communications for Europe (RACE) A program sponsored by the European Community (EC) for the development of broadband networking capabilities.

reset Generally, a change to the original state of operation.

resolution The sharpness and clarity of an image. The term is most often used to describe monitors, printers, and bit-mapped graphic images.

resource Generally, any item that can be used, such as main storage, secondary storage, input/output devices, the processing unit, files, and control or processing programs, or anything else that can be used by a user either directly or indirectly.

resource access control facility (RACF) An IBM program that provides for access control by identifying and verifying the users of the system, by authorizing access to protected resources, by logging the detected unauthorized attempts to enter the system, and by logging the detected accesses to protected resources.

resource definition table (RDT) A VTAM table that describes characteristics of each node available to VTAM and associates each node with a specific network address. This is a main VTAM network configuration table.

resource hierarchy A VTAM relationship among network resources in which some resources are subordinate to others as a result of their positions in the network structure and architecture.

resource manager, resource management The management of critical network resources, such as bandwidth and buffers, at the node level.

resource object data manager (RODM) A resource used in the Network Installation Management environment to represent a file or directory found in that environment.

Resource Reservation Setup Protocol (RSVP) An Internet protocol that enables the Internet to support specified quality-of-service (QoS) classes in IP applications (such as videoconference, multimedia). Using RSVP, an application is able to reserve resources along a route from source to destination. RSVP-enabled routers then schedule and prioritize packets to fulfill the QoS. RSVP is a chief component of a new type of Internet being developed, known broadly as an *integrated services Internet*. The general idea is to enhance

the Internet to support transmission of real-time data.

response (RSP) A reply to some occurrence, or the lack thereof. A message acknowledging the receipt of an inquiry.

response time The lapsed time between the end of an inquiry or demand on a computer system and the beginning of the response.

response-time monitor (RTM) A display of the system's service time, in association with the user's commands.

restore To return a window to its original size.

result handler A routine that the data access manager calls to convert a data item to a character string.

retention In the Multicast Transport Protocol, one of three fundamental parameters that make up the transport's state (along with *heartbeat* and *window*). Retention is a number of heartbeats, and although applied in several different circumstances, is primarily used as the number of heartbeats a producing client must maintain for buffered data should they need to be retransmitted.

return code A code used to identify the action or lack thereof of a program execution.

Reverse Address Resolution Protocol (RARP) (*Illustration*) A TCP/IP protocol for mapping Ethernet addresses to IP addresses. It is typically used by diskless workstations which do not know their IP addresses. RARP enables a computer to discover its IP address by broadcasting a request on a network. In essence, it asks "Who am I?" Normally, a response is provided by a RARP server and is cached in the host.

reverse path multicasting (RPM) Multicasting technique in which a multicast datagram is forwarded out of all but the receiving interface.

RFC *See* request for comments.

RFC Editor RFC publication is the direct responsibility of the RFC Editor, under the general direction of the IAB (RFC 1602).

R

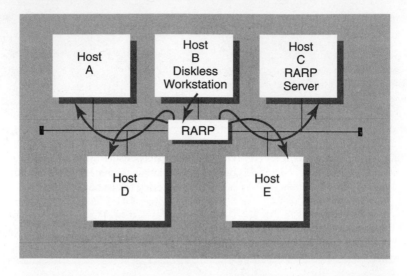

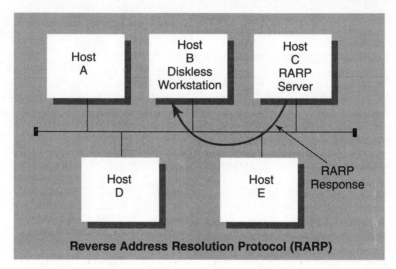

Reverse Address Resolution Protocol (RARP)

The RFC Editor maintains a web page at *http://www.isi.edu/rfc-editor/* and can be contacted at *rfc-editor@isi.edu*.

RFQ *See* request for a price quotation.

RGB monitor Short for red, green, blue monitor; a monitor that requires separate signals for each of the three colors.

RH *See* request (or response) header.

RI *See* ring in.

RIB *See* routing information base.

RIF *See* rate increase factor *and* routing information field.

RII *See* routing information identifier.

ring in (RI) To pass or exchange information between active stations.

ring latency Time required for a signal to propagate once around a ring in a token ring or IEEE 802.5 network.

ring monitor Centralized management tool for token ring networks based on the IEEE 802.5 specification. *See* active monitor *and* standby monitor.

ring topology (*Illustration*) One of the three principal topologies used in LANs. All devices are connected to one another in the shape of a closed loop, so that each device is connected directly to two other devices, one on either side of it. Ring topologies are relatively expensive and difficult to install, but they are robust (one failed device does not usually make the entire network fail). *See* bus topology, *and* star topology.

RIP *See* Routing Information Protocol.

RISC *See* reduced instruction set computer.

RJ-11 Registered Jack-11; a four- or six-wire connector used primarily to connect telephone equipment in the United States. RJ-11 connectors are also used to connect some types of local area networks (LANs), although RJ-45 connectors are more common.

RJ-45 (*Illustration*) Registered Jack-45; an eight-wire connector used commonly to connect computers onto local area networks (LANs), especially Ethernets. RJ-45 connectors look similar to the RJ-11 connectors used for connecting telephone equipment, but they are somewhat wider. Four-pair wire is the standard; Pair 1 is Blue, Pair 2 Orange, Pair 3 Green, and Pair 4 Brown. Colors are always shown with the Base Color first, then the Stripe Color. The RJ-45 is wired as follows:

R

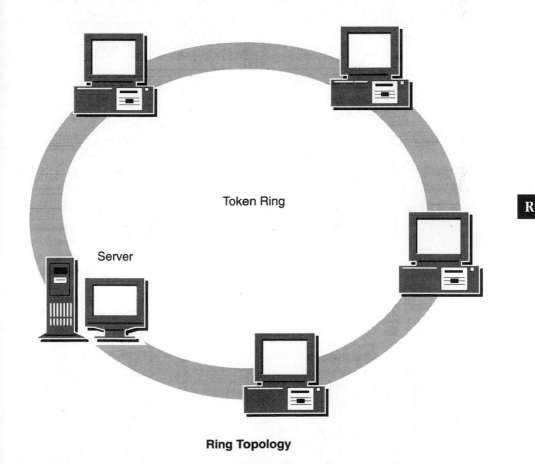

Ring Topology

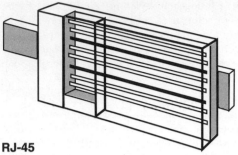

RJ-45

Pin 1 White/Orange Transmit

Pin 2 Orange/White Transmit

Pin 3 White/Green Receive

Pin 4 Blue/White

Pin 5 White/Blue

Pin 6 Green/White Receive

Pin 7 White/Brown

Pin 8 Brown/White

To orient the wires, first hold the cable in the left hand, with the RJ-45 pins facing up—Pin 1 is the furthest away from you. The blue and brown pair are unused.

RJE *See* remote job entry.

RLE *See* run-length encoded.

RLL *See* run-length limited.

rlogin Remote login. A log-on service provided by Berkeley 4BSD UNIX systems that allows users of one machine to connect to other UNIX systems.

RMI *See* Remote Method Invocation.

RMON *See* Remote Network Monitoring.

RO *See* remote office.

robot (*a*) A device that responds to sensory input. (*b*) A program that runs automatically without human intervention. Typically, a robot is endowed with some artificial intelligence so that it can react to different situations it may encounter. Two common types of robots are *agents* and *spiders*.

robotics The field of computer science and engineering concerned with creating *robots*, devices that can move and react to sensory input. Robotics is one branch of *artificial intelligence*. The term *robotics* was coined by the writer Isaac Asimov. In his science fiction book *I, Robot*, published in 1950, he presented three laws of robotics:

1. A robot may not injure a human being, or, through inaction, allow a human being to come to harm.

2. A robot must obey the orders given it by human beings except where such orders would conflict with the First Law.

3. A robot must protect its own existence as long as such protection does not conflict with the First or Second Law.

RODM *See* resource object data manager.

ROM *See* read-only memory.

root account Privileged account on UNIX systems used exclusively by network or system administrators.

root bridge switch A bridge or switch responsible for exchanging topology information with designated bridges in a spanning-tree implementation, to notify all other bridges in the network when topology changes are required. This prevents loops and provides a measure of protection against link failure.

root menu The main menu. That menu from which other menus originate.

root window In the XWindowing environment, the display presented on the screen once the X graphical user interface is visible to the user.

ROSE *See* remote operations service element.

rotary group A group of physical interfaces allocated for dialing out or receiving calls. The group acts like a pool from which any link may be used to dial out or receive calls.

round-trip time (RTT) The time it takes for a transmission to pass between a source and a device, such as a switch. It is usually measured in number of cells (which depends on the buffering capabilities of the device). It is used as a window in flow control.

route An ordered sequence between origin and destination stations that represents a path in a network between the stations.

route extension A path from the destination in SNA, subarea node through peripheral equipment to a NAU.

route map Method of controlling the redistribution of routes between routing domains.

route selection services (RSS) A subcomponent of the topology and routing services component that determines the preferred route between a specified pair of nodes for a given class of service.

router A special-purpose device hardware that connects two or more networks at the network layer (Layer 3) of the OSI model; operated like a bridge but routers can choose routes through a network. Routers spend all their time looking at the destination addresses of the packets passing through them and deciding which route to send them on. Routers use headers and a routing table to determine where packets go. *See* network *and* packet switching.

routine A section of a program that performs a particular task. Programs consist of modules, each of which contains one or more routines. The term routine is synonymous with *procedure, function,* and *subroutine.*

routing Process usually performed by a dedicated device called a *router.* In internetworking, the process of moving a packet of data from source to destination. Routing is a key feature of the Internet because it enables messages to pass from one computer to another and eventually reach the target machine. Each intermediary computer performs routing by passing along the message to the next computer. Part of this process involves analyzing a *routing table* to determine the best path. Routing assumes that addresses have been assigned to facilitate data delivery.

In particular, routing assumes that addresses convey at least partial information about where a host is located. This permits routers to forward packets without having to rely on either broadcasting or a complete listing of all possible destinations. At the IP level, routing is used almost exclusively, primarily because the Internet was designed to construct large networks in which heavy broadcasting or huge routing tables are not feasible.

Routing is often confused with *bridging,* which performs a similar function. The principal difference between the two is that bridging occurs at a lower level and is therefore more of a hardware function, whereas routing occurs at a higher level where the software component is more important. Because routing occurs at a higher level, it can perform more complex analysis to determine the optimal path for the packet.

routing information base (RIB) A collection of output from route calculations.

routing information field (RIF) Field in the IEEE802.5 header that is used by a source-route bridge to determine through which token ring network segments a packet must transit. A RIF is made up of ring and bridge numbers as well as other information.

routing information identifier (RII) Bit used by source route transparent (SRT) bridges to distinguish between frames that should be transparently bridged and frames that should be passed to the source route bridging (SRB) device for handling.

Routing Information Protocol (RIP) (*Illustration*) An early BSD UNIX dynamic routing protocol that has become an industry standard; often used because WIN NT and UNIX systems can understand it. RIP is considered an outdated router protocol. *See* OSPF *and* EIGRP.

Routing Table Maintenance Protocol (RTMP) A protocol that allows an AppleTalk router to obtain and keep information about routes to the various AppleTalk networks.

Routing Table Protocol (RTP) VINES routing protocol based on RIP. Distributes network topology information and aids VINES servers in finding neighboring clients, servers,

R

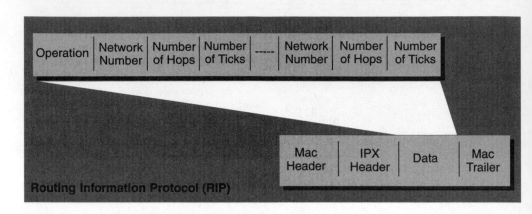

Operation	Network Number	Number of Hops	Number of Ticks	-----	Network Number	Number of Hops	Number of Ticks

Mac Header	IPX Header	Data	Mac Trailer

Routing Information Protocol (RIP)

and routers. Uses delay as a routing metric. *See* SRTP.

routing tables In Internet routing, each entry in a routing table has at least two fields the *IP Address Prefix* and *Next Hop*. The Next Hop is the IP address of another host or router that is directly reachable via an Ethernet, serial link, or some other physical connection.

The IP Address Prefix specifies a set of destinations for which the routing entry is valid. To be in this set, the beginning of the destination IP address must match the IP Address Prefix, which can have from 0 to 32 significant bits.

For example, a IP Address Prefix of 128.8.0.0/16 would match any IP Destination Address of the form 128.8.X.X. If no routing table entries match a packet's destination address, the packet is discarded as undeliverable (possibly with an ICMP notification to the sender). If multiple routing table entries match, the longest match is preferred. The longest match is the entry with the most 1 bits in its subnet mask.

routing update A message sent from a router indicates a network reachability and associated cost information. Routing updates are typically sent at regular intervals and after a change in network topology. *See* flash update.

RPC *See* Remote Procedure Call.

RPL *See* request parameter list.

RPM *See* reverse path multicasting.

RPOA *See* recognized private operating agency.

RPS *See* redundant power supply.

RS-232C A standard interface approved by the Electronic Industries Association (EIA) for connecting serial devices. In 1987, the EIA released a new version of the standard and changed the name to EIA-232-D. In 1991, the EIA teamed up with Telecommunications Industry association (TIA) and issued a new version of the standard called EIA/TIA-232-E. Many people, however, still refer to the standard as RS-232C, or just RS-232.

Almost all modems conform to the EIA-232 standard and most personal computers have an EIA-232 port for connecting a modem or other device. In addition to modems, many display screens, mice, and serial printers are designed to connect to a EIA-232 port. In EIA-232 parlance, the device that connects to the interface is called *Data Communications Equipment (DCE)* and the device to which it connects (e.g., the computer) is called a *Data Terminal Equipment (DTE)*.

The EIA-232 standard supports two types of connectors—a 25-pin D-type connector (DB-25) and a 9-pin D-type connector (DB-9). The type of serial communications used by PCs requires only 9 pins so either type of connector works equally well.

Although EIA-232 is still the most common standard for serial communication, the EIA has recently defined successors to EIA-232 called *RS-422* and *RS-423*. The new standards are backward compatible so that RS-232 devices can connect to an RS-422 port.

RS-422 Balanced electrical implementation of EIA/TIA-449 for high-speed data transmission. Now referred to collectively with RS-423 as *EIA-530*. *See* EIA-530 *and* RS-423.

RS-423 Unbalanced electrical implementation of EIA/TIA-449 for EIA/TIA-232 compatibility. Now referred to collectively with RS-422 as *EIA-530*. *See* EIA-530 *and* RS-422.

RS-449 Popular physical-layer interface. Now known as *EIA/TIA-449*. *See* EIA/TIA-449.

RSA A public-key encryption technology developed by RSA Data Security, Inc. The RSA algorithm is based on the fact that there is no efficient way to factor very large numbers. Cracking an RSA key, therefore, requires an extraordinary amount of computer processing power and time.

For more information, see *http://www.rsa.com*.

RSCS *See* remote spooling communication system.

RSP *See* response.

RSS *See* route selection services.

RSVP *See* Resource Reservation Setup Protocol.

RTM *See* response-time monitor.

RTMP *See* Routing Table Maintenance Protocol.

RTP *See* Routing Table Protocol, Rapid Transport Protocol, *and* Real-Time Transport Protocol.

RTSE *See* reliable transfer service element.

RTSP *See* Real-Time Streaming Protocol.

RTT *See* round-trip time.

RU *See* request (or response) unit.

run (*a*) To execute a program. (*b*) To operate. For example, a device that is running is one that is turned on and operating properly.

run-length encoded (RLE) RLE is a compression method that converts consecutive identical characters into a code consisting of the character and the number marking the length of the run. The longer the run, the greater the compression. It works best with black-and-white or cartoon-style graphics, and is used to compress Windows start-up logos.

run-length limited (RLL) An encoding scheme used to store data on newer PC hard disks.

runtime Occurring while a program is executing.

runtime error An error that occurs during the execution of a program.

R

S/MIME *See* Secure/MIME.

S/T loop ISDN service in the home; made to run short distances from an NT-1.

SA *See* Source address (field).

SAA *See* system application architecture.

SAAL *See* signaling AAL.

SABM *See* set asynchronous balanced mode.

SAC *See* single-attached concentrator.

SACK *See* selective acknowledgment.

sampling rate Rate at which samples are taken. For example, the number of times a particular waveform amplitude values are taken.

SAP *See* service access point.

SAPI *See* service access point identifier.

SAR *See* segmentation and reassembly.

SAR-PDU *See* Segmentation and Reassembly Protocol data unit.

SAS *See* single-attachment station *and* statically assigned sockets.

satellite communication Transmitting data to orbiting satellites in order to relay the data between earth-based stations.

SATF *See* shared-access transfer facility.

satin cable Four parallel wires (0 twists); used for telephone only.

save To copy data from a temporary area to a permanent area such as a floppy or hard disk.

SBus Bus technology adopted by the IEEE as a new bus standard; used in Sun SPARC-based workstations and servers.

Scalable Processor Architecture (SPARC) A RISC technology developed by Sun Microsystems.

scalable How well a hardware or software system can adapt to increased growth. Anything whose size can be changed or altered without a negative effect.

SCAM *See* SCSI Configuration Automatically.

scan To digitize an item such as a picture or document by passing it through an optical scanner.

SCB *See* session control block.

SCE *See* service creation environment.

SCEF *See* service creation environment function.

schema The physical structure of a database system, as described in a formal DBMS language supported by a database management system (DBMS).

SCR *See* sustainable cell rate.

scrapbook In Macintosh environments, a desk accessory (DA) that is similar to the clipboard, but allows more than one item to be stored in it. The user can store objects for future use.

scratchpad RAM A portion of the L1 cache reserved for direct and private use to temporarily store copies of data that reside on slower main memory by a computer's CPU.

screen dump A screen capture capable of being saved as a file.

screen The physical surface of a display device on which information is shown to a user.

script Another term for *macro* or *batch file*; a list of commands that can be executed without user interaction.

script kiddies A derogatory term used by the hacker/cracker community to refer to individuals whose only skill in hacking/cracking is to use prewritten attack software instead of creating or modifying their own software tools.

SCSI Configuration Automatically (SCAM) Provides plug-and-play support for SCSI devices.

SCSI *See* small computer systems interface.

SCTE *See* serial clock transmit external.

SCTR *See* system conformance test report.

SDH *See* synchronous digital hierarchy.

SDK *See* software development kit.

SDLC *See* Synchronous Data Link Control.

SDLLC SDLC feature that performs translation between SDLC and IEEE802.2 type2.

SDRAM *See* synchronous DRAM.

SDSL *See* symmetric digital subscriber line.

SDU *See* service data unit.

SEAL *See* simple efficient adaptation layer.

secondary ring Usually reserved for use in the event of a failure of the primary ring making up an FDDI or CDDI ring.

secondary station A station that responds to commands from a primary station, typically encountered in HDLC networks.

sector The smallest unit that can be accessed on a disk.

Secure Hypertext Transfer Protocol (S-HTTP) An extension to the HTTP protocol to support sending individual messages securely over the World Wide Web.

Secure Sockets Layer (SSL) A protocol developed by Netscape Communications to enable encrypted, authenticated communications via the Internet. SSL is used mostly (but not exclusively) in communications between Web browsers and Web servers. An SSL-protected HTTP transfer uses port 443 (instead of HTTP's normal port 80), and is identified with a special URL method that begins with https to indicate that an SSL connection will be used.

SSL provides three important things: privacy, authentication, and message integrity. In an SSL connection each side of the connection must have a *security certificate*, which each side sends to the other. Each side then encrypts what it sends using information from both its own and the other side's certificate, ensuring that only the intended recipient can decrypt it, that the other side can be sure the data came from the place it claims to have come from, and that the message has not been tampered with. *See* browser, server, security certificate, *and* URL.

Secure/MIME (S/MIME) A new version of the MIME protocol that supports encryption of messages.

security certificate A specially created chunk of information used by the *Secure Sockets Layer (SSL) protocol* to establish a secure connection across the network. In order for an SSL connection to be created both sides must have a valid security certificate. Security certificates contain information about to whom they belong, by whom they were issued, unique serial numbers or other unique identification, valid dates, and encrypted "fingerprints" that can be used to verify the contents of the certificate. *See* certificate authority *and* SSL.

security management One of five categories of network management defined by ISO for management of OSI networks, responsible for controlling access to network resources. *See* accounting management, configuration management, fault management, *and* performance management.

seek time The average time a program or device takes to locate a particular piece of data on a disk or hard drive.

segment (*a*) In networks, a section of a network divided by bridges, routers, hubs, or switches which is one of the most common ways of increasing bandwidth on the LAN. (*b*) A Protocol Data Unit (PDU) consisting of a TCP header and, optionally, some data. Sometimes used to refer to the data portion of a TCP Protocol Data Unit. (*c*) In virtual memory systems, a variable-sized portion of data that is swapped in and out of main memory. (*d*) In token-ring networks, a portion of a LAN that consists of cables, components, or lobes up to a bridge, or an entire ring without bridges.

segmentation and reassembly (SAR) The lower half of the AAL. SAR inserts the data from the information frames into the ATM cell, then adds any necessary header or trailer bits to the data and passes the 48-octet cell to the ATM layer. Each AAL type has its own SAR format. At the destination, the cell payload is extracted and converted to the appropriate PDU. See AAL, ATM layer, CPCS, CS, and SSCS.

Segmentation and Reassembly Protocol data unit (SAR-PDU) The 48-octet PDU that the SAR sublayer exchanges with the ATM layer. It is comprised of the SAR-PDU payload and any control information that the SAR sublayer might add.

segmented address space An address space logically divided into sections, called *segments*.

segment number The identifier that uniquely distinguishes a LAN segment in a multisegment LAN.

segment type (ST) A 2-bit field in the SAR-PDU header that indicates whether the SAR-PDU is a BOM, COM, EOM, or SSM.

select To choose an object so that it can be manipulated in some way.

selective acknowledgment. (SACK) In TCP/IP, an acknowledgment mechanism used with sliding-window protocols. This permits a receiver to acknowledge packets received out of order within the current sliding window.

self-monitoring, analysis and reporting technology (SMART) An open standard for disk drives and software systems that automatically monitors a disk drive's health and report potential problems

semantics In linguistics, the study of meanings.

semiconductor A material that is neither a good conductor of electricity (like copper) nor a good insulator (like rubber). The most common semiconductor materials are silicon and germanium. The basic materials used to manufacture modern day electronic devices.

send pacing Pacing of message units (in SNA) that a component is sending.

sendmail Among the most widely-used UNIX Internet mail packages. Other UNIX Internet mail packages are often designed to operate much like sendmail. Sendmail applies a bizarre series of transformations to mail that are beyond the scope of this book; it runs in two major modes. One is as a *daemon*, the program being detached into background during a startup script, listening for incoming SMTP mail, acting as an SMTP server, and delivering that mail. The other mode is invoked from a mail program or even the command line, allowing sendmail to accept RFC 822 mail over standard input.

sequence number (SN) Part of the header of the SAR-PDU (2 bits in AAL1, 4 bits in AAL3/4). It is used as a sequence counter for detecting lost, out-of-sequence or misinserted SAR-PDUs.

sequence number protection (SNP) A 4-bit field in the header of the AAL1 SAR-PDU that contains the CRC and the Parity Bit fields.

Sequenced Packet Exchange (SPX) A transport-layer protocol (layer 4 of the OSI Model) used in Novell Netware networks by client/server applications. The SPX layer sits on top of the IPX layer (layer 3) and provides connection-oriented services between two nodes on the network. The IPX protocol is similar to IP, SPX is similar to TCP. Together, IPX/SPX provides connection services similar to TCP/IP in Novell-based networks.

Sequenced Packet Protocol (SPP) Developed by Xerox as part of the XNS protocol suite; SPP has been adopted by various other manufacturers. The most popular variant is Novell's SPX. SPP is also a connection-oriented transport protocol; connectionless services are provided by PEP. See SPP.

Sequenced Packet A connection-oriented protocol found in Novell NetWare networks.

Sequenced Routing Update Protocol (SRTP) Protocol that assists Banyan VINES servers in finding neighboring clients, servers, and routers. See Routing Table Protocol (RTP).

sequential access The act of reading or writing information in a sequential order, that is, one record after the other.

S

serial clock transmit external (SCTE) A timing signal designed to compensate for clock phase shift on long cables that the DTE echoes to the DCE to maintain clocking.

Serial Line Internet Protocol (SLIP) The first dial-in protocol for relaying IP packets over dial-up lines as documented in RFC1055, which defines an encapsulation mechanism, but nothing else. *See* Internet, PPP, *and* CSLIP.

serial port A general-purpose port, or interface, that can be used for serial communication for almost any type of device, including modems, mice, and printers, in which only one bit is transmitted at a time. Most serial ports on personal computers conform to the RS-232C or RS-422 standards. The opposite of serial is *parallel*, in which several bits are transmitted concurrently.

serial One by one. Serial data transfer refers to transmitting data one bit at a time. *See* parallel.

server message block (SMB) A message format used by Windows to share files, directories, and devices. NetBIOS is based on the SMB format, and many network products use SMB.

server A computer or software package, often dedicated, that provides a specific kind of service(s) to client software running on other computers. The term can either refer to a particular piece of software, such as a WWW server, or to the physical machine on which the software is running. *See* client *and* network.

server-side include (SSI) A type of HTML comment that directs the Web server to dynamically generate data for the Web page whenever it is requested. The basic format for SSIs is:

<!--#command tag="value"...>

where #command can be any of various commands supported by the Web server. The simplest command is #include, which inserts the contents of another file. This is especially useful for ensuring that boilerplate components, such as headers and footers, are the same on all pages throughout a Web site.

To change a boilerplate element, the user need only modify the include file, instead of updating every individual Web page.

SSIs can also be used to execute programs and insert the results. They therefore represent a powerful tool for Web developers. There is no official standard for SSIs, so every Web server is free to support different SSIs in different ways. However, many SSI commands, such as #include and #exec, have become de facto standards.

Web pages that contain SSIs often end with an shtml extension, though this is not a requirement. The filename extension enables the Web server to differentiate those pages that need to be processed before they are sent to the browser.

service access point (SAP) (*a*) The point of access to services provided by the layers of a LAN architecture. (*b*) A logical addressable point. (*c*) Interface between the layers in the OSI model through which lower layers provide services to the higher layers passing over the protocol data units (PDUs) as defined in IEEE802.2. *See* DSAP *and* SSAP.

service access point identifier (SAPI) A 6-bit field that identifies the point where Layer 2 provides a service to Layer 3 in the OSI model.

Service Advertising Protocol (SAP) (*Illustration*) A NetWare (IPX) protocol used to identify the services available and addresses of IPX servers attached to the internetwork. SAPs are used to update a table in the router known as the *server information table*. *See* IPX.

service creation environment (SCE) A space within Integrated Service Engineering consisting of methods, architectures, interfaces, and tools serving the service creation task.

service creation environment function (SCEF) A major component of the IN architecture.

service data unit (SDU) A unit of information from an upper-layer protocol that defines a service request to a lower-layer protocol.

service features (SF) In telephony, any of a number of special functions that may be specified initially, or added to the user's basic ser-

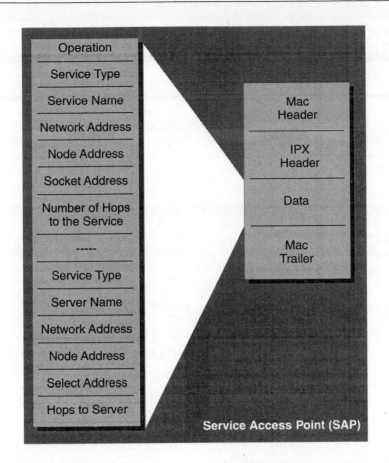

Operation	
Service Type	
Service Name	Mac Header
Network Address	
Node Address	IPX Header
Socket Address	
Number of Hops to the Service	Data

Service Type	Mac Trailer
Server Name	
Network Address	
Node Address	
Select Address	
Hops to Server	

Service Access Point (SAP)

vice. Modern telephone switches are capable of providing a wide variety of service features, such as call forwarding and call waiting.

service level agreement (SLA) An agreement between a service provider and a user that defines, at minimum, how the set of parameters that specifies the quality of service (QoS) to be measured. This guarantees a minimum performance standard to the user.

service primitive Part of a service element. Four types exist: confirm, indication, request, and response.

service profile identifier (SPID) A number that identifies a specific ISDN line. When a user obtains ISDN service, the service provider assigns a SPID to the line. Most service providers in the United States use the Generic SPID Format, which is a 14-digit number. The first 10 digits identify the telephone number, called the *directory number (DN)*. The remaining four digits identify a particular ISDN device, in the case where multiple devices share the same directory number. For example, 91977274630100.

service types There are four service types: CBR, VBR, UBR, and ABR. CBR and VBR are guaranteed services while UBR and ABR are described as best-effort services.

Service-Specific Connection-Oriented Protocol (SSCOP) Part of the SSCS portion of the SAAL. SSCOP is an end-to-end protocol that provides error detection and correction by retransmission and status reporting between the sender and the receiver, while guaranteeing delivery integrity. *See* service-specific coordination function.

S

service-specific convergence sublayer (SSCS) One of the two components of the convergence sublayer (CS) of the AAL that is particular to the traffic service class to be converted. It is developed to support certain user applications such as LAN emulation, transport of high-quality video, and database management.

service-specific coordination function (SSCF) Part of the SSCS portion of the SAAL. Among other functions, it provides a clear interface for relaying user data and providing independence from the underlying sublayers. *See* Service-Specific Connection-Oriented Protocol.

servlet An applet that runs on a server.

session control block (SCB) A control block that contains the parameter values for how a session is to be delivered.

session layer Layer 5 of the OSI reference model. The session layer coordinates the dialog between two communicating application processes by establishing, managing, and terminating sessions between applications; it manages data exchange between presentation layer entities. It corresponds to the data-flow control layer of the SNA model. *See* OSI Model, application layer, data-link layer, network layer, physical layer, presentation layer, *and* transport layer.

Session Management The network-layer protocols of the Internet are fundamentally datagram oriented and unreliable. It is the responsibility of the transport and session layer protocols to enhance the quality of service to that desired by a particular application.

In Internet terminology, these are the protocols of the *Host-to-Host Layer*. These protocols function as intermediaries between the application and network layers thus giving them the session management title. Currently, there are three Internet session management protocols:

The *User Datagram Protocol (UDP)* provides almost no additional functionality over IP. It performs fast, unreliable, datagram delivery. *See* UDP.

The *Transmission Control Protocol (TCP)* provides reliable, stream-oriented delivery for applications such as file transfers and remote logins. TCP is a sliding-window protocol that takes steps to insure reliable data transfer (connection oriented), resending if needed due to network overloads or malfunctions. *See* TCP.

The *Remote Procedure Call (RPC)* is designed for programs to make subroutine calls on other systems. Essentially a request-reply protocol, RPC usually makes heavy use of UDP datagrams, adding its own facilities for insuring data transfer. RPC's most important application is its file sharing via the NFS protocol so its use is mostly limited to local area networks. *See* RPC.

session manager (SM) A third-party product, which permits a user on one terminal to log on to multiple applications concurrently.

session A logical connection between two addressable endpoints that allows them to communicate

set asynchronous balanced mode (SABM) The SABM command is used to place two DXEs in the asynchronous balanced mode. This is a balanced mode of operation known as LAPB, where both devices are treated as equals. Information fields are not allowed in SABM commands. Any outstanding frames left when the SABM command is issued will remain unacknowledged. The DXE confirms reception and acceptance of an SABM command by sending a UA response frame at the earliest opportunity. If the DXE is not capable of accepting an SABM command, it should respond with a DM frame if possible.

SF *See* service features *and* super frame.

SFD *See* start frame delimiter.

SFS *See* shared file system.

SFT *See* system fault tolerance.

SG *See* study group.

SGFS *See* Special Group on Functional Standardization.

SGI *See* Silicon Graphics Incorporated.

SGML *See* Standard Generalized Markup Language.

SGMP *See* Simple Gateway Monitoring Protocol.

SGRAM *See* synchronous graphic random access memory.

shadowing A technique used to increase a computer's speed by using high-speed RAM memory in place of slower ROM memory.

shared Ethernet An Ethernet network configuration in which a number of segments are joined together to form a single collision domain.

shared file system (SFS) A system of file organization much like using directories in MS-DOS or UNIX.

shared memory Memory in a computing or networking device that is accessible to two or more processes, but with access controlled for which process has next access (read/write) to the memory space. The use of shared memory reduces the total memory requirement of a computing system.

shared-access transport facility (SATF) A transmission facility, such as a multipoint link connection or a token-ring network, where multiple pairs of nodes can form concurrently active links.

shareware Software distributed free of charge on the basis of an honor system.

shell (*a*) The outermost layer of a program; another term for user interface. Operating systems and applications sometimes provide an alternative shell to make interaction with the program easier. For example, if the application is usually command driven, the shell might be a menu-driven system that translates the user's selections into the appropriate commands. (*b*) Sometimes called *command shell*, the command processor interface. The command processor is the program that executes operating system commands. The shell, therefore, is the part of the command processor that accepts commands. After verifying that the commands are valid, the shell sends them to another part of the command processor to be executed. UNIX systems offer a choice between several different shells, the most popular being the Cshell, the Bourne shell, and the Korn shell. Each offers a somewhat different command language.

shielded cable Cable that has a layer of shielded insulation to reduce EMI.

shielded twisted pair (STP) A pair of shielded (usually aluminum foil) insulated wires (copper) that are twisted around each other (spiral pattern) to reduce electrical noise. One wire carries the signal, while the other wire is grounded and absorbs signal interference. Commonly found in office buildings. STP cable contains an outside wrap-around conductor to reduce noise further. The shield should be grounded at the hub end. STP generally has an impedance of 150 ohms.

shockwave A technology developed by Macromedia, Inc. that enables Web pages to include multimedia objects. To create a shockwave object, the user uses Macromedia's multimedia authoring tool called *Director*, and then compresses the object with a program called *Afterburner*. A reference is then inserted into the "shocked" file in the Web page. To view a Shockwave object, a browser needs the Shockwave plug-in, a program that is freely available from Macromedia's Web site as either a Netscape Navigator plug-in or an ActiveX control.

For more information, see *http://www.macromedia.com*.

shortcut A special type of file in Windows that points to another file or device.

shortest path first algorithm (SPF) Sometimes called *Dijkstra's algorithm*. SPF is commonly used in link-state routing algorithms such as OSPF. *See* link state routing algorithm.

shortest-path routing Routing that minimizes distance or path cost through application of an algorithm. *See* OSPF, SPF, *and* link-state routing.

S-HTTP *See* Secure Hypertext Transfer Protocol.

SIG *See* SMDS Interest Group.

signaling AAL (SAAL) Service-specific parts of the AAL protocol responsible for signaling. Its specifications, being developed by ITU-T, were adopted from N-ISDN.

Signaling System No. 7 (SS7) A global standard for telecommunications defined by the International Telecommunications Union (ITU) Telecommunication Standardization Sector (ITU-T). The standard defines the procedures and protocol by which network elements in the public switched telephone network (PSTN) exchange information over a digital signaling network to effect wireless (cellular) and wireline call setup, routing, and control.

The ITU definition of SS7 allows for national variants such as the American National Standards Institute (ANSI) and Bell Communications Research (Bellcore) standards used in North America, and the European Telecommunications Standards Institute (ETSI) standard used in Europe. SS7 architecture is set up in a way so that any node could exchange signaling with any other SS7-capable node, not just signaling between switches that are directly connected.

The SS7 network and protocol are used for:

- Basic call setup, management, and tear down.

- Wireless services such as personal communications services (PCS), wireless roaming, and mobile subscriber authentication.

- Local number portability (LNP).

- Toll-free (800/888) and toll (900) wireline services.

- Enhanced call features such as call forwarding, calling party name/number display, and three-way calling.

- Efficient and secure worldwide telecommunications.

 For more information, see www.SS7.com.

signaling Process of sending a transmission signal over a physical medium for purposes of communication.

signal-quality error (SQE) Transmission sent by a transceiver back to the controller to let the controller know whether the collision circuitry is functional.

Silicon Graphics Incorporated (SGI) Founded by Dr. James Clark in 1982 and based in Mountain View, California. Silicon Graphics provides the computer hardware and software used to develop computer graphics such as those used to create special effects and animation in motion pictures. The company merged with MIPS Computer Systems in 1992, Alias Research and Wavefront Technologies in 1995, and Cray Research in 1996.

SIMM *See* single in-line memory module.

simple efficient adaptation layer (SEAL) The original name and recommendation for the AAL5 specification.

Simple Gateway Monitoring Protocol (SGMP) Network management protocol, documented in RFC 1028, that evolved into Simple Network Management Protocol (SNMP). *See* SNMP.

Simple Mail Transfer Protocol (SMTP) (*Illustration*) The protocol standard developed to support the exchange of electronic mail (e-mail) services. The SMTP protocol specifies how two mail systems interact and the format of control messages. *See* client *and* server.

Simple Multicast Routing Protocol (SMRP) Specialized multicast network protocol for routing multimedia data streams on enterprise networks. SMRP works in conjunction with multicast extensions to the AppleTalk protocol.

Simple Network Management Protocol (SNMP) Originally developed for the Department of Defense in the early 80s. SNMP has since evolved into the IETF-defined standard management protocol for managing TCP/IP networks.

SNMP is normally found as an application on top of the *User Datagram Protocol (UDP)*, and is essentially a request-reply protocol running over UDP (ports 161 and 162), though TCP operation is possible. The *agent* is the device

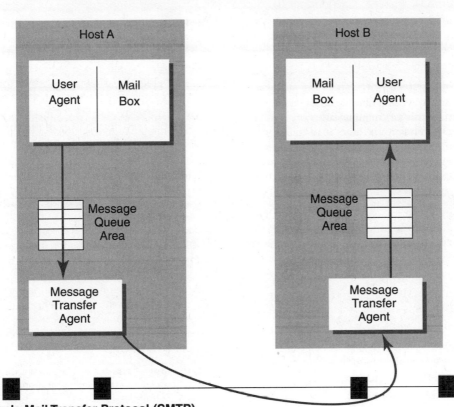

Simple Mail Transfer Protocol (SMTP)

being managed; all that its software has to do is implement a few simple packet types and a generic get-or-set function on its MIB variables.

The management station presents the user interface. Examples of these devices include routers, hubs, and switches. A device is said to be "SNMP compatible" if it can be monitored and/or controlled using SNMP messages.

SNMP Version 1 is documented in RFC 1157.

SNMP Version 2 is documented in several RFCs: RFC 1902 (MIB Structure), RFC 1903 (Textual Conventions), RFC 1904 (Conformance Statements), RFC 1905 (Protocol Operations), RFC 1906 (Transport Mappings), and RFC 1907 (MIB).

SNMP's packet formats are described using *abstract syntax notation 1 (ASN.1)*, one of ISO's "Open" protocols. ASN.1 basically fills the

role of XDR, but does so differently. ASN.1, like all OSI standard documents, is not freely available on-line. An SNMP operation takes the form of a Protocol Data Unit (PDU), basically a fancy word for packet. Version 1 SNMP supports five possible PDUs:

GetRequest/SetRequest supplies a list of objects and, possibly, values they are to be set to (SetRequest). In either case, the agent returns a GetResponse.

GetResponse informs the management station of the results of a GetRequest or SetRequest by returning an error indication and a list of variable/value bindings.

GetNextRequest is used to perform table transversal, and in other cases where the management station does not know the exact MIB name of the object it desires. GetNextRequest does not require an exact name to be speci-

S

fied; if no object exists of the specified name, the next object in the MIB is returned. Note that to support this, MIBs must be strictly ordered sets (and are).

Trap is the only PDU sent by an agent on its own initiative. It is used to notify the management station of an unusual event that may demand further attention (like a link going down). In version 2, traps are named in MIB space. Newer MIBs specify management objects that control how traps are sent.

SNMP communities is the only security architecture found in SNMP that enables an intelligent network device to validate SNMP requests from sources such as the NMS. *See* SNMP.

Simple Protocol for ATM Network Signaling (SPANS) A protocol supported by FORE Systems switches that provides SVC tunneling capability over a PVC network.

simplex When transmission can only occur in one direction, for example, radio.

Simplified Network Management Protocol Management Information Base (SNMP MIB) A standards-based group of management objects used to communicate network management information.

simulation The process of imitating a real phenomenon such as routing, through the use of advanced mathematical data and formulas.

single in-line memory module (SIMM) A small circuit board that can hold a group of memory chips.

single mode A type of fiber optic cable containing only one mode. It is used for longer distances and higher speeds such as long distance telephone lines or for any application that must span more than two kilometers in distance. *See* multimode fiber.

single-attached concentrator (SAC) Used within FDDI or CDDI networks.

single-attachment station (SAS) A device attached only to the primary ring of a FDDI ring.

single-line digital (SDSL) HDSL over a single twisted pair.

single-mode fiber (SMF) An optical fiber in which only the lowest order bound mode can propagate at the wavelength of interest. The lowest order bound mode is ascertained for the wavelength of interest by solving Maxwell's equations for the boundary conditions imposed by the fiber, e.g., core (spot) size and the refractive indices of the core and cladding. The solution of Maxwell's equations for the lowest-order bound mode will permit a pair of orthogonally polarized fields in the fiber, and this is the usual case in a communication fiber. In step-index guides, single-mode operation occurs when the normalized frequency, V, is less than 2.405. For power-law profiles, single-mode operation occurs for a normalized frequency, V, less than approximately where g is the profile parameter. In practice, the orthogonal polarizations may not be associated with degenerate modes. Synonyms are monomode optical fiber, single-mode fiber, single-mode optical waveguide, and unimode fiber.

single-route broadcast The forwarding of specially designated broadcast frames only by bridges which have single-route broadcast enabled. If the network is configured correctly, a single-route broadcast frame will have exactly one copy delivered to every LAN segment in the network.

single-route explorer packet *See* spanning explorer packet.

single-segment message (SSM) A message that constitutes a single PDU.

SIR *See* sustained information rate.

size To make an object larger or smaller.

SLA *See* service level agreement.

sleep mode, sleep state A low-power consumption state of a computer. In the sleep state, the power manager and the various device drivers shut off power or remove clocks from the computer's various subsystems, including the CPU, RAM, ROM, and I/O ports.

sliding window A scenario in which a protocol, such as TCP, permits the transmitting station to send a stream of bytes before an acknowledgment arrives. Sliding-window algorithms are a method of flow control for network data transfers. When the window is full, the transmitter must stop transmitting until the receiver advertises a larger window.

SLIP *See* Serial Line Internet Protocol.

slot (*a*) An opening in a computer where you can insert a printed circuit board. (*b*) Used for the assigned space for particular data in a TDM circuit.

slotted ring LAN architecture based on a ring topology, in which the ring is divided into slots that circulate continuously. Transmissions must start at the beginning of a slot and slots can either be empty or full.

SM *See* session manager.

SMAC *See* source MAC.

SMAE *See* system management application entity.

small computer systems interface (SCSI) A computer peripheral bus, usually used for hard disk drives and CD-ROM readers. The following varieties of SCSI are currently implemented:

SCSI-1 uses an 8-bit bus, and supports data rates of 4 MBps.

SCSI-2 is the same as SCSI-1, but uses a 50-pin connector instead of a 25-pin connector, and supports multiple devices. This is what most people mean when they refer to plain SCSI.

Wide SCSI uses a wider cable (168 cable lines to 68 pins) to support 16-bit transfers.

Fast SCSI uses an 8-bit bus, but doubles the clock rate to support data rates of 10 MBps.

Fast Wide SCSI uses a 16-bit bus and supports data rates of 20MBps.

Ultra SCSI uses an 8-bit bus, and supports data rates of 20 MBps.

SCSI-3 uses a 16-bit bus and supports data rates of 40 MBps. Also called *Ultra Wide SCSI*.

Ultra2 SCSI uses an 8-bit bus and supports data rates of 40 MBps. U2 supports longer cable lengths up to 12meters—four times the earlier cable lengths—due to low voltage differential (LVD) circuitry.

Wide Ultra2 SCSI uses a 16-bit bus and supports data rates of 80 MBps.

Small Office/Home Office (SOHO) A small, remote office with a WAN or MAN connection back to a larger corporate network or the Internet.

Smalltalk An object-oriented operating system and programming language developed at Xerox Corporation's Palo Alto Research Center. Smalltalk was among the first object-oriented programming languages (Simula was the first).

Although it never achieved the commercial success of other languages such as C++ and Java, Smalltalk is considered by many to be the only true object-oriented programming environment, and the one against which all others must be compared.

smart card A small electronic device, about the size of a credit card, that contains electronic memory and possibly an embedded integrated circuit (IC). Smart cards containing an IC are sometimes called *integrated circuit cards (ICCs)*. They can be used for generating unique network IDs in security applications, or for storing digital bank records or medical records.

SMART *See* self-monitoring, analysis and reporting technology.

Smartdrive A disk caching system that provides faster access to data on a hard disk provided by Microsoft with later versions of DOS and used with Windows 3.1.

SMB *See* server message block.

SMDR *See* station message detail recording.

SMDS Interest Group (SIG) An industry forum active in producing specifications in the area of SMDS. It has also joined some of the ATM Forum activities.

SMDS *See* switched multimegabit data service.

SMF *See* single-mode fiber.

SMFA *See* systems management functional area.

S

SMI *See* Structure of Management Information.

SMIL *See* Synchronized Multimedia Integration Language.

SMRP *See* Simple Multicast Routing Protocol.

SMS *See* Systems Management Server.

SMTP *See* Simple Mail Transfer Protocol.

smurf A type of *denial of service (DOS)* attack that does not try to steal information, but instead attempts to disable a computer or network with replies to a ICMP echo (ping) requests.

A smurf attacker sends ping requests to an Internet broadcast address. These are special addresses that broadcast all received messages to the hosts connected to the subnet. Each broadcast address can support up to 255 hosts, so a single ping request can be multiplied 255 times. The source address of the request itself is "faked" to be the address of the attacker's victim. This causes all the hosts receiving the ping request to reply to this victim's address instead of the real sender's address. A single attacker sending hundreds or thousands of these ping messages per second can fill the victim's T-1 (or even T-3) line with PING replies, bring an entire network to its knees.

SN *See* sequence number.

SNA *See* systems network architecture.

SNA distribution services (SNADS) One of three SNA transaction services. *See* DDM and DIA.

SNA network A collection of IBM hardware and software put togetherso as to form a collective composite greater than its parts. The components of the network conform to the SNA format and protocol specifications defined by IBM.

SNA network interconnection (SNI) A connection of two or more independent SNA networks to allow communication between logical units in those networks. The individual SNA networks retain their independence.

SNADS *See* SNA distribution services.

snailmail Paper-based mail, usually delivered through the United States Postal Service.

Because of the speed of e-mail, normal mailing procedures are very slow by comparison.

SNAP *See* Standard Network Access Protocol.

SNI *See* SNA network interconnection.

sniffer A program and/or device that monitors data traveling over a network. Sniffers can be used both for legitimate network management functions and for stealing information off a network. Unauthorized sniffers can be extremely dangerous to network security because they are virtually impossible to detect and can be inserted almost anywhere. This makes them a favorite weapon in the hacker's arsenal. On TCP/IP networks, where they sniff packets, they're called *packet sniffers*.

SNMP MIB *See* Simplified Network Management Protocol Management Information Base.

SNMP *See* Simple Network Management Protocol.

SNMP2 SNMP2 supports centralized as well as distributed network management strategies, and includes improvements in the SMI, protocol operations, management architecture, and security originally documented in the original SNMP specification. *See* SNMP.

SNP *See* sequence number protection.

SNPA *See* subnetwork attachment point.

Socket 7 The form factor for fifth-generation CPU chips from Intel, Cyrix, and AMD.

Socket 8 Socket 8 is a 387-pin ZIF socket with connections for the CPU and one or two SRAM dies for the Level 2 (L2) cache. It is also the form factor for Intel's Pentium Pro microprocessors. The Pentium Pro was the first microprocessor not to use the Socket 7 form factor. The Pentium II microprocessors use an even newer form factor called Slot 1.

socket (*a*) In UNIX and some other operating systems, a software object that connects an application to a network protocol. In UNIX, for example, a program can send and receive TCP/IP messages by opening a socket and reading and writing data to and from the socket. This simplifies program development because the programmer need only worry about manipulating the socket and can rely on the operating system to actually transport messages across the network correctly.

A socket is a network communications endpoint. The analogy is to a wire (the network data connection) being plugged into a socket. Sockets come in two primary flavors.

An *active socket* is connected to a remote active socket via an open data connection. Closing the connection destroys the active sockets at each end-point. A *passive socket* is not connected, but rather awaits an incoming connection, which will spawn a new active socket. A socket is not a port, though there is a close relationship between them.

A socket is associated with a port, though this is a many-to-one relationship. Each port can have a single passive socket, awaiting incoming connections, and multiple active sockets, each corresponding to an open connection on the port.

SOCKS A protocol documented in RFC 1928, 1929 and 1961 for handling TCP traffic through a proxy server. It can be used with virtually any TCP application, including Web browsers and FTP clients. SOCKS provides a simple firewall functionality because it checks incoming and outgoing packets and hides the IP addresses of client applications.

soft A term used to describe things that are easily changed or impermanent.

soft error An intermittent error on a network that causes data to be transmitted more than once to be received.

soft font A font that is copied from a computer's disk to a printer's memory also called *downloadable font*.

software Computer instructions or data.

software development kit (SDK) A programming package that includes one or more APIs, programming tools, and documentation; it enables a programmer to develop applications for a specific platform.

software engineering The computer science discipline concerned with developing large applications.

software licensing Allowing an individual or group to use a piece of software.

SOHO *See* Small Office/Home Office.

Solaris An UNIX-based operating environment, developed by Sun Microsystems, that supports multithreading, symmetric multiprocessing (SMP), integrated TCP/IP networking, and centralized network administration.

SONET *See* synchronous optical network.

sound card An expansion board that enables a computer to manipulate and output sounds.

source A place from which data is taken/sent.

source address (field) (SA) Address of a network device that is sending data.

source code Program instructions in their original form. Source code is differentiated from code of various other forms (for example, object code and executable code). Source code that is the only format is readable by humans.

Initially, a programmer writes a program in a particular programming language. This form of the program is called the source program, or more generically, source code. To execute the program, however, the programmer must translate it into machine language, the language that the computer understands. The first step of this translation process is usually performed by a utility called a *compiler*. The compiler translates the source code into a form called object code. Sometimes the object code is the same as machine code; sometimes it needs to be translated into *machine language* by a utility called an *assembler*.

source MAC (SMAC) MAC address specified in the Source Address field of a packet. Compare with DMAC. *See* MAC address.

source route A route determined by the source. TCP/IP implements source routing by using an option field in an IP datagram.

source routing transparent (SRT) bridge A combination bridge utilizing IBM's source-routing mechanism along with transparent-routing mechanism.

S

source routing A method used by a bridge for moving data between LAN segments. The routing information is embedded in the token.

source-route bridging (SRB) Bridging method originated by IBM and popular in token ring networks. In an SRB network, the entire route to a destination is predetermined, in real time, prior to the sending of data to the destination. Contrast with transparent bridging.

source-route translational bridging (SR/TLB) A method of bridging where source-route stations can communicate with transparent bridge stations with the help of an intermediate bridge that translates between the two bridge protocols. *See* source-route transparent bridging.

source-route transparent bridging (SRT) An IBM bridging scheme that merges the two most prevalent bridging strategies, *source route bridging* and *transparent bridging*. Source-route transparent bridging employs both technologies in one device to satisfy the needs of all end stations. No translation between bridging protocols is necessary. *See* source-route translational bridging.

source (also **session**) **service access point (SSAP)** Service access points, both destination and source, indicate for which upper-layer protocol the packet is intended. Protocols are assigned hexadecimal values that are displayed in the DSAP and SSAP fields of a packet.

spam or spamming An inappropriate attempt to use a mailing list, or USENET or other networked communications facility as if it was a broadcast medium (which it is not) by sending the same message to a large number of people who didn't ask for it. Some people define spam even more generally as any unsolicited e-mail.

The term spam has its origins in one of two Internet legends. The first legend maintains that it comes from a famous Monty Python skit, which featured the word spam repeated over and over in a song. Like the Monty Python song, spam is an endless repetition of worthless text sent via email.

Another Internet legend maintains that spam comes from the computer group lab at the University of Southern California, who gave it the name because it has many of the same characteristics as the lunchmeat Spam: nobody wants it or ever asks for it. No one ever eats it; it is the first item to be pushed to the side of the plate. Sometimes it is actually tasty, like the small percentage of junk mail that is really useful to some people. *See* Maillist *and* USENET.

spanning-tree algorithm (STA) An algorithm used to create a logical topology that connects all network segments, and ensures that only one path exists between any two nodes. A spanning tree is loop free and is a subset of a network. Multicast routers construct a spanning tree from the multicast source located at the root of the tree to all the members of the multicast group.

Spanning-Tree Protocol (STP) Bridge protocol developed by Radia Perlman. It utilizes the spanning-tree algorithm, and enables a switch or learning bridge to dynamically work around loops in a network topology by creating a spanning tree. Switches exchange BPDU messages with other switches to detect loops, and then remove the loops by blocking traffic on selected switch interfaces/ports.

SPANS *See* Simple Protocol for ATM Network Signaling.

SPARC *See* Scalable Processor Architecture.

special character A character that is not a letter, number, symbol, or punctuation mark; a control or formatting character, for example.

Special Group on Functional Standardization (SGFS) The ISO group responsible for publishing the harmonized International Standardized Profile.

spell checker A program that checks the spelling of words in a text document, comparing the spelling against a stored list of words or dictionary.

SPF *See* shortest path first algorithm.

SPID *See* service profile identifier.

spider A program that automatically fetches Web pages for Internet search engines from links on a Web page. Because the program follows links back to a central Web page, it resembles spiders following the strands in a web.

spindle The shaft that rotates in the middle of a disk drive.

split-horizon updates Routing technique used to prevent routing loops. The information about routes is prevented from exiting the router interface through which that information was received.

SPM FDDI-to-SONET physical-layer mapping standard.

spoofing The act of a packet's claiming to be from an address from which it was not actually sent. Spoofing is designed to foil network security mechanisms such as filters and access lists.

spooler A program that controls spooling by placing jobs on a buffer queue and taking them off one at a time as needed.

spooling Simultaneous peripheral operations on-line. Placing jobs in a buffer, a special area in memory or on a disk where a device can access them when it is ready. Spooling is useful because devices access data at different rates. The buffer provides a waiting station where data can wait while the slower device catches up. The most common spooling application is print spooling.

SPP *See* Sequenced Packet Protocol.

spreadsheet A table of values arranged in rows and columns; each value can have a predefined relationship to the other values.

sprite A graphic image that can move within a larger graphic.

SPVC *See* switched or semi-permanent virtual connection.

SPX *See* Sequenced Packet Exchange.

SQE *See* signal-quality error.

SQL Server Generically, any database management system (DBMS) that can respond to queries from client machines using the SQL language.

SQL *See* Structured Query Language.

SR/TLB *See* source-route translational bridging.

SRAM *See* static random access memory.

SRB *See* source-route bridging.

SRT *See* source-route transparent bridging.

SRTP *See* Sequenced Routing Update Protocol.

SS *See* switching system.

SS7 *See* Signaling System No. 7.

SSAP *See* Source (also session) service access point.

SSCF *See* service-specific coordination function.

SSCOP *See* Service-Specific Connection-Oriented Protocol.

SSCP ID According to IBM documentation, in SNA, a number that uniquely identifies a SSCP. The SSCP ID is used in session activation requests sent to physical units (PUs) and other SSCPs.

SSCP rerouting An SNA network interconnection. A technique used by the gateway system services control point (SSCP) to send session-initiation RUs, by way of a series of SSCP-SSCP sessions, from one SSCP to another, until the owning SSCP is reached.

SSCP *See* system services control point.

SSCP-dependent An LUA LU requiring assistance from a SSCP to establish a LU-LU session.

SSCP-independent LU An LU that can activate an LU-LU session (i.e., send a BIND request) without assistance from an SSCP. It does not have an SSCP-LU session. Currently, only a LU6.2 can be an independent LU.

SSCP-LU session In SNA, a session between the SSCP and a logical unit (LU). The session enables the LU to request the SSCP to help initiate LU-LU sessions.

SSCP-PU session In SNA, a session between a SSCP and a PU. SSCP-PU sessions allow SSCPs to send requests to and receive status information from individual nodes in order to control the network configuration.

S

SSCP-SSCP session A session between the SSCP in one domain and the SSCP in another domain. This type of session is used to initiate and terminate cross-domain LU-LU sessions.

SSCS *See* service-specific convergence sublayer.

SSI *See* server-side include.

SSL *See* Secure Sockets Layer.

SSM *See* single-segment message.

SSP *See* System Support Program.

ST *See* segment type.

STA *See* spanning-tree algorithm.

STAC Method of on-the-fly data compression.

stack group A collection of two or more systems that will be configured to operate as a group and support MP bundles with links on different systems.

stack (*a*) In programming, a special type of data structure in which items are removed in the reverse order from that in which they are added, so the most recently added item is the first one removed. (*b*) In networking, short for protocol stack such as TCP/IP.

stand-alone A device that is self-contained; one that does not require any other devices to function.

standard A definition or format that has been approved by a recognized standards organization or is accepted as a de facto standard by the industry. Standards exist for programming languages, operating systems, data formats, communications protocols, and electrical interfaces. Most official computer standards are set by one of the following organizations: ANSI (American National Standards Institute) sets the standards for programming languages and other software related items; ITU (International Telecommunication Union) sets the standards for international communication protocols; IEEE (Institute of Electrical and Electronic Engineers) sets the standards for electrical interfaces and other hardware related items; ISO (International Standards Organization) VESA (Video Electronics Standards Association).

Standard Generalized Markup Language (SGML) A system developed and standardized by the International Organization for Standards (ISO) in 1986 for organizing and tagging elements of a document. SGML specifies the rules for tagging elements.

Standard Network Access Protocol (SNAP) A type of Ethernet framing. SNAP specifies a standard method of encapsulating IP datagrams and ARP messages on IEEE networks. The SNAP entity in the end system makes use of the services of the subnetwork and performs three key functions: data transfer, connection management, and QOS selection.

standby monitor Device that is designated as a backup monitor on a token ring network in case the active monitor fails. *See* active monitor *and* ring monitor.

star topology One of the three principal topologies used in LANs. All devices are connected to a central hub. Star networks are relatively easy to install and manage, but bottlenecks can occur because all data must pass through the hub. *See* bus topology *and* ring topology.

start bit In asynchronous communications, the bit that signals the receiver that data is coming. In communications every byte of data is preceded by a start bit and followed by a *stop bit*.

start frame delimiter (SFD) A specified bit pattern that indicates the start of a transmission frame.

start/stop (transmission) (*a*) Asynchronous transmission in which a start pulse and a stop pulse are used for each symbol. (*b*) Signaling in which each group of code elements corresponding to an alphanumeric character is (1) preceded by a start signal that serves to prepare the receiving mechanism for the reception and registration of a character and (2) followed by a stop signal that serves to bring the receiving mechanism to rest in preparation for the reception of the next character.

stateless Having no information about what occurred previously.

statement An instruction written in a high-level language. A statement directs the computer to perform a specified action. A single statement in a high-level language can represent several machine-language instructions. Programs consist of statements and *expressions*. An expression is a group of symbols that represent a value.

static random access memory (SRAM) A type of memory that doesn't need to be refreshed like dynamic RAM and is faster and more reliable than dynamic RAM.

static route A route that is explicitly (statically) configured and entered into the router's routing table. Static routes will commonly take precedence over routes chosen by dynamic routing protocols.

statically assigned sockets (SAS) Sockets that are permanently reserved for a designated protocol or process. For example, socket 4 is always reserved as the echo socket, used for echoing packets across a network.

station An input or output device that uses telecommunications facilities.

station message detail recording (SMDR) A record of all calls originated or received by a switching system. SMDRs are usually generated by a computer.

statistic Significant data about a defined resource.

statistical time-division multiplexing (STDM) Time-division multiplexing in which connections to communication circuits are made on a statistical basis.

status A condition or state of a resource.

STDM *See* statistical time-division multiplexing.

STM-*n* *See* synchronous transport module-*n*.

STM *See* synchronous transfer mode.

STM-1 *See* synchronous transport module-1.

stop bit In asynchronous communications, a bit that indicates that a byte has just been transmitted. Every byte of data is preceded by a *start bit* and followed by a stop bit.

storage The capacity of a device to hold and retain data in whatever means available.

storage device Specifically, a mass storage device, such as a disk or tape drive. Generally, any device capable of storing data.

store- and forward-packet switching Packet-switching technique used on switches, in which frames are completely processed before being forwarded out the appropriate switch port. This processing includes calculating the CRC and checking the destination address.

store To copy information from a computer's CPU to memory, or from memory to a mass storage device.

STP *See* shielded twisted pair.

streaming A transferring technique so that data can be processed as a steady and continuous stream by the destination device. Because users do not have fast enough access to download large multimedia files quickly, streaming technologies are becoming increasingly important. With streaming, the client browser or plug-in can start displaying the data before the entire file has been transmitted.

Structure of Management Information (language) (SMI) Document (RFC 1155), specifying rules used to define managed objects in the MIB. *See* MIB.

Structured Query Language (SQL) A specialized programming language introduced as a commercial database system in 1979 by Oracle Corporation for sending queries to databases. The original version called SEQUEL (structured English query language) was designed by an IBM research center in 1974 and 1975. Most industrial-strength and many smaller database applications can be addressed using SQL. Each specific application has its own version of SQL implementing features unique to that application, but all SQL-capable databases support a common subset of SQL.

STS-*n* *See* synchronous transport signal-n.

STS-1 *See* synchronous transport signal-1.

study group (SG) End-to-end transmission performance of networks and terminals.

stylus A pointing and drawing device shaped like a pen. A stylus is used with a digitizing tablet or touch screen.

subarea A portion of an SNA network consisting of the subarea node and any attached resources to that node.

subarea address A value defined to identify the subarea node; it is placed in the subarea address field of the network address.

subarea host node A node that provides both subarea function and an application program interface (API) for running application programs. It provides SSCP functions and subarea node services, and is aware of the network configuration.

subarea link A link that connects two subarea nodes.

subarea LU A logical unit that resides in a subarea node.

subarea network Interconnected subareas, their directly attached peripheral nodes, and the transmission groups that connect them.

subarea node A node that uses network addresses for routing and maintains routing tables that reflect the configuration of the network. Subarea nodes can provide gateway function to connect multiple subarea networks, intermediate routing functions, and boundary function support peripheral nodes. Type 4 and type 5 nodes are subarea nodes.

subarea path control The function in a subarea node that routes message units between network-accessible units (NAUs) and provides the paths between them.

subnet A portion of a network that shares a common address component.

subnet mask A configuration parameter that indicates how many bits of an address are used for the host part. It is expressed as a 32-bit quantity, with 1s placed in positions covering the network and subnet part of an IP address and 0s in the host part.

subnetting A method, documented in RFC 950, originally referring to the subdivision of a class-based network into subnetworks. It now refers more generally to the subdivision of a CIDR block into smaller CIDR blocks.

Subnetting allows single routing entries to refer either to the larger block or to its individual constituents. This permits a single, general routing entry to be used through most of the Internet, more specific routes only being required for routers in the subnetted block.

A *subnet mask* is a 32-bit number that determines how an IP address is split into network and host portions, on a bitwise basis. For example, 255.255.0.0 is a standard class B subnet mask, since the first two bytes are all ones (network), and the last two bytes are all zeros (host).

In a subnetted network, the network portion is extended. For example, a subnet mask of 255.255.255.0 would subnet a class B address space using its third byte. Using this scheme, the first two bytes of an IP address would identify the class B network, the next byte would identify the subnet within that network, and the final byte would select an individual host. Because subnet masks are used on a bit-by-bit basis, masks like 255.255.240.0 (4 bits of subnet; 12 bits of host) are perfectly normal.

In a traditional subnetted network, several restrictions apply, which have been lifted by *classless interdomain routing (CIDR).* However, if older, non-CIDR routing protocols (such as RIP version1) are in use, these restrictions must still be observed. Identical subnet masks. Because non-CIDR routing updates do not include subnet masks, a router must assume that the subnet mask it has been configured with is valid for all subnets. Therefore, a single mask must be used for all subnets with a network. Different masks can be used for different networks. Based on this assumption, a router can exchange subnet routes with other routers within the network.

Because the subnet masks are identical across the network, the routers will interpret these routes in the same manner. However, routers not attached to the subnetted network can't interpret these subnet routes, since they lack the subnet mask. Therefore, subnet routes are not relayed to routers on other networks. This leads to our second restriction: *contiguous subnets*.

A subnetted network can't be split into isolated portions. All the subnets must be contiguous, since routing information can't be passed to non-members. Within a network, all subnets must be able to reach all other subnets without passing traffic through other networks. *Variable length subnet masks (VLSM)*, conceptually a stepping stone from subnetting to CIDR, lifted the restrictions of subnetting by relaying subnet information through routing protocols. This idea leads us directly to classless interdomain routing (CIDR).

subnetwork attachment point The unique address maintained by a subnetwork for each of the DTEs attached to it.

subnetwork point of attachment (SNPA) A data-link layer address (for example: Ethernet address, X.25 address, or frame relay DLCI address). SNPA addresses are used to configure a CLNS route for an interface.

subscript (*a*) In programming, a symbol or number used to identify an element in an array. (*b*) In word processing, a character that appears slightly below the line.

subsystem (*a*) Cross-connects between clusters of buildings within a site. (*b*) A secondary or subordinate software system.

super frame (SF) Common framing type used on T1 circuits. SF consists of 12 frames of 192 bits each, with the 193rd bit providing error checking and other functions. SF has been superseded by ESF, but is still widely used. Also called D4 framing. *See* ESF.

Super VGA (SVGA) A set of graphics standards designed to offer greater resolution than VGA.

supercomputer The fastest type of computer available; they are employed for specialized applications that require immense amounts of mathematical calculations.

superscalar Microprocessor architecture that enables more than one instruction to be executed per clock cycle.

supertwist A technique for improving LCD display screens by twisting light rays. The more twists, the higher the contrast..

Super-Video (S-Video) A technology which transmits video signals over a cable by dividing the video information into two separate signals: one for color, and the other for brightness.

supervisor A control program that coordinates the use of resources and maintains the flow of processing unit operations.

support The assistance that a vendor offers to customers.

surf To move from place to place on the Internet while searching randomly for topics of interest.

sustainable cell rate (SCR) A traffic parameter defined by the ATM Forum for ATM traffic management that characterizes a bursty source and specifies the maximum average rate at which cells can be sent over a given virtual connection (VC). SCR can be defined as the ratio of the maximum burst rate to the minimum burst interarrival time. *See* VBR.

sustained information rate (SIR) A flow-control mechanism used in SMDS.

SUT *See* system under test.

SVC *See* switched virtual connection.

SVGA *See* Super VGA.

swap (*a*) To replace pages or segments of data in memory. (*b*) In UNIX systems, moving entire processes in and out of main memory.

switch (*a*) In networks, a device that connects multiple network segments at the data-link layer (Layer 2) of the OSI model. It operates more simply and at higher speeds than does a router. LANs that use switches to join segments are called *switched LANs* or, in the case of Ethernet networks, *switched Ethernet LANs*. (*b*) A small lever or button. (*c*) An option or parameter. (*d*) A device that filters and forwards packets between LAN segments. Switches operate at the data-link layer (Layer 2) of the OSI Reference Model.

switched connection A data-link connection that functions like a telephone.

S

switch fabric The central functional block of any switch design that is responsible for buffering and routing the incoming data to the appropriate output ports

switched line A telecommunications line in which the connection is established by dialing.

switched major node In VTAM, a major node whose minor nodes are physical units and logical units attached by switched SDLC links.

switched multimegabit data service (SMDS) Developed in 1995, SMDS is connectionless service for WAN/MAN service. It is based on 53-byte packets that target the interconnection of different LANs into a switched public network, usually at speeds faster than a T1.

switched network A network that establishes connections by a dialing function.

switched or **semi-permanent virtual connection (SPVC)** A PVC-type connection where SVCs are used for call setup and (automatic) rerouting if the original route is broken. They are also called *smart PVCs*. Commonly used in network designs that require fault-tolerant connections, such as links between PBXs.

switched virtual circuit A connection where control signaling is used to establish and tear it down dynamically. Examples are the telephone system, ISDN, X.25. , and ATM.

switched virtual connection (SVC) A connection that is set up and taken down dynamically through signaling Also known as a *switched virtual circuit*. See permanent virtual connection (PVC).

switching system (SS) (*a*) A communications system consisting of switching centers and their interconnecting media. (*b*) Part of a communication system organized to temporarily associate functional units, transmission channels, or telecommunication circuits for the purpose of providing a desired telecommunication facility. Examples of NATO-owned switching system are IVSN and TARE.

switching (*a*) An electrical switch directs current to one of several wires. Once the connec-

tion is made, the switch appears as part of the wire. It ideally introduces no resistance, no attenuation, no delay. (*b*) A networking switch is designed to behave in much the same way. Its primary feature is speed; like an electrical switch, it is designed to appear much like a wire when relaying data signals.

Switches must implement a normal path selection algorithm; they just do it faster. Layer 2 switches bridge; Layer 3 switches route. Normal bridges and routers will receive an entire packet, analyze its headers, make a forwarding decision, then transmit the packet. The packet is stored in RAM while being processed. These RAM buffers can become bottlenecks in a busy network.

Switches use special silicon chips than can forward packets directly from source to destination without passing through RAM buffers. Consider a typical Ethernet switch, which acts much like a standard IEEE 802.1d bridge. The difference is that as soon as an incoming packet's header has been received, a forwarding decision is immediately made, before the packet is completely received. If the destination Ethernet segment is idle, the packet begins transmission there immediately. As bits are received they are shunted through the switch fabric to the destination interface. On a 10-Mbps Ethernet, the net delay is perhaps one or two microseconds, as opposed to several milliseconds for a typical bridge. This is termed *cut-through switching*.

ATM switches provide a good example of *Layer 3 switching*. When a connection is setup, a routing decision is made based the ATM NSAP address. A virtual path identifier (VPI) is assigned and used in the header of subsequent cells for that connection. The switch fabric is configured to transmit cells bearing that VPI directly to the destination interface.

Sybase One of the dominant software companies in the area of database management systems (DBMSs) and client/server programming environments.

symbolic name A name that may be used instead of an adapter or bridge address to identify an adapter location.

symmetric digital subscriber line (SDSL)
Technology that allows more data to be sent over existing copper telephone lines. SDSL supports data rates up to 3 Mbps. SDSL is called symmetric because it supports the same data rates for upstream and downstream traffic. SDSL works by sending digital pulses in the high-frequency area of telephone wires. Because these high frequencies are not used by normal voice communications, SDSL can operate simultaneously with voice connections over the same wires.

Synchronized Multimedia Integration Language (SMIL) A markup language, based on the *Extensible Markup Language (XML)*, developed by the World Wide Web Consortium (W3C). It enables multimedia content to be divided into separate files and streams (audio, video, text, and images). Once separated, these data can be sent to a user's computer individually, and be displayed together as if they were a single multimedia stream. This will make the multimedia content much smaller, so that it doesn't take as long to travel over the Internet.

synchronous Communication that 36 at regular intervals. Signals along the bus, for example, can occur only at specific points in the clock cycle.

Synchronous Data Link Control (SDLC) A bit-oriented synchronous communications protocol developed by IBM. It is the ISO standard protocol used in IBM's SNA networks. SDLC is similar to HDLC.

synchronous digital hierarchy (SDH) An international standard for synchronous data transmission over fiber optic cables. SDH is the international version of SONET, based on 155 Mbps increments instead of SONET's 51 Mbps increments. See SONET.

synchronous DRAM (SDRAM) A type of DRAM that actually synchronizes itself with the CPU's bus and is capable of running at 100 MHz.

synchronous graphic random access memory (SGRAM) A type of DRAM used in video adapters and graphics accelerators.

synchronous optical network (SONET) (*Illustration*) An optical fiber-based network created by Bellcore in the middle 1980s. It is now an ANSI standard. SONET defines interface standards at the physical layer of the OSI seven-layer model. The SONET ANSI standard defines a hierarchy of interface rates that allow data streams at different rates to be multiplexed from Optical Carrier (OC) levels from 51.8 Mbps (about the same as a T-3 line) to 2.48 Gbps. The international equivalent of SONET, standardized by the ITU, is called SDH.

synchronous time-division multiplexing (STDM) A TDM scheme where the interleaved time slots are preassigned to the users.

Name/Acronym	Bandwidth	Equivalent DS0	Equivalent DS1	Equivalent DS3	comments
DS0	64Kb/s	1	*	*	one phone line
DS1/T1	1.544Mb/s	24	1	*	popular service
DS1C	3.152Mb/s	48	2	*	equipment
E1/CEPT1	2.048Mb/s	32	1	*	European
DS2	6.312Mb/s	96	4	*	equipment
E2	8.448Mb/s	96	4	*	European
DS3/T3	44.736Mb/s	672	28	1	popular service
E3	34.368Mb/s	512	16	1	European
DS4	139.264Mb/s	2016	80	6	long haul radio
STS-1	51.84Mb/s	672	28	1	electrical OC1
OC-1	51.84Mb/s	672	28	1	SONET
OC-3	255.520Mb/s	2,016	84	3	SONET
OC-12	622.080Mb/s	8,064	336	12	SONET
OC-48	2.488Gb/s	32,256	1,344	48	SONET
OC-192	9.953Gb/s	129,024	5,376	192	SONET

S

synchronous transfer mode (STM) A packet-switching approach where time is divided into specific portions or slots, each assigned to a single channels. During its allowed time slot, users can transmit data on each channel.. Basically, time slots denote allocated (fixed) parts of the total available bandwidth. *See* time division multiplexing (TDM).

synchronous transport module-*n* (STM-*n*) An ITU-T–defined SDH physical interface for digital transmission in ATM at n times the basic STM-1 rate. There is a direct equivalence between the STM-n and the SONET STS-3*n* transmission rates.

synchronous transport module-1 (STM-1) An ITU-T–defined SDH physical interface for digital transmission in ATM at the rate of 155.52 Mbps.

synchronous transport signal-1 (STS-1) SONET signal standard for optical transmission at 51.84 Mbps.

synchronous transport signal-n (STS-*n*) SONET signal format for transmission at *n* times the basic STS-1 signal (i.e., STS-3 is at 155.52 Mbps).

SYN-IP Packets used to initiate (or synchronize) a network connection.

syntax The spelling and grammar of a programming language.

sysop (system operator) Anyone responsible for the physical operations of a computer system or network resource.

system application architecture (SAA) A set of architecture standards developed by IBM for program, user, and communications interfaces on various IBM platforms. The main components are: Common Programming Interface (CPI), Common User Access (CUA), and Common Communication Support (CCS). SAA standards were first introduced in the late 1980's. Implementing these standards allows programmers to develop software that is consistent across differing platforms and operating systems.

system bus The bus that connects the CPU to main memory.

System Communications Services A protocol responsible for the formation and breaking of intersystem process connections and for flow control of message traffic over those connections. System services such as the VMS cluster connection manager and the mass storage control protocol (MSCP) disk server communicate with this protocol.

system conformance test report (SCTR) A document written at the end of the conformance assessment process, giving the overall summary of the conformance of the system to the set of protocols for which conformance testing was carried out.

system control block On VAX systems, the data structure in system space that contains all the interrupt and exception vectors known to the system.

system definition The process, completed before a system is put into use, by which desired functions and operations of the system are selected from various available options.

system disk The disk containing the operating system.

system fault tolerance (SFT) The measure of how well a networked or stand-alone computers can withstand events which cause data loss, lock-ups, and system crashes.

system file An essential program that is required whenever you start up a computer.

system generation Synonym for system definition.

system GETVIS area A storage space that is available for dynamic allocation to VSE's system control programs or other application programs.

system image The image read into memory from disk when the system is started up.

system management application entity (SMAE) A service, maintained at the application layer of the OSI model, whose task is to exchange information with other SMAEs at other nodes. In each layer of the OSI reference architecture there is a layer management entity (LME), which carries out management functions specific to that layer. Each of these entities stores data in the management information base (MIB). Upon request from the manager or another agent's SMAE, that information is transmitted.

system menu In a windowing environment, particularly the X windowing environment, the menu displayed when the user presses the system Menu button on the window manager window frame. Every window has a system menu that enables the user to control the size, shape, and position of the window.

system services control point (SSCP) A function within IBM's VTAM that controls and manages an SNA network and its resources. The *domain* of the SSCP consists of the system services control point, the physical units (PUs), the logical units (LUs), the links, the link stations, and all the resources that the SSCP has the ability to control by means of activation and deactivation requests. These focal points within an SNA network manage the network configuration, coordinate with network operators, process problem determination requests, and provide directory services and other session services for end users.

System Support Programs (SSP) IBM licensed program, made up of a collection of utilities and small programs, which supports the operation of the NCP.

system under test (SUT) A test method consisting of (1) One or more processing units (e.g. hosts, front-ends, workstations, etc.) which will run the application described, and whose aggregate performance will be described by the metric tpsB. (2) Any front-end systems needed to communicate with an external driver system. (3) The host system(s), including hardware and software supporting

the database employed in the benchmark. (4) The hardware and software components of all networks required to connect and support the SUT components. (5) Data storage media sufficient to satisfy both the scaling rules and the ACID properties. (6) The data storage media must hold all the data.

systems management functional area (SMFA) The requirements to be satisfied by systems management activities can be categorized into five functional areas: fault management, accounting management, configuration management, performance management, and security management.

Systems Management Server (SMS) A process run under Windows NT to enable a network administrator to create an inventory of all the hardware and software on the network and to store it in an SMS database. SMS can then perform software distribution and installation over the LAN using this database. SMS also enables a network administrator to perform diagnostic tests on PCs attached to the network.

systems network architecture (SNA) A host-based network architecture introduced by IBM in 1974 to support their mainframe computers. It is characterized by the logical channels created between endpoints. SNA has evolved over the years so that it now also supports peer-to-peer networks of workstations. It is similar in many respects to the OSI reference model, but with a number of differences. SNA is essentially composed of seven layers. *See* data-flow control layer, data-link control layer, path control layer, physical control layer, presentation-services layer, transaction-services layer, *and* transmission-control layer.

S

T-1 (*Illustrations*) Digital line consisting of 24, 64-Kbps channels, with a total of 1.544Mbps of throughput available per second. Each channel can be configured to carry voice or data traffic. Most providers will allow you to buy just some of these individual channels, known as *fractional T-1 access*. *See* AMI, B8ZS, *and* DS-1.

T-3 A leased-line connection capable of carrying data at 44.736 Mbps (44,736,000 bits per second). T-3 lines are sometimes referred to as *DS3 lines* and can be multiplexed into 28 T-1 signals. A T-3 line actually consists of 672 individual channels, each of which sup-

ports 64 Kbps. *See* bandwidth, bit, byte, Ethernet, *and* T-1.

TA *See* terminal adapters.

table Data arranged in rows and columns. In *relational database management systems*, all information is stored in the form of tables.

TAC *See* Technical Assistance Center *and* terminal access controller.

TACACS *See* terminal access controller access control system.

TAF *See* terminal access facility.

DS1/T1circuit/line types and applications

Line format/coding	Framing format	Signaling	Application
AMI	SF/D4	in-band	24 voice/modem channels
AMI	ESF	in-band	24 voice/modem channels
AMI	ESF	out-of-band	23 voice/modem or digital/data channels
B8ZS	SF/D4	in-band	24 voice/modem channels
B8ZS	ESF	in-band	24 voice/modem channels
B8ZS	ESF	out-of-band	23 voice/modem or digital/data channels

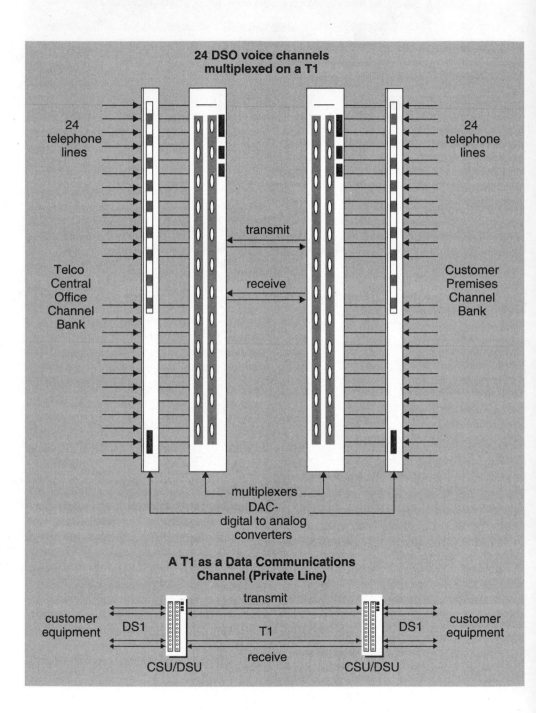

24 DSO voice channels multiplexed on a T1

24 telephone lines

24 telephone lines

transmit

receive

Telco Central Office Channel Bank

Customer Premises Channel Bank

multiplexers
DAC-
digital to analog
converters

A T1 as a Data Communications Channel (Private Line)

transmit

customer equipment

DS1

T1

DS1

customer equipment

receive

CSU/DSU

CSU/DSU

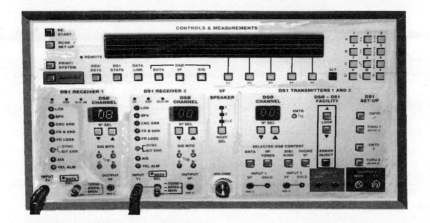

tag RAM The area in an L2 cache that identifies which data from main memory is currently stored in each cache line.

tagged traffic ATM cells that have their CLP bit set to 1. Sometimes called *discard eligible (DE)* traffic. If the network is congested, tagged traffic can be dropped to ensure delivery of higher-priority traffic as a method of QoS. *See* CLP.

TAP *See* trace analysis program.

tape A magnetically coated strip of plastic on which data can be encoded for large storage capacity, ranging from a few hundred kilobytes to several gigabytes. Accessing data on tapes, however, is much slower than accessing data on disks.

tape drive A device, like a tape recorder, that reads data from and writes it onto a tape.

Tape Mass Storage Control Protocol (TMSCP) A protocol supported in Alpha AXP systems running the OpenVMS AXP operating system. It enables all TMSCP-compatible tapes locally connected to an AXP node to be available to all members of the VMS cluster system, thus increasing resource sharing in these systems.

TAPI *See* telephony application programming interface.

target A file, device or any type of location to which data is moved or copied.

target system control facility (TSCF) A service that extends the control, monitoring, and automation capabilities of the NetView program to provide consolidated management for hardware (system) and software (operator) consoles in heterogeneous System/390 environments. TSCF supports both automated and manual operations on a sysplex.

target token rotation time (TTRT) A value that specifies the target rotation time being used by all the stations on the ring.

task control block (TCB) A facility that holds the state of all the system tasks. The kernel, for instance, keeps a list of TCBs with one entry per task.

TAXI *See* transparent asynchronous transmitter/receiver interface.

TBOS Telemetry Byte-Oriented Serial protocol.

Tbyte *See* terabyte.

TC *See* technical committee *and* transport connection.

TC *See* transmission convergence.

TCAM *See* telecommunications access method.

T-carrier TDM transmission method referring to a line or cable carrying a DS-1 signal.

TCB *See* task control block.

TCC *See* transmission control code.

T

TCEP *See* transport connection endpoint.

Tcl *See* Tool Command Language.

TCM *See* time-compression multiplexing.

TCO Total cost of ownership.

T-connector T-shaped device with two female and one male BNC connectors. Used to connect a computer to thin coax cable. With NetSuite Advanced Professional Design, a user can add a T-connector to BNC 10Base-2 ports via the Device Properties dialog. T-connected devices are also noted in NetSuite's work order log.

TCP *See* Transmission Control Protocol.

TCP/IP *See* Transmission Control Protocol/ Internet Protocol.

TCPdump UNIX version of a packet decoder, originally written to analyze TCP performance problems.

TCS *See* transmission convergence sublayer.

TCT *See* terminal control table.

TCU *See* trunk coupling unit.

TD *See* time division.

TDJ *See* transfer delay jitter.

TDM *See* time-division multiplexing.

TDMA *See* time division multiple access.

TDR *See* time-domain reflectometer.

TE *See* terminal equipment.

teamware A category of software that enables colleagues, especially geographically dispersed colleagues, to collaborate on projects.

Technical And Office Protocol (TOP) An OSI-based architecture developed for office communications.

Technical Assistance Center (TAC) Cisco's technical support center.

Technical committee (TC) A group normally concerned with the role of data in the design, development, management and utilization of information systems. Issues of interest include database design; knowledge of data

and processing; languages to describe data, define access and manipulate databases; strategies and mechanisms for data access; security and integrity control; and engineering services and distributed systems.

technical report (TR) A technical description of a particular subject.

telco A telephone company.

Telecommunication Industry Association (TIA) Organization that develops standards relating to telecommunications technologies *See* EIA.

telecommunications Communications (usually involving computer systems) over the telephone network.

telecommunications access method (TCAM) SNA software that runs in System/ 370/390 mainframes and implements the functions of a Type 5 SNA Host Node. Commonly referred to as *VTAM*, this software implements the functions of an SSCP, provides the interface to network operators, and provides SNA support for host-based application programs.

Telecommunications Information Network Architecture Consortium (TINA-CT) A group responsible for assessing both the current and future needs and demands of telecommunication customers. TINA-CT then presents suggestions for ways in which services and products can be designed to meet those needs.

telecommunications management network (TMN) A network that interfaces with a telecommunications network at several points to receive information from and control the operation of, the telecommunications network. A TMN may use parts of the managed telecommunications network to provide for the TMN communications.

telecommunications network (TN) The network infrastructure applied for telecommunications.

telecopy To send a document from one place to another via a fax machine

telematic access unit (TLMAU) A functional entity which provides all of the interworking functions between telematic codes and protocols and IPMS codes and protocols. The TLMAU also supports the DS functionality.

telematics A broad term describing the use of computers and computer systems in telecommunications.

Telemetry Byte-Oriented Serial protocol (TBOS) A port (RS232/RS422) that allows a Central Unit to forward alarm information to a computerized maintenance center.

telephone twisted pair One or more twisted pairs of copper wire in the unshielded voice-grade cable, commonly used to connect a telephone to its wall jack. Also known as *unshielded twisted pair (UTP)*. *See* RJ45.

telephone user part (TUP) In some parts of the world (e.g., China, Brazil), the telephone user part (TUP) is used to support basic call setup and tear down. TUP handles analog circuits only. In many countries, ISUP has replaced TUP for call management.

telephony The science of translating sound into electrical signals, transmitting them, and then converting them back to sound. The term is used to refer to a combination of computer hardware and software that performs functions traditionally done by standard telephone equipment. For example, telephony software used with a modem can convert a computer into a sophisticated answering service.

telephony application programming interface (TAPI) An API introduced in 1993 as the result of joint development by Microsoft and Intel. It is used to connect a PC running Windows to telephone services. TAPI defines standards for simple call control and for manipulating call content.

telephony server application program interface (TSAPI) Developed by Novell and AT&T to enable programmers to build telephony and *computer-telephony-integration (CTI)* applications.

teletype (TTY) An input device that allows alphanumeric characters to be typed in and sent, usually one at a time as they are typed, to a computer or a printer. This is an especially valuable means of communication for hearing-impaired users.

teletypewriter exchange service (TWX) A switched teletypewriter service in which suitably arranged teletypewriter stations are provided with lines to a central office for access to other such stations.

television board A computer expansion board that contains a TV tuner and signal-conversion circuitry. The board translates television signals into a format that can be displayed on a computer monitor.

telex access unit (TLXAU) A device that allows more conventional forms of communication to be distributed as part of the telex messaging network.

telex Tele-typewriter service that allows subscribers to send messages over the *public switched telephone network (PSTN)*.

Telnet An asynchronous, virtual terminal emulation program and protocol documented in RFC 854. It is used in TCP/IP networks, like the Internet, to allow remote access to the network. Telnet operates using the TCP Protocol, and depends heavily on option negotiation. Telnet options are documented in their own RFCs. The organization of these RFCs, and instructions for registering new Telnet options, is found in RFC 855. Many Telnet options exist; a complete, current list can be found in the Internet Official Standards RFC, currently RFC 2400. A copy of this list appears on the next page.

Tempest United States military standard for electronic products that are designed to withstand *electromagnetic pulse (EMP)* radiation. *See* EMP.

template A blank form, sometimes called a *boilerplate*, that shows the layout and formatting of a document. Data can be entered into the template without the need to format it.

TEP Transport endpoint.

terabyte (*a*) One thousand gigabytes, or 2 to the 40th power (1,099,511,627,776) bytes. This is approximately 1 trillion bytes. (*b*) 10 to the 12th power (1,000,000,000,000). This is exactly one trillion. *See* byte *and* kilobyte.

T

Telnet Options

Protocol	Name	Number	State	Status	RFC	STD
TOPT-BIN	Binary Transmission	0	Std	Re	856	27
TOPT-ECHO	Echo	1	Std	Rec	857	28
TOPT-RECN	Reconnection	2	Prop	Ele	...	
TOPT-SUPP	Suppress Go Ahead	3	Std	Rec	858	29
TOPT-APRX	Approx Message Size Negotiation	4	Prop	Ele	...	
TOPT-STAT	Status	5	Std	Rec	859	30
TOPT-TIM	Timing Mark	6	Std	Rec	860	31
TOPT-REM	Remote Controlled Trans and Echo	7	Prop	Ele	726	
TOPT-OLW	Output Line Width	8	Prop	Ele	...	
TOPT-OPS	Output Page Size	9	Prop	Ele	...	
TOPT-OCRD	Output Carriage-Return Disposition	10	Prop	Ele	652	*
TOPT-OHT	Output Horizontal Tabstops	11	Prop	Ele	653	*
TOPT-OHTD	Output Horizontal Tab Disposition	12	Prop	Ele	654	*
TOPT-OFD	Output Formfeed Disposition	13	Prop	Ele	655	*
TOPT-OVT	Output Vertical Tabstops	14	Prop	Ele	656	*
TOPT-OVTD	Output Vertical Tab Disposition	15	Prop	Ele	657	*
TOPT-OLD	Output Linefeed Disposition	16	Prop	Ele	658	*
TOPT-EXT	Extended ASCII	17	Prop	Ele	698	
TOPT-LOGO	Logout	18	Prop	Ele	727	
TOPT-BYTE	Byte Macro	19	Prop	Ele	735	
TOPT-DATA	Data Entry Terminal	20	Prop	Ele	1043	
TOPT-SUP	SUPDUP	21	Prop	Ele	736	
TOPT-SUPO	SUPDUP Output	22	Prop	Ele	749	
TOPT-SNDL	Send Location	23	Prop	Ele	779	
TOPT-TERM	Terminal Type	24	Prop	Ele	1091	
TOPT-EOR	End of Record	25	Prop	Ele	885	
TOPT-TACACS	TACACS User Identification	26	Prop	Ele	927	
TOPT-OM	Output Marking	27	Prop	Ele	933	
TOPT-TLN	Terminal Location Number	28	Prop	Ele	946	
TOPT-3270	Telnet 3270 Regime	29	Prop	Ele	1041	
TOPT-X.3	X.3 PAD	30	Prop	Ele	1053	
TOPT-NAWS	Negotiate About Window Size	31	Prop	Ele	1073	

Protocol	Name	Number	State	Status	RFC	STD
TOPT-TST	erminal Speed	32	Prop	Ele	1079	
TOPT-RFC	Remote Flow Control	33	Prop	Ele	1372	
TOPT-LINE	Linemode	34	Draft	Ele	1184	
TOPT-XDL	X Display Location	35	Prop	Ele	1096	
TOPT-ENVIR	Telnet Environment Option	36	Hist	Not	1408	
TOPT-AUTH	Telnet Authentication Option	37	Exp	Ele	1416	
TOPT-ENVIR	Telnet Environment Option	39	Prop	Ele	1572	
TOPT-EXTOP	Extended-Options-List	255	Std	Rec	861	32

TERENA *See* Trans-European Research and Education Networking Association.

termid SNA cluster controller identification meaningful only for switched lines.

terminal (*a*) A "dumb" device that allows users to send commands to a computer located in different place. Terminals are sometimes divided into three classes based on how much processing power they contain. *Intelligent terminals* are standalone devices that contain main memory and a CPU. *Smart terminals* contain some processing power, but not as much as intelligent terminals. *Dumb terminals* have no processing capabilities and must rely entirely on a remote computer processor. (*b*) In networking, a personal computer or workstation connected to a mainframe computer that is running terminal emulation software so the mainframe thinks it is another terminal.

terminal access controller (TAC) Internet host that accepts terminal connections from dial-up lines.

terminal access controller access control system (TACACS) An authentication protocol that provides remote access authentication and related services, such as event logging. User passwords are administered in a central database rather than in individual routers, providing an easily scaleable network security solution.

terminal access facility (TAF) A service that allows a user to log on to multiple applications, either on their own system or on other systems.

terminal adapter (TA) (*Illustration*) (*a*) A device used to connect ISDN BRI connections to a normal telephone or modem through existing interfaces such as EIA/TIA-232. (*b*) In ISDN, these devices mimic the actions of modems on regular phone lines. Most TAs use the standard Hayes modem AT command set, and can be used as drop-in replacements for modems. A TA operates the same as a modem, except connection and throughput speeds will be much faster. PPP must be configured exactly the same as for a modem setup.

The serial speed should be set as high as possible. The main advantage of using a TA to connect to an Internet Provider is dynamic PPP. As IP address space becomes more and more scarce, most providers are no longer willing to provide static IP. Most standalone routers are not able to accommodate dynamic IP allocation. TAs rely completely on the PPP daemon for their features and stability of connection. This allows easy upgrades on a FreeBSD machine, if PPP is already set up.

However, any problems experienced with the PPP program will to persist. For maximum stability, the kernel PPP option should be used, not the user-land PPP. Motorola BitSurfer and Bitsurfer Pro Adtran, as well as other brandname TAs work well with FreeBSD. Vendors try to make sure their product can accept most of the standard modem AT command set.

terminal control table (TCT) A table that provides a list of the terminals known to CICS.

T

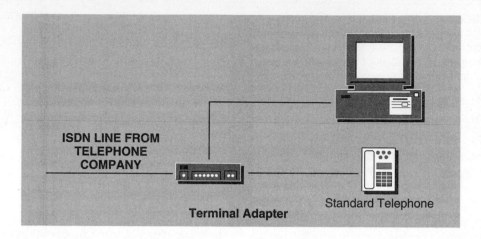

ISDN LINE FROM
TELEPHONE
COMPANY

Terminal Adapter

Standard Telephone

terminal emulation A program that allows a personal computer to access a mainframe computer or bulletin board service. The programs duplicate or "emulate" terminal software needed to make the connection. *See* terminal *and* terminal emulator.

terminal emulator A term generally used to refer to a program that performs some type of simulation; typically this simulation is a type of terminal/protocol. *See* terminal *and* terminal emulation.

terminal equipment (TE) Actual hardware; the terminal.

terminal server Communications processor with connections for multiple modems on one side, and a connection to a LAN or host machine on the other side. The terminal server does the work of answering calls and passing connections on to the appropriate node. Most terminal servers can provide PPP or SLIP services if connected to the Internet. *See* LAN, modem, host, node, PPP, *and* SLIP.

terminal type The type designation of a terminal attached to a computer. UNIX uses the terminal type to set the TERM environment variable so that it can communicate with the terminal correctly. In the SNA environment, the terminal type is required to know how to configure the system correctly.

terminate-and-stay resident (TSR) A program that is loaded into memory, where it

remains after it finishes its task, until it is explicitly removed or until the computer is turned off or reset. The program can be invoked again and again by the users (with the aid of a hot key) or by an application.

terminator (*a*) A device attached to the endpoints of a bus network or daisy chain. (*b*) A character that indicates the end of a string.

texel Texure element. The base unit of a graphic.

text Alphanumeric information in the form of words, sentences, paragraphs. This book, for example, consists of text. Commonly used to refer to text stored as ASCII codes (that is, without any formatting).

text file A file that holds text. Often used as a synonym for ASCII file, in which characters are represented only by their ASCII codes, or without any formatting.

text mode A video display mode in which the screen is divided into rows and columns filled with boxes. Each box can contain one character. Text mode is also called *character mode*.

texture In 3D graphics, the digital representation of the surface of an object. It is possible to define transparency, reflectivity, and other surface characteristics.

TFT *See* thin film transistor.

TFTP *See* Trivial File Transfer Protocol.

TG weight A quantitative measure of how well the values of a transmission group's characteristics satisfy the criteria specified by the class-of-service definition, as computed during route selection for a session.

TG *See* transmission group.

TH *See* transmission header.

thin film transistor (TFT) A type of LCD flat-panel display screen, sometimes called an *active-matrix LCD*, in which each pixel is controlled by one to four transistors. *See* active-matrix.

thinnet A less expensive and thinner version of the cable specified in the IEEE802.3 10Base2 standard.

thread A single, sequential flow of control within a program.

threshold A percentage value set for a resource, usually used to limit a process or action.

throughput The rate of data transferred from one place to another and/or processed in a specified amount of time within a network. Throughput is measured in Kbps, Mbps, and Gbps. It is one of three basic *service-level agreement* parameters

THT *See* token holding timer.

TI RPC *See* transport-independent RPC.

TIA *See* Telecommunication Industry Association.

TIC *See* token-ring interface coupler.

TIE *See* translated image environment.

tile In the X windowing environment, a rectangular area used to cover a surface with a pattern or visual texture.

time-compression multiplexing (TCM) Method of multiplexing that enables a faster half-duplex communication speed (144 Kbits/s for Type II and 160 Kbits/s for Type III) to be used during telco transmissions, rapidly switching the direction, thus providing the appearance of full-duplex service.

time division (TD) A digital transmission method that combines signals from multiple sources.

time division multiple access (TDMA) A technology that works by dividing a radio frequency into time slots and then allocating slots to multiple calls. It delivers digital wireless service using time-division multiplexing (TDM). In this way, a single frequency can support multiple, simultaneous data channels.

Timed Token Protocol (TTP) A protocol that supports an asynchronous as well as a synchronous transmission mode. Asynchronous transmission is the normal case and supported by any FDDI system. Synchronous transmission is an optional feature that offers guaranteed bandwidth.

time-division multiplexing (TDM) A technique used to multiplex data on a channel by a time-sharing of the channel, typically allowing multiple channels to be sent on one wire through time sharing.

TDM splits the total bandwidth (link capacity) from multiple channels into several smaller channels to allow bit streams to be combined as (multiplexed) streams by assigning each stream a different time slot in a set. The bandwidth allocation is done by dividing the time axis into fixed-length slots and a particular channel can then transmit only during a specific time slot regardless of whether the station has data to transmit. Within T-1 and T-3, TDM combines *pulse code modulated (PCM)* streams created for each conversation or data stream.

time-domain reflectometer (TDR) A continuity testing device used to troubleshoot networks. It sends signals through a network medium to check for continuity. It is used to find network-layer problems and to determine the location of breaks in network cabling.

timed-token The rules defining how the target-token rotation time is set with token ring networks..

time-out An event that occurs at the end of a predetermined period of time. Many devices and programs perform time-outs so that they do not sit idle waiting for input.

time-sharing option/extension Base for all TSO enhancements.

T

time-slot interchange (TSI) The period of time during which certain activities are governed by specific regulations. A time interval that can be recognized and uniquely defined.

time-to-live (TTL) A field in the Internet Protocol (IP) that specifies how many more hops a packet can travel before being discarded or returned.

TINA-CT *See* Telecommunications Information Network Architecture Consortium.

title bar In Windows and X-Windows environments, the rectangular bar on top of a window that contains the name of the file, application, or window object. In many graphical user interfaces, including Macintosh and Microsoft Windows interfaces, the user moves (drags) a window by grabbing the title bar.

TL- 1 *See* Transaction Language 1.

TLAP *See* TokenTalk LAP.

TLD *See* top-level domain.

TLI *See* transport-layer interface.

TLMAU *See* telematic access unit.

TLXAU *See* telex access unit.

TM *See* traffic management.

TMN *See* telecommunications management network.

TMSCP *See* Tape Mass Storage Control Protocol.

TN *See* telecommunications network.

TN3270 A client program which emulates the 3270-type terminals that IBM mainframes need for communication. It emulates terminals in the IBM 3270 series that use the *Extended Binary Coded Decimal Interchange Code (EBCDIC)* standard for encoding information. This emulator is required to log on to CMS on the SIUC mainframe.

TNEF *See* transport neutral encapsulation format.

toggle To switch from one setting to another.

token (*a*) A single element within a programming language. (*b*) In networking, a special series of bits that travels around a token-ring network. As the token circulates, stations attached to the network can capture it so that they can transmit data once they have the tokens. (*c*) In security systems, a user ID, usually combined with a password, that allows the user access to a network.

token holding timer (THT) The maximum length of time a station holding the token can initiate asynchronous transmissions. The THT is initialized with the value corresponding to the difference between the arrival of the token and the TTRT (FDDI).

token passing In a token-ring network, the process by which a node captures a token, inserts a message, addresses the token, adds control information, and then transmits the frame and generates another token after the original token has made a complete circuit.

token ring A 4/16 Mbps local area network topology and access mechanism in which all stations attached to the ring listen for a broadcast token or supervisory frame in order to transmit. Stations wishing to transmit data must receive the token first. After a station finishes transmitting, it passes the token to the next node in the ring; the token will continue to circulate until removed by another station wishing to transmit. Token ring networks transmit data in a unidirectional (one-way) manner. The characteristic operating parameters of token ring networks are listed below:

Maximum Number Stations—260 stations on one ring using STP; 72 stations on one ring using UTP

Maximum Distance from Station to MAU—100m (328 ft) when using Type-1 cabling in one contiguous segment; 45m (150 ft) if cable segments are joined by patch cables

Data Rate—4 or 16 Mbps

Maximum Total Ring Length—Varies from vendor to vendor

Transmission Media—Shielded twisted pair

token ring network The token ring network was originally developed by IBM in the 1970s. *See* token ring.

token-ring adapter (TRA) A network interface card (NIC) designed to attach a client workstation to a token ring computer network and operate as a token-passing interface.

token-ring interface (TIC) A coupler controller through which an FEP connects to a token ring network.

token-ring interface coupler (TIC) The hardware interface for connecting front-end processors and controllers to a token-ring network. such as a 3720, 3725, or 3745 communication controller

token-ring subsystem (TRSS) A subset of IBM's token ring network. It is still IBM's primary local area network (LAN) technology and is second only to Ethernet/IEEE 802.3 in general LAN popularity.

token rotation timer (TRT) The timer which counts down between frames arriving at a particular station. The token must be lost if this timer runs out.

TokenTalk LAP (TLAP) On Apple networks, a protocol that manages the tasks of packaging the information for transmission, gaining access to the network, and screening incoming information to make sure that it is "readable".

toner A special electrically charged, dry, powdery ink. It adheres to a drum, plate, or piece of paper charged with the opposite polarity within copy machines and laser printers to produce images.

Tool Command Language (Tcl) A powerful interpreted programming language.

TOP *See* Technical and Office Protocol.

top-level domain (TLD) The suffix attached to Internet domain names. There are a limited number of predefined top-level domain suffixes. Current predefined top-level domains include:

- com—commercial businesses; this is the most common TLD
- gov—United States government agencies
- edu—educational institutions such as universities
- org—organizations (mostly nonprofit)

- mil—military
- net—network organizations
- ca—Canada

topology The physical or logical arrangement of nodes in a local-area network (LAN) or other communications system. There are three main physical topologies used in LANs.

In a *bus topology*, all network devices are connected to a central cable, called a bus or backbone. Bus networks are relatively inexpensive and easy to install for small networks. An example of a bus topology is an Ethernet network.

In a *ring topology*, all devices are connected to one another in the shape of a closed loop, so that each device is connected directly to two other devices, one on either side of it. Token ring and FDDI LANs are an example of ring topologies.

In a *star topology* all devices are connected to a central device such as a switch or hub. Star networks are relatively easy to install and manage, but bottlenecks can occur because all data must pass through the central device.

topology and routing services (TRS) (*a*) APPN control point component that manages the topology database, computes routes, and provides a route selection control vector (RSCV) that specifies the best route through the network for a given session according to its requested class of service. (*b*) A service that maintains information about nodes, transmission groups, and classes of service so that appropriate routes through an APPN network can be calculated.

TOPS *See* transparent operating system.

TOS *See* type of service.

total cost of ownership (TCO) A popular buzzword representing how much it actually costs to own a computer.

TP monitor *See* transaction processing monitor.

TP *See* Transmission Protocol *and* transaction program.

TPF *See* transaction processing facility.

TPI *See* tracks per inch.

T

TPSP *See* transaction processing service provider.

TPSU invocation (TPSUI) A particular instance of a TPSU performing functions for a specific occasion of information processing.

TPSU *See* transaction processing service user.

TPSUI *See* TPSU invocation.

TR *See* technical report.

TRA *See* token-ring adapter.

trace A record of events captured and used to troubleshoot hardware and/or software.

trace analysis program (TAP) A program service aid that assists in analyzing trace data produced by VTAM, TCAM, and NCP. It also provides network data traffic and network error reports.

traceroute Network debugging utility that is documented in RFC792 and attempts to trace the path a packet takes through the network from source to destination by its route. Traceroute utilities work by sending packets with low *time-to-live (TTL)* fields. When a packet can't reach its destination because the TTL value has expired, the last host returns the packet and identifies itself to the sender. By sending a series of packets and incrementing the TTL value with each successive packet, traceroute finds out who all the intermediary hosts are. Traceroute has a variety of options you can use to customize its operation to your networking environment. Here's a short list of common traceroute options:

–m *max-ttl*: *max-ttl* (default 30) sets a limit on how long traceroute keeps trying. If the target host is farther than 30 hops away, you'll need to increase this value.

–n: Numerical output only. Use this if you're having nameserver problems and traceroute hangs trying to do inverse DNS lookups.

––p *port*: Base UDP port. *Port* is the UDP port number that traceroute uses on its first packet, and increments by one for each subsequent packet.

–q *queries*: How many packets should be sent for each TTL value. The default is 3, which is fine for finding out the route.

–w *wait*: Wait is the number of seconds packets have to generate replies before traceroute assumes they never will and moves on. The default is 3.

track A ring on a diskette or hard drive where data can be written (stored). The density of tracks (how close together they are) is measured in terms of tracks per inch (TPI).

trackball A type of pointing device used to input commands. Essentially, a trackball is a mouse lying on its back. To move the pointer, the user rotates the ball with thumb, fingers, or the palm of the hand.

tracks per inch (TPI) The density of tracks on a magnetic storage disk. This determines the amount of data a disk can hold.

traffic The load placed on a communications device or system.

traffic contract An agreement regarding the expected QoS provided by the network

traffic management (TM) The means of providing connection admission congestion and flow control.

traffic shaping A method for regulating non-complying traffic through the use of *queues*. This limits traffic surges that can cause congestion within a network. Data is buffered in the queues and then sent into the network in regulated amounts to ensure that the traffic will fit within the promised traffic envelope for the particular connection. Traffic shaping is used in ATM, frame relay, and other types of networks. Also known as *metering, shaping*, and *smoothing*.

trailer Control information appended to data when encapsulating the data for network transmission. Compare with header.

transaction A sequence of events sent back and forth between a client and a server application, beginning with the client's initial request for a service.

Transaction Language 1 (TL-1) The most widely used management protocol in telecommunications. It manages most of the broadband and access networks in North America and is increasingly being used worldwide for newer management applications.

transaction processing (*a*) A type of computer processing in which the computer responds immediately to any requests for a transaction. (*b*) A set of related operations characterized by four properties: atomicity, consistency, isolation and durability (ACID). A transaction is uniquely identified by a transaction identifier.

transaction processing facility (TPF) (*a*) A software system designed to support real-time applications. (*b*) The high-end member of IBM's family of Transaction Processing Solutions. It is designed as an operating system powered by the S/390 CMOS technology and optimized for delivering the exacting and extreme requirements of highly scalable, mission-critical computing with very high levels of guaranteed 7 x 24 x 365 availability.

transaction processing monitor (TP) A program that monitors a transaction as it passes from one stage to another to ensure that the transaction processes completely or, if an error occurs, to take action.

transaction processing service provider (TPSP) The provider of the OSI TP Service. The TPSP provides the OSI TP Service to all the TPSUIs involved in a particular dialogue tree.

transaction processing service user (TPSU) A user of the OSI TP Service: it refers to a specific set of processing capabilities within an application-process.

transaction program (TP) A program that conforms to LU6.2 protocols.

transceiver Transmitter-receiver. A device frequently used in Ethernet local area networks (LANs), which both transmits and receives analog or digital signals and actually applies signals onto the network wire and detects signals passing through the wire. For many LANs, the transceiver is built into the network interface card (NIC). Some types of networks, however, require an external transceiver. In Ethernet

networks, a transceiver is also called a *media access unit (MAU)*.

Trans-European Research and Education Networking Association (TERENA) Organization, formed by the merging of EARN and RARE, that promotes information and telecommunications technology development in Europe. *See* EARN.

transfer delay jitter (TDJ) A QoS parameter that measures the difference between a single cell's transfer delay (CTD) and the expected transfer delay. It gives a measure of how closely cells are spaced in a *virtual circuit (VC)*. CDV can be introduced by ATM multiplexers (MUXs) or switches.

transistor A device, invented in 1947 by Bell Labs, composed of semiconductor materials that amplify a signal or open or close a circuit. Transistors are the key components in computers and other digital circuits. Modern microprocessors contain tens of millions of microscopic transistors.

transistor-transistor logic (TTL) A common type of digital circuit in which the output is derived from two transistors.

translated image environment (TIE) A shareable library that contains support routines for translated images.

translation table A table used to replace one or more characters with alternative characters.

translational bridging A bridging method between networks with dissimilar MAC sublayer protocols. The MAC information is translated into the format of the destination network at the device bridging between the networks. *See* encapsulation bridging.

transmission control code (TCC) Provides a means to segregate traffic and define controlled communities of interest among subscribers. The TCC values are *trigraphs*, and are available from HQ DCA Code 530.

Transmission Control Protocol (TCP) Documented in RFC 793 as a standardized transport protocol developed for interconnecting IP-based networks. Operating on top of IP, it is responsible for multiplexing sessions, error

T

recovery, end-to-end reliable delivery, and flow control; it guarantees delivery of data and that packets will be delivered in the same order in which they were sent.

The IP protocol deals only with packets, TCP enables two hosts to establish a connection and exchange streams of data. TCP adds a great deal of functionality to the IP service it is layered over:

Streams. TCP data is organized as a stream of bytes, much like a file. The datagram nature of the network is concealed. A mechanism (the *Urgent Pointer*) exists to let out-of-band data be specially flagged. Important features of TCP are:

Reliable delivery. Sequence numbers are used to coordinate which data has been transmitted and received. TCP will arrange for retransmission if it determines that data has been lost.

Network adaptation. TCP will dynamically learn the delay characteristics of a network and adjust its operation to maximize throughput without overloading the network.

Flow control. TCP manages data buffers, and coordinates traffic so its buffers will never overflow. Fast senders will be stopped periodically to keep up with slower receivers.

Full-duplex Operation. TCP usually operates full duplex. The algorithms described below operate in both directions, in an almost completely independent manner. It's helpful to think of a TCP session as two independent byte streams, traveling in opposite directions.

Sequence Numbers. TCP uses a 32-bit sequence number that counts bytes in the data stream. Each TCP packet contains the starting sequence number of the data in that packet and the sequence number (called the *acknowledgment number*) of the last byte received from the remote peer. With this information, a sliding-window protocol is implemented. Forward and reverse sequence numbers are completely independent, and each TCP peer must track both its own sequence numbering and the numbering being used by the remote peer. TCP uses a number of control flags to manage the con-

nection. Some of these flags pertain to a single packet, such as the URG flag indicating valid data in the Urgent Pointer field, but two flags (SYN and FIN), require reliable delivery as they mark the beginning and end of the data stream. In order to insure reliable delivery of these two flags, they are assigned spots in the sequence number space. Each flag occupies a single byte.

Window Size and Buffering. Each endpoint of a TCP connection will have a buffer for storing data transmitted over the network before the application is ready to read the data. This lets network transfers take place while applications are busy with other processing, improving overall performance. To avoid overflowing the buffer, TCP sets a Window Size field in each packet it transmits. This field contains the amount of data that may be transmitted into the buffer. If this number falls to zero, the remote TCP can send no more data. It must wait until buffer space becomes available and it receives a packet announcing a non-zero window size.

Round-Trip Time Estimation. When a host transmits a TCP packet to its peer, it must wait a period of time for an acknowledgment. If the reply does not come within the expected period, the packet is assumed to have been lost and the data is retransmitted. The obvious question is, how long to wait? All modern TCP implementations seek to answer this question by monitoring the normal exchange of data packets and developing an estimate of how long is "too long."

Transmission Control Protocol/Internet Protocol (TCP/IP) (*Illustration*) A set of protocols that allows cooperating computers to share resources across a heterogeneous network. The combined main protocol was developed by the Department of Defense for the Internet. Originally designed for the UNIX operating system, TCP/IP uses several protocols, the two main ones being TCP and IP, mistakenly thought of as one protocol. TCP provides for the reliable transmission of data. IP provides connectionless datagram service. *See* IP, TCP, Internet, *and* UNIX.

transmission convergence (TC) One of the two PHY sublayers that are responsible for

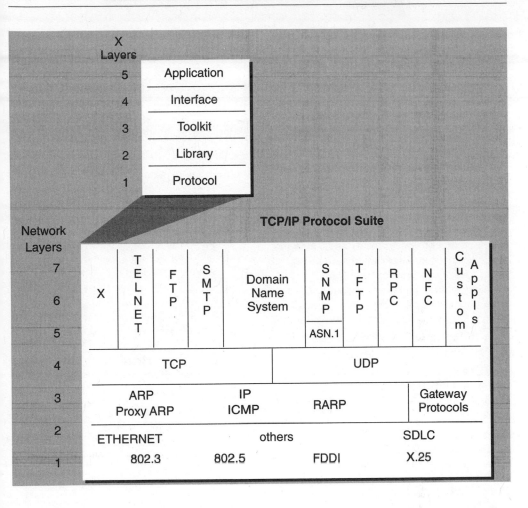

adapting the ATM cells into a stream of bits to be carried over the physical medium. *See* PM.

transmission convergence sublayer (TCS) Part of the ATM physical layer, responsible for cell delineation, rate decoupling, transmission frame adaptation, and transmission frame generation and recovery.

transmission group (TG) A single link or a group of links between adjacent nodes logically grouped together. In SNA, these nodes are adjacent subarea nodes. In APPN, it is a single link. The transmission group may be either the channel connection between host and FEP (where the TG1 is always assigned to the transmission group) or a set of SDLC links (single link, parallel links).

transmission header (TH) In SNA, control information, optionally followed by a basic information unit, created and used by path control to route message units and to control their flow within the network.

transmission link *See* link.

transmission priority A rank assigned to a message unit that determines its precedence for being selected by the path control component in each node along a route for forwarding to the next node in the route.

Transmission Protocol The protocol at the Internet's transport layer that governs the transmission of data.

T

transmission subsystem (TSS) A subset of SNA Transmission Control (TC) commands and protocols supported by a particular type of LU.

transparent Without any visible effect to the user. Most computer functions are transparent to the user.

transparent asynchronous transmitter/ receiver interface (TAXI) An interface that provides connectivity over multimode fiber links at a speed of 100 Mbps. TAXI is the chipset that generates 4B/5B encoding on multimode fiber. *See* 4B/5B local fiber.

transparent operating system (TOPS) A type of peer-to-peer local area network designed by Sun Microsystems. It combines Apple Macintosh computers, Windows PCs, and Sun workstations on the same network through the use of a transparent networking software. The network connection does not alter the computer's native interface or operating system.

transparent routing A method used by a bridge for moving data between two networks through learning the station addresses on each network.

transparent services access facility (TSAF) A VM component that provides communications support between interconnected VM systems. Up to eight VM systems can participate in a TSAF collection, which can be considered analogous to a VM local area network (or wide area network).

transport To transmit real-time data over multicast or unicast network services.

transport connection (TC) The functions of transport connection must match the requested class of services with the services provided by the network layer as follows: (1) Select network service which best matches the requirement of the TS user, taking into account charges for various services. (2) Decide whether to multiplex multiple transport connection onto a single network connection. (3) Establish the optimum TPDU size. (4) Select the functions that will be operational upon entering the data transfer phase. (5) Map transport addresses onto network addresses. (6) Provide a means to distinguish between two different transport connections. (7) Transport user's data.

transport connection endpoint (TCEP) A location on the network that represents the user's interface to the Transport Service Access Point (TSAP). Through this endpoint, service is obtained and a connection ID is established, which corresponds to an endpoint within the service access point.

transport endpoint (TEP) Functions that provide an application programming interface (API) to endpoint providers. When a transport endpoint is configured, the user specifies which protocol or set of protocols the provider is to use; the highest-level protocol specified for the endpoint provider determines whether the transport mechanism is connectionless or connection-oriented, and whether it is transactionless or transaction-based. For example, if ADSP is specified as the highest-level protocol in the endpoint provider, the transport is connection-oriented and transactionless.

transport layer The 4th layer of the OSI Model that provides an end-to-end service to its users. The transport layer provides mechanisms for the establishment, maintenance, termination of virtual circuits, transport fault detection and recovery, and information flow control. The transport layer corresponds to the transmission control layer of the SNA model. *See* application layer, data-link layer, network layer, physical layer, presentation layer, *and* session layer.

transport network Part of an SNA network that includes the data-link control and path control layer.

transport neutral encapsulation format (TNEF) A proprietary e-mail transmission format for *rich text format (RTF)* messages used by the Microsoft Exchange and Outlook e-mail clients.

transport service access point (TSAP) The OSI address at the transport layer. Each incoming OSI protocol data unit includes the TSAP destination address. The TSAP is made up of the ShivaPort's NSAP and TSEL addresses (OSI addressing).

transport service data unit (TSDU) The amount of user data, the identify of which is preserved from one end of a transport connection to the other.

transport-independent RPC (TI RPC) A connection that uses XTI as its transport interface instead of sockets.

transport-layer interface (TLI) In AIX environment, the connection responsible for establishing a transport endpoint.

trap An event used in SNMP-managed networks to send data to the network manager. A trap is sent from an SNMP agent.

tree and tabular combined notation (TTCN) A method of expressing the number of tests to perform, to check an equipment for compliance with some specifications.

tree topology A LAN topology that contains tree networks with branches having multiple nodes. A tree topology is similar to a *bus topology*.

Trivial File Transfer Protocol (TFTP) A simple form of the *File Transfer Protocol (FTP)* documented in RFCs 1123 & 1350. TFTP does not require passwords. It is a TCP/IP *User Datagram Protocol (UDP)* standard protocol for file transfer that uses UDP as a transport mechanism and provides no security features Usually used to back up router configuration information and IOS images. TFTP depends only on UDP, so it can be used on machines such as servers to boot diskless workstations, X-terminals, and routers.

TRS *See* topology and routing services.

TRSS *See* token-ring subsystem.

TRT *See* token rotation timer.

true color Any graphics device or software that uses at least 24 bits of information to represent each dot or pixel. Using 24 bits means that more than 16 million unique colors can be represented, thus providing a true color palette.

TrueType An outline font technology developed jointly by Microsoft and Apple.

trunk coupling unit (TCU) A physical device in token ring networks that enables a station to connect to the trunk cable.

trunk up-down (TUD) A protocol used in ATM networks that monitors trunks and detects when one goes down or comes up.

TSAF *See* transparent services access facility.

TSAP *See* transport service access point.

TSAPI *See* telephony server application program interface.

TSCF *See* target system control facility.

TSDU *See* transport service data unit.

TSI *See* time-slot interchange.

TSR *See* terminate-and-stay resident.

TSS *See* transmission subsystem.

TTCN *See* tree and tabular combined notation.

TTL *See* time-to-live *and* transistor-transistor logic.

TTP *See* Timed Token Protocol.

TTRT *See* target token rotation time.

TTY *See* teletype.

TUD *See* trunk up-down.

tunneling The practice of encapsulating a datagram from one protocol into a second protocol and using the second protocol to trasverse a network. At the destination, the encapsulation is stripped off and the original message is reintroduced to the network. Tunneling is also referred to as encapsulation.

TUP *See* telephone user part.

TVX In fiber distributed-data interface (FDDI), a timer that times the period between valid transmissions on the ring; used to detect excessive ring noise, token loss, and other faults.

tweak To make small changes that fine-tune a piece of software or hardware.

twisted pair Two conductors that wrap around each other to form a pair in order to reduce noise. Typically used in telephone system cabling.

T

two-way simultaneous (TWS) A mode within SDLC that allows a router configured as the primary station to utilize a full-duplex serial line connection.

TWS *See* two-way simultaneous.

TWX *See* teletypewriter exchange service.

type The second field in the name of an AppleTalk entity.

type 2.0 (T2.0) node A node that attaches to a subarea network as a peripheral node and provides full end-user services but no intermediate routing services.

type 2.1 (T2.1) node An SNA node that can be configured as an endpoint or intermediate routing node in a T2.1 network, or as a peripheral node attached to a subarea network. It may act as an end node, network node, or intermediate node in an APPN network.

type 2.1 end node A type 2.1 node that provides full SNA end-user services, but no intermediate routing or network services to any other node; it is configured only as an endpoint in a network.

type 2.1 network A collection of interconnected type 2.1 network nodes and type 2.1 end nodes. A type 2.1 network may consist of nodes of just one type, namely, all network nodes or all end nodes; a pair of directly attached end nodes is the simplest case of a type 2.1 network.

type 4 node An SNA subarea node that provides routing and data link control functions for a type 5 node. Type 5 nodes control type 4 nodes.

type 5 node An SNA subarea node that contains an SSCP and controls type 4 and type 2 SNA node types. A node that can be any one of the following:

■ Advanced Peer-to-Peer Networking (APPN) end node

■ Advanced Peer-to-Peer Networking (APPN) network node

■ Interchange node

■ Low-entry networking (LEN) node

■ Migration data host

■ Subarea node

type of service (TOS) A value used to indicate the quality of the service desired. An abstract or generalized set of parameters, which characterize the service choices provided in the networks that make up the Internet. This type-of-service indication is used by gateways to select the actual transmission parameters for a particular network, the network to be used for the next hop, or the next gateway when routing an Internet datagram. *See* class of service (COS).

U

UA *See* unnumbered acknowledgment.

UART *See* universal asynchronous receiver-transmitter.

UBR *See* unspecified bit rate.

UCT *See* Universal Coordinated Time.

UDA *See* universal data access.

UDP *See* User Datagram Protocol.

UI *See* user interface.

UIML *See* User Interface Markup Language.

UL *See* Underwriters Laboratories.

ULP *See* upper-layer protocol.

ULSI *See* ultra large-scale integration.

Ultra ATA The newest version of the AT Attachment (ATA) standard, which supports burst mode data-transfer rates of 33.3 MBps. A computer must be equipped with Ultra DMA, a protocol that supports faster data transfer rates to and from hard disk drives, to better take advantage of the high speeds now available in data transfer.

Ultra DMA A protocol developed by Quantum Corporation and Intel. It supports burst mode data-transfer rates of 33.3 MBps, which is the speed necessary to take advantage of new, faster Ultra ATA disk drives. It is twice the speed of the previous disk drive standard for PCs.

ultra large-scale integration (ULSI) Technology utilizing the placement of over one million circuit elements on a single chip.

UMB *See* upper memory block.

UNBIND A request to deactivate a session between two logical units (LUs).

UNC *See* universal naming convention.

uncompressing Expanding a compressed or packed file to its original size. When down-loaded software or large files are compressed, the data can be transferred at a higher speed. Compressed files often have a trigger that permits the file to uncompress automatically upon download.

underflow A condition that occurs when a computer tries to represent a number that that is too close to zero. Programs resolve underflow conditions by either reporting an error or approximating the number and resuming processing.

Underwriters Laboratories (UL) An independent agency responsible for the testing of product safety.

undo To go back to the preceding screen or reverse the effect of a command. This feature is an invaluable tool because it allows the user to attempt commands with a much less risk, because any changes to data can be removed. The undo command is supported by most software products.

UNI *See* user-network interface.

unicast The method of sending a packet or datagram to a single address. This type of point-to-point transmission requires the source to send an individual copy of a message to a single destination. *See* anycast, multicast, broadcast, *and* IP multicasting.

unicast address Address specifying a single network device.

unicode Officially called the *unicode worldwide character standard*. A standard for setting up binary codes for text or script characters, which represents each character as an integer. Unicode can represent more than 65,000 unique characters, using 16 bits. Although this might be too much for some languages, those such as Greek, Chinese, and Japanese require a great variety of characters.

uniform resource identifier (URI) A generic term that refers to all names and addresses related to, or on, the World Wide Web. A URI is used to identify any point on the Web, whether it is a picture, a video clip, or any other object of interest.

uniform resource locator (URL) Strins that specifies how to access network resources, such as HTML documents. Part of the more general class of *universal resource identifiers (URIs)*. The most important use of URLs is in HTML documents, to identify the targets of *hyperlinks*. When using a Web browser, every highlighted region has a URL associated with it; this URL is accessed when the link is activated by a mouse click. *Relative URLs* specify only a portion of the full URL—the missing information is inferred though the context of the source document. URLs are documented in RFC 1738. Relative URLs are documented in RFC 1808. URIs are documented in RFC 1630.

The URL http://www.netcerts.com/white papers/wpapers.asp can be translated as:

http:// HyperText Transfer Protocol (HTTP) is to be used to retrieve the document. Other possible values for this field include https (use secure HTTP), ftp (use the File Transfer Protocol), and gopher (use the Gopher Protocol).

www.netcerts.com This is a *hostname*, to be resolved using the Domain Name Service (DNS)

/whitepapers/wpapers.asp A directory and filename, to be passed along in the HTTP request to identify the specific document that the user is requesting to be opened on the server.

uniform resource name (URN) An Internet resource with lasting significance. A URN resembles a Web page address or a URL.

uninstall To take away a certain program, application, or files that were added to a computer when the application was originally installed. Uninstalling may not be entirely effective, and the directories used by the program may remain, because in Windows technology, programs may write to many areas in the Registry or overwrite areas; no history or record of these writes/overwrites is kept, so it is impossible to revert to the previous value when the program is removed.

uninsured traffic The difference between the insured rate and maximum rate for a VCC. This traffic can be dropped by the network if congestion occurs. *See* CLP *and* maximum rate.

uninterruptible power supply (UPS) An electrical device that acts as a backup power source in case of a power loss or surge. When the UPS senses a loss of power supply from its original or main source, a backup battery is triggered, thus giving the computer user time to save files that might be lost and to properly shut down the computer.

unipolar Fundamental electrical characteristic of internal signals in digital communications equipment that only have one polarity.

unity gain The balance between signal loss and signal gain through amplifiers.

universal asynchronous receiver-transmitter (UART) A programmed microchip that controls a computer's interface to its attached serial devices. Every computer contains a UART that provides it with the RS-232C data terminal equipment (DTE) interface so that it can exchange data with modems and other serial devices, and manage serial ports, as well as internal modems.

Universal Coordinated Time (UCT) Also Coordinated Universal Time or Universal Time Coordinated. The standard time common to every place in the world.

universal data access (UDA) Microsoft's framework for a single uniform application program interface. This is a high-level specification developed for accessing data objects regardless of their structure, in different software makers' databases, both relational and non-relational.. One of the main components of UDA is the *ActiveX Data Objects (ADO)* interface.

universal naming convention (UNC) Also, Uniform Naming Convention. A PC format for specifying the location of resources and identifying shared peripheral devices on a local-area network (LAN). UNC uses the \\servername\shared-resource-pathname format.

universal network The idea of a single network that is interconnected with other networks such as the Internet, cable TV, data networks, and video broadcast networks. This universal network allows all smaller interconnected networks to work together.

universal product code (UPC) A computer-readable binary code, in the form of scannable bars. It was first widely used in 1973, when the grocery industry adopted it as a way to automatically associate prices with products at the checkout register. It has since been applied to cataloging and inventory control as well.

universal serial bus (USB) An external bus standard for plug-and-play interfaces between a computer and add-on devices such as mice, modems, keyboards, audio players, joysticks, telephones, scanners, and printers. USBs support data transfer rates of 12 Mbps (12 million bits per second). A single USB port can connect up to 127 devices.

UNIX An operating system developed in 1969 at Bell Laboratories by Ken Thompson and Dennis Ritchie. UNIX became the first operating system written in the C language, and was designed to be a small, flexible system used exclusively by programmers

unnumbered acknowledgment (UA) A data-link control command used in establishing a link and in answering receipt of logical link control frames.

unnumbered frames HDLC frames used for various control and management purposes, including mode specification, link startup, and shutdown.

unreachable A node that cannot be found.

unreliable delivery model One of Internet's earliest design decisions was that the fundamental transport protocol (the IP Protocol) would be based on an assumption of *unreliable delivery*. This means that an IP packet can be legally discarded at any time, without any notification to the sender or receiver. No guarantee is made that any particular packet will be delivered. Instead, network reachability takes a statistical form—there is a pretty good chance that any one packet will be delivered,

and if a group of packets is transmitted, most of them should arrive at their destinations.

unshielded twisted pair (UTP) The most common kind of copper telephone wiring, consisting of two unshielded copper wires twisted around each other. Because the cost is so low, UTP cabling is widely used for local-area networks (LANs) and telephone connections that require short-distance wiring. Even though UTP is inexpensive and easy to work with, it does not offer as high bandwidth or as good protection from interference as coaxial or fiber optic cables.

unspecified bit rate (UBR) One of the best-effort service types in asynchronous transfer method (ATM) networks; (the other is ABR). Realistically, no traffic parameters are specified by the source, so network management makes no actual quality commitment.

unzipping An action similar to extracting, decompressing, or uncompressing a compressed or packed file.

UPC *See* universal product code *and* usage parameter control.

upgrade To move up to the latest version available of hardware or software. Upgrades usually contain better features, and are designed to replace preceding versions.

upline dump In DECnet for OpenVMS, a function that allows an adjacent node to dump its memory to a file on a system.

upload The transmission of data from one computer or computer system to another. The receiving system is usually larger, such as a server, bulletin board service, mainframe, or network. An upload can be successfully performed only if the receiving computer or computer system is set up to receive or *download* the sent data.

upper memory block (UMB) A block of memory in the DOS upper memory area, allocated and managed by a special memory managers such as EMM386.EXE. UMBs can be used by TSRs and device drivers as well.

upper-layer protocol (UPL) A protocol operating at a higher layer in the OSI reference

U

model, in relation to other layers. The term sometimes refers to the next-highest protocol (relative to a particular protocol) in a protocol stack.

UPS *See* uninterruptible power supply.

upward compatible Software that can run on systems that were designed for it, as well as more powerful systems. This feature is important because it allows the user to move data to a newer, larger, and more sophisticated computer without running the risk of losing data or having to convert it. Upward compatibility is also referred to as *forward compatibility*.

URI *See* uniform resource identifier.

URL *See* uniform resource locator.

URN *See* uniform resource name.

usage parameter control (UPC) A form of traffic control that checks and enforces user's conformance with the traffic contract and the QoS parameters. Commonly known as *traffic policing*, it is performed at the UNI level.

USB *See* universal serial bus.

USENET A worldwide bulletin board system of discussion groups, where a collection of notes on various subjects can be posted. USENET can be accessed through almost any online service. The USENET contains thousands of newsgroups, which cover a variety of interests, and is used daily by millions of people around the world.

user An individual who uses a computer. This includes expert programmers as well as novices. An *end user* is any individual who runs an application program.

User Datagram Protocol (UDP) A connectionless transport protocol defined in RFC768. It provides no guarantee of packet sequence or delivery and is thus termed an *unreliable protocol*. It functions directly on top of IP and does not provide error-recovery services. Instead it offers a direct method of sending and receiving datagrams over an IP Network, while making no provision for acknowledgment or guarantee of packets received. This requires that error processing and retransmission be handled by other protocols.

user interface The junction between a user and a computer program. An interface is a set of commands or menus through which a user communicates with a program. A *command-driven interface* is one in which the user enters commands. A *menu-driven interface* is one in which the user selects command choices from various menus displayed on the screen.

User Interface Markup Language (UIML) A language that allows a user to create a Web page that can be sent to any kind of interface device—a smart phone that has no keyboard and a small display, or a PC that has a very large display as well as a keyboard.

user privileges Privileges granted to a user by the system manager or administrator

username For security purposes, a name used to identify the user of a computer. A username and a password are usually required to gain access to a multi-user computer system.

user-network interface (UNI) An ATM Forum specification that defines an interoperability standard for the interface between ATM-based products, located in a private network, and the ATM switches, located within the public carrier networks. This specification refers to two standards being developed, one between a user and a public ATM network, called *public UNI*, and one between a user and a private ATM network, called *P-UNI*. It is also used to describe similar connections in frame relay networks. *See* NNI, Q.920/Q.921, *and* SNI.

UNI 2.0 specifies the physical (PHY) and the ATM layers, the ILMI, OAM (traffic control), and for PVC support.

UNI 3.00, an upgrade of UNI 2.0, adds traffic control for PCR and operation over current transmission systems, as well as other features.

UNI 3.1, is a corrected version of UNI 3.0; it also includes SSCOP standards. *UNI 4.0* refers to signaling issues in ABR, VP, and QoS negotiations. It is important to note that UNI3.1 and UNI4.0 are not entirely compatible because of differences in the information elements (IEs) between the two specifications.

utility Typically, a small program that performs a very specific task, usually related to managing system resources. Operating systems contain a number of utilities for managing disk drives, printers, and other devices.

UTOPIA Universal Test and Operation Physical Interface. An interface to provide connectivity at the physical level among ATM entities.

UTP *See* unshielded twisted pair.

uuencode A set of algorithms used for encoding and decoding files transferred between users on a system or a network. It can also be used over the Internet, especially on e-mails containing attachments. Originally, uuencode was developed to be used between users of UNIX systems, and its name stood for *UNIX-to-UNIX encode*. Since then, it has become a widely used protocol for transferring files between different platforms such as UNIX, Windows, and Macintosh. Uuencode is usually available for use in most operating systems as well as in most e-mail applications. It is easily downloaded from many Web sites.

U

V

V.22 CCITT V.22 communications. *See* CCITT.

V.22bis CCITT V.22bis communications. *See* CCITT.

V.24 ITU-T standard for a physical layer interface between the DTE and DCE; essentially the same as the EIA/TIA-232 standard.

V.25bis The V Series Recommendations from the ITU-T. They include the most commonly used modem standards and other telephone network standards.

V.32 The V Series Recommendations from the ITU-T that provide 4, 800 and 9,600 bits per second at 2,400 baud.

V.32bis The V Series Recommendations from the ITU-T that provide 14,400 bits per second or fallback to 12,000, 9,600, 7,200, and 4,800 bits per second.

V.34 ITU-T standard that specifies a serial line protocol. V.34 offers improvements to the V.32 standard, including higher transmission rates (28.8Kbps) and enhanced data compression.

V.35 The interface standard used by most routers and DSUs that are connected to T-1 carriers in the United States. It is also an ITU standard for high-speed synchronous data exchange over a telephone network interface.

V.42 CCITT V.42 communications. *See* CCITT.

V.90 Approved by the International Telecommunication Union (ITU) in February, 1998 to be a standard for 56-Kbps modems. The competition between X2 from 3COM and K56flex from Rockwell Semiconductor, two 56 Kbps technologies, was resolved in the V.90 standard. Future modems will conform to the V.90 standard. Furthermore, most users who have purchased 56-Kbps modems will be able to upgrade their modem support to V.90 through software.

vaporware A derogatory term used to designate software and hardware products that have been announced and advertised but are not yet available.

variable In programming, objects that have the ability to represent numeric values, characters, character strings, or memory addresses. They enable programmers to write flexible programs. Instead of a programmer's entering data directly into a program, he can use variables to represent the data. The variables are then replaced with real data when the program is executed, allowing the program to process different sets of data.

variable bit rate (VBR) QoS class defined by the ATM Forum for ATM networks. VBR is subdivided into a *real time (RT) class* and *non-real time (NRT) class*. VBR (RT) is used for connections in which there is a fixed timing relationship between samples. VBR (NRT) is used for connections in which there is no fixed timing relationship between samples, though they still need a guaranteed QoS. *See* available bit rate (ABR), CBR, *and* UBR.

variable bit rate-non-real time (VBR-nrt) One of the service types for transmitting traffic where timing information is not critical. It is characterized by the average and peak cell rates, and is well suited for long data packet transfers.

variable bit rate-real time (VBR-rt) One of the service types for transmitting traffic that depends on timing information and control. It is characterized by the average and peak cell rates. It is suitable for carrying traffic such as packetized (compressed) video and audio.

variable-length subnet mask (VLSM) In IP addressing, a means of allocating addressing resources to subnets according to their individual need. Typically, exterior gateway protocols (EGPs) depend on the IP address class definitions, and actually exchange network numbers (8-, 16-, or 24-bit fields) rather than IP addresses (32-bit numbers), while RIP and

IGRP exchange network and subnet numbers in 32-bit fields. The distinction between network number, subnet number, and host number is a matter of convention and is not exchanged in these routing protocols. More recent protocols such as OSPF, BGP, and EIGRP carry either a prefix length (number of contiguous bits in the address) or subnet mask with each address, indicating to which portion of the 32-bit field the address being routed.

variable MTU A link that does not have a well-defined MTU, such as an IEEE 802.5 token ring link. Many links, for example Ethernet links, have a standard MTU defined by the link-layer protocol or by the specific document describing how to run IP over the link layer.

VAX *See* virtual address extension.

VAXcluster configuration A highly integrated organization of OpenVMS systems that communicate over a high-speed communication path. This configuration has all the functions of single-node systems, plus the ability to share CPU resources, queues, and disk storage. Like a single-node system, the VAXcluster configuration provides a single security and management environment. Member nodes can share the same operating environment or serve specialized needs.

VBA *See* Visual Basic Applications.

VBI *See* vertical blanking interval.

vBNS *See* very high-speed backbone network service.

VBR *See* variable bit rate.

VBR-nrt *See* variable bit rate-non-real time.

VBR-rt *See* variable bit rate-real time.

VBScript Visual Basic Scripting Edition. A scripting language developed by Microsoft as a subset of its Visual Basic Applications (VBA) programming language. It is much simpler than Visual Basic and resembles Javascript. VBScript allows Web authors to include interactive controls on their Web pages.

VC *See* virtual channel *and* virtual circuit.

VCACHE The disk cache system in Windows 95. VCACHE replaces the SmartDrive system used in older versions of Windows. VCACHE is a 32-bit driver, as opposed to SmartDrive, which is only a 16-bit driver. Depending on available disk space and application requirements, VCACHE can significantly change the size of the disk cache.

VCC *See* virtual channel connection.

VCI *See* virtual channel identifier.

VCL *See* virtual channel link.

VCN *See* virtual circuit number.

VCNS *See* VTAM common network services.

VCPI *See* virtual control program interface.

Veronica The Very Easy Rodent Oriented Netwide Index to Computerized Archives; a program that enables you to search for Gopher sites, and to then search the files of the Gopher sites. Similar to *Archie*, which is an equivalent program for FTP servers, Veronica serves Gopher sites. Veronica is an indexing *spider* used to create an indexes of file names and directories of all Gopher servers. Veronica's database is updated constantly with the names of most menu items on thousands of Gopher servers. Most major Gopher menus can search the Veronica database. A user then queries Veronica, which checks the query against its index. *See* Gopher.

versatile interface processors (VIP) Network interface modules for high-end routers

vertical blanking interval (VBI) A blank area used for the transmission of closed-caption and HTML-formatted information. This area is a part of a television transmission signal that contains no viewable content; its original purpose was to allow time for the television's electron gun to move from the bottom to the top of the screen as it scans images.

verti-port Also referred to as *miniportal*. A Web site focusing mainly on specific matters, such as a particular industry, subject matter, or target group. One example of a verti-port would be the online retailer Amazon.com, which specializes in books.

very high-speed backbone network service (vBNS) Sponsored by the National Science Foundation (NSF) and implemented by MCI, vBNS is an experimental wide area network. vBNS is designed to serve as a platform for testing new, high-speed Internet technologies and protocols, and it has replaced NSFnet. Because of the new *Abilene network* (based on POS), it is questionable whether groups will continue to support the vBNS network, which is ATM-based.

very large-scale integration (VLSI) The process of placing thousands of transistor on one microchip.

VESA *See* Video Electronics Standards Association.

VESA Local-Bus (VL-Bus) A local bus architecture created by the Video Electronics Standards Association, which is a standard interface between a computer and its expansion slots. The local bus provides faster data flow between the devices controlled by the expansion cards and the computer's microprocessor, thus increasing total system performance, because the data flows at almost the speed of the processor.

vestigial side band (VSB) A method, created by Zenith, for converting digital data for transmission over coaxial cable. The FCC chose VSB as a standard for digital TV.

VFAT *See* virtual file allocation table.

VGA *See* video graphics array.

VG-AnyLan A 100 Mbps technology, developed by Hewlett-Packard, based on the demand priority access method. The IEEE 802.12 VG specification calls for 4-pair UTP category 3, 4, and 5, with 2-pair STP and fiber possibilities in the future.

VIC *See* voice interface card.

video (*n.*) A display of images and text on a computer monitor. (*v.*) Displaying images and text on a computer monitor.

video adapter Also known as a *display adapter* or *video board*. A board that plugs into a PC to give it display capabilities depen-

dent upon both the logical circuitry and the display monitor. A video adapter's purpose is to allow data to be sent to the display and then constantly refreshed.

Video Electronics Standards Association (VESA) An organization of video adapter and monitor manufacturers whose goal is to standardize video protocols. A line of video standards that offer greater resolution and more colors than VGA has been developed by VESA, and these standards are known as *Super VGA (SVGA)*.

video graphics array (VGA) A graphics display system designed by IBM for PCs. VGA is the standard for PCs, providing a resolution of 720 x 400 pixels in text mode. In graphics mode, VGA provides a resolution of 640 x 480 or 320 x 200, and depending on whether the monitor is set for 16 or 256 colors, respectively.

video RAM (VRAM) A special-purpose memory used by video adapters. Two different devices can simultaneously access VRAM; while the video processor provides new data, RAMDAC can access VRAM for updates. VRAM is more expensive than normal RAM, but it yields better graphics performance.

videoconferencing A person-to-person discussion, involving either individuals or groups, in which participants are at different sites, using computer networks to transmit audio and video data. The effect of videoconferencing simulates a meeting held with all participants in the same room. Video conferencing requires special telephone interconnections with wide bandwidth, because of the transmission of audio and video data. The growth of video conferencing has been slow because of the high cost of hardware. Additional information can be found in the current standards H.320, H.321, and H.323.

video-on-demand (VoD) A technology that enables a customer to remotely select and play a video, transmitted over communications links. Some uses for VoD are entertainment, education, and videoconferencing. VoD is not yet widely implemented because its biggest obstacle is its lack of a network infrastructure,

V

necessary to handle the large amounts of data required by video.

VIP *See* versatile interface processors.

virtual Not real. Something that is a mere simulation or illusion of a real environment. A realistic image that is merely conceptual.

virtual address extension (VAX) Computer systems using VAX feature an operating system that supports *virtual memory (VMS)*.

virtual channel (VC) The unidirectional flow of ATM cells between connecting (switching or end-user) points that share a common identifier number (VCI). This number is unique and has significant meaning to the two endpoints of an ATM connection. *See* virtual circuit.

virtual channel connection (VCC) A logical circuit made up of virtual channel links (VCLs); it is sometimes called a *virtual circuit connection*. VCCs carry data between two end points in an ATM network.

virtual channel identifier (VCI) A 16-bit value in the ATM cell header that provides a unique identifier for the virtual channel (VC) that carries that particular cell.

virtual channel link (VCL) Connection between two ATM devices. A virtual channel connection (VCC) is made up of one or more VCLs. *See* virtual channel connection (VCC).

virtual circuit *(Illustration)* A connection set up across the network between a source and a destination. A fixed route is chosen for the entire session and bandwidth is dynamically allocated. These are logical circuits created to ensure reliable communication between two network devices. A virtual circuit is defined by a VPI/VCI pair, and can be either a *permanent virtual circuit (PVC)* or a *switched virtual circuit (SVC)*. Virtual circuits are used in frame relay and X.25. In ATM, a virtual circuit is called a *virtual channel*. Sometimes abbreviated VC. *See* PVC, SVC, VCI, virtual route, *and* VPI.

virtual circuit number (VCN) Also called a *logical channel identifier (LCI)* or *logical channel number (LCN)*. The VCN is a 12-bit field in an X.25 PLP header, which identifies an X.25 virtual circuit. The VCN allows the DCE to determine how to route a packet through the X.25 network.

virtual connection A circuit or path between points in a network that appears to be a discrete, physical path, but is actually a managed pool of circuit resources from which specific circuits are allocated as needed to meet traffic requirements.

virtual control program interface (VCPI) An interface that manages memory past the first megabyte on PCs with 80386 or later processors. Depending upon requirements by the applications design, VCPI can allocate memory to an application as either *expanded* or *extended memory*. Some memory managers and DOS extenders support the VCPI standard.

virtual file allocation table (VFAT) In Windows for Workgroups and Windows 95, a virtual installable files system driver. Located between applications and the *file allocation table (FAT)*, VFAT operates in protected mode and also serves as an interface.

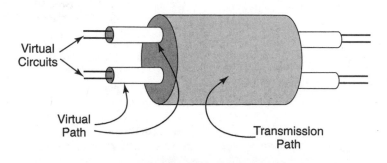

Virtual Circuits

Virtual Path

Transmission Path

virtual LAN (VLAN) A local area network with a definition that maps workstations on some other basis than geographic location (for example, by department, type of user, or primary application). Users on physically independent LANs are interconnected in such a way that it appears as if they are on the same LAN workgroup. VLANs offer significant benefits in terms of efficient use of bandwidth, flexibility, performance, and security. VLAN technology functions by logically segmenting the network into different *broadcast domains* so that packets are only switched between ports that are designated for the same VLAN. VLANs are configured through software rather than hardware, which makes them extremely flexible. One of the biggest advantages of VLANs is that when a computer is physically moved to another location, it can stay on the same VLAN without any hardware reconfiguration. *See* LANE.

The figure below depicts VLAN membership as a departmental function; however, users could also be combined in VLAN topologies based upon a common protocol or subnet address.

The following links are useful to assist you in learning more about virtual LANs:

VLAN Interoperability

http://www.cisco.com/warp/public/537/6.html

Configuring Routing between VLANs with IEEE 802.10 Encapsulation

http://www.cisco.com/univercd/cc/td/doc/product/software/ios113ed/113ed_cr/switch_c/xc802.htm

virtual LAN internetwork (VLI) A network composed of virtual LANs (VLANs). VLANs are most commonly used within campus area network (CAN) environments.

virtual machine In Java applications, software that performs a program's instructions and acts as an interface between compiled Java binary code and the microprocessor. The virtual machine behaves as if it were a separate computer, because it is a self-contained operating environment. A Java program has little possibility of damaging other files or applications because the VM has no contact with the OS. Furthermore, regardless of the hardware and software in the system, a Java applet will run the same in any VM, provided it is a Java VM.

virtual memory A type of memory supported by some operating systems, jointly with hardware. An alternate set of memory addresses, used by programs to store instructions and data, rather than using real addresses. Also known as *logical memory*. The virtual addresses are converted into real memory addresses when the program is executed. This allows programmers to use a larger range of memory or storage addresses for stored data when the program is implemented by a computer and its operating system.

virtual memory system (VMS) A multi-user, multitasking, virtual memory operating system, virtual memory system was developed by DEC, and runs on DEC's VAX computers. VMS originated in 1979 along with the first VAX minicomputer.

virtual path (VP) A set of virtual channels (VCs) grouped together, between crosspoints (i.e., switches).

virtual path connection (VPC) A concatenation of virtual path (VP) links. A grouping of virtual channel connectors (VCCs), which share one or more contiguous VPLs. *See* VCC *and* VPL.

virtual path connection identifier/virtual channel identifier (VPCI/VCI) A combination of two numbers, one for identifying the virtual path (VP) and one for the virtual channel identifier (VCI).

virtual path identifier (VPI) An 8-bit value in the cell header that identifies the VP and, accordingly, the virtual channel to which the cell belongs. The VPI, together with the VCI, is used to identify the next destination of a cell

V

as it passes through a series of ATM switches on its way to its destination. ATM switches use the VPI/VCI fields to identify the next VCL that a cell needs to transit on its way to its final destination. The function of the VPI is similar to that of the DLCI in a frame relay network. *See* DLCI, VCI, *and* VCL.

virtual path link (VPL) Within a virtual path, a group of unidirectional VCLs with the same end points. Grouping VCLs into VPLs reduces the number of connections to be managed, thereby decreasing network control overhead and cost. A VPC is made up of one or more VPLs.

virtual private dialup network (VPDN) A feature that allows a private network dial-in service to span across to remote access servers (defined within most discussions as the network access server [NAS]). Usually, a Point-to-Point Protocol (PPP) client dials into a local NAS. The NAS determines that it is to forward that PPP session to a home gateway router for that client, which then authenticates the user and starts the PPP negotiation. After PPP setup is completed, all frames are sent via the NAS to the client and home gateway. This integrates several protocols and concepts. The NAS begins authentication with the client when it first dials in. From there it can be either statically configured to pass off the call, or use *authentication, authorization, and accounting (AAA)* to have the daemon *terminal access controller access control system (TACACS+)* or remote authentication dial-in user service (RADIUS) pass that information on. The PPP client is forwarded across a layer 2 forwarding (L2F) tunnel riding on top of *User Datagram Protocol (UDP)*. The home gateway has a virtual template configured to handle the incoming call and uses authentication for both the tunnel setup (that uses CHAP) and the client. From there, the network can also pass on specific user information within the authorization segment (per-user configuration) for the client. A virtual-access interface is then brought up for that session, cloned from both the VT and per-user configuration. The protocols running within PPP are transparent to the NAS.

For more information, see the following sites:

http://www.vpdn.com/

http://www.cisco.com/univercd/ cc/td/doc/product/software/ ios113ed/113t/113t_3/vpdnmib.htm

http://www.cisco.com/univercd/ cc/td/doc/product/access/ap/ ap_ts3/ap_ts3sw/apswvpd.htm

virtual private network (VPN) Network resources provided to users, on demand, by public carriers (via the Internet for example) so that users view this partition of the network as a private network. The advantage of the VPNs over the dedicated private networks is that the former allow a dynamic allocation of network resources through encrypted network connections so the entire network is "virtually" private.

Virtual Reality Modeling Language (VRML) A language for describing three-dimensional objects on the World Wide Web, as well as user interactions with them. VRML produces a three-dimensional space that appears on the display screen and allows the user to interact with it as if it were in real time—as the user presses keys to turn left, right, up or down, rotate, go forward or backward, or otherwise move, the images simulate the impression of movement in real space. The new VRML 2.0 is known officially as ISO/IEC 14772.

virtual ring Entity in an SRB network that logically connects two or more physical rings together either locally or remotely. The concept of virtual rings can be expanded across router boundaries.

virtual route (VR) In SNA it is either (*a*) a logical connection between two subarea nodes that is physically realized through an explicit route or (*b*) a logical connection that is contained wholly within a subarea node for intranode sessions.

virtual route (VR) pacing A flow control technique used in SNA by the virtual route control component of path control at each end of a virtual route. This pacing controls the rate at which path information units (PIUs) flow over the virtual route.

virtual routing node A representation of a node's connectivity to a connection network, defined on a shared-access transport facility, such as a token ring.

virtual source/virtual destinations (VS/VD) One of three types of feedback that an ATM switch can provide.

virtual storage A type of storage which is composed of processor, speed, main memory, DASD, and specialized programs. Virtual storage does not exist in reality; it is a concept.

virtual storage access method (VSAM) A file management system for IBM operating systems. By using an inverted index of all records added to each file, VSAM speeds up access to data in files, allowing an enterprise to create and access records in the sequential order by which they were entered. VSAM is composed of processor, speed, main memory, DASD, and specialized programs. Virtual storage does not exist in reality; it is a concept.

virtual storage extended (VSE) Software operating system controlling the execution of programs.

virtual telecommunications access method (VTAM) A set of programs that control communication between nodes and application programs in SNA. It provides single-domain, multiple-domain, and interconnected network capability. VTAM is the software component by which Systems Network Architecture's communication network between LUs is controlled. SDLC and token ring are some of several protocols supported by VTAM. Data transmission between channel-attached devices is controlled by VTAM, and it performs routing functions as well.

For more information, see *http://www.plr-services.com/VTAM.HTM*

Virtual Terminal Protocol (VTP) An ISO application for establishing a virtual terminal connection across a network.

virtualization Process of implementing a network based on virtual network segments, where devices are connected to virtual segments independent of their physical location and their physical connection to the network.

virus A piece of programming code that may be loaded onto a computer, usually without user knowledge, to cause unexpected damage to the computer. Viruses are spread through downloading programs from infected Web sites or diskettes. Frequently, the source from which a virus comes is not aware that there is a virus present. Viruses are often inactive until executed by a computer. Programs that check a computer for viruses and take appropriate action to deactivate them are called *antiviral programs*.

Visual Basic Applications (VBA) A programming language based on the BASIC programming language and developed by Microsoft. Visual Basic Applications was among the first products that provided a graphical programming environment. By simply dragging and dropping *controls* like buttons and dialog boxes, and then defining their appearance and behavior, the VBA programmer can add a significant amount of code to his program.

Visual C++ An application development tool introduced in 1993 by Microsoft for C++ programmers. Visual C++ is for object-oriented programming of 32-bit Windows applications within an integrated development environment (IDE).

VLAN *See* virtual LAN.

VLAN Membership Resolution Protocol (VMRP) A protocol that uses GARP to provide a mechanism for dynamic maintenance of the contents of the port egress lists for each port of a bridge, and for propagating the information they contain to other bridges.

VLAN-tagged frame A tagged frame whose tag header carries VLAN identification information.

V

VLAN Trunk Protocol (VTP) A protocol that allows each device (router or LAN-switch) to transmit advertisements in frames on its trunk ports. These advertisement frames are sent to a multicast address to be received by all neighboring devices. However, they are not forwarded according to normal bridging procedures. These advertisement frames list the sending device's management domain, its configuration revision number, the VLANs, which it knows about, and certain parameters for each known VLAN. Once a device receives these advertisement frames, all devices in its same management domain learn about any new VLANs now configured in the transmitting device. This allows a new VLAN to be created or to have its configuration altered on only one device within a domain. The resulting changes are automatically advertised throughout the domain.

VL-Bus *See* VESA Local-Bus.

VLI *See* virtual LAN internetwork.

VLSI *See* very large-scale integration.

VLSM *See* variable-length subnet mask.

VM/SNA console support (VSCS) A VTAM component for the VM environment that provides Systems Network Architecture (SNA) support. It allows SNA terminals to be virtual machine consoles.

VME bus VersaModule Eurocard bus. A 32-bit bus widely used in industrial, commercial, and military applications. It was developed by Motorola, Signetics, Mostek, and Thompson CSF. A 64-bit version, called the VME64, is available.

VMRP *See* VLAN Membership Resolution Protocol.

VMS *See* virtual memory system.

VoD *See* video-on-demand.

voice interface card (VIC) An interface card installed in a slot in a voice network module to provide the connection to the telephone equipment or network. There are three types: FXS, FXO, and E&M interfaces. Each VIC provides two ports of the same type. Plug-in cards used in 2600, 3600, and AS5300 series routers to route voice over IP.

voice network module A network module that installs in a slot in a Cisco 3600 series router, converts telephone voice signals into a form that can be transmitted over an IP network, and provides one or two slots for voice interface cards.

voice-over-IP (VoIP) A feature that carries voice traffic, such as telephone calls and faxes, over an IP network, simultaneously with data traffic.

VoIP dial peer Software object that ties together an IP address and a telephone number at a remote site reached over the IP network.

VoIP *See* voice-over-IP.

volume A determined amount of storage on a disk or tape; a synonym for the storage medium. A disk may contain more than one volume, or a volume may span more than one disk.

VP *See* virtual path.

VPC *See* virtual path connection.

VPDN *See* virtual private dialup network.

VPI/VCI *See* virtual path identifier/virtual channel identifier.

VPI *See* virtual path identifier.

VPL *See* virtual path link.

VPN *See* virtual private network.

VR *See* virtual route.

VRAM *See* video RAM.

VRML *See* Virtual Reality Modeling Language.

VS/VD *See* virtual source/virtual destinations.

VS *See* virtual storage.

VSAM *See* virtual storage access method.

VSB *See* vestigial side band.

VSCS *See* VM/SNA console support.

VSE *See* virtual storage extended.

VSE/Advanced Functions The basic operating system support needed for a VSE controlled installation.

VTAM *See* virtual telecommunications access method.

VTAM application program A program that has opened an access (or method) control block (ACB) to identify itself to VTAM and that can therefore issue VTAM macroinstructions.

VTAM common network services (VCNS) VTAM's support for shared physical connectivity between Systems Network Architecture (SNA) networks and certain non-SNA networks.

VTP *See* virtual terminal protocol; VLAN Trunk Protocol (VTP).

V

W

W3C *See* World Wide Web Consortium.

WAD file A file that comes with Id Software games; it contains information about game levels, game objects, creatures, graphic images, and sound. Typically, these files are several megabytes in size.

WAIS *See* wide-area information servers.

wait state A time-out period during which a CPU or bus lies idle. Wait states are sometimes required because different components function at different clock speeds. For example, if the CPU is much faster than the memory chips, it may need to sit idle during some clock cycles so that the memory chips can catch up. Likewise, buses sometimes require wait states if expansion boards run slower than the bus.

Wallet A small software program used for online purchase transactions. Currently, CyberCash allows the consumer to get free Wallet software, which allows several methods of payment to be defined within the wallet.

WAN *See* wide area network.

WAN Protocols WAN devices have their own set of protocols, which are used during wide-area transmission. Some typical WAN logical protocols are *High-Level Data Link Control (HDLC), Point-To-Point Protocol (PPP), Public Data Network (PDN) X.25, Frame Relay,* and *Switched Multimegabit Data Service (SMDS).*

WAP *See* Wireless Application Protocol.

warez Pronounced way-rez. Commercial software that has been pirated and made available to the public via a BBS or the Internet. Typically, the pirate (also called a *cracker*) has figured out a way to deactivate the copy protection or registration scheme used by the software manufacturer. Note that the use and distribution of warez software is illegal. In contrast, *shareware* and *freeware* may be freely copied and distributed.

warm boot Resetting a computer that is already turned on. This returns the computer to its initial state, and any data or programs in main memory are erased. A *cold boot* is turning a computer on from an off position.

watchdog packet Ensures that a client is still connected to a NetWare server. If the server has not received a packet from a client for a certain period of time, it sends that client a series of watchdog packets. If the station fails to respond to a predefined number of watchdog packets, the server concludes that the station is no longer connected and clears the connection for that station.

watchdog spoofing When a router assists a NetWare client by sending IPX watchdog packets to a NetWare server to keep the session between client and server active.

watchdog timer (*a*) Hardware or software mechanism used to trigger an event or an escape from a process unless the timer is periodically reset. (*b*) In NetWare, a timer that indicates the maximum period that a server will wait for a client to respond to a watchdog packet. If the timer expires, the server sends another watchdog packet (up to a set maximum). *See* watchdog packet.

WAV A format for storing sound files. Developed jointly by Microsoft and IBM, support for WAV files was built into Windows, thus making it the de facto standard for sound on PCs. WAV sound files end with a .wav extension and can be played by nearly all Windows applications that support sound.

waveform Electrical techniques used to convey binary signals.

wavelength The distance an electromagnetic wave can travel in the amount of time it takes to oscillate through a complete cycle.

wavelength division multiplexing (WDM)
A type of multiplexing developed for use on optical fiber. WDM modulates each of several data streams onto a different part of the light spectrum. WDM is the optical equivalent of FDM. With the increase in packing density a new technology is *dense wave division multiplexing (DWDM)*.

WDM *See* wavelength division multiplexing.

wearable computer Some inventors and other theorists not only believe you could wear a computer; they believe there's no reason why you shouldn't. Assuming you remembered to wear it, a wearable computer is always available. Currently, several companies sell wearables and there is considerable literature on the subject. Some wearable computers are basically desktop or notebook computers that have been scaled down for body-wear. Others employ brand new technology. Both general and special purposes are envisioned. A number of wearables have been designed for the disabled.

Web *See* World Wide Web.

Web browser *See* browser.

Web farm Also called a *server farm* or *server cluster*. A group of computers acting as servers and housed together in a single location. (*a*) A Web site that has more than one server. (*b*) An Internet service provider (ISP) that provides Web hosting services using multiple servers.

Web page A document on the World Wide Web. Every Web page is identified by a unique *Uniform Resource Locator (URL)*.

Web portal A Web site or service that offers a broad array of resources and services, such as e-mail, forums, search engines, and online shopping malls. One of the most useful Web portal sites available for those in the telecommunication field is NetCerts for example.

Web server A program that, using the client/server model and the Web's Hypertext Transfer Protocol (HTTP), serves the files that form Web pages to Web users (whose computers contain HTTP clients that forward their requests).

webcam A video camera, usually attached directly to a computer, whose current or latest image is requestable from a Web site. A *live cam* is continually providing new images that are transmitted in rapid succession or, in some cases, in streaming video. Also called a *home-cam*.

webcasting Using the Internet, and the World Wide Web in particular, to broadcast information. Unlike typical surfing, which relies on a pull method of transferring Web pages, webcasting uses push technologies.

Webmaster An individual who manages a Web site.

WebTV Now owned by Microsoft, WebTV was one of the first entries in the much-publicized convergence of the Web with television. A set-top box similar to a cable TV box must be purchased and an access service acquired. This allows the user to browse Web pages using a WebTV's browser.

weighted fair queuing (WFQ) Part of a suite of protocols used to deliver QoS.

well-known-port A designated port assigned to TCP/IP applications and the programs that reside on top of TCP and UDP.

WFQ *See* weighted fair queuing.

whiteboard An area on a display screen that multiple users can write or draw on. Whiteboards are a principal component of teleconferencing applications because they enable visual as well as audio communication.

Whois An Internet directory service that returns information about a domain name or IP address. It is used to look up records in InterNIC's main database for second-level domains. Whois can be used as a program, by Telneting to *ds.internic.net*, or by going to *http://rs.internic.net/cgi-bin/whois*. Whois performs generic, string-based searches on several databases maintained by InterNIC, the most important of these being the domain registration database. Whois provides information about who owns an Internet host or domain and whom you can contact regarding that host or domain. A Whois request displays a contact name, mailing address, telephone number, and network mailbox for all users and organizations that are registered with one of the official Whois servers, such as the Internet Network Information Center (InterNIC) database.

 You can go directly to the Network Solutions Whois web interface at *http://www.network solutions.com/cgi-bin/ whois/whois.*

wide area network (WAN) Generally, a data communications network that spans geographically separate areas, such as from one building to another or from one region to another. Usually WANs are furnished by third parties, such as phone companies or public data networks. They cover long-haul areas and usually utilize public telephone circuits; WANs are managed and sold to users. WANs have transmission capacities in the Kbps range, compared to LANs, which are in the Mbps range. WANs are often made up of routers, DSUs, and digital leased lines to provide internetwork connections. Frame relay, SMDS, and X.25 are examples of WANs. *See* WAN Protocols, Internet, internet, LAN, *and* network.

wide-area information servers (WAIS) An Internet system in which specialized subject databases are created at multiple server locations, kept track of by a directory of servers at one location, and made accessible for searching by users with WAIS client programs.

wildcard mask An address mask specified when setting up access lists. It is used in conjunction with an IP address to determine which bits in an IP address should be ignored when comparing that address with another IP address.

WIMP *See* windows, icons, menus, and pointing device.

Win32 The Windows API for developing 32-bit applications.

window (*a*) An enclosed, rectangular area on a display screen. Most modern operating systems and applications have graphical user interfaces that let a user divide the display into several windows. Within each window, a different program can be run or different data displayed. Windows are particularly valuable in multitasking environments, which allow the user to execute several programs at once. By dividing a display into windows, a user can see the output from all the programs at the same time. To enter input into a program, the desired window is clicked on to make it the foreground process. (*b*) One of the fundamental elements of the transport's state that can be controlled to affect the QoS provided to the client. It represents the number of user-data carrying packets that may be multicast into the Web during a heartbeat by a single member.

window manager A program in the X windowing system that controls size, placement, and operation of windows on the root window. The window manager includes the functional window frames that surround each window object as well as a menu for the root window.

window-based program A program written for use with a windowing system; either an X-Window environment or a Microsoft Windows environment.

Windows 95 A major release of the Microsoft Windows operating system, premiered in 1995. Windows 95 represents a significant advance over its precursor, Windows 3.1. In addition to a new user interface, Windows 95 also includes a number of important internal improvements. Perhaps most important, it supports 32-bit applications, which means that applications written specifically for this operating system should run much faster.

Windows 98 An upgrade of Windows 95. Windows 98 offers support for a number of new technologies, including FAT32, AGP, MMX, USB, DVD, and ACPI. Its most visible feature, though, is the *Active Desktop*, which integrates the Web browser (Internet Explorer) with the operating system. From the user's point of view, there is no difference between accessing a document residing locally on the user's hard disk or on a Web server halfway around the world.

W

Windows CE A downsized version of the Windows operating system designed for small devices such as personal digital assistants (PDAs) (or handheld PCs in the Microsoft vernacular). The Windows CE graphical user interface (GUI) is very similar to Windows 95, so devices running Windows CE should be easy to operate for anyone familiar with Windows 95.

windows, icons, menus, and pointing device (WIMP) A user interface made famous by the Macintosh computer and later imitated by the Windows operating systems. Most people now use the term *graphical user interface (GUI)* to refer to this type of interface, but it's important to note that when the first GUIs were invented in the 1970s, WIMP was just one possible variation.

windows internet naming service (WINS) A system that determines the IP address associated with a particular network computer. This is called *name resolution*. WINS supports network client and server computers running Windows and can provide name resolution for other computers with special arrangements. Determining the IP address for a computer is a complex process when DHCP servers assign IP addresses dynamically. For example, it is possible for DHCP to assign a different IP address to a client each time the machine logs on to the network. WINS uses a distributed database that is automatically updated with the names of computers currently available and the IP address assigned to each one. DNS is an alternative system for name resolution suitable for network computers with fixed IP addresses.

Windows NT The most advanced version of the Windows operating system. Windows NT is a 32-bit operating system that supports pre-emptive multitasking. There are actually two versions of Windows NT: Windows NT Server, designed to act as a server in networks, and Windows NT Workstation for standalone or client workstations.

WinFrame A technology developed by Citrix Systems that turns Windows NT into a multiuser operating system. Together with another Citrix technology called ICA, WinFrame enables a Windows NT server to function like a minicomputer.

WINS *See* windows internet naming service.

Winsock Windows Socket. An application programming interface (API) for developing Windows programs that can communicate with other machines via the TCP/IP protocol. Windows 95 and Windows NT come with a dynamic link library (DLL) called winsock.dll that implements the API and acts as the glue between Windows programs and TCP/IP connections.

Wireless Application Protocol (WAP) A specification for a set of communication protocols to standardize the way that wireless devices, such as cellular telephones and radio transceivers, can be used for Internet access, including e-mail, the Web, newsgroups, and Internet Relay Chat (IRC).

wiring closet Specially designed room that serves as a centralized junction point for wiring a data or voice network.

WISCNET A TCP/IP network that was founded in 1990 by 24 public and private colleges and universities in the State of Wisconsin to bring Internet access to their faculty, staff, and students.

 For more information, see *http://www.wiscnet.net/*.

word processing The process of using a computer to create, edit, and print documents.

word processor A program or computer that enables you to perform word processing functions.

workgroup computing A collaborative effort by a workgroup having individual computers connected to a network that allows them to send e-mail to one another, share data files, and schedule meetings. Sophisticated workgroup systems allow users to define workflows so that data is automatically forwarded to appropriate people at each stage of a process.

workgroup switching Method of switching that provides high-speed (100-Mbps) transparent bridging between Ethernet networks and high-speed translational bridging between Ethernet and CDDI or FDDI.

workgroup A collection of workstations and servers on a local area network (LAN) designed to communicate and exchange data with one another.

workstation (WS) A type of computer used for engineering applications (CAD/CAM), desktop publishing, software development, and other types of applications that require a moderate amount of computing power and relatively high-quality graphics capabilities. In networking, a workstation is any computer connected to a local area network, whether a NetPC or a personal computer.

World Wide Web (WWW) A graphical, point-and-click-based interface to the Internet. Before the Web, individual Internet computers had windowing systems and graphical capabilities, but network tools, like e-mail, FTP and Telnet, were still text based. With the Web's graphical interface, it is now possible to jump from one document to another simply by clicking a mouse button. A user can connect to a Web site, download a graphical page, use a mouse to click on an item of interest, and load another page. Applications called *Web browsers* make it easy to access the World Wide Web; two of the most popular are Netscape Navigator and Microsoft's Internet Explorer.

World Wide Web Consortium (W3C) An international consortium of companies involved with the Internet and the Web. The W3C was founded in 1994 by Tim Berners-Lee, the original architect of the World Wide Web. The organization's purpose is to develop open standards, so that the Web evolves in a single direction rather than being splintered among competing factions.

worm A special type of virus that can replicate itself and use memory, but does not attach itself to other programs.

wrap Action taken by an FDDI or CDDI based network to recover in the event of a network failure. Wrapping occurs as the stations on each side of the failure reconfigure themselves, creating a single logical ring out of the primary and secondary rings, in essence wrapping the network back around itself.

wrapper Software that accompanies resources or other software for the purposes of improving convenience, compatibility, or security. For example, a wrapper is used to compress and encrypt software that is being sold over the Internet. The term can also apply to hardware; the casing around a Pentium II CPU is called a wrapper.

write To copy data from main memory to a storage device, such as a disk.

write-back cache A caching method in which modifications to data in the cache aren't copied to the cache source until necessary. Write-back caching yields somewhat better performance than *write-through caching* because it reduces the number of write operations to main memory. With this performance improvement comes a slight risk that data may be lost if the system crashes. A write-back cache is also called a *copy-back cache*.

WS *See* workstation.

WWW *See* World Wide Web.

WYSIWYG What You See Is What You Get. Pronounced wizzy-wig. A WYSIWYG application is one that enables the user to see on the display screen exactly what will appear when the document is printed. This differs, for example, from word processors that are incapable of displaying different fonts and graphics on the display screen, even though the formatting codes have been inserted into the file. WYSIWYG is especially popular for desktop publishing.

WYSIWYP What You See Is What You Print. Pronounced wizzy-whip. The ability of a computer system to print colors exactly as they appear on a monitor. WYSIWYP printing requires a special program, called a *color management system (CMS)*, to calibrate the monitor and printer.

W

X

X application An application program that conforms to X protocol standards.

X library A collection of C language routines based on the X protocol.

X protocol A protocol that uses TCP as a transport mechanism. It supports asynchronous, event-driven distributed window environments. It can work across heterogeneous platforms.

X server A server of connections to X terminals in a distributed network that uses the X Window System. It may be seem like a server of applications in multiple windows, but applications in the remote X server computer make client requests for the services of a windows manager that runs in each terminal. X servers are typically installed in a UNIX-based operating system in a mainframe, minicomputer, or workstation.

X terminal A terminal and machine specifically designed to run an X server. In this type of environment, X clients are run on remote systems. A diskless terminal especially designed to provide a low-cost user interface for applications that run a network X server as part of a distributed X Window System. These terminals allow users simultaneous access to several different applications and resources in a multivendor environment through the implementation of X Windows.

X toolkit A collection of high-level programs based on programming from the X library.

X.121 ITU-T standard describing an addressing scheme used in X.25 networks.

X.2 A technology developed by US Robotics (now 3COM) for delivering data rates up to 56 Kbps over plain old telephone service (POTS). It was long believed that the maximum data transmission rate over copper telephone wires was 33.6 Kbps, but X2 achieves higher rates by taking advantage of the fact that most

phone switching stations are connected by high-speed digital lines. X2 bypasses the normal digital-to-analog conversion and sends the digital data over the telephone wires directly to your modem where it is decoded.

X.3 An ITU-T recommendation that defines various PAD parameters used in X.25 networks. *See* PAD *and* X.25.

X.21 A protocol used primarily in Europe and Japan, as an ITU-T standard for serial communications over synchronous digital lines such as x.25.

X.21bis ITU-T standard that defines the physical-layer protocol for communication between DCE and DTE in an X.25 network. Virtually equivalent to EIA/TIA-232.

X.25 For packet-switched WAN technology, a standard approved by the CCITT (now the ITU), which defines Layers 1, 2, and 3 in the OSI reference model and is based on an IBM product called *synchronous data link control (SDLC)*. ISO further modified it to become *high level data link control (HDLC)*. HDLC was adopted by CCITT as part of its X.25 network access standard, where it is known as *link access protocol (LAP)*; a later version known as LAPB. X.25 level 3 is an extension of X.25 level 2 to provide networking functions.

X.25 Level3 *See* PLP.

X.25 Protocol *See* PLP.

X.28 Adopted as a standard by the Consultative Committee for International Telegraph and Telephone (CCITT), as a commonly used network protocol. It is the ITU-T recommendation that defines the terminal-to-PAD interface in X.25 networks.

X.29 A standard that allows computers on different public networks (such as CompuServe, Tymnet, or a TCP/IP network) to communicate through an intermediary computer at the network layer level. X.29's protocols correspond closely to the data-link and physical-layer protocols defined in the Open Systems Interconnection (OSI) communication model.

X.75 The ITU-T specification that defines the signaling system between two PDNs. X.75 is essentially an network-to-network interface (NNI).

X.400 The messaging (notably e-mail) standard specified by the International Telecommunications Union-Telecommunication Standard Sector (ITU-TS). It is an alternative to the more prevalent e-mail protocol, *simple mail transfer protocol (SMTP)*.

X.500 The ITU-T recommendation covering the implementation of addressing databases for devices attached to a network. The basis for Novell's and Banyan's directory services. It is a standard way to develop an electronic directory of people in an organization so that it can be part of a global directory available to anyone in the world with Internet access. Such a directory is sometimes called a *global white pages directory*. A user can look up people in a user-friendly way by name, department, or organization.

X.509 The most widely used standard for defining digital certificates. X.509 is actually an ITU recommendation, which means that it has not yet been officially defined or approved. As a result, companies have implemented the standard in different ways. For example, both Netscape and Microsoft use X.509 certificates to implement secure sockets layer (SSL) in their Web servers and browsers, but an X.509 Certificate generated by Netscape may not be readable by Microsoft products, and vice versa.

XAPIA X.400 API Association

X-CV An X interface between a customer TMN and a VASP TMN.

XDSL A technology for bringing high-bandwidth information to homes and small businesses over ordinary copper telephone lines. It can be synchronous or asynchronous; the X represents the various forms of digital sub-scriber line (DSL) technologies, which includes ADSL, R-ADSL, HDSL, SDSL, or VDSL. All DSL technologies run on existing copper phone lines and use modulation to boost transmission rates, whereas the different approaches (ADSL, RADSL, HDSL, SDSL, and VDSL) are best suited to different applications. *See* Digital Subscriber Line.

Xenix A version of UNIX that runs on PCs. Xenix was developed by Microsoft Corporation and is compatible with AT&T's System V definition.

Xeon A line of Pentium II chipsets from Intel, introduced in 1998. Unlike previous Pentium II chips, which used a Slot 1 form factor, Xeon chips use Slot 2. This allows for faster data transfers between the CPU and L2 cache. Xeon chip speeds start at 400 MHz.

Xerox Best known for its copier machines, Xerox Corporation has also had a profound influence on the computer industry. During the '70s and '80s, its Palo Alto Research Center conducted pioneering work on user interfaces. Many of its inventions, such as the *mouse* and the *graphical user interface (GUI)*, have since become commonplace. Xerox continues to do groundbreaking research, especially in the area of document management.

Xerox Network Standard (XNS) A protocol suite originally designed by PARC. Many PC networking companies, such as 3Com, Banyan, Novell, and UB Networks, used or currently use a variation of XNS as their primary transport protocol.

XI An SNA X.25 interface.

XID Exchange identification. Request and response packets exchanged prior to a session between a router and a token ring host. If the parameters of the serial device contained in the XID packet do not match the configuration of the host, the session is dropped.

XIPC A middleware product that manages interprocess communication (IPC) across programs in a network. A process is a unit of work associated with a particular user request (for example). Completing that work usually involves creating other processes or communicating between processes.

XJACK A type of connector for notebook computer modems that allows a standard telephone connector to snap into the modem. Internal modems for notebook computers come on a slim PCMCIA card.

XMI *See* XML metadata interchange.

XML Extensible Markup Language. A new specification being developed by the W3C that enables a flexible way to create common information formats and share both the format and the data on the Web, intranets, and elsewhere. XML is a pared-down version of SGML, designed especially for Web documents. It enables designers to create their own customized tags to provide functionality not available with HTML. For example, computer makers might agree on a standard or common way to describe the information about a computer product (processor speed, memory size, and so forth) and then describe the product information format with XML.

XML metadata interchange (XMI) A proposed use of the Extensible Markup Language (XML) that is intended to provide a standard way for programmers and other users to exchange information about metadata. Specifically, XMI is intended to help programmers using the Unified Modeling Language (UML) with different languages and development tools to exchange their data models with each other.

XML Query Language (XQL) A way to locate and filter the elements and text in an extensible markup language (XML) document. XML files are used to transmit collections of data between computers on the Web. XQL provides a tool for finding and/or selecting out specific items in the data collection in an XML file or set of files. It is based on the pattern syntax

used in the extensible stylesheet language (XSL) and is proposed as an extension to it.

Xmodem An error-correcting protocol for modems that was created in 1978 by Ward Christensen and has since become a de facto standard. Modems that agree on using the Xmodem protocol send data in 128-byte blocks. If a block is received successfully, a positive (ACK) acknowledgment is returned. If an error is detected, a negative (NAK) acknowledgment is returned and the block is resent. Xmodem uses the checksum method of error checking.

XMS Extended Memory Specification. A procedure developed jointly by AST Research, Intel Corporation, Lotus Development, and Microsoft Corporation for using extended memory and DOS's high memory area, a 64K block just above 1MB.

Xon/Xoff A protocol for controlling the flow of data between computers and other devices on an asynchronous serial connection.

X-PP X interface between two PNO TMNs.

XQL *See* XML Query Language.

XRemote A unique protocol developed to optimize support for X Windows over a serial communications link.

X-VP X interface between a VASP TMN and a PNO TMN.

X-Window Sometimes referred to as "X" or as "XWindows." An open, cross-platform, client/server system for managing a windowed graphical user interface in a distributed network. Developed at the Massachusetts Institute of Technology (MIT), the original design intent was to provide distributed computing support for the development of programs. It supports two-dimensional bitmapped graphics, and almost all UNIX graphical interfaces, including Motif and OpenLook, which are all based on X-Window.

X

Y2K *See* Year 2000 problem.

Yahoo! Yet Another Hierarchical Officious Oracle. A directory of Web sites organized in a hierarchy of topic categories. It was the first such directory with a large following and, by all accounts, continues to be the most popular Web directory. As a directory, it provides both new and seasoned Web users the reassurance of a structured view of hundreds of thousands of Web sites and millions of Web pages. The directory was started by David Filo and Jerry Yang at Stanford University. The two began compiling and categorizing Web pages in 1994.

Year 2000 problem The year 2000 (also known as "Y2K") is the pervasive problem for anyone who depends on a program in which the year is represented by a two-digit number, such as "97" for 1997. Many programs written 10 or 15 years ago, when storage limitations encouraged such information economies, are still running in many companies. Dates ending in "00" were translated by the computer as meaning "1900." This problem affected a vast amount of software, particularly accounting and database systems. A worldwide effort to correct this problem resulted in the almost flawless transition to the year 2000.

Yellow Book The specification for CD-ROMs and CD-ROM/XA.

Ymodem An error-correcting asynchronous communications protocol for modems that uses larger data blocks for greater efficiency. It was designed by Chuck Forsberg, and extends Xmodem. Unlike Xmodem, a batch mode is provided, along with an increase in the transfer block size and support for batch file transfers. A user can specify a list of files and send them all at one time.

yottabyte Equal to 1,024 *zettabytes*; approximately 10 to the 24th power or (1,000,000,000,000,000,000,000,000) bytes (2 to the 80th power bytes). The name "yotta" was supposedly chosen because it's the second-to-last last letter of the Latin alphabet and also sounds like the Greek letter "iota."

z coordinate The third-dimensional coordinate (*z*) in a *volume pixel*, or *voxel*, which together with *x* and *y* coordinates, defines a location in a three-dimensional space.

Z Object Publishing Environment (Zope) A Web site builder and application server that uses the idea that it is "publishing" objects rather than merely providing content that will be added to a Web page. Zope's proponents believe that it is competitive with site builders and application servers such as ColdFusion and the Netscape Application Server. Zope is free software with open source code.

Z39.50 An American National Standards Institute (ANSI/NISO) standard communications protocol for the search and retrieval of bibliographic data in online databases. It is used on the Internet to search the online public access catalogues (OPAC) of library holdings, as well as to link disparate OPACs into a single "union" OPAC.

zap A precise and immediate correction for a computer programming problem. When a bug is detected after the software is released, the only way to fix the already compiled code is to overlay the bad code with a sequence of good code. This overlaying is known as zapping and the fix itself is a zap. IBM provides its mainframe software customers with a special program for applying zaps that is called SuperZap.

zero code suppression Line coding scheme used for transmission clocking, which substitutes a one in the seventh bit of a string of eight consecutive zeros. *See* ones density.

Zero Insertion Force (ZIF) A socket that connects the computer motherboard to the data bus in Intel's 486 and Pentium microprocessors, up to Pentium II. It is designed for ease of manufacture and to easily enable computer owners to upgrade the microprocessor.

zettabyte Equal to 1,024 *exabytes*, or 2 to the 70th power bytes. Approximately 10 to the

21st power (1,000,000,000,000,000,000,000) bytes.

ZIF *See* zero insertion force.

ZIP A popular data compression format that enables files to take up less space in storage or take less time when sent to someone over the Internet. Files that have been compressed with the ZIP format are called ZIP files and usually end with a .zip extension. Several popular tools exist for zipping: PKZIP in the DOS operating system, WinZip and NetZip in Windows, MacZip for Macintosh users, and Zip and UnZip in UNIX systems.

Zip drive A small, portable, high-capacity floppy disk drive, trademarked and developed by Iomega Corporation, used primarily for backing up and archiving personal computer files. Zip disks are slightly larger than conventional floppy disks, and about twice as thick, with the capacity to hold up to 100 megabytes of data or the equivalent of 70 floppy diskettes.

ZIP storm Broadcast storm that occurs when a router running AppleTalk propagates a route. It currently has no corresponding zone name, so the route is typically forwarded by downstream routers, and a ZIP storm ensues. *See* ZIP.

ZIT *See* Zone Information Protocol.

Zmodem An asynchronous communications error-correcting protocol for modems that provides faster data transfer rates and better error detection than Xmodem. In particular, Zmodem supports larger block sizes and if a block arrives and an error is detected, a "NAK" (negative acknowledgment) is returned and the block is resent, enabling the transfer to resume where it left off following a communications failure.

zombie An abandoned and sadly out-of-date Web site that for some reason has been moved

Z

to another Web address. A ghost site. Zombies contribute to *linkrot*, or the degradation of hyperlinks in active Web sites.

Zombie computer A computer, typically Solaris-based, that has been compromised and has had a DDoS program installed without the knowledge of its owner that will control the generation of packets towards the intended victim. Zombie computers are also known as agents since they respond to commands from other systems. *See* handlers.

Zombie network A term used in a DDoS attack that describes the linking of multiple zombie computers into a "virtual" disributed network allowing hackers to coordinate their operation to initiate a DDoS against a target. Key in this network is the installation of one of the four commonly acknowledged DDoS programs: TRN, TRN2K, Trinoo, and Stacheldraht.

Zone Information Protocol (ZIP) An AppleTalk protocol that maintains a table in each router, called the *zone information table*, that lists the relationship between zone names and networks.

zone name A name defined for each zone in an AppleTalk network. A LocalTalk network can have just one zone name. Ethernet and token-ring networks can have multiple zone names, called a *zone list*.

zone of authority In the domain name system, the group of names authorized by a given name server.

zone In AppleTalk, a logical grouping of devices in an AppleTalk internet that makes it easier for users to locate network services. The network administrator defines zones during the router setup process.

zoo A Web site that holds collections of Internet viruses. These sites may be illegal in certain countries. Integralis, sellers of MIMEsweeper, a content security product, uses the term on their Web site.

Zope *See* Z Object Publishing Environment.

ZV port Zoomed video port. A port that enables data to be transferred directly from a PC card to a VGA controller. This technology supports the delivery of full-screen motion video and multimedia to notebook computers. The ZV port allows special software and a version of the PC card called a *ZV port card* to provide a separate dedicated, point-to-point bus or path from continuously arriving video signals directly to the display controller so that they do not need to be handled by the main bus or the CPU.

APPENDIX

Data Communications

Everyone who has ever had to deal with data communications has shuddered at least once. Telecommunications engineers, data processing personnel, and vendors alike all throw data communication terms around as though they were going out of style. The interesting point is that many of them really don't understand what they are talking about. Many people think: "If I learn the buzzwords, everyone will think I know what I'm talking about." Nothing could be further from the truth; these folks make complete fools of themselves in front of knowledgeable professionals. However, there is really no a mystique associated with the use of data communications. Although some complexities do exist in this technology, the basics are fairly straightforward. If you can surmount the initial hurdle of setting up a data transmission, the rest can be fairly well assimilated.

In 1997, for the first time in the history of the telecommunications industry, data was carried across the networks in an equal share as voice. This showed the heavy emphasis on the growth of data communications. As we begin the new millennium, the growth of voice on the networks is averaging between 3 and 4 percent per year. However, data is growing at a rate of 30 percent per year. It will take 12 years to double the amount of voice carried on the network today at the current growth rate, whereas the data is doubling approximately every 90 days. It is important to understand that the data world grew out of the voice world. Voice traditionally paid for the data transmissions on the network, and still today, 90 percent of all the revenues generated across the wide area networks are the result of voice usage. But that will all change quickly as we enter the new millennium. The use of the analog dial-up network is where it all started. In order to communicate from a terminal, computer, or other piece of equipment, you merely have to put the pieces together in the proper order:

- Select and deal with the transmission media

- Use communicating devices that will present the proper signal to the line (the communicating device is called the DCE)

- Add a device called the data terminal equipment (DTE)

- Set up or abide by accepted rules (protocols)

- Use a pre-established alphabet that the devices understand

- Ensure the integrity of information before, during, and after transmission

- Deliver the information to the receiving device

This appendix demystifies the elements involved in all data communications processes. Later chapters focus on specific technologies, using the concepts and terminology introduced here.

Concepts

Like learning computer programming, learning data communications technology is a nonlinear process. That is, whatever starting point one chooses, one almost has to use terms that will be defined elsewhere. The usual solution to this problem is *iterative teaching*: teach a basic set of concepts, then go back and both use and expand on those concepts, refining them along the way. Our basic set begins with a discussion of some important concepts that permeate the world of data communications.

The material in this Appendix originally appeared in the *Voice and Data Communications Handbook, Third Edition*, by Regis J. "Bud" Bates and Donald W. Gregory (McGraw-Hill: 2000).

Those concepts include:

- Standards
- Architectures
- Protocols
- Error detection
- Plexes
- Multiplexing
- Compression
- Standards

A *standard* is a definition or description of a technology. The purpose of developing standards is to help vendors build components that will function together or that will facilitate use by providing consistency with other products. This section discusses what standards are, why they exist, and some of the ways they could affect you. Specific standards are mentioned in other sections where applicable.

There are two kinds of standards: de facto and de jure.

De facto means *in fact*. If more than one vendor "builds to" or complies with a particular technology, one can reasonably refer to that technology as a standard. An excellent example of such a standard in data communications is IBM's Systems Network Architecture (SNA). No independent standards organization has ever "blessed" SNA as an "official," or de jure, standard. But dozens, if not hundreds, of other vendors have built products that successfully interact with SNA devices and networks.

Note that de facto standards rarely become standards overnight. SNA was available for some time before vendors other than IBM could or would provide products that supported it.

Moreover, some technologies become standards because the creating vendors intend them to become standards (e.g., Ethernet), while others become standards despite the creating vendors (e.g., Lotus 1-2-3 menu structure).

De jure means *in law*, although standards do not generally have the force of law. In some parts of the world, when a standard is set, it in fact becomes law. If a user or vendor violates the rules, the penalties can be quite severe. A user who installs a nonstandard piece of equipment on the links could be subject to steep fines and up to one year in prison. These countries take their standards seriously. In the United States, no such penalties exist; we are more relaxed in this area. But a standard is a de jure standard if an independent standards body (i.e., one not solely sponsored by vendors) successfully carries it through a more or less public standards-making procedure and announces that it is now a standard.

You might well ask, "What's the difference? And who cares, anyway?" But understanding which technologies fall into which category, if either, can be a factor in deciding what to buy. Generally, de facto standards are controlled by the vendors that introduced them. For example, Microsoft Windows is a de facto standard; many vendors provide programs that comply with and operate in this environment. But if it decides to change the way a new version of Windows works, Microsoft in theory can obsolete all of those programs. (In practice, Microsoft is most unlikely to do this, at least intentionally, because much of its market power stems from the fact that all those other products are built to its standard. Were Microsoft to make such a change, it is likely that those other software providers would look elsewhere for a target operating system. Microsoft's stock would drop precipitously, to say the least!)

One reason that vendors often build to de facto standards is that the standards-making process tends to be somewhat lengthy. A minimum of a 4- to 12-year period to come out with a new or revised standard is not at all uncommon in the industry. With product cycles under one year in some areas of the communications industry, waiting for finalization of a standard before introducing a product could result in corporate suicide. Ethernet is a good example of a standard that started as a de facto standard. Intel, Xerox, and Digital Equipment Corporation (DEC) introduced Ethernet with the intent of making it a de jure standard. But that process took years, and the final result was slightly different than the technology originally created by the three vendors. Nonetheless, many networks were created based on Ethernet before the 802.3 de jure standard was finalized, bringing profit to its creators and operating environments to their customers.

In the real world, the standards-making bodies rely in large part on vendors to develop the details of new and revised standards. In fact, most standards bodies have vendor representatives as full participants. It is a fascinating political process with much pushing and pulling to gain advantage in the market. The vendors participate for several reasons, not the least of which is to get the jump on competitors that are not as close to the process. Other reasons include the ability to state in marketing materials that they contributed to or were involved in testing of a new standard, as well as the opportunity to influence the actual details of a standard to favor technology that the vendors are most familiar with.

To be fair, it should be stated that the primary goal of most of those involved in the standards process is to define a good and useful standard. But when the process produces a dual standard, as in the case of the Ethernet and Token Ring local area network standards, one can presume that the "best" was compromised somewhat in favor of what could be agreed on.

Even de jure standards (usually identifiable by virtue of their unintelligible alphanumeric designations, such as X.25, V.35, V.42 bis, etc.) change in ways that significantly affect the market—and you. One set of standards that affects thousands of users is the set of modem standards, discussed later. But beware a vendor that trumpets compliance with a "new standard!" The vendor's claim might be legitimate, but if no other vendors have products available in the same space, the company might simply be hyping its own product in hopes that it eventually will become a standard. Or there might be a standard under development but not yet approved. In the latter case, if that standard changes before final approval, the vendor's current products will instantly become nonstandard without changing in any way!

In the recent past, the standards committees were working on a new modulation technique to speed up data communications. The standards committees were locked in discussion about the rules to be applied. Yet, at the same time, every modem manufacturer began producing a new modem that was advertised and sold as compatible or compliant with the new V.Fast or V.34 standard. It was not yet a completed standard, but the manufacturers wanted to get their products on the shelves as quickly as possible and corral their piece of the market. So they produced a product with a disclaimer that offered a free or minimal cost upgrade to the V.34 standards if the standard changed. This is a classic example of industry leaders setting the pace before the standards were completed.

Architectures

As with constructing a building, an overall design is needed when planning a communications environment. For a building, that design is described by architectural drawings. A communications architecture is a coordinated set of design guidelines that together constitute a complete description of one approach to building a communications environment.

Several communications architectures have been developed. Some of the best-known include IBM's SNA and DEC's DNA. The newest architecture to run away with the industry and the fancy of all developers is the Internet architecture using TCP and IP protocols. Every day new applications and protocols are being developed to run on the Internet architecture. This includes voice, data, streaming audio and video, and multimedia applications.

The data communications architectures were modeled after the voice architectures. This is understandable, because data is merely a logical extension of the dial-up voice network. Devices are therefore constructed to fit into the overall voice network operation. Data equipment is designed and built to mimic the characteristics of a human speech pattern. Now, however, we see that voice is data and data is, too! This paradigm shift marks the true convergence of voice and data onto a single architecture. The world appears ready to embrace the technologies that will fall out from this convergence.

Protocols

Protocols are key components of communications architectures. Architectures are guidelines on how environments connecting two or more devices can be constructed, so most components of a given architecture in a network will be found on each communicating computer in that network. Protocols provide the rules for communications between counterpart components on different devices.

There is one aspect of protocols that also applies to hardware: whether they are synchronous or asynchronous. These key characteristics are covered in the following section.

Transmission Protocols (Synchronous vs. Asynchronous)

All lower-level data communications protocols fall into one of the two following categories: synchronous or asynchronous. The words themselves are based on Greek roots indicating that they either are "in" or "with" time (*synchronous*) or "out of" or "separated from" time (*asynchronous*). The underlying meanings are quite accurate, so long as one understands to what they must be applied.

All data communications depend on precise timing, or clocking. But how does the equipment determine precisely when the middle of a bit time occurs? The answer is clocking; equipment at both ends of a circuit must be synchronized during transmission so that the receiver and the sender agree regarding beginnings, middles, and ends of bits during transmissions. There are two fundamentally different ways to do this clocking: asynchronously and synchronously.

Simply put, asynchronous transmissions are clocked (or synchronized) one byte at a time. Synchronous transmissions are clocked in groups of bytes. But the differences in how these two approaches work go beyond the differences between individual bytes and groups of bytes.

Asynchronous communications is also called start/stop communications and has the following characteristics.

Every byte has added to it one bit signaling the beginning of the byte (the *start bit*) and at least one bit (possibly two) added at the end of the byte (the *stop bits*). Bytes with 7 data bits typically also include a parity bit (which is an error-checking bit), whereas 8-data-bit bytes

usually do not. Thus, generally speaking, 10 or 11 total bits are actually transmitted for every asynchronous byte. To get 7 usable data bits, we must transmit approximately 10 to 11; strictly speaking, we use a 30 to 35 percent overhead. Fig. A.1 shows the layout of a data byte in an asynchronous form. This was a special concern when data communications was initially used in the late 1950s and early 1960s. Back then, the cost per minute of a dial-up line was $0.60 to $0.65. Using that value, 30 cents of every dollar were spent just to provide the timing for the line. This amount of waste concerned everyone.

This also makes nominal speed calculations for such connections easy: dividing the rated speed of the circuit (e.g., 9600 bits per second) by 10 bits per byte gives a transmission speed in characters per second (e.g., 960 cps). As a rule, we divide the bits per second by 10 to get the nominal speed of an asynchronous circuit. (*Nominal* here means best-case; in the real world, circuits rarely deliver 100 percent of their nominal capacity. But it's a starting point for capacity calculations.)

The bytes are sent out without regard to the timing of previous and succeeding bytes. That means that none of the components in a circuit ever assume that just because one byte just went by, another will follow in any particular period of time. Think of a person banging away on a keyboard. The speed and number of characters sent in a given period does not indicate in any way how many or how quickly characters can be sent in the succeeding similar period.

Clocking is controlled by data terminal equipment (DTE). For example, when a personal computer is used to dial into CompuServe, clocking on bytes going toward the service is generated by the sending PC

Figure A.1 *To send 7 usable bits of data, we must use 1 start, 1 parity, and 1 or 2 stop bits.*

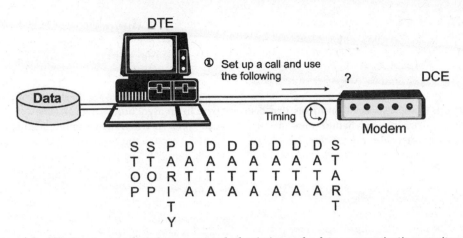

Figure A.2 *The data terminal equipment controls the timing to the data communications equipment (modem), as the bits are sent in an asynchronous protocol—a start bit and 1 or 2 stop bits help to set the timing.*

(see Fig. A.2). That first start bit reaching the modem begins the sequence, with all succeeding bits in the same byte arriving in lockstep at the agreed-on rate until the stop bit is received. Then clocking stops until the beginning of the next byte arrives. Any intervening devices (especially modems) between the communicating DTEs take the clocking from the data sent by the originating DTE for any given byte.

Most PC and minicomputer terminal communications employ asynchronous techniques. The default communications ports on PCs (the "serial" or COM ports) only support asynchronous communications. To use synchronous communications on a PC, a special circuit board is required.

Synchronous communications have the following characteristics:

■ Blocks of data rather than individual bytes (characters) are transmitted.

■ Individual bytes do not have any additional bits added to them on a byte-by-byte basis, except for parity.

However, bytes are sent and clocked in contiguous groups of one or more bytes. Each group is immediately (with no intervening time) preceded by a minimum of two consecutive synchronization bytes (a special character defined by the specific synchronous protocol, of which there are many) that begin the clocking. All succeeding bits in the group are sent in lockstep until the last bit of the last byte is sent, followed (still in lockstep) by an end-of-block byte. This layout of the synchronous characters (SYN) is shown in Fig. A.3.

Clocking is controlled by data communications equipment (DCE). Specifically, on any given circuit one specific DCE component is optioned (i.e., configured) at installation time as the master device. When the circuit is otherwise idle, the master generates the same syn-

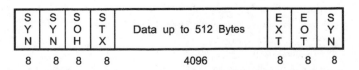

S Y N	S Y N	S O H	S T X	Data up to 512 Bytes	E X T	E O T	S Y N
8	8	8	8	4096	8	8	8

Figure A.3 *The layout of the data transmitted synchronously. In this case, the block size is 512 bytes.*

chronization character mentioned above on a periodic basis to all other DCE devices so that all DCE clocks on the circuit are maintained in continuous synchronization.

Except in cases where smaller numbers of bytes (fewer than about 20) are sent at a time, synchronous communications makes more efficient use of a circuit, as can be seen from Table A.1.

Generally speaking, all circuits running at greater than 2400 bits per second actually operate in synchronous mode over the wire. This is simply because building modems to reliably operate asynchronously at higher speeds over analog circuits is much more difficult than taking this approach. Asynchronous modems that run faster than 2400 bits per second actually incorporate asynchronous-to-synchronous converters; they communicate asynchronously to their respective DTEs but synchronously between the modems as shown in Fig. A.4. This doesn't normally impact performance: when smaller groups of characters are sent, there is time to include the additional overhead for synchronous transmission. When larger groups are sent, the reduced overhead of synchronous transmission comes into play. In practice, these higher-speed modems actually communicate with other modems at even higher than their rated speeds; the extra bandwidth is used for overhead functions between the modems.

Error Detection

We mentioned at the beginning of this appendix that ensuring the integrity of the information was one of the key responsibilities of a data communications environment. This does not mean that the data must be kept honest. Rather, it means that we must somehow guarantee with an extremely high degree of probability that the information is received in exactly the same form as it was sent.

More precisely, there are two tasks required: detecting when transmission errors occur and triggering retransmissions in the event that an error is detected. It is the responsibility of protocols to trigger and manage retransmissions. Here we discuss some of the various approaches that have been developed to detect errors in the first place.

All of the code sets used in data communications (see the following) are designed to use all of their bits to represent characters (letters, numbers, other special characters). A not-so-obvious implication of this fact is that every byte received in such a code set is by definition a valid code. How can we detect whether the received code is the code that was sent?

The solution is to somehow send some additional information, some data about data (sometimes described as metadata) along with the primary data. All error-checking approaches depend on sending some additional data besides

Table A.1 *Comparison of the utilization of the circuit.*

Data Bytes	Asynchronous Bits	Synchronous Bits	Synchronous Savings
1	10	32	-220%
5	50	64	-28%
10	100	104	-4%
20	200	184	8%
30	300	264	12%
100	1000	824	18%
1000	10,000	8024	20%
10,000	100,000	80,024	20%

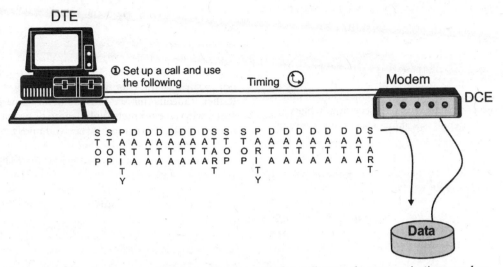

Figure A.4   The data communications equipment (modem) will set up the communications synchronously. Blocks are used to create the synchronous transfer.

the original application-related data. The additional data is created during the communications process, used to check the underlying data when it is received, and then discarded before the information is passed to its final destination.

In order of increasing reliability, the major methods used to detect data communications errors include:

- Parity bit, or vertical redundancy checking (VRC)

- Longitudinal redundancy checking (LRC)

- Cyclic redundancy checking (CRC)

Suppose you are my rich aunt and that I am living in Paris (to further my cultural education, of course) and have run out of money. I've called you (collect, of course) to request that you electronically transfer some money into my account at the Banque de Paris. In a fit of generosity, you have decided to send me $1000.00. If the network used is not perfectly reliable and appropriate error detection methods are not applied by the transmitting financial service, a change in a single character—for example, changing the period after the first three 0s to another 0—could result in your sending me considerably more money than you intended: a total of $1,000,000.

What are the chances of my getting my inheritance early in this way? Not very high, given the odds that only the decimal point would change, and only to a 0 (out of either 126 or 254 other possibilities). But consider the probability of detecting the error, assuming that it has occurred. Using parity bits, the likelihood of detecting this kind of error (which requires several bits to be wrong at one time to change an entire character) is about 65 percent. A somewhat better method, longitudinal redundancy checking, would up the odds of detection to about 85 percent. But the cyclic redundancy checking method improves the odds of detecting and correcting such a multibit error to 99.99995 percent.

Because the networks used to send monetary amounts generally use CRC techniques, it doesn't look as though I'm going to get rich because of their errors. But let's examine these methods in a bit more detail anyway.

Parity Bit/Vertical Redundancy Checking (VRC)

The parity bit approach to error detection simply adds a single "parity" bit to every character (or byte) sent. Whether the parity bit is set to 0 or 1 (the only two possibilities, of course) is calculated by the sending digital device and recalculated by the receiving device. If the calculations match, the associated character is considered good. Otherwise, an error is detected.

This is much simpler than it sounds. Two approaches are typically used: even and odd parity. Other forms of parity exist, such as mark or space parity. It makes no difference which is used; the only requirement is that the sending and receiving devices use the same approach. To illustrate even parity, consider the ASCII bit sequence representing a lower-case letter a: 1100001. Because we are using even parity, we require that the total number of 1 bits transmitted to the receiver to send this a, including the eighth parity bit, be equal to an even number. Their position in the underlying byte is irrelevant. If we count the 1s in the 7-bit pattern, we get 3, an odd number. Therefore we set the parity bit to 1, resulting

in 11100001, an 8-bit pattern with an even number of (i.e., four) 1s. (The parity bit is sent last. In our illustrations the bits farthest to the right are sent first, so we show the parity bit being added at the left.) Figure A.5 shows an ASCII illustration of the word *hello*, complete with even parity bits. As you can see from the illustration, the bytes are represented as vertical sets of numbers, thus vertical redundancy checking: if we orient the digits vertically, we add a vertical bit that is redundant to help check the correctness of the underlying byte. The vertical orientation is arbitrary, of course. However, when we illustrate longitudinal redundancy checking, you will see that there is a reason for this display approach.

Having gone to the trouble of describing parity bits, we must confess that they are of limited use in data communications. Parity checking will catch 100 percent of errors where the number of bits in error is odd (1, 3,

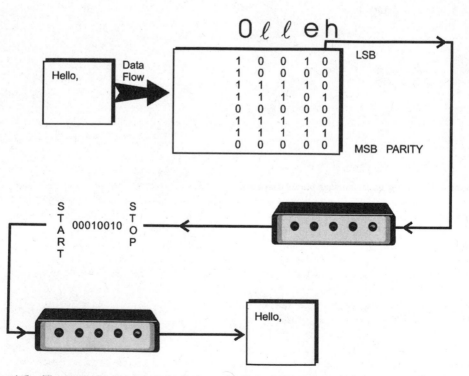

Figure A.5 *The vertical redundancy check shows the flow of data. The parity bit is added after each character is generated.*

5, etc.) . . . and none of the errors where the number of bits in error is even. Put another way, if an error occurs (and communications errors rarely affect only a single bit), there is only about a 65 percent chance that parity checking will detect it. (The probability is better than 50 percent because there are somewhat more one-bit errors than any one type of multibit error, whether the numbers of the latter are odd or even.)

Parity checking is used extensively inside computers. There it makes sense because it is entirely plausible that errors would occur one at a time (if they occur at all). Parity checking does well in this environment. Also, some networks (e.g., CompuServe) still have users set their communications software to use parity checking. But even CompuServe uses a more sophisticated protocol for file transfers. Some more sophisticated error detection protocols are described in the following paragraphs.

Longitudinal Redundancy Checking (LRC)

The concept of LRC follows directly from VRC, taking VRC a step further. This example uses 8-bit rather than 7-bit bytes. But LRC checking needs to operate on a group of bytes, rather than on one byte at a time. For this example, it doesn't really matter what the bits represent, so let us create a set of eight 8-bit bytes. As you will see, although the bit patterns do not matter for the example, the number of bytes used does (see Table A.2).

If we only use VRC (odd parity), as described above, we produce the pattern shown in Table A.3. But of course, we said that VRC only catches about 65 percent of errors, hardly acceptable. But what if we apply odd parity checking across the bytes in addition to vertically? In that case, the completely filled-in Table A.4 would be generated.

Adding both the horizontal and vertical checking, together referred to as longitudinal redundancy checking, improves the odds of detecting errors to about 85 percent. Not bad, although we wouldn't want to trust our money to such a transmission. But there is another disadvantage to LRC. Using 8-bit bytes for every eight data bytes, an additional two LRC bytes must be transmitted. That works out to 20 percent added overhead for error checking (2 LRC bytes divided by the 10 total bytes transmitted in the set), not counting any degradation due to time required to compute the check bytes. This is not an efficient error-checking mechanism. In fact, considering that error checking is only one of several sources of transmission overhead, it is abysmal.

LRC does have one advantage over cyclic redundancy checking (CRC), the approach discussed next: far fewer computational resources are required for calculating the LRC bytes than for calculating a CRC (unless the CRC is implemented with hardware). In fact,

Table A.2   Setting up for vertical parity checking.

1	0	1	0	1	0	1	0
0	0	1	0	0	0	1	0
1	1	1	0	1	1	1	0
1	0	1	0	0	0	1	0
0	1	1	0	0	1	1	0
1	1	1	0	1	1	1	0
0	1	1	0	0	1	1	0
1	0	1	0	1	0	1	0

Table A.3 *The parity bit is inserted in VRC.*

1	0	1	0	1	0	1	0
0	0	1	0	0	0	1	0
1	1	1	0	1	1	1	0
1	0	1	0	0	0	1	0
0	1	1	0	0	1	1	0
1	1	1	0	1	1	1	0
0	1	1	0	0	1	1	0
1	**1**	**0**	**1**	**0**	**1**	**0**	**1**

Table A.4 *The vertical and longitudinal redundancy checks are inserted here.*

1	0	1	0	1	0	1	0	1
0	0	1	0	0	0	1	0	1
1	1	1	0	1	1	1	0	1
1	0	1	0	0	0	1	0	0
0	1	1	0	0	1	1	0	1
1	1	1	0	1	1	1	0	1
0	1	1	0	0	1	1	0	1
1	1	0	1	0	1	0	1	0

until recent generations of PCs became available, with their vastly more powerful CPUs, CRC checking for asynchronous data communications in the PC environment was not practical because of its computationally intensive nature. Now, however, it is routinely used. Read on to see why.

Cyclic Redundancy Checking (CRC)

Although no practical error-checking algorithm can guarantee detection of every possible error pattern, CRC comes close. A complete explanation with examples of how CRC works would (and does, in several data communications textbooks) require several pages of somewhat hairy binary algebra. Rather than put you through that, we'll describe some of the method's key characteristics and indicate how this method is used.

Like the previously described approaches to error detection, CRC relies on on-the-fly calculation of an additional bit pattern (referred to as a *frame check sequence*, or FCS) that is sent immediately after the original block of data bits. The length of the FCS is chosen in advance by a software or hardware designer on the basis of how high a confidence level is required in the error-detection capability of the given transmission. All *burst errors*, or groups of bits randomized by transmission problems, with a length less than that of the FCS will be detected. Frequently used FCS lengths include 12, 16, and 32 bits. Obviously, the longer the FCS, the more errors will be detected.

The FCS is computed by first taking the original data block bit pattern (treated as a single huge binary number) and adding to its end (after the low-order bits) some additional binary 0s. The exact number of added 0s will be the same as the number of bits in the desired FCS. (The FCS, once calculated, will overlay those 0s.) Then, the resulting binary number, including the trailing 0s, is divided by a special previously selected divisor (often referred to in descriptions of the algorithm as P).

P has certain required characteristics:

- It is always 1 bit longer than the desired FCS.

- Its first and last bits are always 1.

- It is chosen to be "relatively prime" to the FCS; that is, P divided by the FCS would always give a non-0 remainder. In practice, that means P is normally a prime number.

- The division uses binary division, a much quicker and simpler pro-cess than decimal division. The remainder of the division becomes the FCS.

Specific implementations of CRC use specific divisors; thus the CRC-32 error-checking protocol on one system should be able to cooperate with the CRC-32 protocol on another system; the CRC-CCITT protocol (which uses a 17-bit pattern, generating a 16-bit FCS) likewise should talk to other implementations of CRC-CCITT. Selection of a specific P can be tuned to the types of errors most likely to occur in a specific environment. But, unless you are planning on engineering a new protocol, you needn't worry about the selection process; it already has been done for you by the designers of your hardware or your communications software. Figure A.6 illustrates the CRC creation process.

CRC is typically used on blocks or frames of data rather than on individual bytes. Depending on the protocol being used, the size of the blocks can be as high as several thousand bytes. Thus, in terms of bits of error-checking information required for a given number of bytes of data, CRC requires far less transmission overhead (e.g., CRC-32 sends four 8-bit bytes' worth of error-checking bits to check thousands of data bytes) than any of the parity-based approaches.

Although binary division is very efficient, having to perform such a calculation on every block transmitted does have the potential to add significantly to transmission times. Fortunately, CPUs developed in the last few years are up to the challenge. Also, unlike with most other check-digit types of error correction, the receiving device or software does not have to recalculate the FCS in order to check for an error. Instead, the original data plus the FCS are concatenated together to form a longer pattern, then divided by the same P used as a divisor during the FCS creation process. If there is no remainder from this last division, then the CRC algorithm assumes that there are no errors. And, 99.99995 percent of the time, there aren't.

Plexes—Communications Channel Directions

The next area of discussion is the directional nature of your communications channel. Three basic forms of communications channels exist.

One-Way (Simplex)

This is a service that is one way and only one way. You can use it to either transmit or to receive. This is not a common channel for telephony (voice), because there are very few occasions where one person speaks and everyone else listens. Feedback, one of the capabilities that we prize in our communications, would be eliminated in a one-way conversation. Broadcast television is an example of simplex communications.

Designing an efficient data communications application using a simplex channel can require quite a bit of ingenuity. A good example is stock ticker tape radio signals. Bear in mind that in a true simplex system (such as this one) there is absolutely no feedback possible from the receiver to the transmitter. How then does someone using such a signal get useful, timely information? After all, unless one is simply gawking at the symbols as they go by, it is not practical to wait for on average half of the symbols to go by in order to find out that

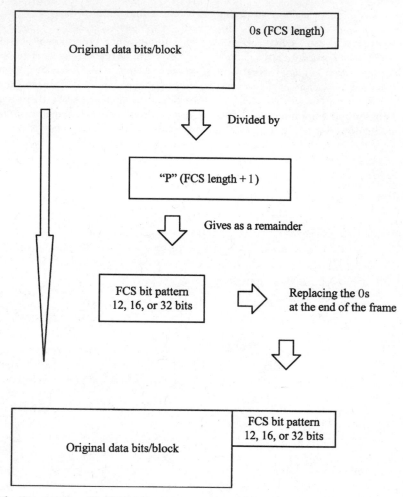

Figure A.6   The creation of a CRC cycle.

the particular stock in which you are interested just went up or down a bit.

The answer is a combination of communications and computer technology. The applications that implement this technique memorize locally (on a PC) the entire repeating communications stream once, then accept each new symbol/price combination received as an update to the local "database." The user inquires against that local database, getting what appears to be instant information, even though it might have been received several minutes ago. Naturally, the computer must be set to continually receive;

otherwise, the user will have no assurance that the data is even remotely current.

Another approach requires the user to specify in advance to the software a set of symbols to collect. As that stock information goes by, the program snags only the specified information for retention and local query. This is not any faster than the previous approach, but it does require less local storage capability.

Two-Way Alternating (Half Duplex)

This is the normal channel that is used in conversations. We speak to a listener, then we listen while someone else speaks. The telephone conversations we engage in are normally half duplex. Although the line or medium (air, in this case) is capable of handling a transmission in each direction, most human brains can't deal well with simultaneous transmission and reception.

Many computer and communications configurations use half duplex technology. Until a few years ago, most leased-line multidrop modems were half duplex. One of the key differentiators among such modems was their turnaround time, that is, how quickly a pair of such modems could reverse the channel direction. This was measured in milliseconds—the fewer, the better. Entire communications protocols were built around this technology (e.g., IBM's Bisynchronous Communications or BSC). All-block mode (e.g., IBM 3270s) terminals still operate in half duplex mode only, even if full duplex facilities are available. This simply means that at any given time, the terminal is either sending to its associated computer or receiving from it, not both at once. This does not cause a problem because the entire system is designed around this behavior, and it works quite well. Of course, almost half of any given circuit's raw capacity (if the capacities of the two directions are added together) is wasted. (IBM's more recent SDLC-protocol-based front end processors can talk to one terminal and receive from another at the same time, minimizing this waste, but the individual terminals are still functioning as half duplex devices.)

With some technologies, half duplex can be used so effectively that the one-way-at-a-time characteristic of the circuit is invisible; it appears to be full duplex (see below). An excellent example of such an approach is local area network communications. Most actual LAN technologies, including both Ethernet and Token Ring, are actually half duplex on the wire. But the information moves so quickly, and the responses are so fast, that the path appears to an observer to be full duplex.

Two-Way Simultaneous (Duplex) or Full Duplex

True full duplex communications make maximum use of a circuit's capacity—if the nature of the communications on that circuit takes advantage of it. In data communications, a circuit is implemented and used in full duplex mode if a device can send to a computer and receive from the computer at the same time. Although we mentioned that human conversation is typically half duplex, there is an exception to this: conversation among teenagers, who seem to be able to speak and listen (somewhat) at exactly the same time.

A common example of full duplex communications is that seen when one dials into an on-line information system such as CompuServe or Prodigy. Most such systems allow users to continue typing at a keyboard even while the service is sending information to the user for display on the screen. Were the connection not a full duplex one, this simultaneous bidirectional communication would not be possible.

One of the points that confuses some people is that the terms *simplex*, *half duplex*, and *full duplex* can refer to varying levels of a communications architecture. If the three levels are considered to be three points on an increasing scale of capability, one can say that a given level of a communications architecture must rely on lower levels with at least the capability of that given level, as presented in Table A.5.

What does this table mean? It means that a wide-area analog data circuit built to handle full duplex communications (requiring the telephone company to support simultaneous communications in both directions, and use of full duplex modems) can fully support half duplex or simplex communications. But if a similar circuit is implemented with half duplex modems, then full duplex communications on that circuit will not work, although simplex will. A citizens band radio provides a half duplex channel—two directions, but only one way at a time. Simplex would work—one sender could lock down a key and just keep sending—but full duplex would be impossible.

Air is a full duplex channel. But a simplex signal such as the output from a stereo speaker system has no trouble traveling this full duplex channel.

Table A.5 *Comparing the capability and directionality of the circuit.*

This Capability Level	Requires All Lower Levels to Have at Least the Following Capability	But Can Also Function Without Impairment on Top of Levels with the Following Capabilities
Simplex	Simplex	Half or full duplex
Half duplex	Half duplex	Full duplex
Full duplex	Full duplex	(no additional levels)

Compression

Although compression is not exactly a modulation technique, it does (usually) produce faster transmissions. To understand how compression works, consider first how human beings communicate. Most human communication is inherently redundant. This does not imply waste; rather, human beings use that redundancy as a continual cross-check on what information is really being sent and meant. For example, in face-to-face conversation much more information is being sent than just the words. Facial expressions, tones of voice, limb positions and movement, overall carriage of the body, and other less obvious cues all contribute to the information stream flowing between two people having a conversation. But much of the information is duplicated. For example, anger can be communicated by the words themselves; but it can also be conveyed by tone of voice, facial expression, involuntary changes in the color of one's complexion, the stress in the voice, arm movement, and other cues. If some of these items were removed, the message received might be just as clear but the total amount of raw information might be reduced.

In data communications, compression is a technique applied either in advance to information to be transmitted or dynamically to an information stream being transmitted. The underlying technology is essentially the same in both cases: removal of redundant information, or expression of the information in a more compact form, is used to reduce the total number of bytes that must pass over the communications medium in order to reduce the time the medium is occupied by a given transmission to a minimum.

A detailed discussion of compression techniques is beyond the scope of this book. But in this section we describe two very basic approaches in order to elucidate the fundamentals of the technology. Later, during the discussion of modems, we will briefly identify and describe the power of some compression techniques that are often built into such devices.

The simplest form of compression is the identification and encoding of repeating characters into fewer characters. For example, consider the transmission of printed output across a network to a printer. A typical report contains a very high number of blank characters, often occurring consecutively. Suppose every such string of four or more consecutive blanks (which are of course themselves ASCII characters) is detected and replaced with a 3-byte special character sequence encoded as follows:

- The first character is a special character (one of the nonprint characters in the ASCII code set, for example) indicating that this is a special sequence.

- The second character is one occurrence of the character that is to be repeated, in this case a blank.

- The third character is a 1-byte binary number indicating how many times the character is to be repeated. With 1 byte (using binary format), we can count up to 255, high enough to get some real savings!

How much can we save? Look at Table A.6. We'll assume that on average, blanks occur in 10-byte consecutive streams, a very pessimistic assumption.

As can be seen from the table, the savings depends on the number of occurrences of the character to be repeated. In practice, this is a reasonably powerful technique. In the example, we addressed only blanks. In practice, any character except the special character would be fair game.

But what if we actually want to send that special character? After all, unlike print jobs, many transmissions must be able to handle every possible code; there are none left over that are "special." No problem—we add the following rules:

- We'll never try to compress multiple occurrences of the special character.

- Every time we encounter the special character as input during the encoding process, we'll simply send it twice. If the receiving hardware sees this character twice, it drops one of the occurrences.

With this approach, we only have to select a special character that is unlikely to occur frequently. If it then does occur frequently in a particular transmission, our compression algorithm doesn't break; it will just be very inefficient for that one transmission.

Note how the overall redundancy is squeezed out of a transmission using this approach. But, just as in human communications, eliminating redundancy increases the risk that some information will be misinterpreted. In human communication, if the reddening of an angry person's face and other visual cues were not visible (e.g., if the conversation were on the telephone) and the speaker was otherwise very self-controlled, the listener might misinterpret angry words as being a joke; after all, many American subcultures routinely use affectionate insults without anger. Unrecognized anger is a very serious loss of information. In data communications without compression, omission of a single space in a series of spaces might cause a slight misalignment on a report, but will most likely not seriously distort its meaning. If compression is used and the binary count field is damaged— i.e., changed to another binary digit—dozens or even hundreds of spaces or other repetitive characters might be either deleted or added to the report, seriously compromising its appearance and perhaps distorting its meaning. Consider the havoc that could be wrought on

Table A.6 Quick analysis of compression benefits.

Total Characters in Print Stream Before Compression	Blanks in Print Before Compression	Total Characters in Streamprint Stream After Compression	Percentage Savings
1000	10	993	1
1000	100	930	7
1000	500	650	35
50,000	2000	48,600	3
50,000	5000	46,500	7
50,000	20,000	36,000	28

a horizontal bar chart! The error-checking techniques discussed earlier become much more important in a system that uses compression!

Another more sophisticated method of compression requires pattern recognition analysis of the raw data rather than just detection of repeating characters. Again, some special character must be designated, but now it precedes a special short code that represents some repetitive pattern detected during the analysis. For example, in graphics displays capable of showing 64K (65,536) colors, every screen pixel has associated with it two

8-bit bytes (which together can represent 65K different values) indicating the color assigned to that pixel. If someone sets the screen to display white on a blue background, the 2-byte code for blue is going to appear thousands of times in the data stream associated with that display. The repeating 1-byte compression algorithm described earlier will not detect anything to compress. But if analysis shows that a 2-byte pattern occurs many times in succession, a more sophisticated approach might assign a specific character (preceded by the special character) to represent precisely 20 (or some other specific number of) consecutive occurrences of that 2-byte sequence. The savings can be considerable, but they again depend on the characteristics of the data being transmitted.

A third, very computationally intensive approach to compression has been designed especially for live transmission of digitized video signals. Unlike most other compression methods, this approach does not involve movement of representations of the entire digitized data stream from one point to another. Video signals consist of a number of still frames composed each second (visualize 30 photographs per second, in the highest-quality case). Although the first picture must, of course, be sent in its entirety, special equipment and algorithms must then continuously examine succeeding video frames to be transmitted, identifying which pixels have changed since the last "picture" was taken. Then, information addressing just the changed pixels is sent to the receiver, rather than the entire new frame. The receiving equipment uses this change information

combined with its "memory" of the previous frame to continuously, locally build new versions of the picture for display. This approach is particularly fruitful for pictures that in large part remain static; for example, video conferencing. In video conferencing, usually the only moving features of the picture are the human beings. The table(s), walls, and other room fixtures stay still, therefore requiring transmission only once. Frequently, only the lips move for long periods of time.

One other compression-related concept is worth mentioning: lossy vs. lossless compression. "What?" I hear you ask. Does lossy mean what it sounds like? Would we ever tolerate transmission that loses information? The answer, for some applications, is yes. Moreover, you have probably settled for information loss when working daily with computers, and it caused you no hardship at all. If you use a personal computer with a video graphics adapter (VGA) screen, but display any type of graphic that inherently has Super VGA (SVGA) level resolution, your VGA screen loses the additional definition in the image that is visible only when an SVGA controller card and monitor are used. And in fact, this example, while not involving compression as such, demonstrates precisely the type of situation where lossy compression would be tolerated: transmission of video images. Some compression algorithms used for transmission of video images lose some of the resolution of those images. However, if the received image is acceptably precise, the maintenance of the speed of the moving image might be more important.

Multiplexing

The paths available for moving electronic information vary considerably in their respective capacities or bandwidths. If a company requires many paths over the same route (for example, many terminals each requiring a connection to one distant computer), it often makes sense to configure one large-capacity circuit and bundle all the smaller requirements into that one big path. The process of combining two or more communications paths into one path is referred to as multiplexing. There are three fundamental types of *multiplexing*, all of which have significant variations. These main types are:

- Space-division multiplexing (SDM)

- Frequency-division multiplexing (FDM)

- Time-division multiplexing (TDM)

SDM

SDM is the easiest multiplexing technology to understand. In fact, it is so simple it would hardly rate its own special term, except that it is the primary method by which literally millions of telephone signals reach private homes. With SDM, signals are placed on physically different media. Then those media are combined into larger groups and connected to the desired end points.

For example, telephone wire pairs (which of course are also used for data communications), each of which can carry a voice conversation, are aggregated into cables with hundreds or even thousands of pairs (see Fig. A.7). The latter are run as units from telco COs out to wiring center locations, from there splitting out to individual customer buildings.

The biggest advantage of SDM is also its biggest disadvantage: the physical separation of the media carrying each signal. It is an advantage because of the simplicity of managing the bandwidth; one only must label each end point of the medium appropriately. No failures (other than a break in the medium) can affect the bandwidth allocation scheme. But because there is a direct physical correlation between the physical link and the individual communications channel, a provider has some difficulty in electronically manipulating the path to achieve efficiencies of technology or scale. For example, probably the largest single factor blocking the conversion of the overall telephone network to all-digital technology is the embedded base of copper wire (and analog amplifiers) supplying telephone service to millions of homes and businesses.

FDM

FDM is inherently an analog technology. It achieves the combining of several digital signals onto (or into) one medium by sending signals in several distinct frequency ranges over that medium.

One of FDM's most common applications is cable television. Only one cable reaches a customer's home, but the service provider can nevertheless send multiple television channels or signals simultaneously over that cable to all subscribers. Receivers must tune to the appropriate frequency in order to access the desired signal. Figure A.8 demonstrates the combining of signals on a cable television coaxial cable.

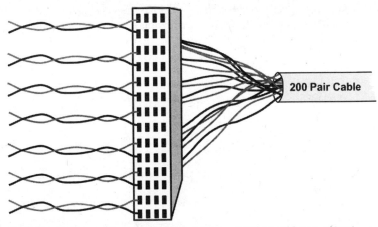

200 Pair Cable

Figure A.7   Individual pairs are bundled together into much larger cables on a 1-to1.

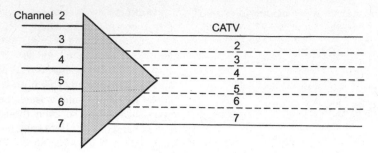

Figure A.8 *Frequency-division multiplexing breaks the whole bandwidth into separate full-time channels.*

Certain modems have built-in FDM capabilities. Users can modify, with controls on the modem, how much bandwidth each connected digital device will be provided.

TDM

Time-division multiplexing is a digital technology. It involves sequencing groups of a few bits or bytes from each individual input stream one after the other and in such a way that they can be associated with the appropriate receiver. If this is done sufficiently quickly, the receiving devices will not realize or care that some of the circuit time was used to serve another logical communication path. The really high-speed communications technologies covered in later chapters all, without exception, use some form of TDM, so it is worthwhile to try to understand it.

Consider an application requiring four terminals at an airport to reach a central computer. Each terminal communicates at 2400 bits per second, so, rather than acquiring four individual circuits to carry such a low-speed trans-

mission, the airline has installed a pair of multiplexers (see below), a pair of 9600-bit-per-second modems, and one dedicated analog communications circuit from the airport ticket desk back to the airline data center, as illustrated in Fig. A.9.

The time-division multiplexers work together to merge the data streams onto the 9600-bit-per-second circuit in such a way that each terminal appears to have a dedicated 2400-bit-per-second circuit. The multiplexer has enough buffer (or storage) space so that as any of the four clerks presses a key, that keystroke is stored locally (in the multiplexer or *mux*) until the time slot assigned to that clerk's terminal comes along. The flow of information for four hypothetical clerks named Ellen, Joe, Susan, and Allan is shown in Table A.7.

As an example, we'll assume that Joe is inquiring as to the available of space on XXXXX Airlines flight 243. As part of this inquiry, he types the letters *XA243*. At the same time, Susan is seeing where there is space at

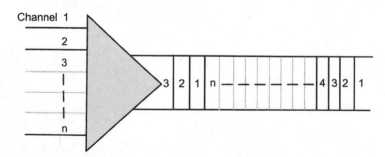

Figure A.9 *In time-division multiplexing, the entire channel is allocated for short periods of time.*

Table A.7 *The flow of information for the various time slots used.*

Byte	From
1	Ellen
2	Joe
3	Susan
4	Allan
5	Ellen
6	Joe
7	Susan
8	Allan

the *Compris* hotel in Chicago, so she types Compris. The other two clerks are out to lunch; their terminals are inactive. Those letters will be interspersed among others typed by their colleagues. TDM assigns time slots to each configured device, whether or not the slots are used. If the data stream is to be interleaved one byte at a time, the data stream toward the computer resulting from this typing might look as shown in Fig. A.10 (the information on the right goes toward the computer first).

This is not really a form of compression, because the same number of bytes is sent as is typed. In fact, as can been seen from the figure, there is a certain inefficiency here. Those

4-byte blocks are being pumped out by the multiplexer no matter whether anyone types a character or not. The first position in each 4-byte block is reserved for Ellen's characters, while the fourth position is reserved for Allan. Because Ellen and Allan are both at lunch, their blocks are empty—and wasted. Joe is a slower typist than Susan, so even though he types fewer characters, his last character goes at the same time as Susan's last; some of his slots are empty. He "missed the train."

In real life, many more slots would be empty because the capacity of the line is 240 characters per second—per clerk! No one can type that quickly. Also, in real life, multiplexing is more commonly done at the bit level rather than at the byte level. This would be harder to illustrate understandably, so we use bytes in the example. But the principle is identical.

Next, we modify the example to assume that the characters typed (*XA243* and *Compris*) are coming back from the computer instead of being typed. In such a case, they will be coming at "wire speed"; the computer can pump them out far faster than the line can absorb them, so we are now talking about wasting some time (Fig. A.11).

Were the multiplexer configured for only two clerks' terminals, the information from the computer could appear much more quickly (Fig. A.12).

This, in effect, is what a variation on a TDM called a statistical time-division multiplexer (STDM), does. The sending STDM analyzes the data stream on the fly to determine which ports

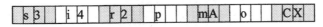

Figure A.10 *The use of TDM and the data time slots for two.*

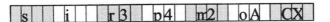

Figure A.11 *The time wasted on the circuit can be compensated for using TDM techniques.*

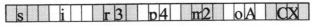

Figure A.12 *The TDM is now configured for only two users, so the data will be less wasted.*

or "tail circuits" are active—that is, how much service they require. If they are inactive, or less active (slow typists?), they are provided fewer of the time slots (or bandwidth). This allocation changes dynamically depending on the traffic pattern. Again, this is not compression, because all the information is sent. Nonetheless, it seems like compression because extending this technique allows overcommitting the line. If 10 terminals are connected to a 9600 circuit via an STDM, each terminal can be set to 2400 bits per second. So long as not all terminals are busy at full speed at every moment, the STDM can make it look as though each terminal has its own 2400-bit-per-second circuit, even though the aggregate bandwidth required to support these settings without using an STDM would be 24,000 bits per second!

Paradoxically, STDM techniques are used more at lower speeds than on the really fast multimegabit circuits. At very high speeds, the equipment is so busy just performing TDM functions that too much extra computer power would be required to do the on-the-fly analysis for STDM.

Codes

The concept of a bit—an electronic expression of a 1 or 0—should now be clear. However, how do you get from 1s and 0s to transmitting your resume over wires?

The alphabet must be built up from sets of 1s and 0s. Specifically, we employ one or more sets of codes or alphabets, standard definitions of patterns of 1s and 0s that we will agree to use to represent letters, numbers, and other symbols that we wish to transmit and receive.

The alphabets most frequently used are either American Standard Code for Information Interchange (ASCII), which is fairly universal, or Extended Binary Coded Decimal Interchange Code (EBCDIC), which is an IBM alphabet. These two code sets, or alphabets, are used to convert a series of 1s and 0s into an alphabetic or numeric character.

ASCII

One character (also known as a byte or octet) must be represented as a consistent bit pattern by both sender and receiver. As we use a keyboard (standard typewriter keyboards are known as *QWERTY keyboards* because of the sequence of the first row of alphabetic keys), we create a stream of combination of letters, numbers, and symbols.

When ASCII (usually pronounced *ass-key* with a mild accent on the first syllable) was originally defined for use by the United States government, the bit pattern was defined to be seven data bits long. With 7 bits, it is possible to differentiate 128 different patterns. So, to recreate these typed characters with 1s and 0s, we can use a combination of up to 128 possible ASCII characters (Fig. A.13).

Using the combinations in this table, we should be able to transmit just about everything we presently understand in our vocabulary. And, in fact, for many years, the 7-bit ASCII was used for most non-IBM mainframe communications. But there were two factors that caused this form of ASCII to become less popular.

First, most computers handle data in 8-bit chunks (rather than 7) to represent characters. The terms *byte* and *octet* almost always refer to 8-bit, not 7-bit, patterns. Second, while 7-bit ASCII can indeed represent all the English letters and numbers, with some symbols left over for special characters and control information, there are many other characters used in written communication that cannot easily be expressed in a 128-character code set. Accented characters in the Romance languages, character graphic drawing symbols, and typographical indications in word processors (bolding, underlining, etc.) are just a few examples of symbols difficult to handle with standard ASCII.

Extended ASCII

Extended ASCII is a superset of ASCII. Extended ASCII is the code used inside virtually all non-IBM computers, including personal computers. It is an 8-bit code set, doubling the possible distinguishable characters to 256. The 7-bit ASCII codes are present in extended ASCII in their original form with a 0 prefixed to the base 7 bits. Another 128 characters are also available with the same base 7 bits as the original ASCII, but with a 1 prefixed instead.

				Bit 7	0	0	0	0	1	1	1	1
				Bit 6	0	0	1	1	0	0	1	1
				Bit 5	0	1	0	1	0	1	0	1
Bit 4	Bit 3	Bit 2	Bit 1	Col	0	1	2	3	4	5	6	7
				Row								
0	0	0	0	0	NUL	DLE	SP	0	@	P		p
0	0	0	1	1	SOH	DC1	!	1	A	Q	a	q
0	0	1	0	2	STX	DC2	"	2	B	R	b	r
0	0	1	1	3	ETX	DC3	#	3	C	S	c	s
0	1	0	0	4	EOT	DC4	$	4	D	T	d	t
0	1	0	1	5	ENQ	NAK	%	5	E	U	e	u
0	1	1	0	6	ACK	SYN	&	6	F	V	f	v
0	1	1	1	7	BEL	ETB	'	7	G	W	g	w
1	0	0	0	8	BS	CAN	(	8	H	X	h	x
1	0	0	1	9	HT	EM	)	9	I	Y	i	y
1	0	1	0	A	LF	SUB	*	:	J	Z	j	z
1	0	1	1	B	VT	ESC	+	;	K	[	k	{
1	1	0	0	C	FF	FS	,	<	L	\	l	|
1	1	0	1	D	CR	GS	-	=	M	]	m	}
1	1	1	0	E	SO	RS	.	>	N	^	n	-
1	1	1	1	F	SI	US	/	?	O	_	o	DEL

Figure A.13   The ASCII code set.

But whereas ASCII is a standard, extended ASCII is ... well, not quite standard. While the original 128 characters communicate well from vendor to vendor, even in extended ASCII, every application defines its own use of the additional 128 characters. For example, you can easily write out ASCII text from most word processing programs, with the result being readable by most other word processors. But if you attempt to read a document created by a word processor in its native form with another, different word processor, you will only be successful if the latter specifically contains a translation module for material created by the first.

Nonetheless, the lion's share of non-IBM communications is now conducted using extended ASCII. Virtually all personal computers use it, including IBM's. If you set your communications protocol to *N,8,1* (no parity, eight data bits, one parity bit), those eight data bits are encoded in using extended ASCII.

EBCDIC

IBM, not a company to follow the herd, realized early on that 128-code ASCII did not contain enough patterns for its requirements. So,

IBM created an entirely different code set, one twice as large as the original ASCII code set. IBM's 8-bit, 256-character code set, used on all of its computers except personal computers, is called Extended Binary Coded Decimal Interchange Code or EBCDIC. (Most people pronounce it *eb-sub-dick* with a mild accent on the first syllable.)

As with ASCII, certain of the characters are consistent wherever EBCDIC is used. But other characters vary depending on the specific communicating devices. In Fig. A.14, the white space can be used differently depending on the EBCDIC dialect in use.

Unicode

Two hundred fifty-six codes might seem to be all anyone would need. But consider the requirements of Chinese, which has thousands of characters. Or the Cyrillic alphabet, which, although it does not have a terribly large number of characters, does not overlap any of those defined in ASCII or EBCDIC. Another code set, called Unicode, is now being implemented in some products. Unlike the 8-bit extended ASCII and EBCDIC code sets, Unicode uses 16 bits, or 2 bytes, per character. While only 1s and 0s are

Figure A.14 The EBCDIC code set.

Columns are selected by bits 4 3 2 1 (second hex digit); rows are selected by bits 5 6 7 8 (first hex digit).

Bits 8765 \ 4321	0	1	2	3	4	5	6	7	8	9	A	B	C	D	E	F
0	NUL	SOH	STX	ETX	PF	HT	LC	DEL			SMM	VT	FF	CR	SO	SI
1	DLE	DC1	DC2	DC3	RES	NL	BS	IL	CAN	EM	CC		IFS	IGS	IRS	IUS
2	DS	SOS	FS		BYP	LF	EOB	PRE			SM		DC4	ENQ	ACK	BEL
3			SYN		PN	RS	UC	EOT						NAK		SUB
4	SP										¢	.	<	(	+	|
5	&										!	$	*	)	;	¬
6	-	/									¦	,	%	_	>	?
7											:	#	@	'	=	"
8		a	b	c	d	e	f	g	h	i						
9		j	k	l	m	n	o	p	q	r						
A		~	s	t	u	v	w	x	y	z						
B																
C	{	A	B	C	D	E	F	G	H	I						
D	}	J	K	L	M	N	O	P	Q	R						
E	\		S	T	U	V	W	X	Y	Z						
F	0	1	2	3	4	5	6	7	8	9						

used, this allows up to 65,536 (2 to the 16th power) separate character definitions. Of course, each character takes up as much storage and transmission time as two eight-bit characters. But Unicode is a truly international code set, allowing all peoples to use their own alphabets if they wish.

Modulation

How does the transmission process work? How does the data get onto the voice dial-up telephone line? We use a device to change the data. This device, known as a modem, changes the data from something a computer understands (numeric bits of information) into something the telephone network understands (analog sine waves, or sound). A modem generates a continuous tone, or carrier, and then modifies or modulates it in ways that will be recognized by its partner modem at the other end of the telephone circuit. The modems available to do this come in variations, each one creating a change in a different way. Remember that the word modem is a con-

traction for *modulation/demodulation*. In order for the communications process to work, we need the same types of modems at each end of the line operating at the same speeds. These modems can use the following types of modulation schemes (or change methods):

Amplitude Modulation (AM)

Amplitude modulation represents the bits of information (the 1s and 0s) by changing a continuous carrier tone. Figure A.15 illustrates amplitude modulation. Because there are only two stages of the data, 1 or 0, you can let the continuous carrier tone represent the 0 and the modulated tone represent the 1. This type of modem changes the amplitude (think of amplitude as the height or loudness of the signal). Each change represents a 1 or a 0. Because this is a 3-kHz analog dial-up telephone line, the maximum amount of changes that can be represented and still be discrete enough to be recognizable to the line and the equipment is about 2400 per second. This cycle of 2400 changes per second is called the

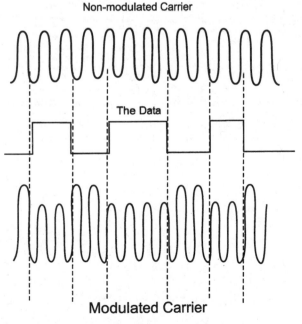

Non-modulated Carrier

The Data

Modulated Carrier

Figure A.15   The concept of amplitude modulation.

baud rate. Therefore, the maximum amount of data bits that can be transmitted across the telephone line with AM modulation is 2400 bits per second. Most amplitude modulation modems were designed to transmit 300–1200 bits per second, although others have been made to go faster.

As we look at the different ways to change the 1s and 0s generated by the computer into their analog equivalents, we have another choice in the process. Voice communications (or human speech itself) is the continuous variation of amplitude and frequencies, so we could choose to use a modem that modulates the frequency instead of the amplitude. An explanation of this type of modem follows.

Frequency Modulation (FM)

Frequency modulation is provided by an FM modem. This modem represents the 1s and 0s as changes in the frequency of a continuous carrier tone. Because there are only two states to deal with, we can represent the normal frequency as being a 0 and slow down the continuous carrier frequency when we want to represent a 1 to the telephone line (Fig. A.16). The modem uses the same baud rate on the telephone line as the amplitude modulation technique, that being 2400 baud or discrete changes per second. These modems modulate

1 bit of information per cycle change per second, or a maximum of 2400 bits per second. Note that the baud rate and the bits per second rate are somewhat symmetrical. Although both AM and FM modems are designed around what was once considered pretty fast transmission rates, we have continually been unsatisfied with any rate of speed developed. We want more and more, faster and faster.

Because we (as humans) and our creations (the computers) are never satisfied with the speed of transmission over the telephone line, we demanded faster. Throughput was expensive under the old dial-up telephone network. Therefore we asked for additional speed to get more throughput and less cost. The engineers came up with a new process that modulates on the basis of phases.

Phase Modulation

If we can change the phase of the sine wave as it is introduced to the line, at positions of 0, 90, 180, and 270 degrees, we can encode the data with more than 1 bit of information at a time. A phase modulation technique allows us to transmit a di-bit of information per signaling-state change. This gives us 4800 bits per second of throughput.

The di-bit represents the information as shown in Table A.8.

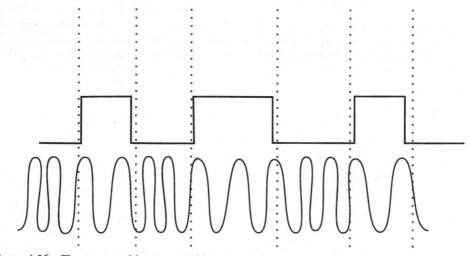

Figure A.16 *The concept of frequency modulation (FM) for data modems.*

Table A.8 *The four phases in phase modulation cause 90° shift when a di-bit is received.*

Bits	Phase
00	0
01	90
10	180
11	270

As you can see, two bits of information at 2400 baud gives us the 4800 bits per second. This was a step in the right direction. But we wanted more; so a combination of phase modulation and amplitude modulation was developed.

QAM

Called quadrature with amplitude modulation (QAM), this combination allows us to use up to 16 possible steps of phase and amplitude modulation. QAM is mostly used with 4 bits of information per baud rate, thereby producing 9600 bits per second of throughput across an analog telephone line. Theoretically, the system should be able to produce 38,400 bits per second of information (4 phases at 4 bits per phase at 2400 baud = 38,400 bits per second). However, in practice, line rates can rarely support sustained throughput across the telephone network at this speed. Also, the telco limits the bandwidth to 3 kHz, and we use 2400 baud. If we try to send more data at a higher baud rate, the band limitation (band-pass filters) will strip the frequencies that go beyond the filters. This is a function of the telco equipment on the line at the CO. Thus we usually have to settle for analog data transmission at slower speeds.

The driving force behind improving modulation techniques has always been to increase the speed possible over an analog circuit. Why? In addition to the obvious reason (i.e., accomplishing the task more quickly improves productivity), the cost of communications over dial circuits is directly proportional to the amount of time those circuits are in use; going faster saves money. But, when the absolute best available modulation technology is in use, one has not yet necessarily squeezed the absolute best transmission volumes out of a circuit. One can push it even further by using compression.

V.90 Modems

Practically all new PCs and laptop computers sold today have a new modem integral to them. The use of modem technology has become commonplace. However, as modems have dropped in price, the ability to go faster has increased. Today, the new modem technology is asymmetrical in that it transmits at one speed and receives data back at a different rate. The world was looking for better ways of moving data, but had to deal with the limits of the wires in the local loop. Over the decades, the cost of modems has dropped while the ability to move the data was going in an upward fashion. Something had to be done because the amount of data we were moving was escalating exponentially. Enter the 56 Kbps modem (V.90 standard), which operates at a 33.6-Kbps transmit rate and a 56 Kbps receive rate.

The rated speeds can be misnomers because in North America, the FCC and the Canadian CRTC limit the speed that a telco can offer to a customer to no greater than 53 Kbps. The rate was selected years ago when we were still trying to drive modem communications at 9.6 Kbps. So the arbitrary decision was something that no one ever thought would occur. Alas, here we are with a modem that can achieve 56-Kbps and the regulators have capped it. Moreover, the asymmetrical rate of speed facilitates access to one of the most commonly used networks today—the Internet. The 56 Kbps modem works well because the user has little data to send (typing <www.tcic.com>, for example, requires very little data) but lots to receive (a Web page can be millions of bytes large). So the different speeds allow for dial-up communications on a telephone company circuit (a voice channel) in one direction and a digital-access method for the return path at a much higher rate of speed.

Typically, however, when a user accesses the network with these modems, they will transmit at between 28.8 and 33.6 Kbps upline and receive approximately between 38 and 45 Kbps downstream. One can get a slightly better response from the 56-Kbps modem, but there are still limitations that must be dealt with.

A note that puts this all in perspective though—in the early 1980s we were transmitting data at between 4800 and 7200 Bps, and the modems were expensive (hundreds to thousands of dollars at the time). Here, in a mere decade, we have achieved quantum leaps in technological advancements, and we have seen the cost drop exponentially to a few dollars. What we can expect is faster and better, but cheaper, through the new millennium.

Devices

DTE versus DCE

A basic of data communications is that every communicating device is either a terminal-type device (data terminal equipment, or DTE; also sometimes referred to as data circuit terminating equipment, or DCTE) or a communications-type device (data communications equipment, or DCE). DTEs use communications facilities; their primary functions lie elsewhere. DCEs provide access or even implement communications facilities. Their only role is moving information.

You might presume that some cosmic requirement is satisfied by this overall categorization. But in fact the nitty-gritty reality of cabled communications is the primary cause of this division. Although we will get into cabling standards later, consider the following situation:

Two devices, A and B, must be connected. The connection will be via two wires, numbered one and two. Let us assign wire number one to transmit the data, and number two to receive. But wait! If A transmits on number one, and B also transmits on number one, and if they both receive on number two, neither will listen to what the other is sending. It would be as though two people each spoke into opposite ends of the same tube at the same time, with neither putting the end to his or her ear.

The solution seems simple: have A transmit on wire one, B listen on wire one, A listen on wire two, B transmit on wire two. But now let us introduce device C. How should C be built? If it is configured as is A, it cannot communicate with A; if it is configured as is B, it cannot communicate with B.

But devices are not configured at random. For example, terminals do not usually connect directly to terminals; printers are never connected directly to printers; and so on. Perhaps if one broad category of devices usually connects not to another in that category but rather to a device in another category, we could standardize on only two default configurations. This is what was done with DTEs and DCEs.

Categories and Examples of DTEs

The grouping is not perfect. Some devices routinely connect to both DTEs and DCEs (e.g., multiplexers). Such devices do not clearly fall into either category, and must be configured depending on the specific installation requirements. But for the most part, any data processing device that can communicate falls cleanly into one of these two categories. Most of the devices covered in this book are DCE devices. Here are some examples of the DTE devices to which we provide data communications services:

- Computers (mainframe, mini, midi)

- Terminals (CRTs, VDT, teletype)

- Printers (laser, line, dot matrix)

- Specialized (bar code readers, optical character recognition)

- Transactional (point of sale equipment, automated tellers)

- Intelligent (personal computers)

The remainder of this section will focus on DCEs and ways of connecting components.

Modems

As mentioned earlier, *modem* is a contraction of two words (*modulator* and *demodulator*). The role of the modem is to change information arriving in digital form into an analog format suitable for transmission over the normal telephone network. Naturally, modems work in pairs (or sets of at least two), and a second modem at the other end of the communications path must return the analog signal to a digital format useful to terminals and computers.

Dozens of manufacturers make modems, and hundreds of models exist. The market can be divided in many ways:

■ Speed

■ Supported standards

■ Leased line versus dial-up

■ Two-wire versus four-wire

■ Point-to-point versus multipoint (multidrop)

■ With or without compression capability

■ With or without error correction capability

■ Manageable or nonmanageable

Entire texts could be (and no doubt have been) written just on this topic.